HEARTS OF DARKNESS

HEARTS OF DARKNESS

The European Exploration of Africa

Frank McLynn

HUTCHINSON
London Sydney Auckland Johannesburg

First published in Great Britain in 1992 by
Hutchinson

Random Century Group Ltd
20 Vauxhall Bridge Road, London SW1V 2SA

Random Century Australia (Pty) Ltd
20 Alfred Street, Milsons Point, Sydney, NSW 2061, Australia

Random Century New Zealand Ltd
PO Box 40–086, Glenfield, Auckland 10, New Zealand

Random Century South Africa (Pty) Ltd
PO Box 337, Bergvlei, 2012, South Africa

A catalogue record of this book is available from
the British Library

ISBN 0–09–177082–3

Set in Ehrhardt by Raven Typesetters, Ellesmere Port, South Wirral
Printed and bound in Great Britain by Mackays of Chatham PLC,
Chatham, Kent

Contents

Illustrations

(following page 180)

PICTURE CREDITS: Mansell Collection: 1, 2, 3, 4, 5, 7, 8, 11, 12, 16, 17; Mary Evans Picture Library: 6, 9, 10, 13, 14, 15; Fotomas Index: 18.

The maps on pp. 36, 50, 63, 65, 74, 96, 105, 122 were drawn by Richard Sanderson for *Africa and its Explorers*, edited by Robert I. Rotberg, and are reprinted by permission of Harvard University Press, Copyright © 1970 by the President and Fellows of Harvard College. Those on pp. 15, 21, 24, 29, 41, 71, 83 are reprinted with the agreement of Christopher Hibbert from his book, *Africa Explored* (Allen Lane), 1982.

For Lucy

Preface

'Africa will always be the Africa of the Victorian atlas, the blank unexplored continent the shape of the human heart.' The African heart so described by Graham Greene acquired a new layer of meaning when Conrad portrayed the Congo under King Leopold as a heart of darkness, a place where barbarism triumphs over humanity, nature over technology, biology over culture, id over superego. Yet perhaps the 'objective correlatives' of the hearts of darkness were the European explorers themselves, men driven by dark forces and pathological drives to attempt a mission seemingly impossible, in the teeth of dangers from hostile tribesmen, wild animals and, most of all, killer diseases.

The story of the explorers has often been told, either through biography or narrative history, but the approach adopted in this book is to isolate key themes and view the explorers from a comparative angle. If it did not sound pretentious, one would be tempted to describe the book as a *sociology* of African exploration rather than a history; in other words to stress the *common* problems and experiences faced by the explorers rather than their unique exploits.

It is often objected by Africans that the very notion of European exploration and discovery of Africa is patronising. 'There was nothing to discover, we were here all the time,' Dr Hastings Banda is said to have declared. But this is a somewhat specious view of exploration. Whatever their achievements, Africans knew nothing of the wider world and little of their own. Before the coming of the explorers, no one knew how the Zambezi watershed linked with the Congo or the Niger with the Nile. The exploration and discovery of Africa meant integrating the continent, for better or worse, into a general system of knowledge and a world system of economics. The explorers were precursors of imperialism, which in turn engendered the modern African nation-states. Graham Greene's romantic/nostalgic view of Africa notwithstanding, it is not the intention here to glorify the great European travellers and discoverers. Given that Africa, in common with the rest of the Third World, is still in the grip of *economic* imperialism, it could even be argued that the legacy of the explorers was ultimately baneful. But that is another story.

Introduction

It requires an effort of the imagination to appreciate that, at the beginning of the nineteenth century, the interior of Africa was almost entirely unknown to Europeans and all other inhabitants of the 'civilised' world. The only comparable *terra incognita* was the great icy landmass of Antarctica but this was uninhabited. South America, in many respects geographically homologous, and possessing a similar wide variety of exotic fauna, had been well combed through by the *conquistadores*, even though there remained pockets of unexplored territory, as in the Xingu river basin and Mato Grosso province in Brazil. Orellana and Aguirre charted the length of the Amazon within seventy years of the American continent's discovery and a full 300 years before the mysteries of the Nile and the Congo were solved. Australasia, settled by the British only in 1788, would be fully explored long before Africa's last secrets were laid bare. The continent of Africa was known to Europeans 5000 years before the New World, but lay unexplored when Lewis and Clark crossed the northern landmass and Alexander Mackenzie put the finishing touches to the map of the far north. More was known about the Arctic north than about places just 100 miles inland from the slave forts on the Gold Coast.

How can this be explained? Africa was Nature's last great redoubt. The technological revolution that enabled Europeans to conquer the Americas, when their Norse forebears had failed 500 years earlier through lack of technical superiority over the indigenous peoples, was not enough to permit the conquest of Africa. A second technological revolution, associated with European industrialisation, urbanisation and the cult of science – those high-water marks of nineteenth-century capitalism – was needed before Africa could be tamed. Africa threw up unprecedented obstacles to penetration by 'the lords of humankind' in Europe.

From the very earliest times Africa south of the Sahara was regarded as a land of mystery. *Ex Africa semper aliquid novi* ('Out of Africa there is always something new') remarked the tireless polymath of the Roman world, Pliny the Elder. The mysterious continent always beckoned to the restless and the curious. Herodotus, 'the father of history', went up the Nile as far as the first cataract and brought back many strange legends, including a story, regarded by modern historians as probable, of a circumnavigation of the continent by the Carthaginians. But no traveller in the Ancient World got farther south than Tibesti in present-day Chad, west of the Nile valley. An expedition sent by the emperor Nero to follow the Nile to its sources got bogged down in the floating vegetation of the *sudd.*

The conquest of North Africa by the Arabs in the seventh century seemed to portend a genuine breakthrough into the regions south of the Sahara. Caravan routes were established across the mighty desert to trade with tribes like the Hausa, Bornu, Songhai and Mandingo, who were all eventually converted to Islam. A flourishing commerce developed: salt, cloth and beads were taken south and exchanged for slaves, ivory, gold, nuts, leather, palm-oil spices and peacock feathers. Sensing that Africa contained great wealth, in the eighth century AD the Muslim traders tried to establish a permanent foothold on the savannah. Africa struck back. No matter how many times the Arabs tried, their horses and camels succumbed to mysterious diseases. The Arabs retreated to their familiar desert. By the fourteenth century individual Muslim explorers had got as far south as Timbuktu on the Niger, but these were no more than individual forays. The disease barrier held the intruders at bay.

Arabs had meanwhile gradually made their way down the east coast and established entrepôts at Sofala, Kilwa and Malindi. It was to these dots on the African coast that Milton referred in *Paradise Lost* (Book XI):

> Nor could his eye not ken . . .
> Mombasa and Quiloa and Meilind.
> And Sofala, through Ophir, to the realm
> Of Congo and Angola further south.

But by the time Milton wrote, these Arab outposts were but a memory and had long since silted up with disuse.

The first European steps in Africa were taken by Prince Henry the Navigator. For nearly fifty years he sent his Portuguese captains ever farther south, bribing them to risk the legendary dangers of the Atlantic, which the wary seafaring Arabs called the Green Sea of Darkness. By the time of Henry's death in 1460, his admirals had ventured as far south as Cape Verde. After his death the voyages continued. Ever southwards pressed the Portuguese, adding a smidgin to knowledge each time: Sierra Leone by 1462; the Bight of Biafra and Fernando Po by 1473; the mouth of the Congo by 1482. In 1486 Bartolomé Dias became the first European to double the Cape of Good Hope. Eleven years later Vasco da Gama rounded the Cape and pressed on to India. Just when it seemed that the Portuguese pioneering voyages might lay bare the secrets of the continent, European enterprise and capital were diverted away to the far richer pickings of the New World and the Far East. Da Gama's opening of the route to the East, and the almost simultaneous discovery of the New World, brought about a loss of interest in Africa. A few brave souls still persisted. Drawn by tales of the legendary Prester John, often confused with the historical King Monomotapa, the Portuguese under Francisco Barreto tried to strike inland from the coast of Mozambique in 1572, but they met the same fate as the Arabs earlier.

Thereafter Africa became the focus for the fanciful imaginations of Europe. The great Portuguese epic poet Camoens, for example, used Vasco da Gama's great voyage as the inspiration for his *Lusiads* – a bizarre attempt to fuse modern discovery and Vergilian epic, complete with the illogical 'co-presence' of Christianity and Olympian gods.

Africa as stimulus to the creative imagination was the other side of the coin from Africa the unknown. One of the most eloquent testimonies to European ignorance of the continent was provided by the geographer Richard Hakluyt, who in his *Principal Navigations of the English Nation*, written at the very end of the sixteenth century, was reduced to citing ancient sources for his 'discourse' on Africa.

The year of the Botany Bay landings in Australia, 1788, can also be regarded as the start of the planned exploration of the African interior. In that year nine enlightened British merchants founded the African Association to increase knowledge and to grow rich or, rather, richer. Clearly the first step was to consolidate the early Arab discoveries and send an expedition to the semi-legendary city of Timbuktu.

It is not recorded whether the founding fathers pondered deeply on the obstacles to European penetration of Africa. Had they done so, the reflection might have given them pause. A glance at the map would have shown a state of geographical knowledge not much advanced on that of Roman times, when the Alexandrian astronomer and geographer Ptolemy produced a map showing Africa merging with Antarctica, the source of the Nile and the fabled Mountains of the Moon far to the south of the Equator, and the Niger running across Africa from Ethiopia to West Africa. Nor were the Europeans any closer to conquering the diseases that had kept out interlopers from the interior of the continent. And knowledge of the tribes of the interior was minimal. Ignorance of Africa from latitude 15°N south to the Limpopo valley, where lived 80 million black Africans, was total.

In just a few areas knowledge had advanced since the Ancient World. Thanks to Islam, North Africa as far as the southern edges of the Sahara was better known than in the days when it was a province of Rome. The Dutch had established a toehold in South Africa in 1652, and the Cape Colony then founded had fanned out as far as present-day Port Elizabeth. Ethiopia, however, was a region apart. Converted to Christianity in the fourth century AD, its people had a high proportion of Caucasian blood. Isolated on two sides by a mountain barrier and an extension of the Sahara desert, Ethiopia enjoyed easy access to the Red Sea, and this salient geographical fact aligned the country with Arabia more naturally than with Africa.

There were dozens of compelling reasons why Europeans fought shy of Africa. Sea power availed them little, since there were few deep bays or gulfs along the African shore. Most of the continent's rivers were unnavigable because of sand bars at their mouths or rapids a short distance upstream. There seemed no real opportunities for plunder and Africa appeared devoid of the precious metals that had made the New World such a magnet to the *conquistadores*. Indeed most of human life in Africa was at the subsistence level. Much of the land in tropical Africa was of poor quality owing to unreliable rainfall and unproductive soil – one reason for the relatively sparse population of the continent. Only in the forest areas were there settled communities of any size; these were the Negro races properly so-called, who lived by fishing and harvesting root crops. The savannah was the homeland of bands of nomads – the Bantu – who extended from the southern limit of the tropical forest to South Africa; they lived on the very margin of existence. One of the reasons European explorers so often ran into violent trouble was that they had no real conception of the economic razor's edge on which most African societies lived. In a context where every tribe produced only a limited agricultural surplus, each major expedition was liable to impose a heavy burden on local resources and to cause local inflation. Africa did not pose any greater military threat to the Europeans than did the aboriginal inhabitants of the Americas; rather less indeed, since there was no central organisation comparable to that of the Aztec and Inca empires.

On paper, nineteenth-century Africa presented a picture of political variety and diffusion every bit as complex as that analysed by Aristotle in his *Politics*. Ancient empires, city-states, quasi-feudal baronies and nomadic bands were all represented. But in fact nineteenth-century Africa was for the most part a spectacle of 'politics without the state', to use the language of political science. Overwhelmingly its people lived in small communities bound together by the dynamics of proximity, kinship, neighbourhood and the village. The ethos of the village was even more important than that of the tribe. The tribal system itself was of awesome complexity: there were over 700 different tribes, each with its own distinctive culture, different ways of growing food, settling disputes or burying the dead. This made social intercourse particularly difficult. Trade goods in high demand in one village might be worthless in the next. Linguistic difficulties compounded the problem, for Africa was a veritable tower of Babel: in most areas there was a multiplicity of tongues; only in East Africa did Swahili establish itself as a *lingua franca*. The sole overarching culture seemed to be that of primitive religion: most Africans worshipped spirits, whether of dead ancestors, inanimate objects or natural phenomena.

In such a fragile social system where the survival of adults was largely a matter of chance and infant mortality was high, polygamy was a necessity. This custom meant that there was no surplus of unmarried women but it was one that deprived the community of the advantages of natural selection since it also meant that couples with undesirable traits could propagate. Traditional African society was ill-equipped to deal with external buffets; even a marginal change in its ecosystem could have catastrophic consequences. The dislocation caused by the explorers was only the latest in a long line of events: the Portuguese interventions in Angola and the Congo after 1545; the conquest of the Songhai state by the Moroccans in 1589; the Great Trek of 1836; the tribal shunting or 'crushing' (*mfecane*) caused by the expansion of Shaka's Zulu empire at the beginning of the nineteenth century; and, most of all, the Arab slave trade. In Africa there was a palimpsest of successive conflict: African against African; Arab against African; African against European; Arab against European; later, European against European.

In more senses than one, then, to penetrate the interior of Africa was to enter a chaos world. Since tsetse flies abounded almost everywhere, preventing the rearing of domestic animals, all travel in the interior and all transport of goods depended on human muscle. The problems of human porterage were legion, and to the more thoughtful European traveller in Africa the use of porters was morally problematical. Africa's climate was also inimical to the white man and all his works. The heat, with temperatures frequently over 100°F, produced weird effects. Screws worked loose from boxes, horn handles dropped off instruments, combs split into fine laminae and the lead fell out of pencils. Signal rockets were spoiled, hair ceased to grow, nails became as brittle as glass, drawers on desks refused to open and boxes once opened would not shut. Flour lost more than 8 per cent of its weight and the proportion of loss in the case of other provisions was even higher.

Rainfall and humidity provided chronic problems in Central Africa. In the heart of the continent April alone afforded a respite from precipitation, but to 'compensate' the days were excessively hot and the nights very cold; shortage of wood would add to the miseries of African porters as they huddled together for warmth at night. During the other months the rain could be incessant. The days were damp and humid and the nights very cold. Even when the sun did break through the clouds, its rays were insupportable. On the east coast Africa was at the mercy of the monsoon winds which blew north-east and south-west for six months of the year and brought a dry wind and a wet wind. There was the *Masika Miku* or 'Greater Rain' and the *Masika M'Dogo* or 'Lesser Rain'. The greater rains began in March, with the heaviest fall in April and May, and continued until September, with gradually diminishing force. Then in October the lesser rains took over and went on until the end of November. The only reliable dry months were December, January and February. Nor was rain itself the only threat from the elements. When Samuel Baker explored Lake Albert in the 1860s a storm arose of such ferocity that Baker, confronted by waves of oceanic steepness, gave himself up for lost.

The explorers also had to deal with fever, for which they had no explanation and no answer, until the coming of quinine. A particular puzzle was that it struck down sedentary Europeans as well as peripatetic explorers. Some thought the origin of fever was inadequate sanitary arrangements and impure water. Others speculated that the wet wind of the monsoon was the culprit. There was even a theory that the prevalence of fever must be due to the disturbance of the soil, especially during excavation for building purposes.

No continent could match Africa when it came to the profusion and variety of dangerous animals. These creatures attacked the explorers, their porters and their animals. A Swahili porter once had the end of his nose bitten off by a hyena; the brute had dashed up to him as he lay sleeping in a group around the camp fire and tried to drag him off. His comrades awoke at his cries and drove the assailant off with firebrands; it was found that the hyena had bitten the end of his nose clean off. The victim found the piece and stuck it on again with a strand of fibre. However, the fibre slipped as the flesh knitted and the piece finally grew on the man's face an inch to the left of its original position, so that he had one nostril complete and in the right place, while the other seemed to grow out of his cheek.

In his missionary village at Ribe in East Africa, Charles New, one of the earliest explorers, had his pet dog taken by a leopard which walked calmly into his house while his back was turned. Animal pests came in all shapes and sizes. In the Nile regions a bird about the size of a thrush, but with a powerful beak like the New Zealand kea, used to attack both camels and donkeys. It pecked holes in them; the resulting wound festered, the animals lost their appetites, pined away and died. Even when boys were employed to ward them off, the tenacious birds managed to crawl under the donkeys' bellies to peck them.

Henry Morton Stanley, greatest of all African explorers, was later to sum up the challenge posed to the white man by Africa:

> Fatal Africa! One after another, travellers drop away. It is such a huge continent, and each of its secrets is environed by so many difficulties – the torrid heat, the miasma exhaled from the soil, the noisome vapours enveloping every path, the giant cane-grass suffocating the wayfarer, the rabid fury of the native guarding every entry and exit, the unspeakable misery of the life within the wild continent, the utter absence of every comfort, the bitterness which each day heaps upon the poor white man's head, in that land of blackness, the sombrous solemnity pervading every feature of it, and the little – too little – promise of success which one feels on entering it.

Such thoughts were far from the minds of the founding fathers of the African Association. In their blissful ignorance they took comfort from one of the exotic sensations of the eighteenth century: the Abyssinian travels of James Bruce of Kinnaird. Bruce, descended from the legendary Robert of Bannockburn, was a tall, massively built, self-assertive cross-grained and boastful individual. His arrogance was such that in 1763 he left behind in Europe a sixteen-year-old fiancée and, on returning from Africa *eleven* years later and finding her married, challenged the husband to a duel for the alienation of his ex-fiancée's affections.

Such was the man often credited with being the first European to explore Abyssinia. In fact, two Portuguese Jesuit priests, Jeronimo Lobo and Pedro Paez, had been there first and visited the mighty Tisisat Falls on the Blue Nile. But since their discoveries were little known and their discoveries sketchy, Bruce reckoned that he could explore the country more thoroughly and then insinuate himself as the true 'discoverer' of the country. Bruce, in short, was the first example of the 'me first' syndrome which so bedevilled African exploration and led so many of the explorers to claim they were the 'first' to see such a natural feature, even when they they knew they had obscure predecessors. He knew both the Abyssinian languages, Amharic and Tigrinya, and his Arabic was so fluent that he could pass himself off as an Arab (thus anticipating Richard Burton by nearly 100 years). His preparation for the life of an African traveller had been thorough but, at thirty-eight, when he set out for Abyssinia, he was already an old man by the standards of African exploration.

In 1769 he set out from Cairo (where, from 1763 to 1765, he had been

Consul-General) and proceeded south via the Nile, Aswan, the Red Sea and Massawa, where he arrived in September. The local ruler, nominally a vassal of the Ottoman empire, sent a message to the *ras* (prime minister) of Abyssinia to ask for instructions on whether to let this strange European proceed. The answer came that a physician was required at court. Accompanied by three Ethiopian guides and his *fidus Achates*, the Italian Luigi Balugani, Bruce set out for the interior. This meant climbing 6000 ft through the mountains of Tigre province.

In the days before Addis Ababa had been built Gondar was the capital of Abyssinia. Following an interview with the chief minister Ras Michael on 14 May 1770, Bruce was received by the emperor Takla Hayamot and given permission to proceed farther south. The key to this smooth passage into Abyssinia was the friendship Bruce struck up with the young emperor's grandmother, Mentwab, whose grandchildren he treated for smallpox. The influential dowager empress Mentwab opened many doors for Bruce and even persuaded Hayamot to make Bruce commander of the country's élite fighting force, the Black Horse.

Civil war was raging in Abyssinia at the time between the Tigre clans loyal to Hayamot and the rebellious Galla tribe of the south under chief Fasil. Hayamot gathered an army to put down the insurrection and invited Bruce to accompany him on the mission of chastisement. This was extremely good news for Bruce. It meant that he could explore the legendary Tisisat Falls under cover of the army. But things did not work out quite so smoothly. When Bruce was only 20 miles from his goal, the defection of two of his commanders to the rebels led the emperor to patch up a peace and return to Gondar.

Bruce was warned that he was known as a 'vizier' to the emperor and so would be executed if he fell into rebel hands. Nevertheless, he was determined to achieve his objective. He pressed on unprotected, with his original party, to the Tisisat Falls, which he found 'one of the most magnificent sights in the creation'.

Furious that he was not the first European to glimpse this awesome sight, Bruce ridiculed Father Lobo's careful figures on height, length and approachability of the falls. In fact Bruce was tilting at windmills; the 'inaccuracies' he detected were the results of the different seasons. Bruce saw the falls in flood, whereas Lobo had seen them in the dry season. Later research established that the Jesuit's statistics and description were the more accurate. And though Luigi Balugani accompanied him to the falls, Bruce took advantage of the Italian's death at Gondar the following year to cut him out of his narrative altogether. In Bruce's account of his Abyssinian travels there is only one explorer to achieve 'firsts': Bruce himself.

Since the emperor had meanwhile made peace with the rebels, the way was clear for further explorations. Bruce returned with the army to Gondar, then asked and obtained permission for further travels in the south while the emperor went north to Tigre to head off another threatened rebellion. Bruce waited for the rainy season to end, then on 27 October 1770, still accompanied by Balugani, he struck south in hopes of finding the Abbai, the headstream of the Blue Nile. He enlisted the help of the Galla chief Fasil, who permitted him to travel in the country of the warlike Gallas provided he went among them as 'governor' of Ghish province.

Early in November Bruce came to the banks of the Blue Nile, then considered the main stream of the mighty river. In the distance loomed a range of mountains Bruce took to be Ptolemy's Mountains of the Moon. On the fourteenth of the month he came to what he took to be the true source of the Nile at the village of Ghish, but he was not in fact even at the fount of the Blue Nile, let alone the White Nile; *Caput Nili* in the case of the Blue is usually held to be at Lake Tana; in any case, the other Jesuit, Pedro Paez, had preceded Bruce at Ghish.

On his return to Gondar Bruce was forced by political instability to remain there until Christmas 1771, when conditions improved sufficiently for him to leave. After many hardships Bruce's party arrived at Sennar in April 1772, to find the town the prey of half a dozen different pestilences: smallpox, epilepsy, fever, ague, dysentery, apoplexy. Delayed there by a suspicious king, Bruce did not leave until September. He next reached Aswan via Shendi, having taken, on 11 November, a farewell bathe in the Nile; some premonition told him he would not see the river again. He was lucky to reach Aswan, as his caravan suffered cruelly from shortage of food and water, and he himself suffered guinea worm infestation in the leg, which left him in agony from inflamed and bleeding feet. His neck was covered in blisters and his face so swollen he could scarcely open his eyes.

After a long convalescence in Aswan, Bruce sailed down the Nile to Cairo, and thence to Alexandria and Marseilles, where he arrived on 25 March 1773. When he crossed to England he was stupefied by his reception. He was widely regarded as a liar and a charlatan. Horace Walpole poured scorn on his braggadocio. Particular animus came from Samuel Johnson, who in *Rasselas* (a romantic fantasy based on the account of Abyssinia by Paez, whose admirer and translator Johnson was) had depicted Ethiopia as a primitive arcadian utopia. Johnson started a whispering campaign to the effect that Bruce had never been in Abyssinia at all. Bruce's tale of the Abyssinians' cutting raw steaks from their cattle was regarded as self-evidently fatuous. The anti-Bruce canards were given substance by his refusal to publish. Not until 1790, sixteen years after his arrival back in England, did he bring out his exhaustive five-volume *Travels to Discover the Source of the Nile*.

But by the 1790s British interest in Africa had already shifted from Ethiopia. For the next half-century it was the West Coast that was to play magnet to the explorers.

I
THE ACHIEVEMENT

I

West Africa and the Niger

The first attempt by the African Association to solve the riddle of the Niger ended in fiasco in 1791 with the death of its envoy Daniel Houghton. He was the first in a long line of victims claimed by West Africa's perils, both human and insect-borne. Houghton was an Irishman, and his successor in the search for the Niger sources was also a Celt: the Scotsman, Mungo Park. Born at Foulshiels on the Yarrow, Park studied medicine in Edinburgh during 1789–91, and was named assistant surgeon on the *Worcester* bound for Sumatra in 1792. He obtained this post through the influence of Sir Joseph Banks, the wealthy English botanist who had sailed round the world in the *Endeavour* in 1768–71 as Captain Cook's scientific adviser. When the African Association accepted his services in 1795, Park was just twenty-four. He exemplified two of the perennial truths about African exploration: that the Celt as natural 'outsider' was better equipped than the Anglo-Saxon for African exploration; and that penetrating the Dark Continent was a job for a young man. To an extent also he bore out a third tenet relating to African exploration: that filling in the great white space on the map enabled men of humble origins to rise rapidly in the world. Park was no proletarian, but as the seventh of twelve children in a middle-class family of reduced circumstances, he was aware that he had to work hard for worldly success.

As founder-member of the African Association, Banks had no difficulty securing the West African commission for his intrepid protégé, who described his motivation as follows: 'I had a passionate desire to examine into [sic] the productions of a country so little known, and to become experimentally acquainted with the modes of life and character of the natives.' The salary he was to receive from the African Association was not large (£271 a year when actually launched on the expedition) but was an improvement on his pay as surgeon's mate. His orders were simple:

proceed up the Niger, explore it as far as practicable, then exit from the interior via The Gambia, if possible.

Unlike later explorers, Park did not set out with a panoply of equipment. There was a certain amateurishness in the way he packed no more clothes than if he were going on a Continental holiday. He sailed from Portsmouth in May 1795 and spent the time until December learning Mandingo at an English factory on the river Gambia.

At the beginning of December Park set out from his base at Pisania with a slave named Johnson and a Mandingo interpreter called Demba. Park made a mistake that many later explorers made: he started for the interior on a horse (his companions rode donkeys). With amazing insouciance, he packed no more scientific equipment than a sextant, a magnetic compass and a thermometer. His armaments, too, contrasted starkly with those of later travellers: his entire arsenal consisted of a couple of fowling pieces and a brace of pistols.

On 3 December 1795 Park bade farewell to white men and headed into the 'boundless forest'. At once he was faced with that permanent headache of African explorers: the demand for tribute or passage money from tribal chiefs. Park found himself divested of much of his cache of tobacco before being allowed to proceed.

He reached Medina, capital of the Wuli, where he was well received by King Jatta. Jatta warned him he would suffer Houghton's fate if he proceeded into the territory of his neighbours, but Park persisted. Jatta shrugged and provided a guide. Park then threaded his way through a number of towns, such as Konjour, Koojar and Joag, gaining all the time in his knowledge of West African cultures. By making lavish gifts and displaying his skills as surgeon, he won over the Bondu chief in Fatteconda, who had been a thorn in Houghton's side. He then crossed eastern Bondu to Kajaaga, the country of the Seraluli. On Christmas Day 1795 Park received the worst possible present. A squad of horsemen, armed with muskets, informed him that all his possessions were forfeit to the ruler of Kajaaga, since he had not asked permission before entering his territory. Park bought the raiders off with a handful of gold and was then rescued from his predicament by an envoy from the neighbouring Khasso people who invited him to the royal court at Tessee as a guest.

Park crossed the Senegal river into Khasso and entered Tessee. But he found Khasso to be the fire to Kajaaga's frying pan. At first he was forbidden to leave, then allowed to do so only after being mulcted of a large part of his trade goods.

From Korriakary, the principal town of Khasso, he made his way to Guemon, capital of Kaarta. At each stage of his journey he was cautioned not to proceed further, but persisted. On 18 February 1796 he entered

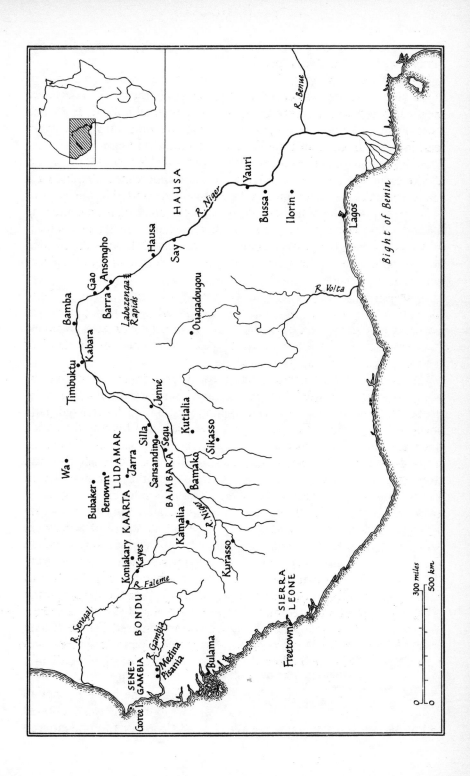

Ludamar, having already travelled 560 miles from Pisania. Ludamar was dangerous territory, for its rulers were Islamic and it was 'Moors' who had done for Major Houghton.

Ali, ruler of Ludamar from his encampment at Benowm, treated Park with contempt and, when told the white man did not speak Arabic, feigned boredom. Park was put under 'hut arrest', accused of being a spy, and threatened with execution or the loss of his right hand and his eyes. There was a rumour that Fatima, Ali's wife, wished to be converted to Christianity. She sent some of her women to Park's hut to find out about Christians. In particular she wished to know if Park was circumcised. Park agreed to give 'ocular demonstration' to one particularly beautiful female.

This period of arrest with Ali was arguably the worst time in Park's life. 'Never did any period of my life pass away so heavily,' he recorded. He bore stoically the threats and insults of Ali's acolytes and the ravages of hunger and thirst – for the chief kept him on short commons and sometimes even on a starvation diet. An interview with the supposed proselyte Fatima proved especially disappointing. Ali capped his tyranny by taking Park's servant Demba into slavery.

In July, in desperation, Park decided to escape to Segu. He crept out of the encampment one morning before dawn with a stolen horse. He was robbed by three mounted 'Moors' and left destitute, but at least they did not take him back to Ali. But his plight was grim. His horse was on its last legs, he had little food and no goods with which to barter for provisions or security. Worst of all was the aching thirst and the scorching sun.

He stumbled on through the wilderness, relieving the pangs of hunger and thirst by munching bitter herbs. He composed his mind for death, which seemed inevitable. Saved by the onset of rain, he laid in stores of water by spreading his clothes on the ground, then used the saturated garments as a sponge from which he squeezed liquid as and when he needed it. Eventually he staggered into a Fulani village, where an old woman took pity on him and fed him and his horse.

Similar acts of kindness from the Fulani in the next few days enabled Park to reach Oussebou by 6 July. He passed on to Doolinkeabo, then fell in with two black travellers who took him to the Niger at Segu.

> Looking forwards, I saw with pleasure the object of my mission – the long sought-for majestic Niger, glittering in the morning sun, as broad as the Thames at Westminster, and flowing slowly to the eastward. I hastened to the brink, and having drunk the water, lifted up my fervent thanks to the Great Ruler of all things, for having thus far crowned my endeavours with success.

The black ruler of Segu, Munsong, was well disposed, but explained to

Park that to help him openly would mean retaliation from the powerful Islamic slave-traders, who feared and hated Europeans as potential commercial competitors. After three days of skulking in a hut on the north bank of the river (he could not appear openly in Segu on the south bank), Park found a guide for the overland journey to Sansanding.

The Muslims of Sansanding proved as hostile to him as Ali of Ludamar had been. He was able to proceed only through the intercession of the headman, whose tribe lived in uneasy symbiosis with the slavers. But now Park's journey reached a crisis, as did the fever that assailed him. Sleepless from constant attacks of mosquitoes, and with his horse at its last gasp, Park reluctantly concluded that his original aim, to reach Timbuktu via Jenné, was suicidal. With a heavy heart, on 30 July 1796, he began to retrace his steps.

To avoid those who had tormented him on the outward journey, from Segu Park swung south to Kamalia. His six-week slog to that town was a nightmare. He trekked on through torrents as the rainy season sliced a swathe across the Niger valley. Because of famine he was turned away from several villages. Once again hunger and thirst gnawed at him. He risked attack by crocodiles by swimming across swollen streams. He was robbed of everything except the clothes he stood up in.

At Kamalia, reached on 16 September, he was taken under the wing of a trader called Karfa Taura, who promised to take him to The Gambia as soon as practicable. This did not happen for a further seven months. Park made the most of his enforced stay in Kamalia by writing up a minute anthropological study of its people. Finally, on 19 April 1797, Karfa's party set out for the coast. In mid-June Karfa, true to his promise, delivered Park to Pisania in The Gambia after an eight-week journey of 500 miles.

Hailed as a man who had come back from the dead, Park secured passage on an American slave-ship, the *Charleston*, which disembarked him in Antigua. Thence Park secured passage on the *Chesterfield Packet* and arrived at Falmouth on 22 December 1797.

Park's discoveries, if not quite the sensation of the hour in the twelve months between the Nore and Spithead mutinies and the Battle of the Nile, were nevertheless received with considerable interest. Not so the explorer himself, whose dour, gauche and socially maladroit personality did not commend itself to London society. Park decamped to Scotland to write up his *Travels* and get married. His marriage led to a rift with Banks, for the *éminence grise* had set up for his protégé an expedition into the Australian outback, which Park renounced at the promptings of his wife.

In 1799 Park took his final examinations as a surgeon. All now seemed set fair for a prosperous practice as a country doctor. Yet if Banks had disowned him, the African Association had not. In 1803 it tempted him back into the African arena with an offer to chart the full course of the Niger. Though now a family man, Park had not made enough money in his practice to be able to resist the offer. Though his wife opposed the venture, Park stubbornly persisted and even learned Arabic to make himself a more complete West African explorer.

In January 1805 he received his commission from the Secretary of State Lord Camden. He could draw £5000 in expenses, his wife would be paid £1000 a year in his absence, and on completion of the chart of the Niger he would receive a further £5000. Two Scotsmen, Alexander Anderson and George Scott, were to accompany him.

For all that, the expedition was not well planned. Storms at sea delayed the party, so that by the time they quit Pisania on 4 May, they had only three weeks to reach the Niger before the rains came. Park might have done well to heed the Jeremiahs, since he already had vivid experience of West African travel in the wettest and hottest months of the year. But he seems to have been buoyed up to overweening confidence by the number of white men he had in his party. In addition to Scott and Anderson, at Pisania he had signed on two press-ganged sailors, four carpenters released from the prison hulks at Portsmouth on condition they built roads for the party, and thirty-five NCOs and rankers from the Royal African Corps garrison at Goree, under the command of Lieutenant John Martyn, a bibulous Irishman. The Royal African Corps was reckoned the scum of the earth as its ranks were filled by men who had opted for service in the tropics rather than face a flogging in their own regiments. Acting as guide for the party was an African trader called Isaaco.

The expedition very soon lurched into disaster. The clothing issued to the soldiers became stifling in day temperatures of 135°F. Troopers in full pack fainted clean away. The pack animals, mainly asses, stuck fast in the quagmires formed by churned-up rice-fields. Mosquitoes and bees assailed the expedition, as did extortionate chiefs and villainous local guides. The heavy rains which came at the beginning of June brought on fever. The first fatality was soon recorded, and by 19 August more than thirty men had died, including Scott.

A fever-ridden Park was reduced to supporting invalids in their saddles as they swayed on the back of the asses which squelched through cloying mud. Villagers plundered the belongings of all stragglers and, unlike on his first journey, this time Park had many visitations from animals dangerous to man. Lions made daylight assaults on the pack-animals; on one occasion a pack of voracious wild dogs besieged the encampment for a whole night; while crossing a stream Isaaco was seized by a crocodile and escaped being taken only by gouging the brute in the eye.

On 19 August, after fourteen horrendous weeks that had seen all his beasts of burden wiped out, together with thirty-three out of forty-five Europeans, Park glimpsed again the Niger he had first seen nine years earlier. He and his men launched their boats at Bamako and travelled downstream to Segu, where he renewed acquaintance with Munsong, who supplied them with rotting canoes for the proposed journey to the mouth of the Niger. Park's men patched these up, caulked them, and fashioned a flat-bottomed boat out of the previously keeled canoes.

Yet only four white men now remained to sail this improvised Noah's Ark that Park absurdly dubbed 'HM Schooner *Joliba*'. Only the drunken Lieutenant Martyn and three soldiers survived. The intrepid party floated down past Jenné, Lake Debo and Kabara, the river port of Timbuktu, Bamba, Gao, Ansongho, Labezenga rapids, and into Hausa country. The river was now a mile wide. They had encountered hostility before, but at Bussa the bellicosity of the locals deepened. It seems that Park's floating flat-bottom was mistaken for a Fulani slave-boat. At all events the Bussa showered the craft with arrows. Park and his companions returned the fire with musketry. It is certain that this battle brought on their deaths, including that of Anderson, but oral testimony, which is all we have, is unreliable on exactly how they occurred. Some say the boat overturned during the fighting and pitched Park and the others into the water. Others say Park and Martyn leaped from it as they could not control it in the fierce currents at Bussa. Still others contend that the white men continued fighting until they ran out of ammunition, then linked arms in a suicide pact and plunged into the river. A view friendly to the Bussa, however, holds that Park's boat simply capsized in the flooded river after he had ignored local advice.

Two of the Four Horsemen of the Apocalypse prevented an early follow-up to Park's pioneering on the Niger. First, African explorations were shelved until the conclusion of the war with Napoleon. Then fever destroyed a British pincer movement, whereby Tuckey, a Royal Navy lieutenant, would advance up the Congo river in hopes of linking up with another party travelling overland from The Gambia and the Niger watershed (1815–16). The following year two German explorers, Blumenbach and Freudenberg, blazed a trail from Cairo to Fezzan before succumbing to dysentery. The British took this opportunity to penetrate to the Niger from Fezzan. Joseph Ritchie and George Francis Lyon tried to follow in the Germans' footsteps, but Ritchie soon joined the swelling list of those brought low by Africa's diseases. Lyon turned back just in time and staggered back to Tripoli a scarecrow. It was not until 1821 that someone from the British Isles had the courage to take on Park's mantle: Hugh Clapperton, a native of Annan, was determined to master the Fezzan route to the Niger. Giving him support were another Scot, Walter Oudney, and Major Dixon Denham.

All three were in their early thirties. Clapperton had gone to sea at thirteen and was a tall, strong, tough, imperious character. He got on well with Oudney, who had just been appointed consul in Bornu, but there was an immediate clash of temperaments and personalities between Clapperton and Denham, a veteran of the Peninsular War, who resented having to co-operate with 'civilians' and liked to throw his weight around. So acute was the conflict that Clapperton and Oudney began their journey to Murzuk in March 1822 without the detested Denham. Nevertheless, Denham managed to squeeze in a trip to Europe and still catch up with them by the end of October at Murzuk, where they had been prostrated with fever for six months. The old quarrels broke out anew, so that Clapperton and Oudney were glad to leave their 'comrade' behind once again when they shook off the dust of Murzuk in mid-November. With them went William Hillman, an English carpenter.

At Gatrone Denham caught up with them again. The Scots were making slow progress because of debility; Oudney was the worse case: he was suffering from aggravated bronchitis. Hillman was also ill and had to be hoisted on and off his mule. The caravan travelled with an Arab convoy for protection.

Still bickering with the high-handed Denham and assailed by fever, the two Scots seemed visited by 'malice domestic, foreign levy'. The country beyond Tejerri shocked the travellers with evidence of the most dreadful holocausts. Hundreds of human skulls and skeletons littered the arid plains. But this in no way drew the Europeans together or diminished the tension between Denham and Clapperton. Fiery letters were exchanged in which the one accused the other of exceeding his authority. Denham even spread a false rumour that Clapperton had homosexual relations with his servant. The two Scots took care to keep the cross-grained Englishman at arm's length and virtually sent him to Coventry.

On 12 August 1823 they reached Bilma, the capital of Tibboo, where they rested four months. But after this oasis came the most dreadful desert yet. It took thirteen days' agonised toil over sands that gave way beneath the feet to emerge from the wilderness and 27 January 1824 found them in scrubland, populated by an abundance of ostrich and gazelle. Next day they were at Beere-Kashifery, where they were grudgingly received.

On 1 February they set off again. Because of the depredations of the Arabs in the caravan, the explorers' party was taken for marauding

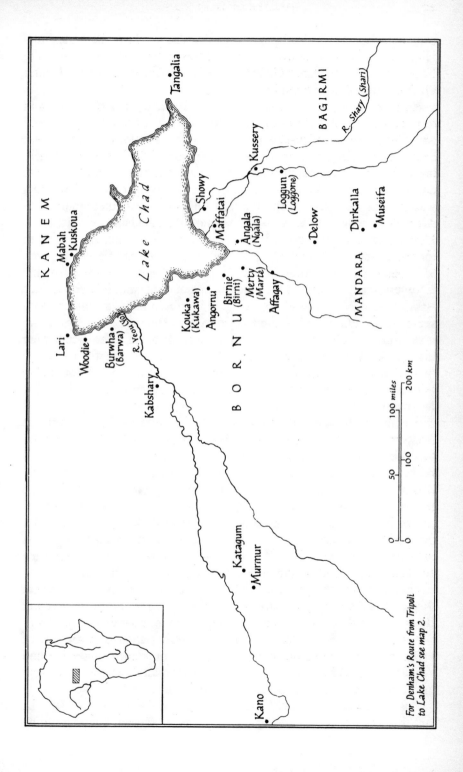

KANEM

Tangalia

BAGIRMI

R. Shary (Shari)

Kussery

Showy

Maffatai

Loggun
(Loggone)

Mabah
Kuskoua

Lake Chad

Angala
(Ngala)

Delow

Dirkalla

Museifa

MANDARA

Lari

Woodie

Burwha
(Barwa)

R. Yeou

Kouka
(Kukawa)

Angornu

Birnie
(Birni)

Merty
(Marté)

Affagay

B O R N U

Kabshary

50   100

100 miles

200 km

Katagum

Murmur

Kano

For Denham's Route from Tripoli
to Lake Chad see map 2.

Tuaregs, and the local people fled before them. Three days later they reached Lake Chad at Lari.

The days by the lakeside at Lari were idyllic. The region round about was a wildfowl paradise and the lake was full of fish, allowing the travellers to gorge themselves on first-class protein. It was a wrench to leave and proceed along the lake to Kouka. The impression that they had blundered into a game reserve was strengthened by the fauna they now encountered: herds of elephant, wild red cattle, gazelle, guinea-fowl, monkeys, wild hogs; less welcome were the lions, one of whom killed a camel from the caravan.

They entered Kouka on 17 February. The ruler was a considerable local potentate, who accepted their assurances of friendliness and, in return for gifts of firearms, loaded the explorers with provisions. Here they remained for two months. Denham made side trips to the towns of Birnie and Angornu and to Lake Chad. He found his whiteness a stigma as striking as if he had leprosy; women, especially, hastened to get out of his way.

When Boo-Khaloom, the leader of the Arabs, took his men south on a slaving expedition in April, the ruler of Kouka tried to prevent the white men from accompanying them. Clapperton and Oudney remained behind, but Denham browbeat the ruler, who acquiesced with the proviso that his adviser Maramy should shadow Denham wherever he went.

Denham then took part in an attack on a Fulani stronghold. Boo-Khaloom and his allies seemed at first to have won the day, but the Fulani counterattacked and drove the invaders from the field. Denham was caught up in the rout and his horse was shot under him. He was quickly surrounded by the Fulani and would have been killed at once had they not coveted his clothes and therefore refrained from ruining them by spear thrusts. They stripped Denham naked and began arguing about who should have the spoils. In the confusion Denham slipped away. The alarm was raised. His pursuers followed him through a wood, where his flesh was torn by prickly undergrowth. He made a lucky escape across a river and next morning fell in with Barca Gana and Boo-Khaloom, still fighting a desperate rearguard action against the Fulani. It was then that Denham had occasion to bless the ruler of Kouka. Maramy rode up and pulled him up behind him on his horse. They reached Delow safely, but not before Denham witnessed the death of Boo-Khaloom from wounds received in the battle.

The raid had been a disaster. Forty-five Arabs perished on the field of battle and many more from the after-effects of wounds and poisoned arrows. Denham himself was soon in hot water with London, where the War Office was stupefied that an officer and gentleman should have taken part in such a savage foray.

Not a whit abashed by his experiences, on his return to Kouka after the raid Denham at once set out on another raiding expedition, led by the ruler in person. This time he was accompanied by Oudney. The Kouka armies were on a punitive mission against their rebellious vassals the Manga, who lived on the far side of the river Gambaron. But once they took the measure of the opposition and realised that the Manga could put 12,000 bowmen with poisoned arrows into the field against them, they patched up a face-saving peace formula and returned to Kouka.

In Kouka Oudney and Clapperton suffered grievously from fever, but Denham's robust health enabled him to hunt, learn Arabic and take notes on Islamic culture which later, in book form, laid bare for the world the strange and cruel customs of Muslim Africa.

In December 1823 Clapperton and Oudney had recovered sufficiently to leave Kouka for Kano, to the south-west. One month later Denham set out in the opposite direction, for Loggun. He was in good spirits as he had a congenial companion in the shape of the newly arrived Ensign Toole of the 80th Regiment. Toole had made the difficult journey from Tripoli to Bornu in three and a half months. Even more welcome to Denham than Toole's having proved his calibre as a traveller was his preparedness to defer: he was a junior officer and Denham his superior, and that, as far as both were concerned, was that.

The two soldiers reached Kussery without mishap but Toole's fever compelled a halt. Kussery turned out to be a hell on earth: the ravages of the insects were so fearsome that the locals, like Bluebeard, constructed houses with seven connecting chambers, so that the winged pests could not penetrate to the inner sanctum. Tired of standing fire-watches over his companion – for fire alone would repel the noxious clouds – Denham manhauled Toole to Loggun, 30 miles to the south. Toole now badly needed rest if he was to survive, but the ruler of Loggun ordered the white men on their way, on the grounds that he could not protect them against slavers. The inevitable happened: Toole died at the end of February 1824; Denham buried him in a tomb of thornbushes to prevent hyenas digging him up.

Loss of his friend affected even Denham's mighty constitution. Returning to Kouka, he tossed feverishly, scarcely consoled by the news that Oudney, too, had just died of fever.

Once he had recovered, Denham's stock with the ruler rose high as a result of two incidents. Some long-delayed supplies for the expedition came in, among which were a dagger, two gold watches and a parcel of rockets, which delighted the ruler. As if this was not enough, Denham used candlewax to extract a fishbone from the gullet of the chief's son. His reward was to be allowed to accompany a Kouka expedition to the east side of Lake Chad.

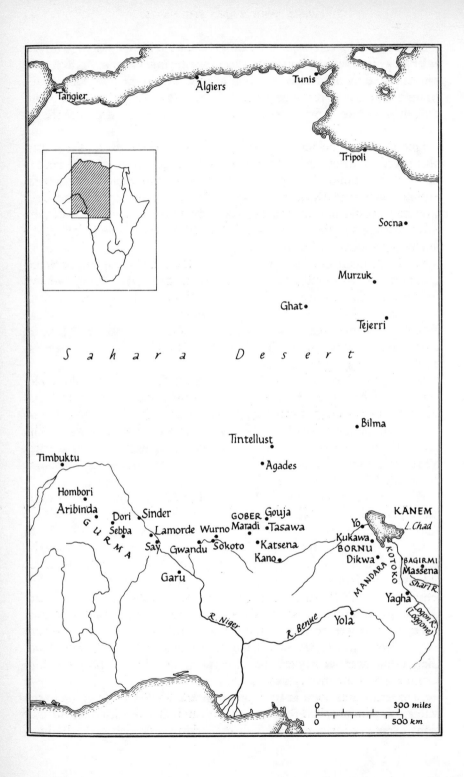

Once again the veteran warrior Barca Gana led the caravan, but he was as unlucky for Denham this time as on the previous foray. Once again he was defeated by the Fulani and had to return to Kouka. Denham made another attempt to explore Lake Chad, with a single guide, but his dragoman turned coward when they reached the lake and insisted on turning back.

Denham now decided to head for home. He crossed the desert northwards to Murzuk and thence to Tripoli. He returned to England in June 1825, submitted a report before Lord Bathurst and published his explorations in the *Narrative*. He seemed to be the one explorer the Dark Continent could not kill off, but Africa had not yet finished with him. After two years in the 'White Man's Grave', Sierra Leone (1826–8), he finally succumbed to fever and died.

While Denham and Toole were heading for Lake Chad, the two Scots, Clapperton and Oudney, were making for Kano, again in the protective cover of an Arab caravan. On the way to Bedigana Clapperton noticed the ravages of the recent Fulani invasions. The evidence of man's inhumanity to man seems to have angered him, for outside Bedigana he intervened when a Bornuese was beating up a black man, and himself thrashed the aggressor.

But he had anxieties enough on his own account. On 12 January Oudney died of fever at Murmur and Clapperton proceeded to Kano alone. Kano was a large town of 40,000 inhabitants, but for all that was no more than an assemblage of square, clay huts built on a swamp. The deepest part of the swamp, complete with ducks, doubled as a town park. Kano's importance was not architectural but commercial, as the town was the greatest emporium in West Africa.

When he had done with the merchants, potters, weavers and snake-charmers of Kano, Clapperton pressed on to the town of Sokoto, like Kano a Fulani stronghold. This was his farthest west; he then decided to return. Suffering intermittently from fever, he obtained from the governor of Sokoto an escort to take him through the war-torn provinces of Gobir and Zamfara. The governor, at Clapperton's prompting, wrote a letter to George IV suggesting trade between Britain and the Fulani. Clapperton returned via Kano, Murmur and Kouka to Tripoli and thence to England, where he arrived the same month as Denham (June 1825) only to find Lord Bathurst keen to sponsor a second expedition. Clapperton was instructed to 'ascertain the source, progress and termination of the mysterious Niger'.

Clapperton was soon at sea again, *en route* for West Africa, this time with a companion called Richard Lander, an innkeeper's son and former manservant aged twenty. Before disembarking at Wydah in the Bight of

Benin, Clapperton additionally enrolled in his party a fellow naval-officer Captain Pearce, two surgeons (Dr Dickson and Dr Morrison), Columbus, a West Indian mulatto, and a Hausa from Gobir named Pasko, whom he planned to use as guide and interpreter.

Starting from Badagry in December 1825, the party struck inland. Almost at once Clapperton and Lander were prostrated with fever. They were the lucky ones. Within a month the two surgeons and Columbus were dead.

Rising from their sick-beds, Clapperton and Lander trekked on to Katunga, within striking distance of the Niger, where they arrived on 22 January 1826. Here they were detained for seven weeks, since the local chief was reluctant to let them go and toyed with the idea of placing them under 'hut arrest'. But on 30 March the travellers reached Bussa on the Niger, where Mungo Park had died. Striking north, the caravan headed for Kano. They made slow progress; both men again had frightening bouts of African fever. On reaching Kano, they lit out at once for Sokoto, but fever and impassable roads drove them back to Kano, where they spent a miserable two months (August and September 1826).

On 11 October Clapperton set out for Sokoto, where Pasko and the invalid Lander joined him just before Christmas. At this point Clapperton decided he could no longer condone Pasko's habitual thieving, so dismissed him.

At Sokoto Clapperton went down with dysentery. Lander nursed him faithfully and after five weeks Clapperton seemed to recover; it proved merely a false dawn for two days later Clapperton died.

Lander set his course for home. He wanted to return to the coast at Badagry, but the chief of Sokoto vetoed this, so Lander was forced to travel across the desert to Fezzan with the Arabs, whom he disliked. He and Pasko set off across the burning sands of the Gobir Bush. Suffering frightfully from thirst all the way, Lander staggered into Kano in May 1827. Here he picked up trade goods owed to Clapperton and turned south towards the Niger, hoping to trace the course of the river to Benin, but he was detained in Zaria in July by a hostile ruler and forced to amend his plans and aim instead for Badagry.

Another anxious four-month journey brought Lander to Badagry in mid-November, but although he was so close to the British presence, Lander had to wait two months for a ship. He was sickened by African brutality, cruelty and the cults of fetish and human sacrifice. The Portuguese traders, jealous of his presence, plotted against him; he was accused of sorcery by the witchdoctors and forced to 'prove' his innocence in the traditional way by drinking a bowl of poison. He summoned enough strength to walk back to his hut, where he vomited up the poison and so survived. Relief came to him shortly afterwards in the form of the British brig *Maria*, and at Cape Coast Castle (the principal British base in the Bight of Benin) he was able to take ship to England, where he returned after an absence of thirteen months.

Lander found it hard to settle down in England. He married and had a child but his health was poor, so that a brief spell in the Excise Department was succeeded by an equally unsatisfactory berth as a weighing-porter. From this limbo he was rescued at the end of 1829 by John Barrow, first chairman of the newly merged Geographical Society and African Association. Barrow recommended him to the Colonial Office 'to settle once and for all the problem of the Niger'. Lander was experienced and, better still, he was cheap. All he required was £200 a year (half for himself, half for his wife) and the assistance of his younger brother John.

The Landers disembarked in the surf of Badagry roads in March 1830. Delays in getting the expedition under way gave Lander time to modify his preconceived idea of the local people. Instead of noble savages, the Africans he encountered were drunken bullies, importunate freeloaders and deceitful skrimshankers. In the circumstances it was hardly surprising that he formed a deep dislike of them, amounting to detestation.

To escape from the grasping clutches of chief Adele of Badagry, the Landers signed a useless chit, authorising the chief to draw on the Royal Ordnance in England such weapons and military impedimenta as he required. The reluctant Adele then allowed the two whites to proceed into the interior. The Landers shook the dust of Badagry off their shoes with gusto and plunged into the wilderness with a small retinue of guides and interpreters, including Pasko from the first expedition.

They made good progress and were at Katunga six weeks after leaving Badagry. Forewarned that exploring ventures aroused suspicions, the Landers conveyed to the chiefs they met that their purpose in coming to West Africa was to retrieve the personal papers of a British subject who had died at Bussa many years before. The ruler of Katunga eased matters by sending messengers to warn neighbouring tribes to the north that white men were coming among them, and to assure them they were peaceful.

Again the Landers made further good progress and were at Bussa by 7 June. They pressed on upstream to Yauri, reached on 27 June. Now in Islamic country, the Landers were received with coldness and hostility. The Emir of Yauri was inclined to keep them as prisoners, but the Landers smuggled out a message to Bussa, asking for the ruler's assistance. A canoe, suitable for a voyage downstream to the mouth of the Niger, was sent and, presumably, the Emir of Yauri did not think a war with his neighbour over two white devils was worth while.

The chief of Bussa welcomed the returning travellers with all the appearance of joy and sent a message to his brother-in-law downstream at Wawa to request a larger canoe. This was not forthcoming, so for the next few months the Landers were based in Bussa, anxious to get transport downriver and grimly aware that the attitude of Bussa's ruler towards them was changing, and not for the better.

In September an invitation arrived for the white men to visit the kingdom of Nupe, whose monarch remembered the gifts Clapperton had brought. There ensued another month of frustration while the 'sultans' of Wawa and Patashie shuttlecocked the Landers to and fro between them without ever providing the requested river transport. In desperation the white men finally purloined two canoes and surreptitiously paddled downstream until they came eventually to the kingdom of Nupe.

From there the explorers made their way downstream in painfully slow stages. They soon needed to replace the stolen canoes, but serviceable river craft were not available and not even the most sumptuous gifts could tempt local chiefs to part with them.

Finally they changed boats and proceeded downstream in a larger, though still leaky, canoe. All the way down the Niger they were plagued with requests for tribute or passage money. Gales and thunderstorms on the river, attacks by hippos and crocodiles, and thinly veiled threats of consequences if the white men did not accept local 'hospitality' (i.e. long stopovers in riverine villages) completed their woes.

At Egga, in the bend of the Niger, the Landers needed all their assertiveness. Wishing to detain them, the Muslim chief painted a terrifying picture of the perils downstream. Richard and John's rowers attempted mutiny and were pressed back into service only when Richard claimed to have learned from secret sources that the chief of Egga intended to enslave them.

On 23 October the travellers narrowly avoided confrontation with villagers who mistook them for Fulani raiders. Next day they reached Kasunda where they were received with kindness, but were again warned about warlike tribes farther downstream.

25 October 1830 was a memorable day in the annals of African exploration. The day before, the travellers had noticed that the direction of the river was changing to SSW and that mountains now surrounded them. At dawn on the 25th they suddenly caught sight of a vast river flowing into the Niger from the east. They had come to the confluence of the river with its mighty tributary, the Benue. They were the first Europeans ever to set eyes on it.

Fêted and lionised at the town of Damugoo, the explorers embarked on

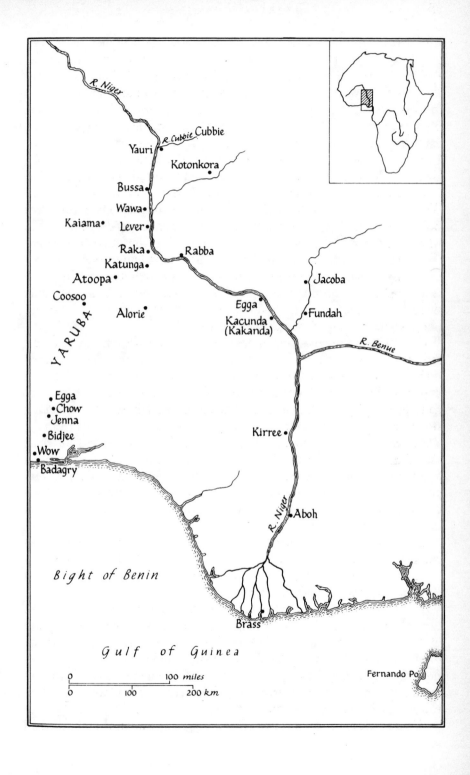

the broad river on 4 November 1830, confident that they were near journey's end. But they forgot, or had never heard, Odysseus's warning that the time for supreme vigilance is at the very end of a journey. By now the Landers were used to being overhauled by war canoes, which invariably turned out to contain nothing more than excited or rambunctious tribesmen. When yet another flotilla bore down on them, the travellers treated its advent cavalierly. Suspicions were allayed by the European clothes of the canoeists and the Union Jacks on their pennants, but, too late, John and Richard realised that these were the pirates they had been warned about all the way down the river.

The pirates overpowered the two canoes and sank the one on which the brothers were sailing. The Landers swam ashore, only to be informed by their rescuers that they were now prisoners of the king of Ibo. Next day the luckless travellers were conveyed to the monarch. He told them that by ancient custom their lives and possessions were forfeit to him; however, as he liked white men, he would accept a ransom equal in value to the price of twenty slaves.

Complicated negotiations ensued. Eventually one of the emirs of the Brass river came forward with the ransom money, after taking verbal surety from the master of the brig *Thomas*, then at anchor in the Brass delta. Released on 12 November, the Landers were conveyed downstream to the town of Brass in a large forty-oared canoe, which got them to their destination three days later. The Emir of Brass then demanded a refund of the redemption money. Richard promised to obtain it from the *Thomas*'s captain next day; the Emir meanwhile held John as a hostage.

The master of the *Thomas* proved to be a blackguard and refused to put up a penny as ransom, although he did promise to take the Landers as far as the island of Fernando Po if they could escape the clutches of the Emir. Richard returned and explained to the Emir that the *Thomas*'s master would not put up the ransom money, and so he and his brother would have to wait for the next British ship to arrive. He did not tell the ruler about the captain's ancillary offer. Having thus lulled the Emir, Richard and John stole away and boarded the *Thomas*. By the end of the month they were at Fernando Po, where they transshipped to England via Rio de Janeiro.

The Landers arrived in England in June 1831. If they had expected to be treated as heroes for charting the Niger down to its many deltas, they were sorely disappointed. Their sole tangible reward was £1000 from the publisher John Murray for their journals. Some Liverpool merchants nevertheless took Richard on as leader of a new commercial expedition to the Niger, and so by October 1832 he was back in the Delta.

His final Niger venture was a chapter of misfortunes. The naval officer sent out to make an Admiralty survey quarrelled with him; the expected ivory trade proved disappointing; his old friend Pasko was poisoned by the Igala when Lander sent him up to the confluence with the Benue; and fever once again cut a swathe through the white men in the expedition. Lander's only success was to steam 100 miles up the Benue in the *Alburkah*, which he hoped would take him all the way to Lake Chad, but navigation difficulties and food shortages forced him back. Instead, he then tried to proceed up the main Niger waterway, but this time the engine failed and he was compelled to return to Fernando Po.

Lander now made the mistake of sending the *Alburkah* back up the Niger under the command of the ship's surgeon while he went to Cape Coast Castle to obtain more trading goods. This meant that to rejoin the ship he had to travel up the Niger by canoe. Large numbers of hostile tribesmen, armed with flintlocks – evidently renegades who detested King Boy of Brass's friendly policy towards whites – attacked Lander's party. After a five-hour running fight in which three of his men were killed and he himself was wounded, Richard beat a retreat to Fernando Po. A few days later, on 2 February 1834, he died of his wounds at the age of thirty. His brother John died soon afterwards in London, aged thirty-two, from the delayed effects of tropical illness contracted in Africa. The career of the Landers showed clearly two things about African exploration: it was a young man's game, and it virtually assured such young men an early death.

The next man to attempt to solve the mystery of the Niger was Alexander Gordon Laing. A native of Edinburgh and former schoolmaster, in 1825 Laing was a major in the Royal African Corps, with seven years' service in the West Indies and two in Sierra Leone already behind him. Unpopular with his regiment, he obtained permission from the Governor of Sierra Leone to go freelancing in the interior. His secret ambition was to reach Timbuktu and discover the source of the Niger.

He left Sierra Leone and proceeded up the river Rokelle in April 1825. He passed through the towns of Ma Bung, Mayassa and Koolooga, then out of the territory of the Muslim Mandingos into that of the 'pagan' Koorankos. Here he was welcomed like royalty, and even more so at Falabe, the capital of the Soolima people. Laing asked permission to press on to the source of the Niger, and heard the usual grisly stories about savage and hostile tribes there. It seemed that the Soolima and Kissi, who lived in the area around the fount of the Niger, were ancient enemies. Given that his leave was about to expire and that to reach the source of the Niger was going to be more troublesome than he expected, Laing reluctantly abandoned his plans and made his way back to Sierra Leone.

Shortly after Laing had returned to England to prepare an account of his travels, Lord Bathurst, the Colonial Secretary, proposed that Laing should guide an expedition across the desert from Tripoli to Timbuktu and the upper Niger. It was a commission Laing accepted with alacrity. Once at Tripoli he struck south via Fezzan, Ghadames, Ensala, and then crossed the desert of Tenerounft with an Arab caravan. But when success seemed within his grasp, his convoy was ambushed by Tuaregs of the Ahagger sept and Laing came within an ace of being butchered in his sleep. He took a gunshot wound, then in the ensuing mêlée sustained serious wounds and was left for dead. The Arabs carried him to Timbuktu, which he entered on 18 August 1826, where he underwent a long convalescence. His body had been striated with sword cuts, his right hand almost severed, his jaw broken. He had five deep gashes in his scalp and the lobe of his ear had been hacked off. In this Muslim city he was treated with tolerance so long as he made outward obeisance to Islam.

On 26 September 1826 he started the homeward journey but again he was set upon by Tuaregs from the Barabich sept. This time the Tuaregs made no mistake; they strangled Laing, and ripped up and made a bonfire of his papers. So perished the records of the first European to dwell in Timbuktu.

Money was added to the list of motives for exploring the Dark Continent when the French Société de Géographie offered a 10,000-franc prize to the man who could reach Timbuktu and return with an account of it. The challenge was taken up by René Caillié, the first African explorer in a line of those from humble backgrounds whose most famous representative was H.M. Stanley. René's father was a convict, his mother died early and after a few years in a charity school young René was apprenticed to a cobbler.

At an early age he developed a monomania about Africa. At the age of sixteen he left his apprenticeship, took a job as a manservant and accompanied his master to Senegal. At Dakar the officer died, as did most of the Frenchmen who had come out to Africa. His zest for Africa heightened rather than diminished by these early experiences, Caillié decided to throw in his lot with the British, who were said to be mounting an expedition into the interior from The Gambia. He slogged 1300 miles to Goree but arrived too exhausted even to apply to His Majesty's representatives. He then shipped out to Guadeloupe and spent six months trying to amass the capital for an African venture.

Arriving back in The Gambia at the end of 1818, he learned that the British expedition, under a Major Gray, had still not left. He applied to join and was accepted on the understanding that he would not be paid. Having endured agonies of thirst on the first leg of the journey inland,

Caillié went down with fever and had to be invalided back to St Louis on the coast. After a period working as a cook there, shortage of funds forced him to return to France, where he worked for a wine merchant. He painfully accumulated the money for a store of trade goods and eventually returned to Senegal in 1824, the same age as the century. His short experience with the Gray expedition had convinced him that he travels fastest and safest who travels alone. The key was not to make oneself a target for Africa's many marauders and to this end he decided to dress as a Muslim and assume the identity of an Islamic postulant.

In August 1824 he departed from St Louis, bearing a small bundle of goods on his head. He moved up the Senegal river and lived for a time with the Braknas, to whom he explained his Islamic ambitions. After enduring great hardships with them, Caillié returned to St Louis, convinced he now knew enough about Muslim customs to make the journey to Timbuktu. There still remained the question of money, but this was solved by a tempting offer from the British to be manager of an indigo factory. While he worked and saved, Caillié rehearsed and perfected the story he would tell the Timbuktu Arabs and honed his knowledge of the Koran. Finally, in March 1827, he headed for the mouth of the Rio Nunez. At Kakande he joined a small caravan.

His Arabic persona held up well and on 10 May, after covering 200 miles in three weeks, he reached Kambaya. By mid-June he was across the Niger at Kouroussia. He passed through the country of the Ouassoulous to the Mandingo village of Tieme (reached 3 August 1827) where, however, he fell seriously ill; prostrated by fever, he had to endure the secondary agonies of a foot painfully swollen from parasite infection. It took him until November to recover from this double affliction; then he promptly went down with an agonising attack of scurvy.

Finally, on New Year's Day 1828 Caillié left Tieme with a caravan bound for Jenné. At Jenné Caillié repeated his story and was subjected to intense cross-questioning before his credentials were accepted. The chief of Jenné, whom the Arabs called in to make the final decision, accepted Caillié at face value and decreed he should be lodged with the Arabs at their expense until an opportunity arose for him to go to Timbuktu.

At length Caillié won over the Arab sherif, who arranged passage for him to Timbuktu on a canoe. On 23 March 1828 he set off down the river Bani on to the Niger, where passengers were transferred to a 100-ft-long canoe. Proceeding at the tortoise pace of 2 mph, the crew alternated punting, paddling and rope hauling. As the only white among the passengers, Caillié was abused by the blacks who had no pity on him even when he became feverish. Beyond Saferre, he was forced to hide under matting in the covered part of the canoe so that his pale skin would not attract the attention of the marauding Tuaregs.

So at last, painfully slowly, Caillié came to Kabara, the port for Timbuktu where a party of slaves arrived to escort him across the desert to his destination. Caillié caught his first sight of the city at sunset, which after all his travails engendered 'an indescribable feeling of satisfaction'.

But the satisfaction changed to disappointment when a closer inspection showed Timbuktu to be nothing more than a collection of dingy houses built of earth. The legendary city turned out to be a one-horse town, where food was dear and the inhabitants apathetic. There was a black king, but he was a figurehead; the real power in the land were the Tuaregs, who rode into Timbuktu whenever the fancy took them to pillage, loot and prey on the town's women. They would then demand payment as the price of their leaving.

Knowing of Laing's fate at the hands of the Tuaregs and fearing that he might be their next victim, Caillié left Timbuktu in May and headed north across the Sahara by a circuitous route. In a caravan of 400 persons and 1400 camels, Caillié endured heat, thirst, sandstorms, monotonous food and bullying from his 'protectors'. Both the humans and the camels came close to expiring from thirst before they located the all-important wells of Telig.

There was a long stop-over at El-Karib where a violently sick Caillié lay in misery in a tent, short of water and unable to chew because of scurvy. At last on 12 July the caravan left El-Karib. Eleven days later they were at the oasis of Tafilet where water was plentiful and dates, melons and apples abundant. Tafilet was the end of the road for the caravan and so Caillié then made his way by mule across the Atlas mountains to Fez, and thence via Meknes and Rabat to Tangier. Still in disguise, he slipped surreptitiously into the house of the French vice-consul, then, after a week of being treated like the prodigal son, emerged in the garb of a sailor to board a ship for France.

There he was greeted like a hero. He obtained his 10,000-franc prize and was additionally granted a pension of 3000 francs a year. But there were many sceptics and critics. Some criticised his Arab disguise, much as they did Richard Burton's after his journey to Mecca in 1853. Others doubted that he had ever been to Timbuktu and claimed he had discovered Laing's papers and invented the story of his own journey to Timbuktu. Caillié married, retired to a farm near Mauze and was even elected mayor, but the stress of controversy took its toll. He declared that the charge of charlatanry was more painful even than the aching thirst he endured in the Sahara and he died of consumption aged thirty-eight.

It took the German explorer, Heinrich Barth, to prove that Caillié had indeed been to Timbuktu. Barth resembled his friend Richard Burton in his erudition and linguistic talent: he was fluent in Arabic, English, Spanish and Italian and had read Classics at the University of Berlin. He did not of course possess Burton's exceptional ability as a linguist but it is arguable that as an African explorer he surpassed Burton's achievement.

Born in 1821 he spent the years after university in an arduous apprenticeship as an African traveller. First he crossed North Africa from Morocco to Egypt, then went up the Nile as far as Wadi Halfa. When the German ambassador in London asked that one of his compatriots should accompany the Englishman, James Richardson, his official superior, on a new expedition to Lake Chad, Barth's name was at the top of his list. Another German, Adolph Overweg, a Prussian astronomer, was also selected.

Barth and Richardson did not see eye to eye on the aims of the expedition. Richardson, a veteran of travels to Murzuk, Ghadanes and Ghat, was a middle-aged campaigner against slavery. To him Africa was important only as the source of the detested slave trade. To Barth scientific exploration was the lodestone; after Chad he hoped to journey to the Nile, to Zanzibar, or to Timbuktu.

The trio of Barth, Richardson and Overweg left Tripoli on 24 March 1850. They made slow but sure progress south, through Murzuk, Ghat, Basakat, Selufiet to Tintellust, which they reached in September. Here Barth left his companions for a side-trip to Agades. Barth was one of the earliest in a long line of discoverers who had to be the 'first' at everything; here the aim was to be the first Christian in Agades. Perhaps partly for this reason, when he returned to Tintellust after three weeks and travelled south to catch up his comrades at Tagetel, the differences he had with Richardson on the aims of the expedition hardened into mutual antipathy to rival the Denham/Clapperton hatred.

In January 1851 the expedition split into three. Richardson headed for Kukawa, Overweg for Gobir, while Barth made for Tasawa. This was the first village Barth had seen in black Africa proper, and it entranced him. When he moved on to Kano in February he found that delightful too. Already Barth was displaying the quality of empathy some students of his life feel was his most noteworthy characteristic.

In March he continued to Bornu to learn that Richardson had died on the road to Kukawa. The administrative problems involved in obtaining Richardson's effects from the ruler of Kukawa were legion and were not solved until Overweg joined Barth in Kukawa in May. The Prussian decided to stay and explore Lake Chad; released from his chores, Barth left Kukawa with a horse and a band of 'dark companions' at the end of May.

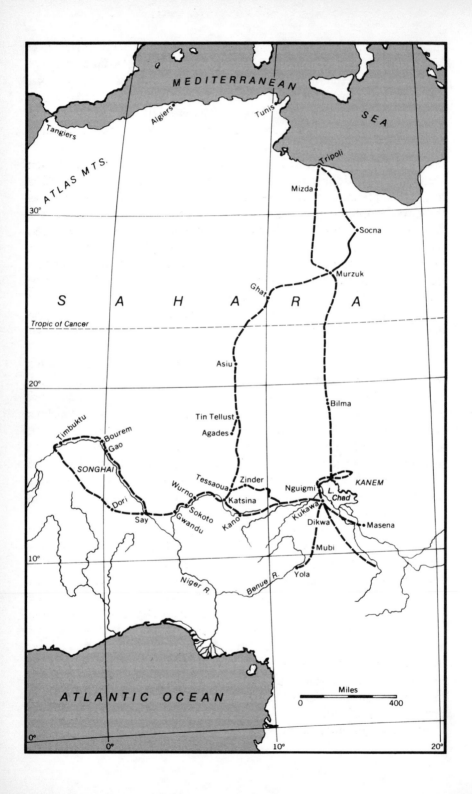

In the middle of June he reached the Benue, now in flood with the onset of the rainy season. He crossed the river and entered Yola, a large town of beehive huts, but the ruler made it clear he was not welcome. Barth beat a retreat to Kukawa, where he pondered the idea of a circumnavigation of Lake Chad. On 11 September he met Overweg at the village of Yo. The two men headed north along the lake shore, marvelling at the military precision of the elephant herds they encountered.

It was not just in his quarrel with Richardson that Barth resembled Denham. He had the major's selfsame propensity for getting involved in local wars. He and Overweg fell in with a band of Arab raiders who in three weeks uplifted 300 cattle, 1500 sheep and goats and fifteen camels. The Arab camp was fiercely attacked in retaliation but the enraged pastoral tribesmen were beaten off with heavy loss. Not content with this incident, Barth and Overweg then switched to another band of warriors, this time commanded by the ruler of Kukawa, who was bent on chastising his vassals in Mandara. Barth rationalised his awkward moral position on the grounds that he could not otherwise travel so far south. The army cut deep into Mandara territory, accepting the fealty of the local ruler, but also pillaging when the fancy took it.

On 7 January 1852 they marched back to Kukawa. Resting there for one month, Barth set out in March to chart the southern shores of Lake Chad, crossing the Loggun and Shari rivers to Massena, the dilapidated capital of Bagirmi. While he was there, a letter arrived from Kukawa announcing that the British government had appointed Barth to the expeditionary command left vacant on Richardson's death. He returned to Kukawa in August, intending to make Timbuktu his goal. He arrived barely in time to witness Overweg's death from fever. The Prussian was only twenty-nine.

Barth left Kukawa for Timbuktu on 25 November 1852 with a small party. He made a leisurely progress alone the well-trodden road to Sokoto, and on 20 June 1853 recorded his first sight of the Niger. Barth's route took him through Say, Champagore, Sebba, Dori, Lamorde, Kubo, Isaye, Bambara, Saramayo and so at last to Kabara, the port of Timbuktu, where he arrived on 17 September 1853. Barth entered Timbuktu in the guise of a Muslim merchant. As extra insurance he bought the protection of a rich Muslim, Sheikh el-Bakay, with sumptuous presents. He then spent seven months travelling between his protector's encampment and Timbuktu, which he found exactly as Caillié had described it. Because of local suspicions towards him, Barth was a virtual prisoner for these seven months, and probably only the loyal friendship of Sheikh el-Bakay saved him from assassination.

At last Barth obtained permission to leave and set off on the return journey to Kukawa on 19 April 1854. The return itinerary was slightly different: Gogo, Garu, Sinder, Say, Guandu, Sokoto, Wurmu, Kano and Bundi. In Kukawa there were further administrative problems arising from the expedition's debts. Subventions sent out from Europe solved these, and in mid-1854 Barth departed for the north. He reached Tejerri on 6 July and was in Tripoli a month later. Travelling via Malta and Marseilles, he arrived in London on 6 September 1855 to the plaudits of Palmerston and Lord Clarendon.

Barth's five-year sojourn in the heart of West Africa, during which he covered 10,000 miles of territory, made him the most complete African explorer to date. It may be hyperbole to state, as one of his admirers has, 'in terms of exploration no single man ever equalled Heinrich Barth', but he was the first European to enter Yola and describe the Fulani kingdom of Adamana. He charted the Benue river and disproved the current theory that it flowed into Lake Chad. He was also the first European to enter deeply into African culture and the first to bring back scientific results of abiding value. Significantly, too, he was the first great African explorer to live past forty. He died in Hamburg in 1865, aged forty-four.

2

From the Cape to the Zambezi

If the exploration of Africa began on the west coast of the continent, its second stage started in South Africa. Two different impulses lay behind the northward spread of Europeans, but both were the consequence of the cession of the Cape Province to Britain by the 1815 Treaty of Paris.

When the 150-year-old Dutch colony became British territory, there was an immediate culture clash between the new incoming British settlers and officials and the long-established Afrikaans-speaking farmers of Dutch descent, the Boers. This would have been bad enough in itself, but the coming of British rule had an even more sombre implication for the Boers. By extending the abolition of slavery to its burgeoning dominions, the British Empire at once posed a threat to the very roots of Boer existence. Steeped in the Old Testament, the Boers regarded blacks as the accursed children of Ham; to enslave them was thus part of the natural order of things. To be told that the indigenous African had equal rights was for the Boer like being asked to believe that water ran uphill – and this was quite apart from the consideration that the entire Boer economy was built on slavery.

As soon as the British took steps to make their anti-slavery writ run in Cape Colony, the Boers met in conclave and took a decision that would have been approved by the great social contract theorists Locke and Rousseau. Since civil society did not meet their aspirations, the Boers were prepared to exile themselves from it and live in a 'state of nature'. In a word, they proposed to trek out of Cape Colony and continue their old way of life in the 'virgin' lands to the north and east.

In 1836, taking their inspiration from Moses's leading his people out of Egypt into the Promised Land, the Boers began their exodus. The 'Great Trek' split into two parties. One, under Piet Retief, crossed the Drakensberg mountains and debouched on to present-day Natal. Here they came into collision with the Zulus, recently converted into the most powerful warrior race in Africa by the military genius of Shaka. His successor, Dingaan, alarmed by the power of the Boers' guns and the mobility of their horses, pretended friendship for the interlopers and seemed agreeable to making grants of land for them to settle on.

Then, early in 1838, he invited Retief to his kraal to seal the bargain with a feast. Retief and seventy of his men entered Dingaan's township, trustingly leaving their weapons outside, and were then massacred to a man. Vowing revenge for this treachery, the Boers gathered together a powerful commando to punish Dingaan. On 16 December 1838 a force of 500 Boers under Andries Pretorius formed a laager at Blood River in Zululand and awaited attack by 4000 of Dingaan's assegai-wielding impis. What followed was a classic demonstration of European technological superiority. Wave after wave of Zulus crashed ineffectually against the tight circle of waggons lashed together with thorn bushes. The Boers' elephant-guns doled out fearful punishment on the Zulu warriors, who could not close the range so as to make their numbers tell. When the Boers had mown down thousands of Zulus from long range, they sortied on horseback and drove the survivors in rout into Blood River. At least 3000 Zulus died that day. Dingaan fled and was assassinated by a treacherous aide. The Boers installed a puppet chief, Mpande.

But the Zululand Boers were forced to trek on almost at once, when the British extended their suzerainty over Natal. The heroes of Blood River moved disconsolately on to the high veldt, where the first wave of Boers under Hernan Potgieter had arrived in 1836. Potgieter and his men encountered a human obstacle almost as formidable as Dingaan's Zulus. The Matabele, under Mzilikazi (who had begun his career as one of Shaka's most trusted lieutenants) were a breakaway tribe from the Zulus. When he and his followers moved north, the subsequent tribal 'shunting' triggered the *mfecane* or 'crushing'. At least a million people died in the subsequent population dislocation, and the area of the Orange Free State was depopulated. Mzilikazi himself became the victim of the Boers. A massacre of the white interlopers at Weenen was followed by Matabele reverses at Vegkop and Mosega. Finally, in 1837, as a result of a decisive week-long running battle along the Marico river, Mzilikazi was driven across the Limpopo river into what later became Rhodesia. A second wave of *mfecane* took place. After his defeat, Mzilikazi's original intention was to found a nation on the other side of the Zambezi, but the prevalence of the tsetse fly made this impossible and he had to fall back on southern Rhodesia and raid the Makalala and Manansa tribes.

The Boers meanwhile settled in what later became the Transvaal and the Orange Free State; these territories were recognised as independent Boer republics by the British at the Conventions of Sand River (1852) and Bloemfontein (1854) respectively.

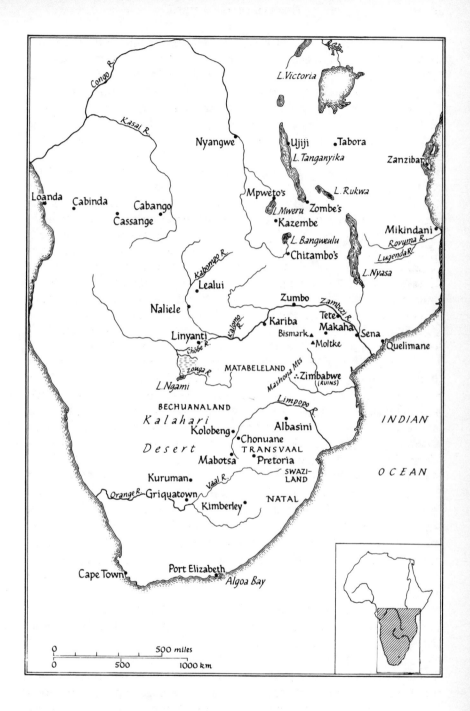

Congo R.

L.Victoria

Kasai R.

Nyangwe

Ujiji   Tabora

L.Tanganyika

Zanzibar

Loanda   Cabinda   Cabango

Mpweto's   L.Rukwa

L.Mweru   Zombe's

Cassange   Kazembe

Mikindani

Rovuma R.

L. Bangweulu

Lugenda R.

Chitambo's

L.Nyasa

Kabompo R.

Lealui

Zumbo   Zambezi R.

Naliele   Tete

Kariba   Makaha

Linyanti   Bismark.   Sena

Moltke

Chobe R.   Quelimane

Zonga R.   MATABELELAND

L.Ngami   Mashona Mts   Zimbabwe   (RUINS)

Limpopo   INDIAN

BECHUANALAND

Kalahari   Albasini

Kolobeng   OCEAN

Chonuane

Desert   TRANSVAAL

Mabotsa   Pretoria

Kuruman   SWAZI-LAND

Vaal R.

Orange R.   Griquatown

Kimberley   NATAL

Cape Town   Port Elizabeth

Algoa Bay

0   500 miles

0   500   1000 km

Part of the map of southern Africa, then, was filled in by migration and settlement rather than exploration in the true sense. The other part was brought into European ken by hunters and missionaries doubling as explorers; of these men David Livingstone was far the most important. His early mentor and father-in-law, Robert Moffat, was an effective bridge between settlement and exploration for he was a confidant of Mzilikazi, who regarded him as the 'chief' of all missionaries in southern Africa. Anyone who came to Mzilikazi's kraal and mentioned Moffat's name was guaranteed preferential treatment from the chief. It was Moffat's talk of having seen the smoke from a thousand distant villages to the north, as yet unvisited, which first fired Livingstone's imagination as explorer.

Born in Lanarkshire in 1813, Livingstone came from a devout Protestant family. There was Jacobitism in the ancestry; his great-grandfather had been 'out' in the '45. His family was poor, and young David was apprenticed at the age of ten as a 'piecer' in a cotton mill. Despite working from 6 a.m. to 8 p.m. the lad devoured books in his spare time. When promoted to cotton-spinner, he began to take lessons in medicine and divinity with a view to becoming a medical missionary. Part-time study made the road long and hard, but at twenty-six he qualified as a physician at Glasgow University and at once offered his services to the London Missionary Society. He was destined at first for China, but the Opium Wars supervened, so he was sent instead to South Africa. His first posting was at Kuruman, 125 miles north-west of Kimberley, where the great Scottish missionary Robert Moffat had his headquarters. But by 1843 Livingstone had his own mission station at Mabotse. Meanwhile he contracted a marriage of convenience with Moffat's daughter Mary, whom he did not love. Yet through Moffat's influence Livingstone was able to press ever farther north, ostensibly spreading the Gospel, first at Chonuane, then at Kolobeng. Here he made his one and only convert, who later lapsed.

By the late 1840s Livingstone was already using his missionary labours as a mask for his true ambition: the exploration and discovery of southern Africa. The obstacle in his path was lack of money, but in 1849 he persuaded the wealthy big-game hunters William Cotton Oswell and Mungo Murray to accompany him on an expedition across the Kalahari desert to find the legendary Lake Ngami.

On 1 June the three friends set out with Hottentot and Griqua guides. They travelled by ox-waggon, and both men and beasts suffered from thirst in the barren desert, plagued also by mirages, scorpions and snakes. The scorpions were the worst pest in the desert. Their stings produced swellings, excruciating pain, intense cold and muscular paralysis and a human could even lose the use of arms and legs from a particularly bad bite. Given average health it took six days for the poison to wear off. Africans proposed various remedies: bleeding, searing with a hot iron, incision and introduction of powdered charcoal; some advocated killing the scorpion and laying its smashed body over the wound it had inflicted. But after two months of these hazards, on 1 August 1849, Livingstone and his companions became the first Europeans to see Lake Ngami.

Livingstone's next exploit was to attempt to meet Chief Sebituane of the powerful Makololo tribe. After being defeated by tsetse flies, fever and the crocodile-infested Zouga river, in April 1851 he set out again with Oswell. Against the pleas of the Moffats, he insisted on taking his wife with him and after further ordeals through hunger and thirst, Livingstone met Sebituane on the Chobe river. The old chief died before Livingstone could disclose his plans for European settlements, but his trip through Makololo territory enabled him to pull off the second great discovery of his life: the Zambezi river. The sight of this vast river conjured visions of a navigable waterway into the heart of Africa, making feasible Livingstone's dream of bringing Christianity and commerce to the Dark Continent.

He returned to Cape Town, sent his family back to England and received London Missionary Society backing for a further foray among the Makololo. By May 1853 he was back among them, to find a new king, eighteen-year-old Sekeletu, on the throne. Sekeletu and his warriors accompanied him on a journey to the upper reaches of the Zambezi near Seshehe. But wherever Livingstone went he could not find a suitable site for European settlement, since the tsetse was endemic in the area. Disappointed, Livingstone conceived instead the idea of a journey to the west coast. Sekeletu provided the men; the march started on 11 November 1853.

Livingstone's party moved from the Zambezi to the Congo watershed, and crossed the Kasai. Almost permanently ill from fever and debilitated from malnutrition, Livingstone finally staggered into Portuguese Angola and safety. After convalescing from malaria and dysentery at St Paul de Loanda, the indomitable Livingstone set out again with fresh porters on 20 September 1854, intending to cross the continent from west to east.

The first stretch of the expedition took a year. In addition to his discovery of the Kasai, Livingstone now recorded the existence of other rivers; the Lulua, Lubilash (Sankuru), Kwilu and Kwango. While crossing the Kasai, he sustained his twenty-seventh bout of fever to date. Livingstone was stoical about the dreadful delirium that accompanied African fever, but a later traveller on the same route vividly recalled its horrors:

Who shall describe the many horrible days and nights that were passed in the midst of racking pain and delirium. Indeed, none but he who has actually experienced it can conceive the lamentable state of weakness to which successive days of African fever will reduce the strongest man! When his legs refuse their office, his head is racked with pain, and his mind is filled with images of horror, the very thought of which will, years afterwards, produce a shudder through his frame.

At the beginning of September 1855 Livingstone arrived exhausted at Sekeletu's capital, Linyanti. Here he recuperated for two months. Then, on 3 November 1855, he set out for the Zambezi, intending to follow the river eastward to the coast. In November 1855 he made one of his most spectacular discoveries. Called *Mosi-oa-Tunya* ('the smoke that thunders') by the local people, the mighty cataracts were promptly renamed Victoria Falls by the dutiful Livingstone.

Accompanied by 114 Makololo, he then pressed on down the Zambezi valley. Beyond the Makololo sphere of influence, Livingstone came upon a warlike tribe at the confluence of the Loangwa. Chief Mpende and his warriors had been fighting the Portuguese continuously for two years and naturally took Livingstone for a Lusitanian. But Livingstone was determined to prove that pacific methods could work in Africa. He told the chief's emissaries, 'I am a *Lekoa*, an Englishman.'

'We do not know that tribe. We thought you were Portuguese.' Livingstone then showed them his hair and skin.

'No, we never saw a skin as white as that,' the emissaries conceded. 'You must be one of the tribe that loves the black man.'

Livingstone agreed and was gratified that Mpende then allowed his party unimpeded transit. He passed safely through Tete, but by taking a short cut across a loop in the Zambezi failed to discover that the river was blocked by ferocious rapids. He crossed over to the south bank of the Zambezi at a critical point and thus missed the Kebrabasa rapids by about fifty miles. These rapids were the most formidable barrier to navigation on the entire river, but Livingstone took back with him to England the erroneous conclusion that the Zambezi was navigable along its whole length, with just one or two minor cascades as obstacles.

On 20 May 1856 Livingstone emerged at the east coast at Quelimane, the first European to have crossed the continent from coast to coast. He had made great discoveries and recorded some acute observations, even though some of his judgements were eccentric, like his conviction that men could suckle infants when their mothers died. Most of all, Livingstone had given heart to his compatriots. There was a pervasive fear among missionaries that Europeans in Africa would be sucked into a black hole of savagery, that missionaries would 'go native' and backslide into barbarism. Some even believed that to survive in Africa one needed to empty one's veins of European blood and replace it with the blood of Africa. To this end it was common for missionaries to bleed themselves; one monk called Brother Carli was bled ninety times.

Livingstone scouted such far-fetched notions. His solution to the European fear of losing one's identity in Africa was to remain detached and find relief in the beauties of nature. The missionary should be aloof from African depravity as was the surgeon from the filthy surroundings in which he had to operate:

> Missionaries ought to cultivate a taste for the beautiful. We are necessarily compelled to contemplate much moral impurity and degradation. We are so often doomed to disappointment. We are apt to become either callous or melancholy, or, if preserved from these, the constant strain on the sensibilities is likely to injure the bodily health.

On his arrival in England in December 1856 Livingstone found himself the lion of the hour. His account of his fifteen years in Africa, *Missionary Travels*, was an immediate success and sold 30,000 copies within months. Always a prima donna, Livingstone resigned from the London Missionary Society in high dudgeon when its directors ventured to disapprove of his long journeys as being 'only remotely connected with the spread of the Gospel'.

Livingstone was impatient to return to Africa at the earliest opportunity. Appointed HM Consul for the east coast of Africa, he was instructed by the Foreign Office to extend the state of knowledge of the geography and resources of the region, to establish friendly trading relations with the locals and continue the work of Christian propaganda – for Livingstone still considered himself a missionary. He was given the use of a small steam-launch, which he christened the *Ma-Robert*, using the African name for his wife. To his great irritation he was also given the services of six British assistants, including his brother Charles; Dr John Kirk was appointed physician and botanist; Commander Norman Bedingfield, RN – a cantankerous individual who had already been court-martialled twice – was naval liaison officer and Livingstone's second-in-command; Thomas Baines was appointed artist and storekeeper; Richard Thornton, geologist; and George Rae, engineer.

It was on this second expedition that Livingstone's failings as a human being most clearly manifested themselves. His superficial optimism about 'all for the best in the best of all possible worlds' masked a deep pessimism. There was also an element of fanaticism in Livingstone that enabled him to overcome extraordinary obstacles; but the dark side of this was an obstinate obsession and a conviction that he alone was right. Most of all, Livingstone was incapable of working with other white men. He was a loner, especially jealous that one of his 'comrades' might try to steal the glory for some African discovery that was really his.

He was very soon at cross-purposes with Thornton and Baines, and he was not above persecuting them mercilessly for some completely imaginary dereliction of duty. They in turn hated the feckless and incompetent Charles Livingstone, whom the doctor felt the need to protect but whom he privately pronounced 'useless'. A tempestuous relationship with Bedingfield led to the commander's early resignation and departure. Kirk too sometimes felt the lash of Livingstone's caustic tongue. He found the doctor's mood swings intolerable. 'He knows how to come round niggers very well,' Kirk wrote, 'but if his digestive system don't go all right, he loses his diplomatic power wonderfully.' Kirk was amazed to hear the man who had been virtually canonised in England in 1856 threaten to break his men's necks if they did not shape up.

Personality clashes were the outward sign of an expedition that was ill-starred from the very beginning. In May 1858 HMS *Pearl* entered the Zambezi by the Kongone mouth. But it was at once discovered that she could not accompany the expedition to Tete, 250 miles inland, as her draught was too deep. The *Ma-Robert* also proved a notable disappoint-ment. This 75-ft paddle-wheeled, flat-bottomed craft, with a capacity for thirty-six men, had been shipped out to Africa in sections and Kroomen had been hired in West Africa as crew. But the ship proved to be a notorious wood-guzzler; it consumed 150 tons in the first year. Livingstone wrote disconsolately of 'perpetual wood-cutting: it wears the heart out of us'. *Ma-Robert* leaked as well as guzzling fuel, and navigation was difficult because of sandbanks and shoals. And because the *Pearl* was not able to travel beyond the Zambezi delta, there was endless toing and froing between Tete and the river mouth.

By the time *Ma-Robert* got to Tete in September Bedingfield had resigned and Thornton and Baines were in disgrace (they resigned finally in 1859). But far worse was in store for Livingstone. To his horror the rumour that there was a waterfall as high as a tree turned out to be true when in November he first came to terms with the Kebrabasa rapids. With ill-tempered reluctance Livingstone grudgingly conceded that the Zambezi was not navigable beyond that point. He took *Ma-Robert* down the Zambezi and up the river Shire. After exploring Mt Morumbala with Kirk, Livingstone then steamed upriver as far as the cataracts on the Shire. These he named Murchison Falls, after his patron Sir Roderick Murchison of the Royal Geographical Society. He returned to Tete in February 1859, impressed by the possibility of European settlements in the Shire highlands.

In March 1859 he left Tete to attempt the second exploration of the Shire. His party reached Chibisa's, where Livingstone and Kirk set off overland to reach the reported large lakes in the hinterland. They reached Lake Shirwa but not the larger 'Nyinyezi' beyond. Livingstone returned to the coast in July, then went back to Chibisa's the following month to attempt to find the larger lake that local lore clearly stated was there. On 17 September 1859 his efforts were crowned with success. To his impressive string of 'firsts' Livingstone added Nyinyezi, which he renamed Lake Nyasa.

Livingstone was impressed by all he saw of the region's fertility and began to conceive the idea that, just as good money drove out bad, so legitimate trade would soon kill off the slave trade. He sent to London for a new steam launch, to be paid for from the royalties of *Missionary Travels*. In November he set off downriver from Tete but on the way the troublesome *Ma-Robert* sank and the party had to proceed by canoe.

Livingstone spent the year 1860 mainly with the Makololo, his faithful companions of 1856, whom he had left at Tete. He set out to escort them back to their homeland, but many Makololo were already well ensconced in the Shire country with new wives and resisted the invitation. Many of those who set out with Livingstone slipped away quietly *enroute* to Sesheke. Livingstone and Kirk arrived at the Makololo capital to find scenes of unbelievable despair and devastation. Their young protégé Sekeletu was smitten with leprosy and lived in walled seclusion. Believing the leprosy to be an effect of witchcraft, he had massacred large numbers of his tribal noblemen and their families, thus setting in train the irreversible decline of the Makololo in this region. The two 'Zambezi doctors' found Sekeletu beyond medical help; he died shortly after their departure on 17 September 1860.

In January 1861 HMS *Sidon* arrived at Kongone with the *Pioneer*, a new 115-ft launch provided by the Admiralty. Less welcome was the advance party from the newly formed Universities' Mission to Central Africa, among whose number was Bishop Charles Frederick Mackenzie. Livingstone's next endeavour was to find a way into the Shire highlands that avoided Portuguese territory and he thought the key might be the Rovuma river, 600 miles north-east of Zambezi. He decided to take the entire party to the Comoro Islands. Then, in March 1861, Livingstone, Kirk, Bishop Mackenzie, Charles Livingstone and the Revd Henry Rowley, as well as a number of naval officers, attempted the ascent of the Rovuma in the *Pioneer*.

After thirty miles the shallowness of the river forced the expedition back. Then fever took a hand. About a third of the Europeans were sick when the *Pioneer* returned to the Comoro Islands. From there the steamer laboured up the Shire to Chibisa's. On 15 July Livingstone led the missionaries inland to find a suitable station.

While scouring the country for a site, Livingstone's party came upon a line of manacled slaves and their black drivers. At sight of the white men the drivers fled into the forest. Livingstone ordered the fetters to be struck from the captives and bade them help themselves to food. A little boy expressed his wonderment: 'They starved us, but now *you* bid us cook food.' The missionaries took the freed slaves into their protective custody when they set up their first station at Magomero. But Livingstone's humane action led to hostilities with the local slaving tribes and soon the missionaries were drawn into local wars on the side of the Makanga tribe. In the privacy of his journal Livingstone expressed regret that he had in any way allowed himself to be inveigled into local politics.

Meanwhile Livingstone, his brother and Dr Kirk set off to explore Lake Nyasa. On 2 September 1861 they reached the lake and began their reconnaissance. After a three-month circumnavigation, on 1 November, during the journey back, Livingstone reached the lowest navigable point of the Shire.

On 31 January 1862 Mrs Livingstone arrived in Mozambique on HMS *Gorgon*, together with the bishop's sister, Miss Mackenzie. The Royal Navy also brought Livingstone a new launch in sections, the *Lady Nyasa*. With no news from Bishop Mackenzie, Livingstone sent Captain Wilson of the *Gorgon* upriver to investigate. He learned that Mackenzie had died of fever after an accident in a canoe. Livingstone scarcely had time to absorb this before his wife died (April 1862).

Still uncowed by these bad omens, Livingstone again attempted an exploration of the Rovuma river. This time he made lengthy and detailed preparations and set out on 9 September 1862 with the galley and cutter from HMS *Orestes*. In these smaller craft Livingstone managed to push 156 miles up-river before admitting defeat. He returned to the coast on 9 October and at once launched into a violent altercation with gunner Young, whom he had left in charge of the party at the coast. Livingstone left in disgust in November for Shupanga and by mid-March 1863 was once again at Chibisa's.

He pressed on to Murchison Falls, where he established a base camp. The *Lady Nyasa* was taken to pieces and a road begun along which it was intended that ox-carts would portage her. But it was already evident that the expedition was disintegrating at a number of levels. Thornton became the next victim of fever, while to escape a similar fate Kirk and Charles Livingstone had to be invalided out. Finally, in July, came news that the expedition had been recalled.

The *Lady Nyasa* now had to be reassembled for the return to the coast;

she was destined never to sail on the lake after which she was named. Before returning Livingstone made a last attempt to explore the northern and eastern shores of the lake. Horace Waller, one of the missionaries, and later to be founder of the Livingstone cult, hired Yao tribesmen to take a boat beyond the cataracts, where the ox-waggon track ended. At the top of the falls the Zambezi men tried to show they were better boatmen than the Makololo, but their experience was exclusively with heavy canoes; the boat was overturned and lost in the cataracts. 'Sic gloria sailing on the Nyasa transit,' remarked Livingstone disconsolately.

Livingstone engaged new guides and reached the lake at the end of August 1863. At the high altitudes the Shupunga men, who were malaria-proof in the delta, succumbed and after some desultory exploration Livingstone beat a retreat to the *Pioneer* in November. This was the occasion for further personal animosities. Waller quarrelled violently with Bishop Tozer, and Livingstone took Tozer's side.

In January 1864 Livingstone said goodbye to his Makololo friends for the last time and travelled downstream to Chibisa's in the *Pioneer*. Once at the coast he took the eccentric decision to take the tiny 110-ft *Lady Nyasa* across 2500 miles of notoriously storm-tossed ocean to Bombay. This perilous journey in the troughs and crests of the ocean swells lasted from 30 April to 13 June 1864. It is one of Livingstone's least-known exploits but arguably the most dangerous and foolhardy.

Livingstone's return to England in 1864 from India marked the end of his career as explorer of southern Africa. His next expedition would take him into Africa's heartland, to the Lualaba, in search of the sources of the Nile. He was still a hero to the British public but in establishment eyes his star had lost much of its lustre. Lord Russell received him coldly and Prince Albert, cousin of King Pedro of Portugal, took umbrage when Livingstone denounced the Portuguese for their role in the slave trade. Livingstone consoled himself by sniping at both Burton and Speke at the famous 1864 meeting of the British Association in Bath; he considered them both to be wrong about the sources of the Nile. Meanwhile he set about finding the money for a third African venture which would prove that he alone possessed the secrets of the fountains of the Nile and the Mountains of the Moon.

It is worth pausing at this point to take stock of Livingstone. A sober assessment indicates that his legend far outran his achievements. He had proved himself selfish, obsessional, ambitious, unforgiving, deceitful and lacking in compassion towards fellow Europeans. Since he was the expeditionary leader in 1858–64, he could be held indirectly responsible for the deaths of a dozen of his compatriots. He had already failed in many of his objectives as an explorer, had disrupted the fragile political system

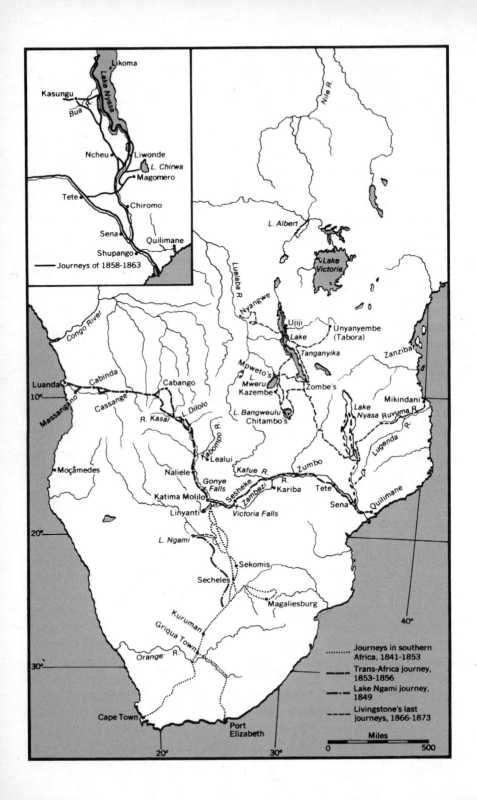

Likoma
Lake Nyasa
Kasungu
Bua R.
Ncheu
Liwonde
L. Chirwa
Magomero
Tete
Chiromo
Sena
Quilimane
Shupango
—— Journeys of 1858-1863

Nile R.
L. Albert
Lake Victoria
Congo River
Lualaba R.
Nyangwe
Ujiji
Lake
Unyanyembe
(Tabora)
Tanganyika
Zanzibar
Luanda
Cabinda
Cabango
Mpweto's
L. Mweru
Zombe's
Mikindani
10°
Massangano
Cassange
L. Dilolo
Kazembe
Lake Nyasa
Ruvuma R.
R. Kasai
L. Bangweulu
Chitambo's
Lugenda R.
Moçâmedes
Kabompo R.
Lealui
Kafue R.
Zumbo
Naliele
Gonye Falls
Sesheke
R.
Kariba
Tete
Katima Molilo
Zambezi
Sena
Quilimane
Linyanti
Victoria Falls
20°
L. Ngami
Sekomis
Secheles
Magaliesburg
Kuruman
Griqua Town
Orange R.
30°
Cape Town
Port Elizabeth
40°
20°
30°

.... Journeys in southern Africa, 1841-1853
———— Trans-Africa journey, 1853-1856
—·—·— Lake Ngami journey, 1849
– – – Livingstone's last journeys, 1866-1873

Miles
0   500

of the Shire, and shown himself careless and insouciant when it came to forward planning. To assert that the Zambezi was navigable for its entire length was a singular error. It was also odd that a man who had experienced the sharp end of capitalism in his youth should have been so eupeptic about its introduction in Africa.

Worst of all his faults, however, was his failure to relate successfully to other human beings as equals. He had little sense of comradeship, was incapable of leading white men by example, as a Shackleton could, and had absurdly high expectations of himself and others. He nursed grudges for decades, to the point where Stanley in 1871 found him still brooding about the 'treachery' of his subordinates on the Zambezi expedition. Possibly his humble beginnings in the cotton mill made him fanatically determined to 'overcome' and rise above the level of the common herd, but what explains his treatment of his wife and children? Having insisted that his family accompany him across the Kalahari desert, while Mary endured two pregnancies when caring for three young children, he then packed them all off to Britain without any means of financial support, simply dumping the problem of their maintenance on others. In Britain the Livingstones survived four penurious years. Mrs Livingstone took to the bottle, and her constitution was probably already weakened when she came out to Africa in January 1861, there to die three months later. All this helps to explain why, between his second and third expeditions, there was something of a question mark against the name of 'St David'.

Two other explorers played a major part in filling in the blanks on the map of southern Africa. Charles John Andersson was born at Wermeland, Sweden, in 1827 to an English father and Swedish mother. Adopting the maternal surname in his youth, while perversely shedding his Swedish given names of Karl Johan, he served his apprenticeship as an African explorer under Francis (later Sir Francis) Galton, the notable scientist-explorer who was a cousin of Charles Darwin. In the late 1840s the two men explored the then unknown regions of South-West Africa: Damaraland, Ovampoland and Ondonga. When Galton returned to England to pursue his spectacular career in meteorology, ophthalmology and eugenics, Andersson set up alone as explorer and lion-hunter. In 1851 on his own resources he organised an expedition to Lake Ngami, discovered two years earlier by Livingstone and Oswell. Having reached the lake, he then pressed on into the unknown country to the north of it. He found the principal disease in these regions to be ophthalmia and suffered from it himself. His journey was also notable for a kind of fanatical crusade against lions. There are lion-hunting incidents on almost every other page of Andersson's three books of African travels.

In 1856 Andersson visited London, but returned to South Africa soon afterwards as superintendent of mining operations with the Walwich Bay Mining Company. But this soon failed to satisfy the restless Andersson. He resigned and set off to reach the goal that would be his abiding lodestone – the river Cunene, marking the boundary between Ovampoland and Portuguese Angola. Unfortunately, while crossing the Okovango river, which flowed east, he was gored by a rhino, which thrust its horn into his thigh and inflicted a gashing wound which left him crippled for months in his tent.

Frustrated this time, he returned to the Cape and married in 1861. He settled down to a lucrative trade, supplying elephant-hunters with cattle across Namaqualand. When a war broke out between the Damaras and the Namaquas, living as he did among the Damaras, Andersson was appointed their war chief and soon defeated the Namaquas. However, the continuing hostility of the Namaquas meant that his herds of cattle were frequently stopped, seized and confiscated.

Matters came to a head when the Namaquas attacked his station at Otjimbingue. While leading a sortie to repel them, he was shot down by a bullet which smashed his leg. Miraculously, he survived and returned nine months later to Cape Town to be told he would be a cripple for life. At first he seemed to reconcile himself to life as an invalid and wrote a massive study of the birds of South-West Africa. The Cunene still beckoned, however, and in May 1866 he left Cape Town for Dawan, to try to put together his ruined business so as to finance another expedition. He proceeded north to Ovampoland to try to institute a trade between the white hunters there and the Portuguese of Angola. This time he actually came within sight of the Cunene river, but he succumbed to fever, was forced to retrace his steps, and died on the return journey in July 1867, aged forty. Andersson's exploits are little known, but it was he, not Livingstone, who was Jan Christian Smuts's favourite explorer of southern Africa.

Karl Mauch was in some ways Andersson's equivalent on the east coast. The son of a poor Bavarian carpenter, his childhood was strikingly similar to Caillié's: both assuaged the privations of boyhood by poring over atlases and books about Africa. Mauch managed to scrape together enough money to train and qualify as a teacher and while he taught he lived like a hermit, devouring books on natural history, geology, astronomy and even Arabic. In 1856, at the age of twenty-seven, he sailed for South Africa. There he fell in with the elephant-hunter William Hartley, who took him north and introduced him to the aged Mzilikazi. In Matabeleland Mauch found gold; added to the ore he had seen in Transvaal and Swaziland, this find convinced him that the goldfields were all outcrops of a single treasure-house of precious metals, which he identified with the riches of Ophir, capital of the Queen of Sheba. Persistent reports of a ruined city beyond the Lundi river convinced him that Ophir was no myth.

It was May 1871 by the time Mauch finally assembled the resources for his great adventure. Heading north out of Transvaal, he crossed the Limpopo river. He then struck north towards the Mashona mountains, excited by the trans-Limpopo lore he picked up, to the effect that the locals had often found iron tools which were quite beyond their own capacity to manufacture. He also began to hear clearer and clearer stories of great stone ruins in the heart of what came to be Rhodesia. On 5 September, after switching superstitious guides in quick succession, he finally reached the ruins of Zimbabwe. Here, it was clear, were the remains of a medieval (not biblical) stone city of African origin. He wandered in an intoxicated daze through the remains of a huge wall, through extensive monoliths and crumbling ruins; at one point he lit on a quite unscathed 30-ft-tall 'tower-like structure'. He made out temple corridors and the remnants of edifices built from smoothly cut granite blocks. Most impressive of all was the elaborate ornamentation on the cross-beams of trimmed stone.

It seemed to Mauch that Zimbabwe must have been the seat of the fabled Monomotapa, often confused with Prester John, and in his enthusiasm he stayed in the environs of the ruins until May 1872, existing on short commons and cursing the savagery of the 'degenerate' Africans of Matabeleland. Finally food shortages forced him north. A month later he struck gold again, at Makaha, and dubbed the claim Kaiser Wilhelm field. He identified two massive landmarks, granite mountains, that he christened the Moltke and Bismarck ranges, before he eventually staggered into Quelimane in tatters at the end of July.

The Portuguese authorities were coolly polite but were not interested in his discoveries. Disappointed, he returned to Germany, hoping for a more sympathetic audience. He was ten years too soon: the German craze for Africa did not begin until the mid-1880s. So far from having his discoveries lauded, Mauch found that Germany did not even consider them of sufficient moment to override his lack of formal academic qualifications. Turned down in applications for university and museum posts, Mauch was forced to accept a lowly post in a cement works in Württemberg. The discoverer of Zimbabwe lived the rest of his brief life in a dingy room above the local railway station. It was noted that he seemed depressed and, shortly after coming to Württemberg, he was found one night with his skull smashed in, lying on the cobblestones beneath his high window. There was no note, but the presumption of suicide was very strong. Africa took its toll on explorers in many different ways, but at the very least it can be asserted that some of them met their end while the balance of the mind was disturbed. This certainly applied to Speke and Emin Pasha and, above all, to Karl Mauch.

3

The Mountains of the Moon

Livingstone's Zambezi expedition was a failure, but it was a momentous one since it had the effect, alongside other factors, of switching British attention from the west to the east coasts of Africa. For the first half of the nineteenth century the tradition of exploring West Africa in the interests of science and commerce was pursued vigorously. The Royal Geographical Society, into which the African Association was merged, carried on that tradition. In 1850 it was still true to say that whereas West Africa was in a trading sense an extension of Europe, East Africa was an extension of Asia in the form of Arab and Indian traders. There was certainly nothing comparable on the east coast to the humanitarian experiments of Liberia and Sierra Leone, where an attempt had been made to create independent African states with European institutions.

The *indirect* impact of Livingstone's Zambezi expedition can be seen if a thumbnail sketch is provided of African exploration in the period 1815–58, excluding southern Africa. After the Napoleonic wars the Colonial Office and Admiralty tenaciously sought accurate geographical information in the interests of the coastal trade of West Africa. They sponsored scientific and commercial investigations staffed by military men and scientists. Above all, the Foreign Office and the Royal Navy, charged with monitoring the anti-slave trade treaties signed with the tribes, needed precise knowledge of the coasts, to prevent illicit slaving ships escaping the naval blockade. Buxton's Niger expedition, despite failing, stimulated both official and private efforts to explore West Africa and lay bare its commercial potential. A Parliamentary Select Committee in 1842 recommended a more active British role in West Africa and a more vigorous exploitation of existing commercial opportunities.

Quinine provided the great breakthrough. The British government's Niger expedition of 1841–2, backed by the aristocratic African Civilisation Society, was supremely well equipped in all areas save the medical.

A staff of experienced naval officers, missionaries and scientists (two botanists, a geologist, a mineralogist and a zoologist) took out specially constructed steamships. No expense was spared. Yet because a third of these Europeans died in Africa, most of them within two months, public dismay led to the recall of the expedition. A dozen years later, in 1854, quinine was tried out on the Niger. Its successful use was a turning point for the European exploration of Africa. The medical investigation of this new febrifuge was an essential part of Livingstone's Zambezi expedition. At this level, at least, the failed venture produced encouraging results.

There were other reasons why a dramatic switch of exploration resources from Africa's west coast to the east coast was evident by the 1860s. Andersson may have been the greater technical explorer of the Galton/Andersson duo that penetrated Damaraland in the late 1840s, but the scientific fame of Galton had the more lasting impact. Galton's *Art of Travel*, published in 1855, was destined to run through eight editions, the last appearing in 1893. It was a thesaurus of African lore and contained advice on everything from how to deal with scorpion stings to how to treat porters. Galton included such homely advice as remembering, when applying a tourniquet, that the main arteries followed the same direction as the seams of sleeves and trousers. He also advised mountaineers to carry a cat with them as a barometric gauge, since felines were alleged to go into convulsions at precisely 13,000 ft above sea-level.

The confidence born of the 'miracle drug' quinine and Galton's 'scientific' nostrums fed into the Livingstone cult created by the 1857 publication of *Missionary Travels*, which made East Africa the sensation of the day. It was also realised that East Africa offered a far more congenial climate for Europeans. The East African plateau was a paradise after the heat and humidity of the Guinea coast. South of a line drawn from Angola to Ethiopia most of the terrain was upland, over 1000 m in altitude; even Lake Victoria turned out to be 1130 m above sea-level. Using Zanzibar as a jumping-off point, East African explorers could very soon find themselves in the cool temperatures of the Kenya and Tanganyika highlands.

Strategic factors also played their part in the switch. The Royal Navy had recently gained control of the Indian Ocean, as well as the Atlantic. By the end of the 1860s the opening of the Suez Canal led to the establishment of further military posts to back up those already in existence, at Aden, Karachi and Socobra, to safeguard the route to India. Conscious of the area's importance, the Indian government (India had just been put under direct rule from London after the Indian Mutiny) encouraged Army officers to spend leaves there. A new breed of explorers arose, equipped with beds, insect-proof tin boxes, fold-up chairs and even cameras.

Finally, East Africa satisfied both the instinct for profit and the romantic sensibility. Not only were expeditions in this part of the world less perilous than in West Africa, but the ivory trade made them potentially far more lucrative. Adventurers and romantics were attracted by the vast herds of game and, furthermore, the discovery by German missionaries of snow-capped peaks in Kenya and Tanzania suggested a factual basis for Ptolemy's legends of the Mountains of the Moon and the sources of the Nile. Some missionaries rolled back the boundaries of the fanciful still farther and claimed that the opening of East Africa was all part of a divine plan. The interior of the Dark Continent had remained unknown for so long, it was argued, because Europe had not had the technology earlier to impose itself on Africa as God intended. Neither would he trust his emissaries until Christian consciences had been aroused to the sin and cruelty of slavery. In some versions of this 'providential' world-view, the abolition of slavery in the United States in the Civil War, occurring as it did at the very same time as Speke's and Burton's great journeys, was further proof of the 'pre-established harmony' demanded by the thesis.

It is clear, at any rate, that missionaries were the pioneer explorers of East Africa. Johann Ludwig Krapf and Johannes Rebmann, in the employment of the Church Missionary Society, made several journeys into the interior in the 1840s, using as their guide a Swahili trader named Bana Kheri. It was from this pair that there came the first reports of a 'slug-shaped' great inland sea of Unyamwezi. These rumours were later seen to be garbled conflations of both Lakes Tanganyika and Nyasa; at the time Krapf and Rebmann did not know whether the reports referred to one lake or several.

Travelling to Taita country and then to the territory of the Chagas, in 1848 Rebmann became the first white man to see the peak of Kilimanjaro, though he was ridiculed by armchair geographers in Europe when he (correctly) described it as snow-capped. Krapf meanwhile explored in Usambara, to the south and south-west of Mombasa. Growing bolder, the two joined forces and visited Chaga country again, hoping to find a route to Unyamwezi. This time Chief Mamkinga set on them and plundered their thirty-strong party. The villain of the piece was Bana Kheri, who for some obscure reason turned on the missionaries and influenced the Chagas against them. Soon afterwards the Swahili trader himself suffered the rewards of treachery when he was killed by the Masai between Chagaland and Mombasa.

In the winter of 1849–50 Krapf set out again to visit the Kamba. He

was beset by illness and a mutiny of his porters and had to return to the
coast, with a distant view of Mt Kenya the sole recompense for his pains.
A wolverine in his appetite for punishment, in April 1851 Krapf tried
once more to penetrate the Kamba area. Kivoi, a chief who had
befriended him on the 1849–50 journey, agreed to build a mission station
on his territory but disaster struck when Kivoi with fifty followers
accompanied the missionary to the agreed site for the headquarters. His
enemies ambushed Kivoi in the forest, killed him and put his men to
flight. Krapf, left alone and destitute, wandered through the forest in a
daze of fever, thirst and hunger. He was shunned by the Kamba, who
blamed him for Kivoi's death, and with difficulty limped back to the coast,
a broken man.

But the journeys of Krapf and Rebmann gave a great fillip to European
interest in the interior of East Africa. Two lessons seemed clear from the
missionaries' experience. It was important not to offend local suscepti-
bilities; Krapf had alienated his Muslim porters by eating pork. And it was
essential to take firearms; the missionaries had eschewed the use of
'magic sticks' and had suffered accordingly.

In Cairo in late 1853 Krapf's traveller's tales fired the imagination of a
man who was then the lion of the hour. Richard Francis Burton, son of a
wealthy but disillusioned ex-Army officer, was a phenomenon even in an
age replete with larger-than-life personalities. After an eccentric and
itinerant boyhood, when he trailed around Europe after his restless
valetudinarian parents and received his education from private tutors,
Burton spent an unsuccessful year at Oxford. He thought it a second-rate
university. The dons were either drones or hacks. The standard of
teaching was abysmal. The pronunciation of Latin and Greek was wrong.
In a word, Oxford did not understand Burton's genius. But, unlike many
self-assigned geniuses, Burton soon proved that he had good claims to the
title. At the very least he had linguistic talents of a very high order. The
seven years he spent as an Army officer in India in the 1840s, after the
Oxford débâcle, saw him adding an oriental language a year to his rapidly
growing inventory of tongues; in the end he mastered twenty-five
languages and was fluent in a further fifteen. Additionally, he was a fine
boxer and a master swordsman.

It was hard for such a multi-talented man, a unique blend of thinker
and man of action, to find a niche. But at thirty-two he suddenly burst
upon public consciousness by an exploit that made him a household
name. Drawing on his unrivalled knowledge of Arabic and the culture of
Islam, he made a journey to Mecca disguised as a Muslim, when certain
death was the penalty ordained for an unconverted infidel who trod the
places sacred to Muhammad. On his return from Mecca Burton rested in

Cairo, and it was there that he met Krapf. Talk of the Mountains of the Moon and the Fountains of the Nile fired his romantic soul and he dreamed of becoming the first European to cross Africa from the Indian to the Atlantic Oceans.

To test his capacity for African exploration, Burton first made a journey to the 'forbidden' city of Harar in Somaliland, where the emir was reputed to execute all infidels on sight. But Harar capitulated to Burton as Jericho to Joshua. It was now time for Burton to put his larger plan into operation. He gathered together three other Indian Army officers, Lieutenants Herne, Stroyan and Speke, hired guides and porters and made camp at Berbera on the Red Sea coast, ready for an initial trek south. Then disaster struck. Hostile Somalis attacked the camp at Berbera. Stroyan was killed; Burton and Speke escaped with their lives but only after being within a hair's breadth of death and having sustained terrible wounds. Ever after Burton bore on his cheek a hideous disfiguring scar where a Somali lance had transfixed his jaw.

After recuperating from his wounds Burton served in the Crimean war, where he was disillusioned by all he saw of the incompetence of Britain's high command. Then he returned to his current obsession: the Mountains of the Moon. Further reports reaching Zanzibar from the Arabs in the interior of East Africa suggested that there was an 'inland sea' or 'slug-shaped' lake called Tanganyika. Burton proposed to chart the limits of this lake, study the ethnography of the tribes in the area and report on trade prospects in the interior. His private ambition was to seek the sources of the Nile, which he imagined would be found in the Mountains of the Moon described by Ptolemy. His employer, the East India Company, agreed to his request for a two-year leave of absence, and the enterprise was sponsored both by the Royal Geographical Society and the Foreign Office, which contributed £1000 to the expenses. Despite some earlier clashes with the younger man, Burton again asked John Hanning Speke to accompany him.

Towards the end of 1856 Burton and Speke arrived at Zanzibar, where Sultan Majid had recently succeeded to the throne. The Omani Arabs had been the power on this coast since the end of the seventeenth century when they defeated and expelled the Portuguese. Seyyid Said, the Omani ruler who died in 1855, had transferred his royal seat from Muscat in Oman to Zanzibar. The island was a flourishing commercial centre and was the principal slave market in the Indian Ocean. By the time Burton and Speke arrived there, the Arabs had established outposts far inland, principally at Tabora (Kazeh) in Unyanyembe (in the heart of what is now Tanzania). There was already a well-established caravan trade across East Africa from Unyanyembe to Bagamoyo, on the mainland coast opposite Zanzibar.

Burton did not strike into the African interior straightaway. First he travelled north to interview Rebmann, who now lived on a mission station near Mombasa. Rebmann advised him not to attempt passage inland from Mombasa, as the fearsome Masai tribe barred the way. Far better would be to go south to the mouth of the Pangani and start from there. Burton investigated this avenue but it proved impracticable. So too did an itinerary beginning from the port of Kilwa to the south of Bagamoyo. In the end Burton plumped for the tried and tested caravan route east from Bagamoyo to Tabora.

It was June 1857 before Burton and Speke finally got under way for the interior. It took them 134 days to get to Tabora. They had under-estimated the difficulties of the march at every level. Personnel problems were uppermost. Said bin Salim, a half-caste Arab, who was caravan leader, proved unreliable and was replaced by a Yao freedman named Sidi Mubarak Bombay. Each African expedition required a hundred or so porters – Burton's highest muster roll was 132 – yet the desertion rates on the Burton/Speke expedition were very high from the first. Burton took thirty donkeys and mules with him, but all very soon succumbed to the tsetse fly or wild animals. The problems that beset Burton are evident from his journal entry for the first day's march:

> At length by ejecting skulkers from their huts, by dint of promises and threats, of gentleness and violence, of soft words and hard words, occasionally combined with a smart application of the *bakur* – the local 'cat' – by sitting in the sun, in fact by incessant worry and fidget from 6 a.m. till 3 p.m., the sluggish unwieldy body acquired some momentum.

But desertions and thefts of stores were not the worst of it. During the four and a half months to Tabora, one or other of the two explorers was always ill, and sometimes both together. Both suffered violently from fever, first malaria, then relapsing fever. Speke was temporarily blinded by ophthalmia; Burton endured agonies from ulcers. At times they were so ill that they had to be carried in hammocks. At others, when crossing mountain ranges, they were so weak that their men had to drag them up the slopes. They forced themselves across constantly changing terrain: swamps, deserts, mountain passes, marshes. Yet even while enduring all this, Burton took detailed notes of the tribal areas through which they passed, laying the foundations for the first anthropological study of East Africa.

Tabora, which they reached on 7 November 1857, was a haven, particularly for Burton, who made a great friend of Snay bin Amir, the principal merchant in the settlement. Burton stunned Snay and the other Arabs by his detailed knowledge of Islam and his ability to recite great chunks of the Koran to them. There was always a thespian side to Burton and he liked nothing better than to repeat by heart the stories from the *Arabian Nights*, acting out the parts as he went. Speke, however, who had no intellectual or indeed any other interests but big-game hunting, quickly became bored. The latent tension between the two men, already in evidence on the 1854–5 Berbera trip, became overt.

As he smoked and drank coffee with the Arabs, Burton became more and more excited at their confirmation of the reality of the great lake or inland sea. His problem was that almost all his porters deserted or took half-pay at Tabora and refused to travel further. It took him five weeks to hire fresh carriers. At last, with the help of Snay and the other Arabs, Burton whipped his recalcitrant porters into line once more for the final push towards the lake. Again illness struck. By the time they reached the lake, Speke had acute ophthalmia and Burton was limping – the lame leading the blind, as one supercilious commentator put it. But at last, on 13 February 1858, they reached their goal. From the summit of the hill Burton beheld his Pisgah:

> The whole scene suddenly burst upon my view, filling me with admiration, wonder and delight . . . An expanse of the lightest and softest blue, in breadth varying from thirty to thirty-five miles . . . the background in front is a high and broken wall of steel-coloured mountains . . . truly it was a revel for soul and sight! Forgetting toils, dangers and the doubtfulness of return, I felt willing to endure double what I had endured; and all the party seemed to join with me in joy.

This was Lake Tanganyika, the longest freshwater lake in the world. Burton and the caravan descended to the village of Ujiji by the lakeside. Intense questioning revealed that there was a river called Rusizi at the head of the lake. If the explorers could demonstrate that the river flowed out of the lake, they could be morally certain in their own minds that they had discovered the source of the Nile.

Burton and Speke set off for the north end of the lake in canoes, but fear of the hostile tribes there caused his paddlers to desert. Burton, suffering from an ulceration of the tongue so painful that he could hardly speak, lacked the strength to go on unaided. Besides, all the people they met were adamant that the Rusizi flowed into the lake, not out of it. Perhaps there was an element of unwillingness to see his pet theories refuted that made Burton unwilling to go the extra miles to see for himself. Disappointed, he returned to Ujiji. He was still convinced that Lake Tanganyika was the source of the Nile though Speke already had serious doubts.

They reached Ujiji on 13 May, left two weeks later and were back in Tabora at the end of June 1858. By this time tensions between Speke and

Burton had become acute. While Burton lay ill in his hut at Tabora, Speke sought permission from his leader to make a side-trip to investigate local rumour that there was a second large lake due north of Tabora. Burton agreed, mainly, as he later recorded: 'To get rid of him!'

Speke left Tabora on 10 July. On 25 August he was back with dramatic news. He had found a second great lake, which he named Victoria Nyanza, and on the basis of his calculations and all circumstantial evidence was convinced that he had found the true source of the Nile. The antagonism between the two men now found a new focus. Burton wanted to be the discoverer of the Nile sources; now this young semi-literate big-game hunter was challenging him in his heart's desire. It is possible that at some level Burton already realised that Speke had scooped the prize – as indeed later proved to be the case – but he found the thought unendurable. His perennial taste for sardonic jeering found expression in a venomous passage directed against Speke in *The Lake Regions of Central Africa*, the book Burton wrote about his East African journeys:

> The fortunate discoverer's conviction was strong; his reasons were weak – were of the category alluded to by the damsel Lucetta, when justifying her penchant in favour of the lovely gentleman Sir Proteus:
>> 'I have no other but a woman's reason:
>> I think him so, because I think him so.'

The sequel was scarcely surprising. Burton wrote:

> Jack changed his manners to me from this date . . . After a few days it became evident to me that not a word could be uttered upon the subject of the lake, the Nile, and his *trouvaille* generally without offence. By a tacit agreement it was, therefore, avoided, and I should never have resumed it, had Jack not stultified the results of my expedition by putting forth a claim which no geographer can admit, and which is at the same time so weak and flimsy, that no geographer has yet taken the trouble to contradict it.

Speke wanted to return to Lake Victoria with Burton to settle the issue once and for all. Burton pointed out that he was ill, supplies were running low, and it was nearly the monsoon season. The explorers quit Tabora on 6 September and struggled through a further four-month nightmare back to the coast. Speke went down with his worst attack of malaria so far. At various stages of his delirium he blurted out the reasons for his hatred of Burton. Burton now discovered that the antagonism went beyond the dispute over the sources of the Nile, and had little to do with the apparent reasons for conflict: Speke's teetotalism as against Burton's liking for alcohol and drugs, and Speke's disdain for his partner's dalliance with the black beauties of Tanganyika. In fact Speke's resentment went all the way

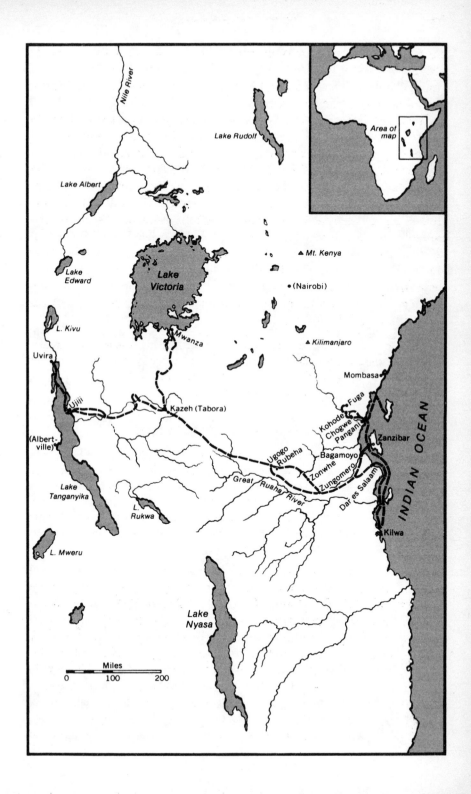

back to the first expedition with Burton. Two things particularly rankled with Speke: he brooded over an apparent imputation of cowardice during the night attack at Berbera; he was also furious that Burton had relegated his (Speke's) diary to an appendix in the book about the expedition, *First Footsteps in East Africa.*

When Speke was well enough to travel, he was carried in a hammock for the rest of the journey. At last, on 30 January 1859, Burton's porters whooped for joy at their first sight of the coastal mango trees. Three days later they reached the coast. After a side trip to cholera-stricken Kilwa, the party made its way across the channel to Zanzibar, from where Burton and Speke caught a ship to Aden, intending to recuperate from their travails. Speke, however, shipped out from Aden within days, after promising the convalescent Burton that he would not approach the Royal Geographical Society in London until the two of them were reunited.

Whether Speke had always intended to double-cross Burton, whether he was talked into it by the malicious homosexual traveller, Laurence Oliphant, whom he met on board the *Furious*, or whether – as is most likely – Oliphant simply strengthened Speke's resolve to persevere with an act of treachery, it is certain that Speke broke his word. Two days after landing in England he spoke at the Royal Geographical Society, egged on by its president Sir Roderick Murchison, who had always hated Burton. The upshot was that Speke was commissioned to go back to Africa without Burton, in command of his own expedition, to settle the issue of the sources of the Nile once and for all. When Burton arrived two weeks later, he was lionised at the Society, given its Gold Medal, but politely informed that the next main expedition to East Africa would be headed by Speke; he himself was offered a picayune re-run of his Somaliland venture as consolation prize.

Indignantly Burton turned down the offer. For the next twelve months he and Speke waged an angry battle by letter and in print, disputing not just African geography but about treachery and the finer points of gentlemanly conduct. Burton may have won the dialectical battle, but Speke garnered all the laurels. By the time Speke set out on his next African expedition, Burton's career was at a nadir. The East India Company, tired of his criticisms and 'insubordination', used the excuse of the reorganisation of Indian administration after the Mutiny to get rid of him. He returned from a nine-month trip to the United States to find himself penniless and without a career. While Speke went from strength to strength in East Africa, Burton was obliged to take a job as consul in Fernando Po, the Spanish island off the West African coast, which Burton dubbed 'the Foreign Office grave'.

As his lieutenant on his great 1860–3 expedition Speke chose an

unassuming Scotsman James Augustus Grant, with the express intention that Grant would never be able to play Mosca to Volpone, as he himself had done with Burton. Aged thirty-two, the same age as Speke, Grant had an even more illustrious pedigree, as he had been wounded during the Indian Mutiny. A good amateur artist and expert botanist, Grant had the additional advantage that he liked big-game hunting. Speke would not have to fear the supercilious basilisk eye from a superior beetling brow, as with Burton, every time he wanted to wander off to slaughter a few dozen of Africa's wildlife.

Speke's intention was to retrace his steps from Zanzibar to Tabora, strike north to Lake Victoria, explore the lake up to the northern shore, and then enter the White Nile at its source, the effluent river of Victoria Nyanza. The expedition would then be met by a relief party travelling up the Nile under an ivory trader called John Petherick.

By 1860 the Upper Nile had been charted for twenty years. The Arabs under Salim Qapudan first found a passage through the great swamps of the Nile in 1840. Into the breach poured missionaries and merchants, fanning out into the southern Sudan as they went. Ivory traders made a killing in more sense than one: whenever they could not kill elephants themselves, they traded cloth, beads and wire for ivory. By 1863 the annual number of boats leaving Khartoum for the southern Sudan was 120.

Powerful tribes like the Bari who at first welcomed the newcomers soon learned their mistake, for Salim Qapudan's Arabs had requited initial Bari hospitality by spreading fire and sword. The Arabs despised blacks and regarded them fit only as fodder for the slave markets, and the cultural gap between African and Arab was widened when the even more 'superior' Europeans arrived. The first white traders arrived in the Bahr-al-Jabal in 1850; for ten years there was an uneasy symbiosis with the tribes, for the newcomers did not know the interior and relied on the locals for supplies of ivory. But in 1860 they overcame this obstacle by penetrating into the interior on their own, locating vast herds of elephants and setting up ivory stations. Taking advantage of this European spearhead, the Arabs advanced as far south as the Bahr al-Ghazal and with their superior firepower soon established themselves as a ruling caste. They became supremely skilful at divide and rule, playing off one potentially threatening tribe against another. The spiral of violence whirled in ever wider loops, reaching into the heart of Africa itself. Most of the explorers' armed encounters with hostile tribes were a consequence of the Arab push farther and farther up the Nile, since the Arab presence all but triggered a *mfecane* of the north; only in a few strongholds did the most powerful confederations, those of the Dinka, Nuer and Azande, hold the intruder at bay. The tribe that felt the full force of the newcomers was the Bari, lying as they did athwart the entrances to the Victoria Nile.

The southward Arab push was eventually halted by the people of Bunyoro, a powerful, populous, centralised kingdom that was a quasi-feudal war machine. Beyond the Bunyoro people to the south-east in turn was the even more powerful land of Buganda, with Karagwe beyond that as the third of the great Central African states. When Speke set out in 1860 no white man had ever seen these great kingdoms; the land of the Bari marked the farthest point south on the Nile reached by Europeans.

The beginnings of Speke's and Grant's expedition were propitious. The new British consul in Zanzibar, Christopher Rigby, who had hated Burton ever since the great linguist had vanquished him in India in the Gujerati examination, went out of his way to help Speke. If Speke's expedition was a success and his theory on the sources of the Nile proved, Burton would be discredited; that was good enough reward for Rigby.

But as Speke and party trekked through Ugogo, the region he had first visited with Burton three years before, they found disturbing signs of the political instability that would hamper African exploration in this area for the next decade or more. As the Arabs attempted to tighten their grip on East Africa between Ujiji and Bagamoyo, more and more tribes challenged their attempt at hegemony. The Gogo, Ngoni, Ha and Nyamwezi were among the foremost martial tribes and their numbers compensated for the technical superiority afforded by the Arabs' firepower. Local inflation, the tendency of the Arabs to try to avoid paying local taxes and tribute in favour of taking what they wanted by force, and food shortages caused by the breakdown of the traditional order through war, led to the fragmentation of East African society. Bands of armed guerrillas – the *ruga-ruga* – arose, dedicated to a nomadic life of plunder. The upshot of all this was that the favourable supply situation Speke had expected on the journey to Tabora did not materialise. At Tabora indeed he was revictualled only on the tacit understanding that he would deploy his fifty riflemen on the side of the Arabs against the Nyamwezi tribe.

True to form, Speke broke this gentleman's agreement. He can scarcely be blamed for this; after all his task was to find the sources of the Nile, not to engage in local politics. But the Arabs, used to a man like Burton who understood their customs, were affronted. When the inevitable happened after Speke turned north, and supplies ran out while porters deserted, Speke had to return cap in hand to Tabora in July 1861 to beg Arab help. A seriously ill Grant, meanwhile, lay marooned in one spot for 109 days without complaint; Speke had chosen his comrade well.

At last, towards the end of 1861, Speke equalled his 'farthest north' of 1858 and entered the kingdom of Karagwe where he was warmly welcomed by king Rumanika. Rumanika's motivation was similar to that of the Arabs of Tabora: he wanted Speke's help against his brother Rogero, for in all the three lacustrine kingdoms the death of a father was followed by a fight for the succession by the surviving sons. Though defeated in 1853, Rogero still lurked around the shores of Lake Victoria as a 'king over the water' and sometimes on the water.

Speke and Grant revelled in a positive cornucopia of big-game in Karagwe, for here were lion, elephant, giraffe, rhinoceros, buffalo, zebra, antelope and hyena in abundance. The explorers marvelled at the fatness of Rumanika's wives, who attained girths the female equivalent of Sumo wrestlers. Obesity was a sign of status and wealth, and royal wives were beaten if they did not stretch their adipose tissue to the limit. Speke measured one of the women and found her bust measurement to be 52 in., her thighs 31 in. Speke, a repressed homosexual, liked to pretend an interest in women when there was no sexual threat. He indulged in some harmless flirtation with a sixteen-year-old princess: 'I got up a bit of a flirtation with Missy,' he wrote, 'and induced her to rise and shake hands with me. Her features were lovely, but her body was as round as a ball.'

Hearing a rumour that there was a white man at the court of Mutesa of Buganda, Speke pressed on alone to the north-west of Lake Victoria, leaving Grant, who had increasing trouble with a painfully ulcerated leg, stranded once more, at the whim of Rumanika's royal physicians. He did not think to carry Grant in a hammock, as Burton had carried him. There is also a suspicion that he did a secret deal with Rumanika, whereby Speke left Grant as a hostage in Karagwe, so that Mutesa could not steal the white man's magic away from the rival kingdom.

Mutesa was intrigued by his first sight of a white man. Though urged by apprehensive courtiers to kill the 'wizard', Mutesa took Speke under his wing, impressed by his guns and his abilities as a marksman, even though he raged inwardly that Speke showed disrespect by remaining seated in his presence. Once again Speke tried his hand at flirtation with dusky beauties. He developed a strong relationship with the formidable queen mother, whose protection was another consideration that gave Mutesa pause when he pondered a bloody exit for his guest.

After much wheedling and cajolery, Speke obtained permission to leave Buganda and proceed to Bunyoro. He sent for Grant, who had been stranded in Karagwe for six months; reluctantly Rumanika released him. Grant arrived at Mutesa's court on 7 July 1862; ten days later he and Speke were on the move again. Mutesa, who had dithered about whether to keep the white men under house arrest at his court, apparently gambled that Kamurasi of Bunyoro would not grant them passage, so that they would be forced to return to his court anyway.

Speke meanwhile demonstrated his dark, selfish side once more by sending Grant on to blaze a trail to Bunyoro while he himself turned aside to track down the sources of the Nile. He wanted no one to share the glory. On 28 July 1862 he came to the spot where Lake Victoria emptied into the Nile. A waterfall 12 ft high and up to 700 yds wide played around a dormitory for somnolent crocodiles and hippopotami. Local fishermen hauled in large fish that tried to jump the falls. Speke thought the scene a perfect idyll: 'We were well rewarded . . . I saw that old Father Nile without any doubt rises in the Victoria Nyanza, and, as I had foretold, that lake is the great source of the holy river which cradled the first expounder of our religious belief.'

After dubbing the cataracts Ripon Falls after the then president of the Royal Geographical Society, Speke rejoined Grant in Bunyoro. This was the third separation of the two companions: Grant had been left to his own devices for three and a half months in Unyamwezi in 1861, six months in Karagwe in early 1862 and now another month in the summer of that year. Thus did Speke interpret comradeship. He had also devolved on to Grant the difficult task of explaining their intentions. As Mutesa had foreseen, Kamurasi was indeed suspicious of a 'wizard' who came to him from the court of his rival Mutesa. He became even more alarmed when Speke spoke of opening a passage to the Nile, for he had very good intelligence of the Arabs to the north and the destruction they had wrought. Nevertheless, after six weeks of indecision, he did as his brothers in the other two kingdoms had done and let the white men go.

Speke was by now seriously short of provisions and could not spare the time to turn aside to investigate rumours of yet another lake to the west, called Luta N'Zige. Throughout the journey to the three kingdoms they had heard stories of a white man just ahead of them and Speke, petrified that this might be Petherick stealing his thunder, now forced the pace to Gondokoro. Hostile tribes, famine and cataracts prevented Speke from following the course of the Nile all the way north (a fact which his enemies later used to good propaganda advantage) but at last, on 13 February 1863, he and Grant staggered into Gondokoro.

Here they found, not Petherick, but the adventurer Samuel Baker, also on the quest of the sources of the Nile. To his fury Speke learned that Petherick was not present at the rendezvous. He had brought up boats and supplies as requested, but Speke's instructions specifically mentioned a meeting in 1862. When the year elapsed without news, Petherick and his wife went off ivory-hunting. All of this meant nothing to Speke; he at once marked Petherick down as an enemy like Burton. When the Pethericks arrived five days later, Speke was sullen, hostile and impatient with their explanations. He also suborned Baker into accepting his viewpoint.

Speke and Grant continued down the Nile, to Fashoda, Khartoum and Cairo. Speke arrived back in England with a flourish: 'The Nile is settled' was his cry. Lionised at first by the public, he soon suffered in general esteem when his arrogance and self-regard became overt. When he inveighed bitterly against Petherick, the Royal Geographical Society investigated the allegations and cleared Petherick completely. Geographers like James McQueen took Speke to task for his failure to establish the source of the Nile beyond doubt, through his insouciance in not cleaving to the shore all the way north. Speke also alienated Murchison and the Royal Geographical Society by refusing to publish his findings in their learned journal, on the ground that this would detract from the sales of a book he was writing for commercial publishers.

Speke had seemed to have won the argument with Burton hands down in 1859, but now all the old doubts resurfaced. When Burton returned from his Fernando Po consulate in the summer of 1864, he joined battle again. Reputations were at stake all round. It was agreed to settle the matter by a debate held under the auspices of the British Association at Bath, with David Livingstone, recently returned from the Zambezi expedition, as umpire and honest broker. The day before the debate was scheduled, in September 1864, Speke shot himself in what was euphemistically termed a 'shooting accident'. There were many suspicious aspects of the case that have never been satisfactorily resolved to this day. Although conscious suicide may be ruled out, the over-confident judgement of 'accidental death' returned by the jury, which was not in possession of half of the material facts, glosses over a legion of problems. It was perhaps a desire not to establish in the public mind the idea that there was some kind of curse on African exploration that led the authorities to rush to judgement. But it has to be conceded that their half-baked assessment of the case is still regarded as authoritative by many eminent Africanists today.

In Speke Africa had clearly claimed another victim, to add to Park, Clapperton, Mauch, Andersson and the rest. Arguably, it had also done for Richard Burton. 'This will finish Burton,' was one opinion when the news of Speke's death was announced. The prophecy was fulfilled: although Burton continued to lead a spectacular life of travel and adventure, in South America, the Middle East and Europe (albeit straitjacketed in consular service) he never undertook a genuine mission of exploration again. After 1864 he made only one visit to the Dark Continent, a singularly ill-advised gold-seeking trip to West Africa in 1881. The irony of Speke's career was that he was completely right about the Nile. Its source was in Lake Victoria; all other theories proved to be blinds or red herrings. The proud Burton, however, could not bring

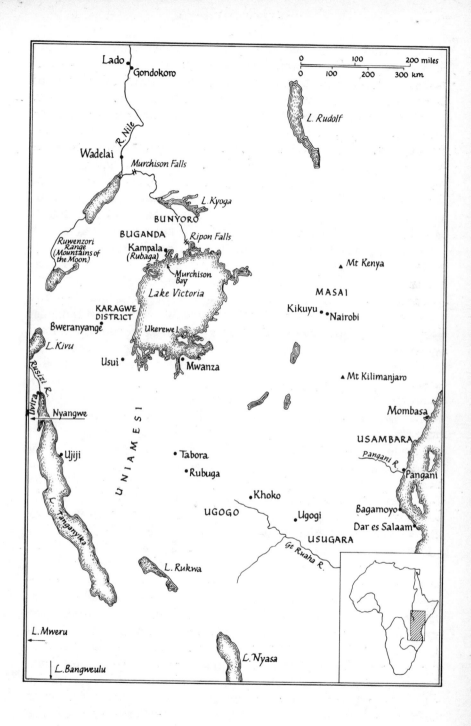

himself to admit the truth of this until 1881, and even then he made his admission of defeat in a footnote to a translation of Camoens. For a while he hoped that the saviour of his Lake Tanganyika theory would be Samuel Baker. If only Baker could find a feeder from Luta N'Zige, and then in turn Lake Tanganyika could be shown to connect with this new lake . . .

Samuel White Baker was possibly the least attractive personality of all the African explorers yet his fairy-tale romance with Florence von Sass has always protected him from merited censure. He managed to combine the faults of Speke with those of Burton – no mean feat. While detesting the black man even more heartily than Burton, he outdid Speke in mania for slaughter. He was also the wealthiest of the explorers. Baker's first expedition into unknown Africa needed no sponsorship from government, newspaper or the Royal Geographical Society; he possessed ample funds himself.

As an African explorer he was a late starter. Born in London in 1821, he inherited substantial legacies from both his father and grandfather. Discipline was unknown to him: he had been spared the rigours of a public school education in favour of private tutoring at home. He developed an early taste for shooting and the chase. On his own admission his greatest delight was 'whole hecatombs of slaughter'. When hunting in Scotland he specialised in killing stags by plunging a 12-in. double-bladed knife into the heart from the shoulder, a method he found more satisfying than simply shooting a stag at bay.

He began his career by managing the family plantations in Mauritius and Ceylon, using this as an excuse to slaughter more elephants than any man before him. An early marriage produced four daughters in quick succession, but his wife died of typhus in 1855. Baker then entered a period of aimlessness, mainly spent boar-hunting in Turkey and the Balkans, when he found himself in the familiar career cul-de-sac of one too proud to take employment yet miserable without it.

In 1860, while on his way to Turkey, he passed through the Balkan town of Widdin and paused at an Ottoman slave market. There, for sale, was a slight, fair girl from Transylvanian Hungary. Baker admitted to a *coup de foudre*. He bought the girl and entered into a form of marriage with her, later solemnised in London. Florence von Sass became the love of his life, and once she had outgrown her initial timidity, she proved herself to be the perfect partner. Utterly devoted to her 'saviour', she came to be a match for him in courage, endurance and strength of character. The two even shared the same sense of humour.

Baker realised that Victorian England would never accept the liaison, so he took an appointment with the Danube & Black Sea Railway

Company so that his partner could be with him. He then supervised the construction of a railway across the Dobrudja, but after a year of this, he decided that the Dark Continent was the proper place for exiles and misfits. With his wife, who had taken the name Florence Baker, he arrived in Egypt with vague ideas of searching for the sources of the Nile.

On 15 April 1861 the Bakers sailed up the Nile from Cairo. At Korosko they crossed the Nubian desert to Berber. Feeling himself in need of a thorough preparation, not least in Arabic, Baker spent a year exploring the Nile tributaries, especially the river Atbara, as far as the Abyssinian mountains. His aim was to reach the Blue Nile this way and thence to Khartoum. He followed the banks of the Atbara to the junction of the Settite or Taccazy river. Then he pursued the latter stream into the Abyssinian mountains in the Base country. Thence he crossed to the rivers Salaam and Angrab, at the foot of the magnificent mountain range from which they flow direct into the Atbara. Having explored these rivers, he passed through an extensive and beautiful tract of Abyssinia on the south bank of the river Salaam. Crossing the Atbara again, he arrived at the frontier town of Gellabat – known to Bruce as 'Ras el Feel'. He then marched due west and reached the river Rahad at about latitude 12°30'. Descending its banks, he crossed over a narrow strip of country to the west, and arrived at the river Dinder. He followed this to the junction of the Blue Nile and descended to Khartoum. He had been away exactly twelve months from the time he left Berber.

Khartoum, the capital of Egyptian Sudan, was at this time governed by a Turk, and the town's élite was a motley collection of Turks, Egyptians, Sudanese and Europeans. The governor received him sullenly, despite the firman Baker bore from the Viceroy of Egypt. The Khartoum élite was hand in glove with the slave-traders of the Upper Nile, who were disturbed to find an interloper coming from the north: Bruce had begun in Ethiopia and Speke and Grant in East Africa. Afraid to snub the orders from Cairo yet frightened of the consequences for their trade in human flesh if Baker was allowed to proceed, the governor tried the methods of the Circumlocution Office: he did nothing. However, the energetic Baker was not a man to be easily thwarted. By December 1862 he had assembled a flotilla of boats and an escort of forty-five soldiers, whom he had personally armed and placed in uniform. On 18 December 1862 the expedition sailed for Gondokoro.

On arrival there the negrophobe Baker had predictable trouble with the Bari tribe, who persuaded his men to desert. Baker's two-fisted methods got the recalcitrants back in line, just in time for the arrival of Speke and Grant on 15 February 1863. The news of Speke's triumph cast Baker down. 'Does not one leaf of the laurel remain for me?' he asked

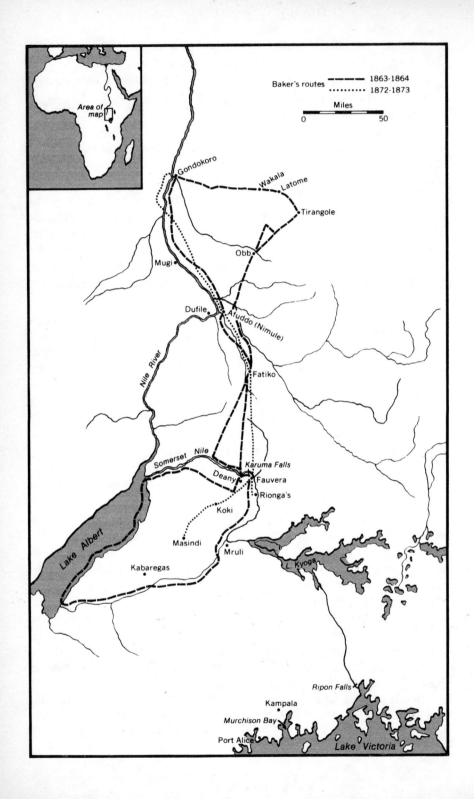

plaintively. To cheer him up, Speke said he had heard of a second lake, called Luta N'Zige, west of Bunyoro, that might feed Speke's Victoria Nile. That was incentive enough for Baker. After bidding farewell to his compatriots he headed south-east on 26 March 1863.

Held up at Abbo by the rains until the river Aswa fell, he did not approach the Karuma Falls until 22 January 1864. Kamurasi was suspicious of Europeans after the raids from slavers claiming to be friends of Speke and did not want to meet him, but contact was made in February 1864 with a chief Baker believed to be Kamurasi himself, although he was in fact the king's younger brother Mgambi; Kamurasi feared to go himself as he suspected treachery. The Nyoro people agreed to provide guides to the lake as long as Baker in return helped in the civil war against Ruyonga, Kamurasi's brother and pretender to the throne. Baker demurred, so presents were exchanged instead of a treaty of alliance. The curmudgeonly Baker's sole response to this was to exclaim: 'It is the rapacity of the chiefs of the various tribes that renders African exploration so difficult.'

Eventually it was agreed that porters and canoes for the lake would be provided. But then came a classic instance of failure to communicate across cultures that was forever to bedevil Baker's relations with African tribes. Mgambi, still posing as Kamurasi, demanded that Baker leave his wife behind. It was the custom in Bunyoro to give visitors pretty women, and he had naively imagined that Baker might like to exchange his woman. Mgambi, astonished at having given offence, was frightened out of his wits when Baker manifested his anger in typical manner. 'Drawing my revolver quietly, I held it within two inches of his chest . . . I explained to him that in my country such insolence would entail bloodshed . . . my wife made him a little speech in Arabic with a countenance almost as amiable as the head of Medusa.'

On 23 February the Bakers left Mruli, made a detour round a great swamp and eventually reached the river Kafu. Baker was entranced by the countryside and its 'comparative civilisation'. He praised the Bunyoro clothes, manufactures, huts and blacksmiths and commented on the plentiful food: simsim, sweet potatoes, beans, finger millet, sorghum, maize and plantains. On 14 March 1864, near Kyanwali, Baker first saw the lake he called Albert, after the Prince Consort:

> The glory of our prize burst suddenly upon me! There, like a sea of quicksilver, lay far beneath the grand expanse of water – a boundless sea horizon on the south and south-west, glittering in the noonday sun; and on the west, at 50 or 60 miles distance, blue mountains rose from the bosom of the lake to a height of seven thousand feet above its level . . . I called this great lake the 'Albert Nyanza'. The Victoria and Albert lakes are the two sources of the

Nile . . . after a toilsome descent of about two hours . . . we gained the level plain below the cliff . . . a walk of about a mile . . . brought us to the water's edge. The waves were rolling upon a white pebbly beach: I rushed into the lake, and thirsty with heat and fatigue, with a heart full of gratitude, I drank deeply from the sources of the Nile.

The Bakers acquired canoes and travelled northward along the eastern shore of the lake, enduring storms, mosquitoes and deserting paddlers. When they reached Bugungu they found the same river they had crossed at Karuma, boiling and tearing along its rocky course, now entering the lake as a sluggish stream. This perplexed Baker, but the locals assured him it was the same river. His guides refused to take him downstream, fearing they would be killed by hostile tribes on the return journey. As Baker could not travel downstream, he decided to fulfil his promise to Speke to explore the doubtful portion of the river between the Karuma Falls and Lake Albert, even though this meant missing the boats at Gondokoro in which they had arranged to travel north.

The Bakers set off up the Victoria Nile. About eighteen miles east of Bukungu they noticed a slight current, then:

when the paddles ceased working we could distinctly hear the roar of water . . . upon rounding the corner a magnificent sight burst suddenly upon us . . . on either side of the river were beautifully wooded cliffs rising abruptly to a height of about three hundred feet; rocks were jutting out from the intensely green foliage; and rushing through a gap that cleft the rock exactly before us, the river, contracted from a grand stream, was pent up in a narrow gorge of scarcely fifty yards in width; roaring furiously through the rock-bound pass, it plunged in one leap of about one hundred and twenty feet perpendicular into a dark abyss below . . . in honour of the distinguished president of the Royal Geographical Society I named it the Murchison Falls.

Next, the Bakers left the canoes at Fajao and marched east, parallel to the Nile. One night they camped upon Patooan, an island in the river, and a place of refuge for people driven from their homes during the war between Kamurasi and Ruyonga. The islands to the east, to within a march of Karuma Falls, were in the possession of Ruyonga and his half-brother Mpuhuka, the deadly enemies of Kamurasi. Because of the war, the Bakers could not proceed farther; porters were unobtainable and the country was deserted. The travellers subsisted on finger millet and local spinach for two months. Kamurasi was nearby and knew of their plight, but did not help the Bakers; he wanted the white men as allies in a war against his enemies. Baker eventually sent a message to Kamurasi, artfully cajoling him into a meeting in person. Kamurasi took the bait and the

Bakers were transported to his camp. Now at last they learned that 'Kamurasi' had been Mgambi; in high dudgeon at the deception, Baker tried to overawe the true Kamurasi by going to meet him in full Highland dress. The sequel showed Baker at his most typically arrogant:

Kamurasi was a remarkably fine man, tall and well proportioned, with a handsome face of dark brown colour, but a peculiarly sinister expression; he was beautifully clean, and instead of wearing the barkcloth common among the people, he was dressed in a fine mantle of black and white goat-skins, as soft as chamois leather. His people sat on the ground at some distance from his throne; when they approached to address him on any subject they crawled upon their hands and knees to his feet, and touched the ground with their foreheads. True to his natural instincts the king started begging . . . disgusted with his importunity I rose to depart, telling him that I should not return to visit him, as I did not believe he was the real Kamurasi. I had heard that Kamurasi was a great king but that he was a mere beggar, and was doubtless an impostor, like Mgambi. At this he seemed highly amused.

Since the *mukama* continued to make demands for presents, Baker steered him on to the subject of Bunyoro's history. Kamurasi explained it had once been a vast empire in Buganda and Kitara, from Karagwe to the Victoria Nile at Bugungu. But he was not deflected for long and kept pestering Baker for military aid in his war against Ruyonga and Mpuhuka. Baker pleaded poor health as an excuse for keeping out of these family quarrels. Kamurasi eventually stormed off in anger and cut off all food supplies. When Mpuhuka's people advanced, however, Baker was forced to act. He cowed the invaders into retreat by running up the Union Jack and warning that this was the emblem of the great White Queen who commanded a million soldiers with fire-sticks. After this Baker moved to Foweira and nursed his fever by constructing a still and making potato whisky. Impressed, Kamurasi declared that he would form a company to manufacture the drink. Finally the Bakers quit Bunyoro on 16 November 1864 and arrived in Gondokoro in February 1865. From there they travelled to Khartoum by May, thence to Cairo, and were in England by the end of the year.

Baker's discovery of Lake Albert was an important contribution to African exploration but, instead of solving, it added a further layer of obfuscation to the debate on the Nile sources. His *Albert Nyanza* was a mine of information on the geography and fauna of Bunyoro, but useless as a political guide. Baker had a stereotypical view of what African 'savages' would be like; despite his experiences, which should have taught him better, he merely reproduced his a *priori* stereotype.

Knighted for his endeavours, Baker was approached by the Khedive of

Egypt in 1869, when the Bakers accompanied the Prince of Wales to the opening of the Suez Canal, to see if he would accept the leadership of an expedition to the upper Nile. Baker accepted on condition that the major objective of the expedition should be the extirpation of the slave trade in the Sudan. The upshot was that Baker arrived in Khartoum in January 1870 as governor of Equatoria province, in command of the best-equipped expedition ever to process to the upper Nile. Baker's mission brought him into immediate conflict with the local élites, and his blinkered negrophobia presaged further trouble as he journeyed south.

It took his expedition, with 1600 men and fifty-eight vessels, until 15 April 1871 before it could break through the seemingly impenetrable barrier posed by the *sudd* – masses of floating vegetation choking the labyrinthine channels of the White Nile between Fashoda and Gondo-koro. By the time he had succeeded, Baker had already served two years of the contract signed by Khedive Ismail and would now have to work extremely fast, for it expired in April 1873.

Yet a further nine months were spent in a war of pacification against the Bari, who had been a thorn in his side on the first expedition. 'I always knew the Bari to be the worst tribe in the Nile basin,' he wrote, 'naturally vicious and treacherous . . . irrepressible vermin.' The hostilities began when Baker demanded that the Bari surrender their cattle to feed his huge expedition. For the Bari, however, cattle were not simply a means of wealth; they represented status, social class, identity itself. In vain did they point this out to Baker, but his one and only concern was to feed his troops. He seized the cattle by force and used his superior firepower against the Bari to devastating effect. This naked use of force saw Baker in his element, but he forgot that he had alienated the very people whom, according to the Khedive's instructions, he was supposed to conciliate.

Even with this compulsory requisition, the country could not sustain Baker's mighty host. Everything seemed to conspire against him. On one occasion Baker's steamer was towing a boat full of sheep to feed his men. A hippopotamus charged the boat, capsized it, and drowned all the sheep. Admitting defeat, Baker sent 1000 troops back to Khartoum to be fed; he accepted that without them and the co-operation of the now sullen Bari he could not carry out his original intention of carrying the sections of a disassembled steamer around the rapids to the navigable Nile; nor could there be a second visit to Lake Albert. In grim and vengeful mood, Baker proceeded south in January 1872 with just over 200 men.

At Fatiko, just north of the Victoria Nile and the Bunyoro border, Baker faced even more formidable enemies in the shape of the Arab slaver Abu Su'ud and his armed retainers, the Danaqla. For once Baker managed to deal sensibly with an African tribe; the Acholi were only too keen to form an alliance with him to drive the Arabs out, and a well-prepared ambush in long grass left 103 Danaqla and 150 of their allies dead. The Acholi were delighted with Baker's help and willingly accepted his nominal suzerainty.

Baker left Fatiko on 18 March, less than a fortnight after his arrival. He was now in a race against the calendar. His grand design had collapsed and there was no longer any question of visiting Buganda. Even to find time for Bunyoro he would have to move faster than ever before. By forced marches he reached Masindi, capital of Bunyoro, on 25 April 1872. Kamurasi was dead and his son Kabbarega reigned in his stead. He was already beginning to gain the ascendancy in the inevitable dynastic civil wars that followed every royal death in the kingdom. He had defeated and killed his brother Kabigumire and was preparing to move against the Old Pretender Ruyonga. Kabbarega was later to prove that he was a great military leader, but at his meeting with the young king, Baker went out of his way to be boorish. As he wrote contemptuously: 'This was Kabba Rega, the son of Kamrasi, the sixteenth king of Unyoro, of the Galla conquerors, a gauche, awkward, undignified lout of twenty years of age, who thought himself a great monarch. He was cowardly, cruel, cunning and treacherous to the last degree.' But Baker viewed Kabbarega as merely an egregious example of black duplicity. 'The negro idea of the 8th commandment is this: "Thou shalt not steal" – from *me*: but he takes a liberal view of the subject when the property belongs to another.'

A second and third round of talks between Kabbarega and Baker revealed no common ground. To have something to show for his four-year stewardship in Equatorial Africa Baker needed at the very least a document from the Nyoro acknowledging Egyptian hegemony in the area. Kabbarega, for his part, was interested in Baker only if he would throw his armed levies into the struggle against Ruyonga. It was the Baker/Kamurasi stand-off of 1864 raised to a new degree. With both sides prepared to use force to get what they wanted, the outcome was inevitable. Relations gradually worsened. At the end of May the Nyoro war drums beat to action. Baker claimed that the signal for war had been given by a hopelessly drunk Kabbarega, though he acknowledged that he had given the king solid grounds for enmity by forcing him to make a humiliating return of some stolen muskets and by pardoning his enemies, the slave-hunters, on condition they entered the Khedive's service. The fact that he ran up the Egyptian flag on Nyoro territory and sent envoys and letters to Kabbarega's mortal enemy, Mutesa of Buganda, did little to further Baker's cause either.

Relations reached their nadir when Kabbarega tried to poison Baker's men. Baker responded with an armed demonstration which ended in a

Nyoro attack on Baker's birthday (8 June). Another surprise attack on 13 June under the cover of grazing cattle led Baker to further fulminations on the unregenerate benightedness of the black man: 'The treachery of the negro is beyond belief; he has not a moral human instinct and is below the brute. How is it possible to improve such abject animals? They are not worth the trouble, and they are only fit for slaves, to which position their race appears to have been condemned.'

Baker decided to take the initiative and to retreat from Bunyoro so suddenly that he would steal a precious advantage on Kabbarega's pursuing hordes. While his wife laid in emergency stores of food, Baker planned the retreat to the last detail. He then set fire to Masindi to cover his movements. There followed a fortnight of tension as Kabbarega's warriors tried to close the gap on Baker's fast-moving forces. The ferocious running battles on the retreat were made more serious by Baker's dire shortage of ammunition. Altogether he took casualties of ten killed and eleven wounded before he was able to transfer his men across the Victoria Nile. His number of effectives was also reduced by the wounds from the sharp poisonous edges of the high grass through which they trekked, in hourly fear of ambush. Thirty of Baker's men suffered grievously from ulcerated legs caused by the poisoned grass.

On the other side of the Nile Baker was greeted as a brother by Ruyonga and had to agree to blood-brotherhood with him. Ruyonga knew all that had taken place: that Baker had refused to join Kabbarega against him and that he had prevented the forces of the slaver Suleiman from linking up with the Nyoro regiments. He therefore provided him with supplies and advised him that Abu Su'ud, his old enemy at Fatiko, had encouraged Kabbarega to eliminate the white man. Nevertheless, despite Ruyonga's pleas that Baker should join forces with him, ready for a second invasion of Bunyoro, Baker decided his first priority was the situation at Fatiko.

A pitched battle was enough to sweep aside Abu Su'ud's irregulars at Fatiko. Baker ordered a strong fort built there; the town became the southernmost Egyptian outpost and a symbol of Baker's futile attempts to bring the powerful kingdoms of Buganda and Bunyoro under the Egyptian flag. Even so, Mutesa misunderstood his intentions. He was reported to be most angry that Kabbarega's 'treachery' had forced Baker to consign to the flames at Masindi the presents earmarked for him (Mutesa) by the Khedive. Baker decided not to bother seeking out and crushing the remnants of Abu Su'ud and his 600 'rebels'. He reasoned thus: 'I have lately had a painful lesson in the treachery of Kabba Rega who, when I had relieved him of his enemies, the slave traders, immediately turned against *me*. These natives [the Acholi] might probably do the same. Negroes respect nothing but force; and the force that now exists, if removed, will leave them free to act against the government.'

Baker's four years in Equatoria had been a fairly comprehensive failure at every level, although this did not prevent him from boasting that he had fought his way from Cairo to the great lakes and suppressed slavery betimes. But his expeditions are of very great importance in the history of African exploration, as they illustrate more clearly than the journeys of other explorers the impact of the white man on indigenous societies, the traces left behind in oral tradition, the limited efficacy of violence and, most of all, the uneasy relationship between explorers and the slave trade.

Baker also had a greater impact on British public opinion than any African explorer since Livingstone. Economic, strategic and philan-thropic interest in the southern Sudan was awakened. By deluging *The Times* with letters when he reached England, Baker further fuelled his own legend. He hit the right note by arguing to a Victorian audience that virtue was its own reward, that the suppression of the slave trade could be a lucrative opportunity for British commerce. There was nothing God's Englishmen liked more than to have confirmed their own conviction that the morally right solution was also the profitable one. Taking his achievements at face value, 'The Thunderer' compared Baker's work with that of the Spanish in Mexico and the British in India.

Baker died at seventy-two in 1893, having lived off his fame for twenty years. He was regarded as England's foremost authority on the river Nile, and the 'grand old man' of Africa exploration. Controversy never dogged him in his lifetime, as it did Burton, Speke and Stanley. His achievements as a pure explorer, as opposed to his huge reputation and vast impact in Africa, were certainly eclipsed by Livingstone and even more by the two men who now followed Livingstone into the breach, Cameron and Stanley. But perhaps it was his very Englishness that served Baker so well. All these other men were Celts, and as such an aura of 'unsoundness' always hovered about them in the deep recesses of the collective unconscious of the English establishment. But in Samuel White Baker they truly recognised 'one of us'.

4

The Lualaba and the Congo

While Speke and Burton clashed over the sources of the Nile and Baker explored Lake Albert, the grand old man of African exploration was preparing for a final foray into the continent that had brought him fame. Livingstone, who despised Burton and Speke and thought they were both wrong about the Nile, had evolved his own theory about Africa's greatest remaining riddle. Burton had tried to disprove Speke's (correct) theory on the origin of the Nile by claiming that it arose at Lake Tanganyika, flowed into the Lake Albert that Baker had discovered, and only then proceeded to the Victoria Nyanza where Speke had located it. Livingstone's solution was even more radical. He postulated an origin in Lake Mweru, and thence to lakes Tanganyika, Albert and Victoria. *Caput Nili* was thus placed farther and farther south. If Speke's pinpointing was Point A, Baker's was point A−1, Burton's A−2 and Livingstone's A−3.

It took Livingstone a long time to amass the necessary resources for a third venture into Africa. The Royal Geographical Society was prepared to put up only £500 for the Nile quest. Livingstone got around this by appealing for funds for an exhaustive survey of the slave trade in the lake regions. This drew more backers, including the industrial chemist James Young, who contributed £1000.

Relieved at last of financial anxiety, Livingstone sailed for India in August 1865 and arrived in Bombay on 11 September. In India he signed on as bearers some black freedmen from a government school at Nasik. He also decided to use buffaloes because they were such good beasts of burden and gave milk, and because he wanted to make one more effort to defeat the tsetse fly. He employed thirteen sepoys to look after the animals, in addition to ten 'Johanna men' – so-called because they came from Anjouan Island (then called Johanna) in the Comoro islands. The party sailed from Bombay on 5 January 1866 and reached Zanzibar twenty-three days later. In March Livingstone set out on another

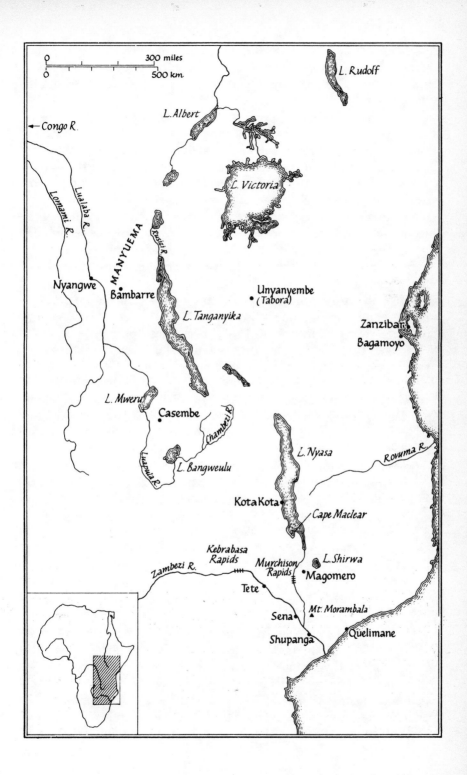

exploration of the Rovuma river, hoping to prove that it was after all a waterway to the interior. There followed yet another nightmare journey. All the animals died, and by June he had discharged all the sepoys he brought from India.

On 8 August he reached Lake Nyasa and began to follow it southwards. By 19 September he had reached Mponda's, at the south end of the lake. From there he proceeded to Marenga's on the western shore of Nyasa. At the end of September he took stock of his expedition: out of thirty-six men and sixteen beasts of burden with which he had left the coast, only nine Nasik men were left. Shortage of porters meant that Livingstone was reduced to hiring carriers for short stretches only. Musa and eight other Johanna men deserted, reached Zanzibar and spread the report that Livingstone had been murdered by a chief called Mazitu. The resulting outcry in England led to the formation of the first of many 'Livingstone relief' expeditions.

Livingstone crossed the Luangwa river on 16 December, but progress was slow in the rainy season and guides were hard to find. He crossed the Chambeze river – an influent of Lake Bangweulu – on 28 January 1867 and trudged through 'dripping forests and oozing bogs' to Chitapangwa on 20 February. Here, assailed by fever, he sent a letter to Zanzibar, in the charge of some Swahili slavers, asking for stores and medicines to be sent to Ujiji. He then trekked on to Lake Tanganyika, which he reached in April. But by now he was too ill to walk a step and could not even write up his journal. He was still feverish on 22 September when he set out for Lake Mweru.

His companion this time was the least imaginable one for the doughty opponent of the slave trade. Hamed bin Muhammad el Murjebi, known as Tippu Tip, was the greatest Arab slaver in the African interior, where he had power to rival that of the Sultan of Zanzibar. Livingstone accepted his protection to travel to Lake Mweru since tribal warfare was raging along the route and only Tippu's firepower guaranteed protection. On 8 November he came to Lake Mweru, then turned south to Casembe where the pioneer Portuguese explorer Francisco José de Lacerda had died in 1799 on his way to the lake. Livingstone was thus able to chalk up another 'first'.

At Casembe he linked up with another party of Arabs for protection against the bloodthirsty ruler of Casembe. But heavy flooding halted the caravan and so Livingstone used the delay to go south to find Lake Bangweulu. Another consideration in his mind was the conviction that too much time spent in the Arabs' company was morally corrupting for his men. However, his bearers did not agree. There was another mutiny, and Livingstone was obliged to press on with just five attendants. He braved hostile country all the way to Lake Bangweulu, which he reached on 18 July 1868, and was thus the first white man to see the lake and the river Luapula, which flowed north to Lake Mweru. After a fortnight's exploration, he set off north.

At the end of September he joined another Arab caravan for the journey to Ujiji. With these companions he reached Kabwabwata on 1 November. But hostilities between the locals and the Arabs delayed the departure for Ujiji until 11 December. On the march Livingstone fell seriously ill again. He developed pneumonia in the right lung, coughed unceasingly, could hardly speak and had to be carried in a litter for the first time in his life. To add to his troubles, his feet were ulcerated and he began to hallucinate, seeing human shapes and faces in the barks of the forest giants. He was fortunate that Muhammad, the leader of the slave caravan, looked after him so well.

The caravan reached the southern tip of Lake Tanganyika on 14 February and trooped into Ujiji a month later. The invalid Livingstone realised to his consternation that every possible mishap had befallen the stores he had ordered from Zanzibar. There were no medicines to begin with; of the stores, some had already been plundered, some had been left in Tabora, while what remained to him was inferior. Livingstone began to deluge Zanzibar with letters, pointing out that he needed more men, stores and medicine to be able to continue his work. By sending out a letter with each caravan that left for the coast, Livingstone managed to dispatch altogether forty-two different pleas for help – this was just as well, for only one of them got through.

To kill time until the expected results materialised, Livingstone accepted an offer of an escort from the Arabs to Manyema, the country to the west of Lake Tanganyika. Having heard tales of a mighty river named the Lualaba, he began to wonder whether this was, after all, the ultimate feeder of the Nile. Taking only a few followers with him, he set out on 12 July 1869 and reached the Manyema country on 21 September. Fever and rain now launched a two-pronged assault, preventing him from reaching the banks of the Lualaba. Additionally, only three of his 'dark companions' – Susi, Chuma and Gardner – remained faithful.

The year 1870 was a black year in Livingstone's life – almost a black hole. For eight months he remained in the town of Bambarre in Manyema. All around him was death, as a cholera epidemic was sweeping along the trade routes of eastern Africa from Zanzibar. He himself was ill much of the time with malaria. From July to October he was confined to his tent with ulcerated feet. In his lucid moments he tried to hire porters for the journey to the Lualaba. But the local traders could spare no man-power from the lucrative ivory-hunting and, as warfare raged between

Bambarre and the Lualaba, it was inadvisable for anyone, without a strong escorting party of Arabs, to attempt the trip. Livingstone's journals for this period are full of despair; he now doubted that he was the agent of Providence and thought, rather, that God frowned on his enterprise.

At last, on 4 February 1871, ten men arrived from Ujiji – part of the reinforcements sent from Zanzibar. To Livingstone's chagrin, all turned out to be slaves. Moreover, Sherif bin Ahmed, the Arab who had brought the men from the coast to Ujiji, used them as free labour to transport his goods and freely pilfered Livingstone's stores all the way to Lake Tanganyika. Further irritation was caused Livingstone when the ten men refused to proceed west and claimed that Dr John Kirk, Livingstone's old comrade on the Zambezi and now acting consul in Zanzibar, had sent them into the interior for the sole purpose of bringing him out. Livingstone solved this conundrum by having his Arab friend Muhammad Bogharib threaten to shoot them if they did not go with the white man.

The reluctant caravan set out on 16 February 1871 and reached Nyangwe on the shores of the Lualaba on 29 March. The Lualaba was another 'first' for Livingstone, but a further four months of frustration were in store for him there. His men refused to go on and, sensing the power that their superior firearms gave them, began to dabble in local politics. Finally, on 15 July, Livingstone's cup was filled to overflowing when the Arabs massacred 400 people in Nyangwe marketplace, basically to assert their credibility as overlords. Revolted and disgusted, Livingstone began to retrace his steps to Ujiji.

On the return journey he was ambushed by the Manyema forest peoples. Two spears missed him by inches. Then came another 'near-miss' described by Livingstone as follows:

> Guns were fired into the dense mass of forest, but with no effect, for nothing could be seen, but we heard men jeering and denouncing us close by. Two of our party were slain. Coming to a part of the forest cleared for cultivation, I noticed a gigantic tree, made higher still by growing on an ant-hill, twenty feet high. It had fire applied near its roots, and I heard a crack that told the fire had done its work, but felt no alarm till I saw it come straight for me. I ran a few paces back, and down it came to the ground one yard behind me, and breaking into several lengths, covered me with a cloud of dust. Three times in one day I was delivered from impending death.

Looking like a skeleton, Livingstone limped into Ujiji in October 1871. To his fury he learned that fresh stores had arrived for him, but that these and the supplies and medicines he had left behind had been sold off by the Arab trader named Sherif to whom they were entrusted. Sherif, a notorious drunkard and speculator, helped himself to Livingstone's cloth and beads, extracting this 'surplus' to spend in the fleshpots of Ujiji, imagining that his 'benefactor' would not survive the journey to the Lualaba. Sherif, a 'moral idiot' in Livingstone's phrase, came up to shake the doctor's hand as if nothing had happened, and claimed to be affronted by the white man's 'boorishness' when Livingstone rounded on him angrily. Livingstone had now just a month's emergency supply of local currency to spend on subsistence, after which he was likely to starve.

For two weeks Livingstone lived in turmoil and mental agony, thinking all this the clearest proof yet that God did not smile on him. Then, one Friday morning, Susi came rushing into the hut or *tembe* where Livingstone lived to tell him that a white man was approaching. Livingstone put on his red woollen jacket and navy cap with a faded gold band around it. As he walked to Ujiji market, a throng of Arabs joined him and walked with him. Already he could hear the firing of guns and the soundings of horns. Winding its way into Ujiji was a large column, with an American flag fluttering in the breeze at its head. Livingstone stopped. A wiry, short-statured young man of pugnacious appearance threaded his way to the front of the column. Cautiously he approached Livingstone. Both men doffed their caps. The young man spoke first:

'Dr Livingstone, I presume?'

'Yes.'

'Doctor, I thank God I have been permitted to shake hands with you.'

'I feel thankful that I am here to welcome you.'

The thirty-year-old 'American' who made such a timely appearance at Ujiji in October 1871 was in fact a Welshman. 'Henry M. Stanley' was a name taken from a New Orleans plantation owner. The man destined to be the greatest of all African explorers was born John Rowlands in north Wales in 1841. He was illegitimate, the son of an unknown father. His mother was a promiscuous woman even by the loose standards currently the norm among the British proletariat; altogether she produced five children out of wedlock by different fathers. Brought up by his grandfather until the age of six, John Rowlands was then consigned on the grandfather's death to the St Asaph Union workhouse. There he remained until the age of fifteen, witnessing all manner of sexual degradation. In later years Stanley wove elaborate fantasies round this period in his life. After unsuccessful periods as apprentice schoolmaster and shop assistant, at the age of seventeen young Rowlands shipped out from Liverpool as a cabin boy. In New Orleans he jumped ship to avoid the routine brutality on board, and was taken under the wing of a rich cotton merchant and landowner. From this man he took the appellation Henry Stanley by which he was to become a household name.

After quarrelling with his protector and living an itinerant life as storekeeper in the Deep South, Stanley was pressurised into volunteering in the Confederate Army at the start of the American Civil War. He took part in the dreadful battle of Shiloh in 1862, was captured by the Union Army and released from prisoner-of-war camp on condition he re-enlisted on the Federal side. Stanley did so, but fell seriously ill and was discharged as medically unfit. After nearly dying of fever, he served for two years in the US Merchant Marine before re-entering the Civil War, this time as a clerk in the Federal Navy. Shortly before the end of the war he deserted and persuaded a young comrade Lewis Noe to decamp with him. After a year in mining camps in the Far West, Stanley persuaded Noe to accompany him to Turkey, where he was sure they would make their fortunes. The Turkish adventure of 1866 turned into a nightmare. Noe was beaten and raped by Turks, and Stanley himself was lucky to escape with his life.

Returning to the United States at the beginning of 1867, the ambitious and highly intelligent Stanley conceived of an escape from the lower depths via journalism. He persuaded the *Missouri Democrat* to take him on as a roving 'special' and in this capacity quickly made a name for himself as war correspondent. He covered General Hancock's campaigns against the Cheyenne and the subsequent treaties of pacification of Medicine Lodge and elsewhere. Here he rubbed up against such legendary characters as Wild Bill Hickok and George Armstrong Custer.

Having made his name as a reporter, Stanley was taken on by James Gordon Bennett, Jr, of the *New York Herald* to cover the British campaign against Emperor Theodore of Abyssinia. On his way out to Ethiopia Stanley bribed the telegraph operator at Alexandria to make sure his copy was sent to London ahead of his rivals'. After General Napier's victory over Theodore at Magdala, Stanley sped back to Alexandria, again bribed the telegraph operator and set off for London. Now came an amazing stroke of luck. Almost immediately after Stanley's copy had been filed, the cable between Malta and Alexandria broke. The upshot was that Stanley scooped all other journalists by a full two weeks. Almost overnight he was as famous as W.H. Russell of *The Times*.

Gordon Bennett was a newspaperman of genius and he had meanwhile realised that a reporter 'finding' Livingstone in Central Africa would have the scoop of the century on his hands. He carefully groomed Stanley for the task. First he sent him on war correspondent assignments in Crete and Spain. Then he summoned him to Paris in October 1869 and gave him his dramatic assignment: 'Find Livingstone.' Yet Bennett's ingenuity did not end there. He intuited correctly that if the tension over Livingstone's uncertain whereabouts could be maintained for a further year, and then a *Herald* man met him in Africa, a global sensation would ensue. He therefore sent Stanley on a long and somewhat pointless assignment to India, via the Middle East, the Holy Land, Georgia, the Caucasus, Asiatic Russia and Persia to Bombay. From there, in January 1871, Stanley took ship to Zanzibar, having been given the green light to proceed with the 'discovery' of Livingstone.

Stanley proved a remarkably fast learner. In an amazingly short time he mastered the intricacies of porterage, *hongo*, and man-management. He was materially assisted by the vast sums of money Bennett put at his disposal – a fact that ever afterwards drew envious sarcasm from his rival explorers. He left for the interior in February with some 200 porters and soldiers. But in the first half of 1871 he evinced the qualities that most differentiated him from his peers: hard-driving ruthlessness and brutality. Stanley later boasted that by getting to Tabora twice as fast as Burton and Speke he revealed himself a natural professional. But he failed to mention the human cost of his achievements. He took on two white assistants and hounded them to death by refusing to stop when they contracted fever. Six months into the expedition both men were dead; but not before in desperation they had attempted to assassinate Stanley. By refusing to halt for adequate rest Stanley also killed off large numbers of his porters, who were debilitated by smallpox and other illnesses, and induced many more to desert. By the time he reached Tabora, Stanley had thinned out his expedition to the point where he urgently needed to hire new porters.

At Tabora Stanley allowed himself to be sucked into a war between the Arabs and the outstanding Nyamwezi commander of irregulars, Mirambo. When Mirambo lured the Arabs into an ambush and slaughtered them, Stanley feared for his own position. Mirambo's warriors stormed down to Tabora and laid it waste, but did not tangle with Stanley and his men who had formed a Rorke's Drift-style redoubt around Stanley's *tembe* and were determined to fight to the last.

Life at Tabora returned to normal as Mirambo and his army withdrew. Stanley hired new porters. But the route to Lake Tanganyika was now blocked, as Arabs fought Nyamwezi in bitter clashes. Stanley therefore headed south into the unknown Gombe and then swung north again at the Malagarazi river. He survived desertions, disease, mutiny and another assassination attempt, this time by his black retainers or *wangwana*. While crossing the Malagarazi his party was attacked by crocodiles, but on the far bank human marauders proved an even more serious trial. After being mulcted of half his trade goods by the powerful Ha tribe, Stanley evaded further exactions by striking into the wilderness and coming to the shores of Lake Tanganyika by a new route. He and his men then descended from the heights into Ujiji for the meeting with Livingstone.

On paper it was unlikely that Stanley and Livingstone would get on. Both were essentially misanthropes and prima donnas who had to be 'first' and resented the presence of any other white men on their expeditions. But their meeting by the lake shore in October 1871, which was designed to be a perfunctory hand-over of supplies and letters, extended into a four-month friendship. Quite apart from Livingstone's joy at having been saved by the younger man's coming – 'You have given me new life,' he told Stanley, and for once this was no explorer's hyperbole – other latent factors favoured the relationship. Both men were Celts, 'outsiders' in English terms, both from humble origins and with a marked distaste for the aristocratic hauteur of the English 'milord'. Both men were abnormally sensitive about being short of stature but, since they were both small, no irrational physical antagonism arose. Most of all the relationship was complementary: each found in the other a fulfilment of a human lack. For the 30-year-old Stanley, the 58-year-old Livingstone was the father he had never known, and he acknowledged as much in his diary. For Livingstone, Stanley acted as surrogate prodigal son. He had quarrelled bitterly with his natural son Robert, and Robert had run away to an early death in the American Civil War. Now here was Stanley, an 'American' who had fought in and survived the selfsame war.

As the friendship deepened over the first two weeks in Ujiji, and Livingstone's health improved, Livingstone invited Stanley to join him on an expedition to the head of Lake Tanganyika, to settle once and for all the question that Speke and Burton had left open: did the Rusizi river flow into or out of the lake; clearly if it flowed in, Tanganyika could not be the Nile feeder. In December Stanley and Livingstone delivered the *coup de grâce* to Burton's theory by establishing conclusively that the Rusizi was an influent.

Stanley tried to persuade Livingstone to return to England with him, but the doctor was adamant that he had to stay and finish his work. Seeing his dire shortage of goods and men, Stanley persuaded him to come back to Tabora with him, there to await fresh porters and stores that Stanley would sent back from Zanzibar. Livingstone agreed. The two men took their followers back to Tabora by a new route, avoiding the Ha and all other troublesome tribes. This involved sailing south from Ujiji, then disembarking and following a north-easterly course to Tabora.

They arrived in Tabora in mid-February. Stanley spent a month in the doctor's company, making meticulous preparations meanwhile for a forced march to the coast. On 14 March 1872 the two men bade one another a sad farewell. For both it meant the end of the only successful human relationship of their lives. Stanley then set out on another hard-driving epic through the torrential rains of the *Masika*. He reached

Bagamoyo on the coast on 6 May, having covered 525 miles in fifty-two days – the fastest rate-per-day over a long distance ever achieved by an African explorer's marching column.

Stanley set out for England at the earliest opportunity. The cable he received from Bennett in Aden said it all: 'You are now as famous as Livingstone, having discovered the discoverer.' Stanley sped to England with his young black servant Kalulu, receiving the plaudits of French geographers all the way from Marseilles to Paris. But when he reached England on 1 August he suffered severe disillusionment. All the jaundiced comments about the English establishment that he and Livingstone had swapped at Ujiji were borne out startlingly. Resentful that a 'Yankee penny-a-liner' had found their hero in Africa when a brace of Englishmen had already failed, the English upper classes at first refused to believe Stanley's story and accused him of being a liar and a charlatan. The Royal Geographical Society acted both grudgingly and insultingly towards Stanley. Only when Livingstone's own family produced unimpeachable evidence that Stanley had indeed met him, did the attitude of the establishment change. Queen Victoria received Stanley at Balmoral and the Royal Geographical Society tried to cover its sceptical tracks by awarding him their highest honour, the Gold Medal. Stanley's own account of his adventures *How I Found Livingstone in Central Africa* was the publishing sensation of 1872.

Livingstone meanwhile waited patiently at Tabora for the promised men and supplies. Stanley was as good as his word. He proved later in the Congo what a superlative administrator he was. Once in Zanzibar, in May 1872, he had not taken long to handpick a party of porters and to oversee the despatch of high-quality trade goods and medicine. The reinforcements reached a delighted Livingstone in August. He now resolved on a twenty-month trek. He would strike south and complete his exploration of lakes Bangweulu and Mweru, which had been hampered before by his lack of manpower. Then he would head north through Katanga, attempt to follow the Lualaba and prove that it was the Nile source, then return to Ujiji.

But it was mid-October before Livingstone returned to Lake Tanganyika from Tabora, and the heavy rains began in November. A combination of errors in calculation, bad weather and faulty instruments led him to lose his way and wander in circles. From 4 January to 13 February 1873 he retraced his steps so often that he travelled less than seventy miles as the crow flies. In addition, he suffered from dysentery and loss of blood from haemorrhoids and increasingly had to be carried in a litter.

Yet he persevered doggedly. All his strength was needed to browbeat the recalcitrant chief Matipa into letting him have canoes. Then he crossed the Kalongosi river which flows into Lake Mweru and climbed the mountains behind. He descended into the country north of Lake Bangweulu and passed over flooded lands to Kabinga's. By now his servants Susi and Chuma were the mainstay of the expedition. The crossing of the Chambezi brought torments from mosquitoes, ants and poisonous spiders to compound the pain from dysentery and haemorrhoids.

By the beginning of April Livingstone was seriously weakening. His men constructed a *kitanda* or litter, with two side pieces 7-ft long, joined by 3-ft cross-pieces lashed at intervals, covered with grass and a blanket. This was slung from a carrying pole, over which was hung a second blanket as protection from the sun. He was now fading fast, as his diary entries indicate. On 10 April he wrote: 'I am pale and weak from bleeding profusely ever since 31 March. Oh, how I long to be permitted by the Over Power to finish my work.' A few days later he wrote: 'Nothing earthly will ever make me give up my work in despair. I encourage myself in the Lord my God, and go forward.'

Livingstone's last diary entry was made on 27 April. On the night of the 30th, at Chitambo's, after learning from Susi that they still had three days' march to go to the Luapula, he let out a sigh and whispered, 'Oh dear, dear.' At midnight he asked Susi to give him a dose of calomel. Then came his last recorded words: 'All right, you can go now.'

At 4 a.m. his men found him kneeling on the bed with his head on the pillow. Victorian piety assumed he had spent his last minutes in prayer, and Susi and Chuma were happy to acquiese in this version. 'They saw the doctor fallen forward as if in the act of praying . . . they felt his cheeks and found him cold.' This happened shortly before dawn on 1 May 1873. The Livingstone legend was already in the making. By an extraordinary act of devotion Susi and Chuma made it seem as though the doctor had indeed been one of God's chosen ones. After drying his body in the sun for a fortnight, they cut out the heart and entrails, buried them under a tree, and embalmed the rest of the corpse. They then wrapped it in sailcloth, enclosed it in a cylinder of bark and lashed it to a pole. Then they started a twelve-month journey to the coast – a courageous exploit that ensured that the names of Susi and Chuma would always be remembered.

When they reached Tabora, Susi and Chuma met a Scotsman very unlike their dead master. The twenty-four-year-old Verney Lovett Cameron had been born in 1844, the son of a minister. A career in the Royal Navy saw him first in the West Indian squadron, where he witnessed some of the naval operations in the American Civil War, then in the Channel squadron, where he attained the rank of lieutenant. Service in the Indian Ocean followed – which engendered a lifelong hatred of the slave trade – and he was decorated for his role in the Abyssinian campaign of 1868. In 1870 he was placed on the steam reserve at Sheerness; in effect at the age of twenty-six he had already been put out to grass.

What saved Cameron from obscurity was Livingstone – or rather the successive waves of 'Livingstone relief expeditions'. The first naval officer to be given his head in this area was Lieutenant William Henn. With the missionary Charles New and Livingstone's son Oswell, Henn was set to plunge into the African interior when Stanley arrived at the coast with the news of the 'finding' of Livingstone. In 1872, however, after hearing Stanley's reports, the Royal Geographical Society decided to send another expedition to Africa to assist Livingstone in his work. Cameron, who had been plaguing the society with requests for adventure since 1870, was chosen to be leader. As comrades in the venture he signed on his friend W.E. Dillon, a naval surgeon, and Cecil Murphy, a lieutenant in the Royal Artillery. Also assured of a place on the expedition was Robert Moffat, grandson of the famous missionary and Livingstone's nephew, who sold his sugar plantations in Natal to join the British adventurers.

Cameron arrived in Zanzibar in January 1873. He experienced immense difficulties in getting together a credible caravan but at last, on 30 May, he departed from Bagamoyo with 192 *pagazis* or regular porters and 34 *askaris* or soldiers. All the white men went down with fever, and Robert Moffat died of it when just a few days inland. Cameron often reflected gloomily on the human toll exacted by Africa. In the case of his own expedition he received a startling demonstration. At Tabora the fever-racked Murphy elected to accompany Susi and Chuma back to the coast with Livingstone's body. Shortly after resuming the journey to Ujiji, Dillon was again attacked by fever and in delirium shot himself. By November 1873, having started with three white comrades, Cameron was alone.

That was not even the worst of it. Disease hung at their heels all the way across Tanzania: fever, dysentery, ophthalmia. In Ugogo they encountered smallpox 'which at times sweeps like a devouring fire throughout large portions of Africa'. Cameron's route lay south of Burton's and north of Stanley's but he became the second explorer (after Stanley) to report on the cornucopia of game in the Gombe area. Sidi Bombay, who was Cameron's caravan master, gave him good advice at the Malagarazi river and advised him not to dicker over the extra fee charged for getting the donkeys across the river. Bombay related that it was Stanley's meanness in refusing to pay this extra *hongo* that induced him to try to get them across himself, leading to the loss of his favourite animal to crocodiles.

But Bombay was no help in a more important area of African travel. Lacking experience, Cameron paid his porters in advance. Mass desertion was the inevitable result. By the time he left Tabora, Cameron's party was down to 100 men, and within days a further fifty had deserted. Cameron himself was suffering grievously from ophthalmia, he was in pain from an injured back sustained by a fall from a donkey and was already down to seven stone in weight. It took him until 21 February to arrive at Ujiji; throughout the march he was short of food, lashed by the rains of the *Masika* and in permanent fear of attack by the *ruga-ruga*.

In Ujiji Cameron took possession of the remainder of Livingstone's papers. After deliberation he decided to complete Livingstone's work by pressing on with the task of exploration. On 13 March 1874 he set out to explore the southern end of Lake Tanganyika, as yet uncharted by Europeans. Bombay nursed him through another fever. The southern tip of the lake was reached on 17 April. All the time Cameron was bedevilled by his men's acute fear of water. As an old salt, he felt impatient with their timidity. 'What would I not have given for a man-of-war's whaler and crew for six weeks!' he exclaimed. He entered the river Lukuga but found it impenetrable because of a barrier of impacted vegetation. Nevertheless he had plotted ninety-six rivers flowing into the lake and one flowing out of it. He abandoned the Lukuga on 4 May and was back in Ujiji five days later.

Cameron now followed the example of earlier travellers and joined up with a party of Arab slave-traders for the march across Manyema. He held a final muster of his now seventy-strong party on the western shores of Lake Tanganyika on 31 May. He was lured onward by talk of the Lualaba river, which the Arabs told him flowed into the Congo. Local lore spoke of people who had gone all the way to the far sea where white men traded. One Arab boasted that he had offered to take Livingstone all the way for 1000 dollars but the doctor jibbed at the price. (The Maria Teresa dollar was the international currency of Africa at this time.) Cameron entertained visions of emerging at the Atlantic, having been the first white man to chart the Congo river.

On 3 August 1874 Cameron arrived at the banks of the Lualaba which he described as 'a strong and sweeping current of turbid yellow water fully a mile wide'. Next day he entered Nyangwe and found it much as Livingstone had described it: the Arabs occupied the high and salubrious right bank, while the Africans lived in rude huts on the mud flats on the other side. But Cameron found all his efforts to obtain canoes and paddlers frustrated by Arab interference.

He was toying with retracing his steps to Bagamoyo when Tippu Tip arrived, after a two-year absence in Katanga. Tippu always got on well, at least initially, with white explorers. He persuaded Cameron to proceed to the Atlantic coast by a more southerly route which would come out at Portuguese Angola, on the ground that the Lualaba/Congo was utterly impassable. Tippu was being disingenuous in the intelligence he gave Cameron; his real aim was to divert the explorer away from Arab-held territory into Portuguese spheres of influence. But Cameron avidly accepted the advice and Tippu's offer of help. On 26 August he accompanied Tippu south to his base camp near the Lomami river in hopes of crossing the Lomami and reaching Lake Sankorra. But when he got to Tippu's encampment on 3 September he found the direct route to Lake Sankorra closed by tribal wars. Baulked again, Cameron accepted Tippu's offer of guides to Urua in Katanga, where there were supposed to be Portuguese traders.

They trekked across barren lands and through villages where the white man was thought to be a devil or spirit and where scarcity of animal protein led the villagers to eat porridge mixed with ants. Then in October came the first serious hostilities with tribal warriors. The proximate cause of the initial outbreak was the theft of Cameron's mascot goat, but it appears that a party of Portuguese slavers had been operating in the area and Cameron's expedition was mistaken for it. At any rate, Cameron was hard pressed and found himself obliged to respond to showers of arrows with a sharp volley. He then retreated to the next village and built a stockade, called Fort Dinah after the purloined goat. Several days of tense sniping and skirmishing ended with a hastily patched-up truce. Cameron made haste to shake off the dust of the region.

He pressed on to Kilemba, where he met a friendly Arab trader, Jumah Merikani. Jumah introduced him to an African trader who had taken the Portuguese name of Jose Antonio Alvez and it was agreed that Cameron would continue his journey westwards with him. While waiting for the tardy Alvez to set out, Cameron explored lakes Mohrya and Kassazi and made some tentative treaties with the local tribes.

In February 1875 Alvez at last consented to depart but after a short journey halted again for a further four months. It was 10 June 1875 before the march resumed, and the pace was still painfully slow. Food was scarce, and Cameron's relations with Alvez deteriorated weekly. Cameron was particularly disgusted with Alvez's cruel treatment of his slaves. At last, in October, they crossed the Kwanza river and came to Alvez's village. Cameron was now free to travel on alone. He obtained new porters and set out again on 10 October.

By now there were plentiful signs of a Portuguese presence in the villages and towns. In some of the larger settlements Cameron was able to sleep between sheets and drink rosé wine. But he was still far from his

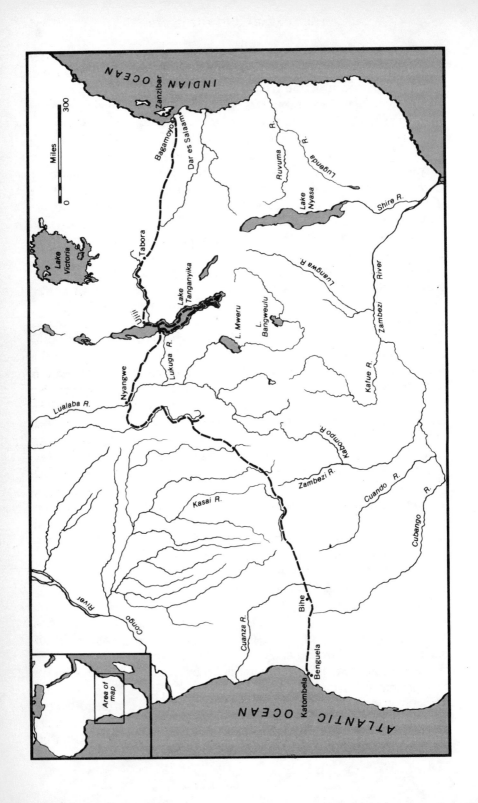

goal, and on the long stretches between human habitation cold and wet took a fearful toll. By early November the expedition was tired, dispirited and disease-ridden, and they were still 125 miles from the coast. Cameron decided to gamble all on an austerity programme. He reduced his men's pay from 8½ dollars to 5 dollars a month, so that they would be keen to get to journey's end and leave his service. Then he selected a small advance party and pressed on to the coast in forced marches.

After six days of gruelling trekking, he reached the coast on 7 November. At the town of Katombela he purchased food in bulk and sent it back to the men in the main party. The rearguard arrived on 11 November, and ten days later the united expedition traipsed into Luanda. Of the fifty-four men who reached the coast, forty-nine (including twenty-three of the thirty-five *askaris*) had come all the way; most of the desertions since Manyema had been by those engaged in the villages they passed through en route. For Cameron the principal reward of the journey was fame. He was the first European to cross Africa from east to west, thus achieving a Scots 'double' (for Livingstone was first west to east). He had accumulated a wealth of geographical, political and anthropological information about Central Africa and had exposed the fragility of the Portuguese hold on the Angola region. He was the first to guess the truth about the Lualaba/Congo connection and the first to point to the mineral wealth of Katanga, source of so many African conflicts in the twentieth century.

The consequences of Cameron's journey were manifold. His discoveries gave Britain the option of a protectorate over the Congo region, which the authorities in London chose not to take up. His expedition alerted the Portuguese to the possibilities inherent in African exploration. Two years later they sent Major Serpa Pinto on a trans-Africa expedition in hopes of building a Portuguese bloc across Africa to link Angola and Mozambique. Most important of all, in terms of long-term impact, Cameron's African traverse opened the eyes of the avaricious Leopold of Belgium to the potential wealth of Central Africa and set him on his notorious career as the 'king incorporated'.

Cameron himself was loaded with honours. He was promoted Commander, given the CB, an Oxford doctorate and the Founder's Medal of the Royal Geographical Society. He was widely consulted as a leading expert on African affairs and became an advocate of the necessary symbiosis of commerce and missionary endeavour. He retired from the Royal Navy and served on the board of a number of companies with African interests. He struck up a notable friendship with Richard Burton and accompanied him on a gold-seeking expedition to West Africa in 1881–2. He then took to writing adventure stories for boys. The fall from a donkey in his early days in Africa proved prophetic, for he died at the age of fifty after being thrown from his horse while returning from a hunt near Leighton Buzzard. He thus joined a long list of explorers who, having survived the rigours of Africa, still failed to die in their beds.

Even as Cameron emerged on the Atlantic coast, another man was on the point of fulfilling his dream of charting the Congo. After his triumph in England in 1872, Stanley entered a limbo period. Still in the employment of Gordon Bennett, who resented the fact that it was Stanley rather than the *New York Herald* who had been given the credit for the 'finding' of Livingstone, Stanley was condemned to three months' inactivity in New York. Having cut him down to size sufficiently, Bennett sent him to Spain to cover the Carlist rising. After four months' reporting from the battlefields of Navarre, Stanley was abruptly reassigned to cover Sir Garnet Wolseley's expedition against the Ashanti. He filed vivid copy on the march to Kumasi, the victory over the Ashanti and the sack of their capital. He was on the way back to England, in February 1874, when he heard of the death of Livingstone. Stanley at once saw a chance to find further fame as an African explorer. He announced that it was his destiny to complete Livingstone's work, though his expression of this contained some choice pietistic Stanleyesque cant: 'Dear Livingstone! Another sacrifice to Africa! . . . May I be selected to succeed him in opening up Africa to the shining light of Christianity! . . . May Livingstone's God be with me, as He was with Livingstone in all his loneliness. May God direct me as He wills. I can only vow to be obedient, and not to slacken.'

After the state funeral of Livingstone's body in Westminster Abbey on 18 April, when he acted as pall-bearer, Stanley asked his friend Edwin Arnold, editor of the *Daily Telegraph*, to persuade the newspaper's proprietor to put up £6000 for an expedition to complete Livingstone's work. With this advance under his belt, Stanley did not find it difficult to 'persuade' Gordon Bennett to put up a matching sum.

Preparations went on throughout the summer of 1874. Stanley decided to take three white companions with him: one was Frederick Barker, a clerk at the Langham Hotel where he was staying; the other two were the Pocock brothers, Frank and Edward, Medway fishermen whom Stanley hired to deal with the boat he was taking with him to conquer Africa's lakes and rivers. The *Lady Alice* was a detachable craft in five sections, each 8 ft long, suitable for carriage by porters.

On arrival at Zanzibar, Stanley hired one Augustus Sparhawk to arrange the details of his expedition; with the largesse from Bennett and the *Daily Telegraph* money was virtually no object. He took his white companions with him on a 'taster' expedition to the mainland to explore the Rufiji river. Then he returned to Zanzibar ready for the journey proper. His aim was to circumnavigate the great lakes of Victoria and Tanganyika and provide the first comprehensive chart of the lacustrine areas, before proceeding to the Lualaba, to follow it wherever it might lead. The expedition Stanley led into Africa in November 1874 was the most lavishly equipped and financed to date. He paid out £1300 in advances to the *wangwana* – his Zanzibari followers. He took with him 18,000 lb of trade goods, stores, and arms – 8 tons divided into loads of 60 lb each for his 300 porters.

Stanley's expedition left Bagamoyo in mid-November 1874. After gruelling marches in the *Masika*, the party came in sight of Lake Victoria on 26 February 1875. Already the toll taken on the travellers had been grievous. Battle and disease had halved their numbers; out of 347 souls who had left Bagamoyo, 181 had been lost through famine, illness, desertion or as victims of tribal spears. Edward Pocock caught fever on his first day on the mainland, never recovered, and died on 17 January. The trek from the coast to Victoria Nyanza saw a veritable roll-call of African diseases: dysentery, bronchitis, pneumonia, ophthalmia, rheumatism, sciatica, asthma, dropsy, emphysema, erysipelas, elephantiasis.

Leaving the bulk of his expedition at Kaduma on the south-east corner of Lake Victoria under the command of Frank Pocock, Stanley took an élite squad with him on the clockwise circumnavigation of the Nyanza. They encountered egregious hostility from the people of Bumbire, but were warmly welcomed on the north-western coast by Mutesa, who was intrigued to meet his fourth white man (Speke, Grant and Chaillé-Long had been Stanley's predecessors). Encouraged by his reception, Stanley completed his clockwise tour of the lake and returned to Kaduma to bring up the rest of his expedition. He had been away fifty-seven days, but in that time a second white man, Frederick Barker, had succumbed to fever. His last hours were spent in laboured breathing and foaming at the mouth.

With his united expedition and with help from Mutesa, Stanley meted out draconian punishment on the hostile islanders of Bumbire (August 1875). Then Stanley returned to Mutesa's court to assist him in a war of pacification against rebel vassals. Stanley also convinced himself that he had converted Mutesa to Christianity, and on the strength of this bogus feat (Mutesa was simply playing with him) sent out a clarion call for English missionaries to come to Uganda.

In December Stanley left for the kingdom of Bunyoro, accompanied by 500 of Mutesa's Buganda spearsmen. But Kabbarega, king of Bunyoro, had recently had a taste of Europeans in the shape of Baker and did not wish to see another; additionally he resented the presence of Ganda warriors on his territory. So Stanley was firmly and none too politely turned back from Bunyoro. He got as far as Lake George before being obliged to turn back into Buganda, whence he made his way south into Karagwe.

Hospitably received there, Stanley spent the early part of 1876 exploring Karagwe. Then he set his course south for Lake Tanganyika. A highlight of this part of his journey was a meeting with Mirambo, the Nyamwezi chief who had so nearly come to blows with him at Tabora in 1871. Without his Arab friends, the white man was regarded as a harmless curiosity.

On 27 May 1876 Stanley once more entered Ujiji, scene of the famous meeting with Livingstone five years before. He then set out on a thorough examination of the three-quarters of the lake he had not visited before (he had explored the extreme north with Livingstone in 1871). After returning from this reconnaissance, Stanley held a muster at Ujiji on 25 August, to find that of the 170 men still on his muster-roll another thirty-eight had deserted. He at once decided to take the remainder as far from temptation as possible. The expedition crossed the lake and on 5 October entered Manyema.

Later that month Stanley became the third great explorer (after Livingstone and Cameron) to link up with Tippu Tip. After accompanying Tippu to Nyangwe, Stanley played on the Arab's love of prestige and fame – he had no need of Stanley's money – to persuade him to accompany him on a sixty-day march north along the Lualaba. This was *terra incognita* even for the Arabs, and Tippu had staked his reputation on his conviction that no man could follow the Lualaba along the entire length of its course. The joint expedition split into a land party and a river party. Stanley's excitement was mingled with uncertainty, for he could still not be certain that the Lualaba flowed into the Congo rather than the Nile or even the Niger.

For two months Tippu and Stanley struggled through damp, dark and dank forests, their clothes wet with perspiration and humidity, their feet forever slipping on clayey soil or feculent bog. There were battles with the forest tribes all the way up to Vinya-Nyara, 125 miles north of Nyangwe. At this point Tippu Tip decided he had had enough. Despite Stanley's pleas he turned for home. As a final favour he forced Stanley's 149 followers into their boats – twenty-three canoes and the *Lady Alice*. On 28 December 1876 Stanley's flotilla launched on to the unknown Lualaba.

January 1877 found Stanley struggling with obstacles from both man and nature. Even while he portaged his boats over the seven cataracts of the falls that afterwards bore his name, he was engaged in continual battles with hostile tribes. But he became aware, as the river gradually swung west, and later south-west, that he was indeed on the Congo. On 1 February, at the confluence of the Aruwimi river, the expedition had its toughest ordeal to date, a hard-fought battle against Soko warriors. Two weeks later, on 14 February, came what Stanley called the 'fight of fights' – an eight-hour running battle with the powerful Bangala confederation on the right bank of the Congo. After surviving this most close-run of all their battles, the adventurers came on 12 March to a kind of lake, surrounded with white cliffs like those at Dover. Stanley called the area Stanley Pool.

Beyond Stanley Pool there were no battles. But the lower Congo, with its fearsome cataracts, proved virtually impassable. Stanley spent weeks making almost no progress: in April he averaged a mile a day. Still refusing to abandon the river he inched forward at a snail's pace. But the perils of trying to take the lower Congo's boiling rapids by frontal assault were graphically demonstrated on 3 June when Frank Pocock and two other men were drowned while trying to shoot the rapids. Stanley had thus lost all five white comrades on his first two expeditions.

At last, nearly dead from starvation, Stanley abandoned the river at Isangila and headed for the coast. A despairing message sent on by courier reached the European trading post at Boma. Supplies were sent back, and in early August the emaciated Stanley staggered into Boma on the Congo estuary. His 999-day epic crossing of Africa had won for him the fame of a Columbus, a Cook or a Marco Polo.

Stanley returned to Europe, where he was again lionised, though his harsh methods increasingly came under scrutiny in the radical press. Tired of service with Bennett, Stanley resigned and took employment with Leopold of the Belgians, who dreamed of a personal empire in Central Africa. Leopold's ambition was to turn the Belgian monarchy into a form of capitalist corporation where he was the sole shareholder. To achieve his aims, he constructed a number of 'front' organisations, with humanitarian and anti-slave-trading aims. Even the cynical Stanley was partly taken in by the monarch's humbug.

In 1879 Stanley returned to the Congo to set up on Leopold's behalf a chain of trading stations that would be the nucleus of an independent state the king wished to set up. From 1879 to 1882 Stanley patiently built roads along the entire stretch of the Congo to Stanley Pool. He went to Europe on leave in 1882, but returned at the beginning of 1883 for a further eighteen months' service, in which he extended Leopold's dominion on the upper Congo. All the warlike tribes on the upper Congo, like the Soko and the Bangala, were brought to heel by the awesome power of Stanley's artillery, including the latest Krupps gun. Stanley even set up a station at Stanley Falls. But he discovered to his chagrin that his success in blasting a passage through the supposedly impassable Lualaba had allowed the Arab slavers to follow in his wake and spread their reign of terror into the upper Congo.

In 1884 Stanley completed his task and returned to Europe. He attended the 1884–5 Berlin Conference where Leopold outmanoeuvred all the great powers and all the great statesmen, Bismarck included, into granting him the personal possession of the Congo area, which was constituted as the Congo Free State. It is important to be clear that this was not a *Belgian* colony – the Free State became the Belgian Congo only in 1908. *L'Etat, c'est moi* was more truly predicated of Leopold than of Louis XIV. For twenty-three years the 'Free State' was the personal fief of Leopold: as one observer put it, he owned the Congo as completely as Rockefeller owned Standard Oil.

But in return for this extraordinary arrangement, Leopold had been forced to strike a secret deal with the French whereby he would never again employ Stanley in Africa; France was angry that Stanley had so comprehensively outpointed its own man, Brazza, in the race for imperial possessions in the Congo area. Stanley, unaware of this, chafed in inactivity in Europe for nearly three years. Then he got a break as lucky in its own way as when he had had the opportunity to outwit Bennett in 1874. After the death of Gordon in the Mahdist rebellion in Khartoum in 1885, a campaign arose to rescue his lieutenant, Emin Pasha, from his beleaguered position in Equatoria province. The British felt guilty at the failure to relieve Gordon, and thought that the rescue of Emin would palliate the collective guilt. Meanwhile a consortium of British capitalists under Sir William Mackinnon had conceived the idea of obtaining in East Africa the same sort of trading monopoly Leopold had acquired in the Congo; there was the additional incentive that Emin was reported to be sitting on a vast cache of ivory in Equatoria.

There was thus from the very beginning an official and an unofficial agenda with the Emin Pasha Relief Expedition, as it came to be known. Mackinnon and his henchmen looked around for a leader for the expedition and concluded that Stanley was the obvious choice. Stanley accepted the appointment with alacrity, but first he had to square things with Leopold, to whom he was still bound by a contract of employment. Leopold agreed to release Stanley to head the Emin expedition on one condition: that Stanley would travel to Equatoria via the Congo and then carry the flag of the Free State on to the Nile. It was an abiding ambition of Leopold to be a second pharaoh and to extend the vague boundaries of the Congo state all the way to the upper Nile.

So now there was not only a latent and an overt motive for the Emin Pasha expedition; Stanley also had two masters to serve. His task was difficult. Emin was cut off from the north by the *mahdiya*, and to the south were the hostile kingdoms of Buganda and Bunyoro. The task of rescue was made even more difficult by the need to follow the Congo route.

Stanley gathered together an unprepossessing band of eight white lieutenants. With these he sailed to Zanzibar in early 1887. There he met Tippu Tip, who agreed to supply porters for the expedition in return for being appointed Belgian governor of Stanley Falls, an area he now controlled. The forces of Stanley, some 800 strong, and those of Tippu Tip were once again reunited and together they sailed from Zanzibar round the Cape to the mouth of the Congo.

The long list of fatalities that was to stain the memory of the Emin expedition began even as the caravan trudged from the coast to the capital of the fledgling Belgian state at Stanley Pool. Once at the Pool, Stanley realised that famine gripped the Free State and that he could look for no help from Leopold. After commandeering a number of steamers belonging to the newly arrived missionaries, Stanley pressed on up the upper Congo. At the confluence of the Congo and Aruwimi he paused to consider his strategy.

Messages sent to Emin had asked him to meet the relief expedition at Lake Albert. In his perennial impulse towards haste, Stanley decided to take a vanguard with him across the unknown Ituri area to Lake Albert, leaving a rear column behind under the command of his unbalanced second-in-command Major Barttelot. He expected to be back at base camp in a matter of months.

But Stanley had underrated the nightmare of the Ituri forest. For seven months his vanguard floundered hopelessly through this green hell of 50,000 acres, most of the time on the brink of starvation and assailed by unseen forest people who shot at them with poisoned arrows. At last, in December 1887, Stanley and his men emerged from the darkness of the forests on to the plains around Lake Albert. Here they waited, fighting further battles with local tribes, until contact was made with Emin in April 1888.

The meeting of Stanley with Emin on the shores of Lake Albert irresistibly recalled the meeting with Livingstone by the waters of Lake Tanganyika. But this encounter was not destined to have such a happy outcome. For a start, the two men had clashing personalities: Stanley a man of action, an energetic voluntarist who believed in making things happen; Emin a scholar and contemplative, fatalistic, resigned to the will of Allah. Emin was in his own way as much of an oddity as Stanley, down to the detail of an assumed name. Born Eduard Schnitzer in Prussia in 1840, he had run away from wife and children, converted to Islam, taken the name Emin Pasha and enlisted in the Egyptian service with the redoubtable Colonel Charles Gordon. His understanding was that Stanley was bringing him extra guns and ammunition to allow him to maintain himself in Equatoria. Stanley's was that he was to bring Emin back to the coast as an exhibit of a task successfully accomplished or, at the very least, that he would settle Emin as manager of Mackinnon's trading company on the shores of Lake Victoria. Emin wanted none of this. He was comfortably settled, with a local wife and children, in Equatoria, and considered that to leave his post would mean abandoning the considerable expatriate Egyptian community in Equatoria.

The two men agreed to suspend their differences and meet again at the same place the following year, when Emin would have had time to consult his followers and Stanley to bring up the rear column. Emin returned to Equatoria, only to be overtaken by a Mahdist revolt which convulsed his province. Stanley fared even worse. After enduring the travails of the Ituri a second time he arrived back on the Aruwimi in August 1888 to find the rear column a hopeless shambles. Major Barttelot had gone mad and dismissed two of the other whites. He had brutalised the *wangwana* and had eventually been shot dead by an irate husband after raising a whip to the man's wife. Barttelot's second-in-command Jameson had been overwhelmed by the dark forces of Africa to the point where he had calmly sketched a cannibal feast and seemed uncomprehending when it was put to him that his action was immoral. Jameson too had died, of fever it was said, before Stanley arrived back. Worst of all, Tippu Tip had not delivered the promised porters.

The energetic, hard-driving Stanley whipped the rear column into order and plunged again into the diabolical greenness of the Ituri. Once again the expedition came within an ace of disaster; starvation was the norm all the way through the wilderness, and on one occasion Stanley seriously contemplated suicide. But at last they won through and the tattered remnants of the Emin Pasha Relief Expedition joined hands with Emin's tatterdemalion followers on the shores of Lake Albert in January 1889.

There now followed acrimonious discussions between Stanley and Emin, Stanley insisting that the Pasha accompany him to the coast, Emin digging in his heels. Stanley in his typically ruthless manner cut the Gordian knot by an 'internal coup' in April 1889 when he disarmed Emin's soldiers and virtually put Emin and his officers under 'camp arrest'. The journey to the east coast with the unwilling Emin began. Again there was dreadful loss of life. Again Stanley used firepower to overawe the hostile tribes he met, this time wheeling the very latest item in military technology, the Maxim gun, into action. The expedition reached Bagamoyo in December 1889 after sustaining the highest fatalities of any

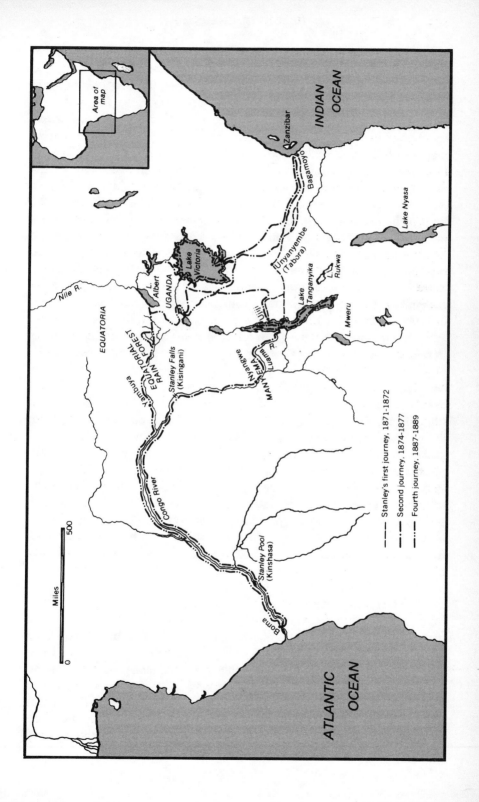

INDIAN OCEAN

Zanzibar

Bagamoyo

Lake Nyasa

UGANDA

Lake Victoria

L. Albert

Nile R.

EQUATORIA

(Unyanyembe (Tabora)

L. Rukwa

Lake Tanganyika

L. Mweru

EQUATORIAL RAIN FOREST

Yambuya

Stanley Falls (Kisingani)

Nyangwe

MANYEMA

Ujiji

Lualaba R.

Congo River

Stanley Pool (Kinshasa)

Boma

ATLANTIC OCEAN

Miles
500
0

Stanley's first journey, 1871–1872
Second journey, 1874–1877
Fourth journey, 1887–1889

Area of map

recorded African expedition. Of some 800 men with whom Stanley had left Zanzibar in spring 1887 only about a quarter remained; of some 500 of Emin's followers who had been forced to make the gruelling march to the coast, only about a half survived.

The initial rapture with which Stanley's exploit was greeted in Britain soon gave way to scepticism, concern and alarm when the full, harrowing picture of the expedition became known. Stanley effectively lost his reputation and became known as a man of blood, even though he continued to be honoured in establishment circles. He served as a Member of Parliament from 1895 to 1900 and was knighted. But when he died in 1904 his enemies had the last word. He was not allowed his dearest wish – to be buried alongside his hero Livingstone in Westminster Abbey – because the Dean, after taking soundings, concluded that he was too controversial a figure to be accorded such a signal honour.

Emin Pasha himself, after a controversial 'accident' at Bagamoyo in December 1889 when he fell from a first-floor balcony – Stanley interpreted this as a suicide bid – fell victim to the increasingly bitter Arab-Belgian rivalry in the Congo. War broke out between Tippu Tip's descendants and the Free State in 1893. Emin, now in the service of the Germans, strayed into the war zone, and was murdered by the Arabs. He was held down on a table while an Arab executioner cut his throat.

On his final African exploration Stanley had considerably added to knowledge of the continent. He laid bare the secrets of the Ituri rainforest and discovered the Ruwenzori mountains. But although the broad brushstrokes in the delineation of the Congo Free State from Stanley Pool to Lake Albert were Stanley's, filling in the close detail remained the task for lesser successors. For example, there remained the charting of all the Congo tributaries to be done. Here sterling work was done by the Revd George Grenfell in the years 1884–5. Indeed, by the end of 1885 the discoveries of Grenfell and the German Wissmann had considerably fleshed out the map of the Congo, whose general bones had first been sketched by Stanley.

The Belgian Lieutenant Vangele continued Grenfell's explorations in 1887. He followed the whole course of the river Mubangi to its junction with the Makwa explored by Junker and the Welle charted by Schweinfurth. By following the Mubangi to the river Kibali, which his compatriot Van Kerkhoven had explored, he completed a satisfactory Belgian double. Indeed it may perhaps better be considered a treble, for east of the Zongo Falls the river Mubangi was surveyed by another Belgian, Georges Le Marinel.

Most notable of the epigones to Stanley was Hermann Wissmann, a lieutenant in the Prussian Army. Born at Frankfurt in 1853, he presented the acceptable face of the Germans in Africa – the unacceptable visage being provided by the notorious Carl Peters. Wissmann came out to Angola with a Dr Pogge in 1880 and, after crossing all the great rivers of south-central Congoland, reached Nyangwe in 1882 and Zanzibar in 1883, thus becoming yet another man to cross Africa from west to east. Together with Dr Pogge in 1881 he reached the middle Kasai where it was flowing nearly due north, and aware that Stanley considered that the Kasai joined the Congo via the Ruiki, Wissmann returned to Congoland from Angola in 1884. Between June 1884 and July 1885 (with his companions the Muellers, von François and Dr L. Wolf), he revealed the main features of the Kasai system: the lengthy Lulua river, the even more important Sankuru, their junction with the Kasai, and the Kasai's confluence with the Kwilu-Kwango and Mfini-Lukenye to form the great Kwa tributary of the river Congo.

Having thus established himself as the greatest Congo explorer after Stanley (though some would assert Grenfell's claims to the title), in 1886 Wissmann ascended the Kasai and Lulua, and crossed over to the Lomami and Tanganyika. Instead of exploring Lake Albert and returning to Zanzibar via Lake Victoria (his original intention), he marched from Lake Tanganyika to Lake Nyasa and emerged at Quelimane on the east coast. From 1888 to 1890 he was busy founding German East Africa and subduing the Arab revolt there. In 1891–3 he conveyed a large steamer in detachable pieces to Lake Nyasa and strengthened the German hold over Tanganyika by first defeating and then making peace with the slave-trading Awemba. Arguably the greatest of the German explorers of Africa by virtue of the range of his travels, and certainly Berlin's finest colonial administrator in the Dark Continent, Wissmann died in 1905.

Of the other Congo tributaries, the river Kwango was first explored by Major von Mechow of the Austrian Army in 1880, but he was halted by the Kigunji rapids. The missionaries Grenfell and Bentley completed the task in 1886, travelling from the rapids to the junction with the Kasai-Kwa.

Most of the minor mysteries left unsolved by Stanley were filled in by Belgians. He himself solved one riddle he had posed on an earlier journey. Near the base of the Ruwenzori mountains was a shallow gulf called Lake Dweru. This was connected by a narrow winding channel with the Katwe bay of Lake Edward. Stanley believed from his 1875–6 venture that here was a great lake with several arms or gulfs called Muta N'Zige ('The killer of locusts'). Stanley finally cleared up the mystery of the lake's name in 1889 on his way home with Emin: the legions of locusts on the wing often dropped into the water from weariness and were drowned. But the lure of Muta N'Zige had acted as a magnet to many eager explorers previously. Wissmann aimed for it, but changed his mind and returned via Nyasaland. The Austrian Oscar Lenz (whose only really important journey was in 1880, from Morocco to Timbuktu), set out in that direction in the mid-1880s with an escort of Arabs, hoping also to make contact with Emin Pasha. He departed with high expectations from Stanley Falls, but soon turned back and completed a somewhat humdrum and routine journey instead, across Africa and down the already charted course of the Congo.

So it was left to the Belgians to complete Stanley's work in the unknown tract between the Aruwimi and Lake Albert. In 1887 Lieutenant Vangele continued Grenfell's exploration of the Mubangi (Oubangi), passed the Zongo rapids while ascending the river at flood, and traced it eastwards as far as its junction with the Mbomu. By 1891 Vangele and Roget had founded a Congo post at Jebir, on Schweinfurth's Welle.

Other Belgians were active in the no-man's land between Congo tributaries and upper Nile; in the 1880s one of them, Lupton Bey, travelled far and wide in the west and south of the Bahr-el-Ghazal. In 1892 Van Kerkhoven traced the Mubangi-Dua-Makua-Welle to its source within 2–3 days' journey of Wadelai on the White Nile. In 1893 the Belgians Le Marinel, Hanolet, Nils and de la Kethulle pressed north from the Mbomu affluent of the Mubangi, explored the Shinko basin, and reached the north-west limits of Bahr-el-Ghazal around Darfur. Other Belgian travellers (Schagestrom, Milz, Daenen, Becker, Charltin, Lothaire, Bricusse), mapped in the Bantu lands between the Welle on the north and the Congo and Aruwimi on the south. Ponthier explored the Welle feeder, the Bomokandi; Helle traced the Mbomu to its source; Milz in September 1892 reached the Nile near Bedden; in June 1893 Captain Delanghe occupied the Muggi, Labore and Dufile on the left bank of the Mountain Nile. Stopped from northward expansion by the *mahdiya* in the Sudan, the Belgians expanded westward towards Lake Chad and the French sphere of influence. By April 1893 expeditions under Hanolet, Van Calster and Stroobart had explored the Bali and Koto affluents of the Mubangi and penetrated across the watershed to Belle within the basin of the Shari.

These journeys were all ripples in the tide of the general scramble for Africa. Until the 1860s British explorers largely had the Continent to themselves. Thereafter the occasional French and German interloper could be discerned, but it was not until the 1880s, when the rush for a place in the African sun began in earnest, that exploration there acquired a truly pan-European flavour, with the Belgians especially to the fore. The fount and origin of all this was Stanley. Since it was arguably Leopold's machinations in the Congo that launched the scramble for Africa, and Leopold's dreams were impossible without Stanley, it was the Welsh workhouse brat made good who 'overdetermined' this Belgian effort. By his pioneering exploration he revealed the bare bones of the Congo, encouraging other explorers to complete his work. But by founding the Free State for Leopold, he provided the 'infrastructure' in which wave after wave of Belgian traveller could operate a kind of microsurgery on the unknown niches and crevices of Leopold's sprawling domain.

5

The Heart of Africa

Once the full nature of the four great African rivers – Niger, Nile, Zambezi and Congo – was known, and all their tributaries explored, there remained just a few unknown patches of territory in Africa's heartland for adventurers to lay bare. The task of putting the last pieces into the jigsaw puzzle that made up the Dark Continent fell to a group of lesser known, but nonetheless significant explorers. Their miscellaneous exploits took place along the Kenya/Ethiopia borders, the Uganda/Equatoria marches and in present-day Cameroon, Gabon and Congo-Brazzaville.

After René Caillié, the next important French adventurer to bestride Africa was Paul du Chaillu. He was the son of a merchant who set up a trading post in Gabon in 1845, dealing in rubber, dyes and indigoes. There, in 1848, du Chaillu senior was joined by his seventeen-year-old son Paul, who spent the next four years learning languages and immersed in local cultures. At twenty-one he had a fully formed plan for an expedition into the rainforests of the interior of Gabon, from which the trade goods reached the coast. But, lacking the money to execute his plans, he went to the United States, ingratiated himself with a number of learned societies and took out American citizenship. In 1855 he returned to Africa with substantial subventions from two learned societies. He then spent the next four years making three long journeys into the interior.

He summed up his experiences as follows:

I travelled – always on foot and unaccompanied by other white men – about 8000 miles. I shot, stuffed and brought home over 3000 birds, of which more than sixty are new species, and I killed upwards of a thousand quadrupeds, of which 200 were stuffed and brought home, with more than eighty skeletons . . . I suffered fifty attacks of African fever, taking, to cure myself, more than fourteen ounces of quinine. Of famine, long-continued exposure to the tropical rains, and attacks of ferocious ants and venomous flies, it is not worthwhile to speak.

Du Chaillu's main fame was due to his being the first white man to observe and shoot a gorilla. The revelation of this 'missing link' created a sensation in mid-Victorian England, beset as it was by doubts and controversies over Darwin's theory of evolution. Du Chaillu can scarcely have been aware of the storm he would cause when, after four years in the jungle, he returned to the United States to lecture on his discoveries. After a multi-state tour in 1860, du Chaillu crossed to England in 1861. He made friends with Richard Burton, but his controversial lectures led to an outbreak of fisticuffs in the hallowed halls of the Ethnological Society when he was called a liar.

Du Chaillu returned to Africa and made a further trip in 1863–5, described in his *A Journey to Ashango-land*. This expedition, though well subsidised and equipped, was plagued with delays and bad luck. Smallpox cut a swathe through the party. Once again du Chaillu shot and captured gorillas. He managed to get a live specimen as far as the coast, but it died on board ship to England. In Ashango country one of his men lost his temper and killed a villager with a spear, whereupon the villagers and their allies attacked the visitors, drove them downstream and chased them for miles in hopes of revenge. Du Chaillu, hit by a poisoned arrow, was forced to retreat in haste, leaving behind his specimens, photographic equipment and plates, trade stores and supplies.

After the Ashango expedition he never returned to Africa. The least neurotic of African explorers, he mainly wanted to be rich and enjoy himself. As soon as the pleasures of Africa paled, he became a boulevardier and writer of children's books. He once played cricket, along with Joseph Thomson, in one of J.M. Barrie's scratch elevens. He died at St Petersburg in 1903.

Ten years passed after du Chaillu's Ashango expedition before another notable Frenchman ventured into the African interior. By 1875 French attitudes were beginning to change. Although not nearly as fervent about suppressing the slave trade in Africa as Britain, France, fuelled by strident nationalism after the débâcle of 1870–1, began to espouse the view that without colonies France would sink to the level of a second-rate power. Thereafter Anglo-French rivalry was a fact of African life and was one of the spectres that hung heavily over the 'scramble for Africa' after 1884.

In 1875 there came forward as France's African standard-bearer Pierre Savorgnan de Brazza, a naval officer born of Italian descent at Rio de Janeiro. At the age of twenty-three he headed an expedition from Dakar to Lambaréné accompanied by Noel Ballay and Victor Hamon. Once in the heart of Africa, Brazza began to follow the course of the Ogowé river on which the main obstacles to rapid progress were the Boone rapids and the necessity to proceed by diplomacy rather than force

through the territory of the Okandas, Galais and Ossieba. After nearly
two years the travellers reached a place where the Ogowé was no longer
navigable. Brazza was undaunted: 'But our task was not yet finished. Our
aim now was to advance towards the east in an attempt to lift the veil from
that huge unknown country separating us from the upper Nile and
Tanganyika, where we believed that Cameron and Stanley were concentrating their efforts.'

On leaving the confluence of the Ogowé and the Passa in August 1877,
the Brazza expedition proceeded on foot through rugged, hilly territory.
After initial difficulties Brazza won over the Bateke tribe, but the
Abfourus barred his way. Since the Alima river flowed into the Congo,
and Stanley had recently passed through the south of the Abfouru
country, Brazza put the blame for their hostility on Stanley. This was the
beginning of a long and sustained rivalry between Brazza and his more
eminent predecessor in the Congo area.

The immediate upshot of Brazza's arrival in Abfouru country was
warfare. A pitched battle in daytime was followed by amphibious attacks
when dusk fell. After spending a dreadful night hove to on the river,
Brazza's party had to withstand an attack from thirty canoes on both
flanks. Superior firepower alone halted the Abfourus, who fought with
conspicuous courage. Short of ammunition and faced with mounting
hostility on the river Alima, Brazza retreated into Bateke country. After a
fruitless solo side trip, having sent Ballay and Hamon down the Ogowé,
Brazza rejoined them and continued on to the coast and then to France.

In 1879 he was back in Africa, ironically sponsored by the French
Committee of Leopold's front organisation, the Association Inter-
nationale Africaine, which was headed by Ferdinand de Lesseps, another
of the Belgian king's creatures. First Brazza founded a trading post called
Franceville near the confluence of the Passa and the Ogowé. Next Brazza
made a shrewd appointment and hired the black Senegalese sergeant
Malamine as his second-in-command for the march to the Congo. Brazza
reached the Congo, but did not recognise it and spent weeks in confusion
on its broad waters. But in August 1880 he had talks with a chief he called
Makoko, in the vicinity of Stanley Pool. Believing him to be paramount
chief of the area, Brazza signed a treaty establishing French sovereignty
on the right bank of the Congo. He then continued down the Congo and
had a memorable meeting with Stanley on the way downriver (Nov. 1880)
before proceeding to the coast. Next he traced the Ogowé to its source
and surveyed the Kwilu-Niari area before being recalled in 1881.

On his third expedition (1883–5) Brazza tried to establish French
authority against the claims of Leopold in the Loango region, and made
several trips up the Ogowé. He spent six months on the river Alima with

the Abfourus, the tribe that had driven him back on the first expedition. Then he journeyed to Stanley Pool for a joyous reunion with his 'Makoko'. Brazza tried to foment discontent against Stanley's successor at Leopoldville on the left bank but in 1885, on the fall of his protector Jules Ferry, he was recalled to France.

In 1887 Brazza went out to West Africa again for five years, as French Commissioner. By now the high tide of conscious imperialism had arrived. French expeditions pushed north and east up the Oubangi to claim most of what is now the Central African Republic. Here France had no competition, but to the north and west French intrusion was challenged by Germany and Britain. Expeditions travelling west to Lake Benue, as also on the southern shore of Lake Chad, were warned off by the British. Bismarck also opposed the French in Cameroon, where he had ambitions. In 1897, after a long fight, Brazza was finally recalled to France following pressure from Leopold and his allied capitalists. He died in 1905, aged fifty-three.

If the French were most active in the areas of West and Central Africa that would eventually be absorbed into their empire, German explorers at first concentrated on the area north and west of the East African lakes, as far west as Lake Chad and as far south as the Congo, with particular emphasis on Bornu, Bagirmi, Wadai and Darfur.

First into the breach was Gerhard Rohlfs, more an old-style adventurer than an explorer proper. Born in Bremen in 1831, he ran away to sea, then fought in the Army in 1850 against the Danes in Schleswig-Holstein. Thus far Rohlfs's career resembled that of a much great explorer, for whom he always entertained a particular antipathy: H.M. Stanley. There followed further spells as a soldier, in the Austrian Army and the French Foreign Legion; desertion from the former was followed in 1861 by discharge from the latter. Rohlfs then explored Morocco in the guise of a Muslim, but he lacked Burton's skill at disguise. His feeble attempts at camouflage were unmasked, he was robbed near Tafilat and left for dead by brigands, with wounds in thigh, arm and foot. Nevertheless, he succeeded in scouring all of North Africa from Morocco to Tripoli, in an area of high risk for Europeans, and acquired valuable information about the trans-Sahara trade routes.

In 1865–7 he crossed the Sahara to Kouka via Murzuk, then struck south to the Bight of Biafra near Lagos, thus becoming the first European to cross Africa from the Mediterranean to the Gulf of Guinea. In 1868 he was in Ethiopia with General Napier's expedition against Emperor Theodore. His final expedition, from Benghazi to Kufra, in 1879, was a smaller-scale affair. Rohlfs was more important as an influence and inspiration than in his own right; his principal protégé was Gustav Nachtigal.

Born in 1834, Nachtigal trained in Germany as a physician and went out to Tunisia for his health. He spent some years as court doctor to the ruler of Tunis and, since the lesions in his lung had healed, was thinking of returning to the fatherland. Then Rohlfs arrived with presents from the King of Prussia for the ruler of Bornu, to thank him for his protection of German travellers in the Lake Chad area. Nachtigal offered to take the presents on; Rohlfs was delighted to devolve his commission.

Nachtigal left Tripoli in January 1869 and headed south in company with an Italian cook called Giuseppe Valpreda. At Muzzuk he met the Dutch woman explorer Alexandrine Tinné, who was murdered by Tuaregs soon afterwards near Ghudamis while trying to cross the Sahara to Sudan. Then he continued south across the arid wastes of south Fezzan, through Murzuk, Quatrun and Tejerri. He was hours away from thirsting to death in this desert until the providential arrival of a camel-driver with spare water-bottles. He then entered Tubu country and reached Tao in Tibesti where he found the Tubu deceitful, grasping and hostile. Only after being mulcted of most of his trade goods was he permitted to continue his journey to Bardai. Here the Tubu proved to be even more cunning and rapacious. Nachtigal and Valpreda were kept prisoners in their tent while the ruler and his acolytes debated long and vociferously over the fate of the Europeans. There were many calls for their execution as spies, especially when the Tubu heard about the slaying of Alexandrine Tinné by the Tuareg. Nachtigal decided the time had come for desperate measures. He bribed the Tubu chief best disposed to his cause to provide camels for his party. Then he stole away under cover of darkness. He was back in Murzuk by the beginning of October.

As no caravan was leaving for Bornu, Nachtigal was obliged to spend six months there in some discomfort until April 1870, when he took passage with a convoy for Kuka and thence travelled east to Wadai and Darfur. After four years of meticulous, painstaking travel Nachtigal filled in all the gaps in European knowledge of the area between Lake Chad and Khartoum and the upper Nile. Returning to Germany in 1874, he was laden with honours, widely recognised as the doyen of German explorers and *the* expert on the Sahara. He died at sea in 1885.

The next eminent German in the heart of Africa was, on paper, the quintessence of the Teutonic 'Herr Doktor'. Born in Riga in 1836, the son of a wealthy merchant, George Schweinfurth was educated at the universities of Berlin and Heidelberg and gained a PhD in botany. He was both a scientific botanist and an accomplished draughtsman; each was a rare qualification among African explorers, and none except Schwein-furth had both. The noted Austrian socialite Marie von Bunsen described him thus: 'He reminded me a little of Stanley, another square set, short figure; a yellowish-brown face, against which the whites of the eyes stood out prominently; he, too, gave one the impression of quiet reserves of strength. On the other hand there is nothing moody or sombre about him; he is unaffectedly pleasant and cultured.'

In 1868 Schweinfurth traced Baker's footsteps by travelling up the Nile to Khartoum and then on to Fashoda. He noted that among the Nubian soldiers he travelled with, Speke's account of his expeditions was known as 'The History of King Kamrasi' but Baker's book was called 'The Book of the Elephant Hunter' – an accurate enough estimate of the respective ways his two predecessors had got inside the idiom of Africa. After tortuous progress through Nile tributaries choked with canopies of intertwining papyrus, reeds, elephant grass and ambatch, he and his party came to the Gazelle river and disembarked at Meshra-er-Req.

Here Schweinfurth awaited the Arab merchants from Khartoum who were to accompany him to the ivory country to the west. When they arrived, the joint convoy set out through the land of the Dinkas, the most expert cattle herdsmen in Central Africa, who worshipped snakes as 'brothers'. Very different were their neighbours the Bongo, who were distinguished, Schweinfurth thought, by their propensity to slaughter any living thing they met: cattle, snakes, hyena, vulture, termite.

After several months with the Bongo, Schweinfurth crossed the river Tondy in November 1868. He made a careful study of the Mittoo and Niam-Niam peoples he encountered, so that it was 5 March 1869 before he crossed the river Linduku, the watershed between the Nile and Congo basins. He was the first European on the Linduku.

A fortnight later Schweinfurth made another dramatic discovery: the great river Welle, which later exploration would establish as a northern tributary of the Congo. The sight of the Welle's ferruginous and turbid waters reminded Schweinfurth strongly of Mungo Park's description of the first glimpse of the Niger. South of the river Welle he encountered Munza, king of the Mangbetu. A memorable interview ensued. Among Munza's auxiliaries were the Akka race of pygmies on whom Schweinfurth took copious notes.

Many different incidents confirmed Schweinfurth as a veteran Africa hand. On one occasion he shot an antelope, which bounded away into tall grass. He expected to hear it fall, but mysteriously it was as though the wounded beast had vanished into thin air. Proceeding into the tall grass, Schweinfurth found that a huge python had seized the antelope and was wrapping itself round it. He disabled the snake with a single shot which shattered its vertebral column, then finished it off with a second shot. He then bore both antelope and python back to camp in triumph.

When Schweinfurth turned for home, he had every reason to be pleased with his achievements. Apart from the two great rivers he had added to the European store of knowledge, he had acquired a veritable thesaurus of information on the Mangbetu, Mittoo and Niam-Niam peoples, including incontrovertible evidence of cannibalism, for Schweinfurth was far too erudite and subtle to be unable to distinguish between fact and fantasy in this controversial area.

The return journey, in company with a Nubian caravan, was marred by a bloody two-day fight with the Abanga tribe. Schweinfurth's detached narration of this incident contrasts admirably with the purple passages of an Andersson, a du Chaillu or a Stanley when in a similar situation:

> I took no personal share in this mild skirmish but those who were present delighted afterwards in telling wonderful stories of the daring prowess I had displayed in penetrating the enemy's ranks. Such reports often follow a traveller's reputation for years, and whoever repeats them is pretty sure to append some marvel of his own fancy. 'When fame paints a serpent, she attaches feet to its body.'

On 24 June 1870 the party crossed the river Tondy. On 3 July they were at Sabby and shortly afterwards arrived at Ghattas, a Coptic settlement between the Dinka and Bongo country. A long halt ended disastrously. On 1 December a fire in Schweinfurth's hut destroyed most of his papers; journals, meteorological records, statistical data, botanical and entomological specimens all went up in the blaze.

In despair Schweinfurth was forced to abandon his planned second foray into the country of the Niam-Niam. On 16 December he commenced a *via dolorosa* to the coast. Dragging his feet, as if reluctant to bid farewell to Africa, Schweinfurth took until the end of September 1871 to reach the shores of the Red Sea and another month to arrive in Sicily. Although he later returned to North Africa, he never saw the true 'Dark Continent' again. But, as though in compensation for all the tribulations he suffered, he was the only African explorer of first importance to be granted more than his biblical span. He died in 1925 in his ninetieth year. His achievements have always been underrated but Winwood Reade, no mean African traveller himself, summed them up like this: 'As an explorer he stands in the highest rank, and merits to be classed with Mungo Park, Denham and Clapperton, Livingstone, Burton, Speke and Grant, Barth and Rohlfs.'

At the Paris Geographical Conference of 1875 Schweinfurth encouraged a German physician named Wilhelm Junker to continue his work. In Cairo Junker recruited a Würrtemberg forester named Kopp and began his travels by journeying from the Red Sea port of Suakin to Kassala through the little-known Baraka valley. From Kassala Junker and Kopp set out on 7 April 1876 for Qedaref province. In Suq-Abu-Sinn they marvelled at the market in all kinds of African commodities but recoiled from the thriving slave trade. From there they proceeded to Khartoum, where they met Romolo Gessi, just back from his circumnavigation of Lake Albert. Gessi invited the Germans to join him on a cruise up the Blue Nile in the steamer *Sofia* which would take them south to Fashoda then through the Dinka territory previously explored by Schweinfurth. Instead of following in his mentor's footsteps south-west towards the Welle, Junker pressed on southwards to Lado and added an impressive tally of peoples to an already lengthy German ethnological list: the Bari, the Mundu, the Bombeh, the Moru and the Abaka.

In June 1877 Africa claimed another victim in young Kopp. Junker now felt alone in more senses than one since, in order to penetrate further into regions untrodden by white men he had, like Denham and Clapperton before him, to seek the protection of morally dubious filibusterers. Junker clothed the horror he felt at this combined ivory/slaving expedition in suitably Germanic abstractions. He also pointed to the greater menaces in Africa. On the return journey from Bahr-el-Ghazal hundreds of men had fallen a prey to starvation and exhaustion. On the return journey from Kalika it was smallpox that carried off his men in dozens. 'Famine and disease', he wrote, 'are the chief causes of the depopulation of Central Africa; in comparison with these the export of slaves is but a small item.'

Junker showed himself particularly learned on the subject of ivory. He distinguished between the dark forest ivory and that obtained from the elephants of the plains, which was quite white and of greater commercial value. He also reported on the jungle drums that could send a message 100 miles in two hours. The drums were hollowed out from the solid trunk of a tree, 5 ft in diameter, and produced two distinct notes. By varying these the drummers could send messages.

Yet Junker was always more affected by the horrors of Africa than Schweinfurth had been. Reporting from the Niambara valley, Junker wrote:

The numbers of skeletons and human bones lying near the road on the march through the valley had already shown what had taken place there. Death had reaped a rich harvest. Famine had allied itself to smallpox. But in the immediate neighbourhood of the zeriba bleached skulls and skeletons and dried uninjured human corpses or parts of them lay about in dozens. Starvation could be plainly read in many of the completely mummified bodies. The poor Negroes were literally reduced to skin and bone, and the skin had been tanned to leather by the tropical sun. The hyenas and vultures must have been left a plentiful repast, for they had left a number of corpses untouched. Driven by hunger, even the hostile natives from the mountains had come to the zeriba seeking help, and had there found death instead of the food they had hoped for.

In revulsion at the horror all around him, Junker made haste to quit Africa. He had been born in Moscow of German parents, and it was there that he retreated to pour balm on a soul polluted by the barbarism of Africa. But the lure of the Dark Continent was too strong. February 1879 found him steaming up the Nile towards Fashoda. At Meshra-er-Req he disembarked for further travel in Dinka territory, having recruited a German factotum named Friedrich Bohndorff.

Junker set up his base in the Ndorama, chief village of the Niam-Niam. In order to reach the source of the Welle, he was again compelled to join a slaving and ivory expedition, this time headed by the Zande chief, Semio. At the Welle he pressed on alone to Mabanga, the new king of the Mangbetu, a nephew of Munza, whom Schweinfurth had known. So rapid was dynastic change in Mangbetu that the late king Munza's village, so graphically described by Schweinfurth, had been reclaimed by the jungle and all traces of it had disappeared.

Junker spent 1881 in the lands of the Amadi north of Lake Albert. At the end of the year he made contact with king Bakangai of the Abarmbo. With escorts provided by Bakangai, Junker departed in January 1882 for a circular tour which took him first to the Kibbi river, then south towards Nepoko, where he confirmed Schweinfurth's findings on the pygmies. On 6 May 1881 he came at last to the Nepoko river, which he tentatively identified (wrongly) with the Aruwimi tributary of the Congo, knowledge of which was common in Europe since the publication in 1878 of Stanley's *Through the Dark Continent*.

For four years Junker crisscrossed the Nile/Congo watershed, from Wadelai to Lado, and from the upper Welle to Lake Kyoga. He spent some time with Emin Pasha and Gaetano Casati in Equatoria. In January 1886 he visited the suspicious Kabbarega of Bunyoro at Kibero. Only in 1888, as the threat from the Mahdists loomed, did he head for the east coast. He arrived at Zanzibar at the end of that year, after a trek via lakes Albert and Victoria, very much the itinerary Stanley took on the Emin Pasha Relief Expedition a year later. Junker died from the delayed effects of African fever in St Petersburg in 1892, aged fifty-two.

Further explorations were made by 'Gordon's lieutenants' – that remarkable group of larger-than-life adventurers employed by Colonel Charles Gordon, later the hero of Khartoum, when he was governor of Equatoria province in the 1870s, in the service of the Khedive. Emin Pasha, Frederick Burnaby, Rudolph Slatkin, Romolo Gessi, Mason Bey, Gaetano Casati, Linant de Bellefonds, Carlo Piaggia: all these men, handpicked by Gordon, made a name for themselves either in African exploration or the wider world. Gordon even tried to recruit Richard Burton as one of his 'men'. The first of them to break trail in the lacustrine area was Charles Chaillé-Long, who was also the first white man since Speke and Grant to see Lake Victoria and visit Mutesa's court. Chaillé-Long had seen action as a colonel in the Union Army in the American Civil War. When Mutesa sent a message expressing a desire to be on friendly terms with the Egyptians to the north, Gordon sent Chaillé-Long to treat with him.

Chaillé-Long travelled from Gondokoro to Fatiko and thence to Foweira, where he arrived on 17 May 1874. He then crossed the Nile, met the Bunyoro pretender Royonga who impressed him mightily, continued across the Kafua and made his way to Mutesa's capital in Buganda where he presented the king with a gilt-and-red bound volume of Burton's *Lake Regions*. He was well received and later bragged that Mutesa had favoured him over later arrivals: 'Neither Stanley nor Linant [de Bellefonds] was received with the honours accorded me.' Gordon followed up the embassy with a further one the next year under Linant de Bellefonds, who was with Mutesa when Stanley arrived in April 1875. Unfortunately, on his way home Linant became snarled up in a tribal war and was massacred with his thirty-six soldiers.

Chaillé-Long's attempts to travel from Murchison Bay to the Ripon Falls via Lake Victoria were frustrated. He marched to Burondogani, travelled down the Nile by canoe, and discovered Lake Kioga, which he named Lake Ibrahim. Near Mruli on 17 August 1874 he was opposed by a fleet of Bunyoro canoes. He and his men directed a well-trained fire on the fleet and dispersed it. After killing eighty-two of Kabbarega's warriors, Chaillé-Long withdrew under cover of night and escaped by the river route to Foweira. He arrived back in Gondokoro on 18 October, having covered the unexplored sections of the Nile from Burondogani to Murli and thence to the Karuma Falls.

Further hostilities occurred on 9 March 1875. Confronted by the Yanbari tribe, who deluged his party with showers of poisoned arrows, Chaillé-Long replied with an elephant gun, which inflicted heavy punishment on his assailants. Meanwhile the Upper Nile itself was proving a hell on earth, for two main reasons. Mosquitoes swarmed in tens of thousands: the howling of bitten dogs was piteous and Chaillé-Long's mosquito net proved no defence against the swarms, who seemed to breach the defences through sheer numbers. The river itself was full of shoals. His men had to plunge into the water to push the steamer forward; they were then in danger from crocodiles and hippos which were present in great numbers and kept away only by constant noise and the firing of rifles.

In 1876 Gordon sent Gessi and Piaggia to make a definitive reconnaissance of Lake Albert to see if the Nile really did flow out of it, as Baker had alleged. Their supplementary instructions were to assist Stanley, if they met him, but to remind him that Lake Albert was within the Egyptian sphere of influence. The two travellers saw nothing of Stanley for, after Kabbarega's hostile demonstration, he turned south towards Lake Tanganyika, as we have seen. Piaggia thoroughly explored Lake Kyoga, which Chaillé-Long had merely touched on. Meanwhile Gessi left Dufile with two lifeboats on 7 March 1876 and arrived at Magungo on the 30th. After making exact preparations, he left on 12 April, coasted down the eastern shore of Lake Albert and then circumnavigated it in two boats. He returned to Magungo on 21 April and was back in Dufile a week later. Gessi was the first to establish the truth about Lake Albert and its connection with the Nile. He disproved Baker's contention that the lake stretched far to the south of Buhuka, for he discovered that about 25 miles to the south the lake terminated in a mass of ambatch and papyrus.

Another genuine explorer among Gordon's men was the American Mason Bey, who in 1877 governed Equatoria province for Gordon and surveyed from Dufile to Lake Albert. On 14 June 1877 he left Magungo in the steamer *Nyanza* and steamed along the west coast of the lake to Kavalli's, then discovered and beat up the river Semliki, before returning along the lake's eastern shore. The whole of the White Nile had now been mapped, and Speke shown to be correct. All that remained was to show the connections between lakes Edward and George and the river Semliki and Lake Albert, and to trace the Ruwenzori mountains which none of these early travellers had yet seen. These final gaps in knowledge were remedied by Stanley in 1889 on his return with Emin.

In the days before he became Stanley's victim, Emin had had a distinguished career in African travelling. In 1877, when Gordon sent him on a peace mission to Kabbarega, lengthy negotiations were needed before the mission was even allowed to tread Nyoro soil, but the wait proved worthwhile. Emin and Kabbarega, as Arabic speakers, were able to converse directly and achieved considerable rapport. Emin failed to cement a permanent alliance only because Egypt continued to support Ruyonga. From Kabbarega's court Emin proceeded to Mutesa's, to inform him that Gordon had abandoned the idea of a route from Equatoria to the Indian Ocean – the principal source of external tension in the lake areas.

In 1878 Emin reluctantly acceded to Gordon's orders to evacuate all Egyptian stations south of Dufile. He proceeded to make his head-quarters at Lado where he was joined in 1885 by the Italian Casati, who had been exploring the Welle some 400 miles west of Arua. When the

Mahdist rising in the Sudan cut Emin off from Egypt, it thereby greatly increased the power and political leverage of Kabbarega in the area. In May 1886 Emin sent Casati as his ambassador to Bunyoro. Kabbarega received him at his capital of Kasingo, and at once showed that he meant to take advantage of Emin's difficulties. He kept Casati a prisoner and laid plans to attack Wadelai and to invite Emin to Bunyoro and assassinate him. Casati remained a prisoner until 1888; there was even an attempt to murder him. But when Stanley arrived at Lake Albert in January 1888, Kabbarega took fright at the thought of a major expedition arriving from Europe and allowed Casati to escape. Casati then shared Emin's fate in being taken back to Zanzibar by Stanley as a trophy against his will.

Surprisingly, Kenya, of all Central African countries the one most congenial to the white man, was the last to be fully explored. Three men completed the task in the 1880s: Joseph Thomson, Harry Johnston and Samuel Teleki.

Joseph Thomson's career got off to an early start thanks to the death of the man he was serving under. He was the son of a quarry owner in Dumfriesshire and had just qualified as a geologist at the University of Edinburgh at the age of twenty-one when he got his lucky break. The Royal Geographical Society became suspicious of Leopold and his true aims after the 1876 Congress in Paris and decided to set up its own African Exploration Fund. An expedition was prepared to explore the country between Dar es Salaam and Lake Nyasa and between lakes Nyasa and Tanganyika, but the leader, Keith Johnston, died before the expedition crossed to the African mainland. Thomson, his deputy, assumed command.

For his caravan leader he had the selfsame Chuma who had borne Livingstone's body back to the coast in 1873. Chuma was a good organiser and a firm disciplinarian, quite prepared to knock together the heads of mutineers. He divided the caravan into five sections, each with a headman. Chief of these was Makatatubu, the equal of Chuma in intelligence but utterly incapable of maintaining discipline. Two other notable headmen were Nasibu, a man of immense strength but a heavy drinker, who needed ten hours' sleep a night to throw off the effects of his carousing, and Asikari, a dandy, dressed in a snow-white robe and gorgeous turban, with a huge shield in one hand and a spear in the other. Thomson and Chuma were prescient administrators. The British consul in Zanzibar, John Kirk, testified: 'No better organised caravan ever left the coast for the interior.'

In July 1879 Thomson struck along the Msendani valley and crossed the Ruaha, then reached the edge of the East African plateau in August. After 350 miles no one on the expedition had died or deserted, no cloth

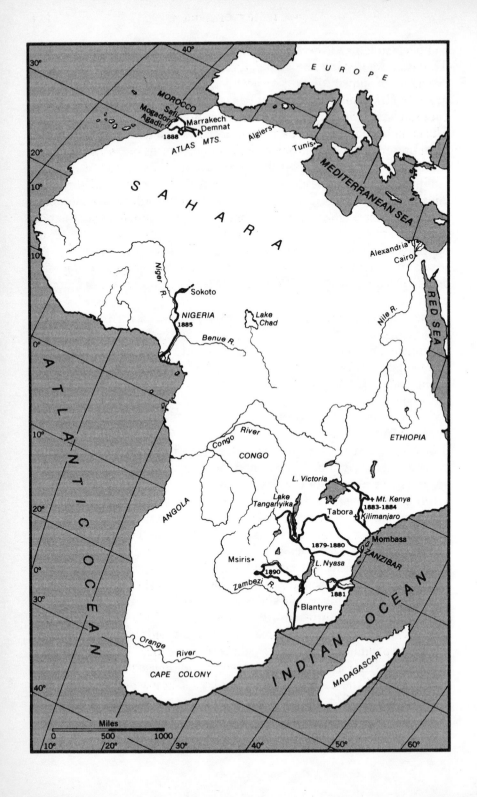

had been stolen and there was no conflict with the local tribes. Already Thomson was laying the foundations for his great reputation as an exponent of exploration by peaceful means. He quoted the Italian proverb: *Chi va piano va sano, chi va sano va lontano* (He who goes softly, goes safely, he who goes safely goes far). And he had little time for those who complained about the hardships of Africa: 'Hard constant work is the great preserver. Sweat out the malaria and the germs of disease, and less will be heard of the energy-destroying climate of the tropics.'

If this sounds smug, it must be conceded that Thomson paraded his own initial shortcomings at some length. He discovered that the *wangwana* would submit uncomplainingly to beatings and physical chastisement but went on strike if he fined them, and returned only on the understanding that future punishment would be physical, not financial. He was struck by the contradictory nature of the *wangwana* and saw them as angels portrayed as devils. Though it was true that they expected three square meals a day for doing nothing, the other side of the coin was that they would endure iron rations uncomplainingly day after day when on the march.

Thomson also evolved a joker's gallery for placating recalcitrant or curmudgeonly tribal chiefs. He did tricks with mirrors and amused a village chief by showing him a photograph album full of shots of nubile young ladies. Chuma won great prestige for his leader by claiming that these were all Thomson's wives.

On 22 September Thomson became the first European to arrive at the northern end of Lake Nyasa. He then set out for Lake Tanganyika but fell ill on the way and was soon tossing feverishly in his tent. In his delirium he quarrelled with Chuma but patched things up when well again. Never again was their close association broken.

On 3 November the caravan arrived at Pambete, Lake Tanganyika, exactly where Chuma had guided Livingstone in April 1867. After he had been saved from a crocodile by the prompt action of his men, Thomson headed north on 10 November to explore the river Lukuga. The very difficult going meant that he did not reach the Lukuga until Christmas Day 1879. He pressed on to Mtoma on the western shore of the lake, and thence made a round-trip to Ujiji across the lake.

Next he decided to return to Liendwe via the Lukuga, Lualaba and Lake Mweru but his men were reluctant to proceed. Unreliable guides, low stocks of ammunition, thefts and exactions by the tribes compounded his problems and on 20 February 1889 he was forced to turn back ten miles short of the Lualaba. He re-entered Mtoma despondently two months after leaving, 'like a sheep from the shearers'.

He then paid off all but ten of his men and went by decked canoe to the recently established Belgian station at Karema; thence he continued to

Liendwe, arriving in April. He had intended to return via Kilwa but tribal wars in the intervening country ruled this out. Instead he marched north-east to the old Arab caravan route via Unyanyembe. He became the first European to visit Lake Rukwa and later met Leopold's agents Carter and Cadenhead, who were killed soon afterwards in a skirmish with Mirambo.

On 26 May Thomson entered Tabora and stayed in the *tembe* where Livingstone and Stanley had lodged in 1872. On 7 June he set off for the coast where he had a better reception at Ugogo than most African travellers, but the price for this was an exorbitant *hongo*. The journey back to Bagamoyo was uneventful but the proof of his 'softly, softly' methods was in the human cost: all but one of his *wangwana* survived the journey.

Thomson began to propagandise for the trade possibilities in Africa. 'Africa is going to be ready to take unlimited quantities of calicoes from Manchester, of nicknacks from Birmingham and of cutlery from Sheffield, and indeed is to give a renewal and impetus to British trade in all its branches. Africa, in short, is to be the future hope of Britain, and a very El Dorado to all traders enterprising enough to enter and establish themselves.'

He returned to Africa in June 1881 on a two-year contract with the Sultan of Zanzibar to explore the alleged mineral deposits of the Rovuma river. He reached the confluence of the Rovuma and the Lujende, found no coal so followed the Lujende, cut back to the Rovuma and thence to the confluence. He then proceeded to the coast by a more southerly route, reaching Tungi Bay on 10 September after a 700-mile expedition accomplished in eight weeks. Hearing that there was no coal on the Rovuma, the Sultan dispensed with the services of Thomson, who returned to Scotland.

But he was back again the following year. In 1882 the Royal Geographical Society appointed him to lead a new expedition to Lake Victoria through Masailand, and to explore Mount Kenya, as yet unvisited by a European. Masailand had a fearsome reputation, largely the product of 'expedient exaggerations' by Arab traders who wished to keep the Europeans out. The Masai, though warlike enough on occasions, were far from the bloodthirsty savages of legend. Indeed Thomson found them largely paper tigers as regards their threat to explorers, but he apotheo-sised the Masai as the true noble savage, and produced quasi-Darwinian explanations for their 'superiority' over the merely 'negroid' Kikuyu.

At Zanzibar Thomson heard the disconcerting news that the German explorer Gustav Fischer had already started for Masailand with 250 men. Fischer was a German in the Carl Peters mould whose hectoring aggression led him into a fight with the Masai, who promptly went on the warpath against other Europeans. Thomson had left Mombasa on 15

March 1883 with just thirty men, so had to turn back to augment his numbers.

It took him until August to assemble 140 men, but once contact was made with the Masai, Thomson demonstrated that only Prussian contumacity would induce them to don their warpaint. He established an immediate rapport with them. Once again he made use of his repertoire of party tricks. He charmed the Masai with mirrors and his own false teeth and treated their sick with an effervescent dose of Eno's Fruit Salts. Indeed, on the march to Lake Victoria, the only attack on his camp came from the Kikuyu. Once again Thomson moved forward very slowly, letting his men's morale and self-confidence gradually improve. He made side trips to climb the mountains of Longonot and Eburu but an attempt to climb Mount Kenya was abandoned, partly through shortage of supplies and partly because the Masai indicated that they would construe such an attempt as an unfriendly act.

Thomson reached Lake Victoria in December 1883. His return to the coast was marked by much illness, and he was laid up for six weeks at Mianzini with dysentery. But once again he had proved his point about pacific approaches:

> My fondest boast is not that I have travelled over hundreds of miles hitherto untrodden by the foot of a white man, but that I have been able to do so as a Christian and a Scotchman, carrying everywhere goodwill and friendship, finding that a gentle word was even more potent than gunpowder, and that it was not necessary, even in Central Africa, to sacrifice the lives of men in order to throw light upon its dark corners.

After 1884 Thomson was more an agent of imperialism than an explorer proper. His 1885 visit to Nigeria left him with feelings of marked distaste for the 'inferior' blacks of West Africa, whom he contrasted unfavourably with his beloved Masai. A close friend of J.M. Barrie, Thomson had a caustic wit, and he used it to effect in his animadversions on West Africa. Referring to Nigerian cannibalism, he remarked:

> The only circumstance which serves to maintain an air of romance about the Niger negro is the knowledge we possess that he still loves his neighbour, to the extent of becoming at times literally one flesh with him.

A visit to Morocco in 1888 left Thomson with a pointed disdain for Islam. His last African venture was in 1890, when he travelled through modern Zambia and Malawi as an agent of Cecil Rhodes. Further adventures were cut short by an early death from pneumonia, but already, in terms of area covered, Thomson had travelled more widely than any African explorer except Stanley. Thomson had a certain reputation for leaving tasks half-done and for combining energy with boredom. Perhaps he suffered in public esteem for making light of the 'ordeal' of African exploration. He once told J.M. Barrie that the most dangerous journey he had ever undertaken in his life was crossing Piccadilly Circus in heavy traffic.

As Thomson was coming down from the Kenya highlands to the coast in 1884, another explorer was heading into the interior in the opposite direction. Where Thomson's objective had been Mount Kenya, Harry Johnston's target was the even loftier peak of Mt Kilimanjaro. There were similarities between Johnston and Thomson, and not just because the assonance of their names confused the Kikuyu into thinking they were brothers. Born in the same year as Thomson, Johnston was, like him, a writer and a propagandist for British imperialism. A diminutive figure, he was closer in physical appearance to Thomson's friend, the tiny J.M. Barrie. Unlike Thomson, Johnston was destined for a long, honour-laden life as one of the most distinguished servants of the British empire in Africa.

A talented amateur artist, keen botanist and zealous zoologist, Johnston was chosen by the Royal Society to head its 1885 Kenya expedition on the strength of his travels in the Congo in 1882–3, where he had met Stanley, and where Johnston produced the first of a notable multi-volume *oeuvre* on Africa. When he arrived at Zanzibar in 1884, Johnston found a disastrous famine raging through the lands of the African littoral, the result of local overpopulation.

Johnston did not have Thomson's knack with the *wangwana*. When Mabruki and Asmani proved refractory, he avenged himself on them by freeing their slaves and threatening them with a thrashing. Nor did he have Thomson's patience. His main fault as an African explorer was obstinacy and pig-headedness. He foolishly made his base for the assault on Kilimanjaro in the village of Chief Mandara, unaware that Mandara did not command any of the routes to the higher regions near the snowline of the peak. Flushed with the advent of the white man and his guns, Mandara raided his neighbours' women and cattle. Mandara boasted to the victimised Kiboso, Kirua and Maranu peoples that his tame white man would 'pickle them alive' if they retaliated. Not a whit abashed by the threat, Mandara's enemies did so. The result was full-scale warfare along the route Johnston wished to take to the peak.

Relations between Johnston and Mandara turned sour when Johnston condemned his host's slaving raids and refused to stay on as his adviser. Mandara riposted by demanding *hongo* when Johnston collected botanical specimens and by gloating when a hyena carried off the white man's favourite milch cow. He then tried to starve Johnston out, hoping to get his trade goods in return for food. Johnston, though in a parlous state, bluffed it out and was saved when the Kiboso resumed hostilities against

Mandara. With the boot now on the other foot, Mandara withdrew his blockading warriors and sought help from the white man. Johnston demurred, but Mandara was convinced of his integrity. When his advisers cautioned him not to ask the explorer for medicines lest Johnston take the opportunity to poison him, Mandara is reputed to have replied: 'A black man might do so, but a white man never would.'

The botch Johnston made of his relations with the tribes meant that his expedition was ultimately unsuccessful. But Johnston was a fast learner and developed a talent for quick thinking in awkward situations. On the return journey his interpreter said of a chief with whom they were parleying, 'This man plenty devilly.' The chief then asked in Swahili what kind of adjective was 'devilly'. Improvising rapidly, Johnston pointed to his jacket: 'Something like this.' The chief then replied that as part of his *hongo* he wanted two 'devilly'. When the Masai appeared hostile, Johnston told them that his caravan was riddled with smallpox and promptly produced an albino bearer to 'prove' it. The Masai at once decamped in terror.

The final piece in the Kenyan jigsaw puzzle was supplied by Count Samuel Teleki when he discovered lakes Rudolph and Stephanie during an expedition to the far north of Kenya in 1887-8. Teleki was a Hungarian nobleman, wealthy, corpulent and Falstaffian, with a taste for big-game hunting. He had an able assistant in the shape of Ludwig von Höhnel, who ensured that the Teleki expedition was superlatively equipped and armed for the long trek to the Ethiopian border. Money was no object: Teleki was the only explorer, other than Baker, to make discoveries of major importance while on a self-financed trip. As his headman Teleki engaged Manwa Sera, who had distinguished himself on Thomson's Masailand trip both for steadfastness and for having a taste for violence, which made other *wangwana* reluctant to serve with him. Manwa Sera proved as bad as his reputation. He abducted a village girl during the march and then called on his fellow *wangwana* to take arms against the villagers when they protested. As von Höhnel commented scathingly, Manwa Sera 'acted the part of a Paris and Achilles alike in the imbroglio'.

Teleki was as much a negrophobe as Baker. In his 'hawkish' attitudes he was encouraged by Frederick Jackson, the English adventurer who so angered Stanley by organising an Emin Pasha Relief Expedition to rescue *him*. Jackson was ferociously critical of Thomson for not having used force against the Masai in 1883-4. On *his* Emin expedition of 1889, to Lake Victoria, he blasted a passage to the lake and refused to pay any *hongo* at all. Teleki dithered in his attitude to the tribute. At first, when passing through Masailand, he allowed himself to be gulled by a Swahili trader into paying what he later realised was an absurdly high level of *hongo*. He then decided to be all in all a Jackson man. This accounted for the many nasty skirmishes he had with the Kikuyu.

Teleki's methods were usually brutal. He liked to provide 'proofs of toughness' by firing off rockets around his camp every night, as the most efficacious way of scaring off the locals. He called the bluff of the Meru tribe by refusing to pay *hongo* and threatening to move out without making any purchases either. Faced with the unpalatable prospect of attacking a large, well-armed column, the Meru waived their demand for tribute and settled for normal commercial transactions. Teleki also flogged mutineers mercilessly and sent out bounty hunters after deserters, who were dragged back into camp in chains.

Towards the end of 1888 he discovered the wide expanse of Lake Rudolph and, a little later, the much smaller Lake Stephanie. He also outshone Thomson by climbing Mt Kenya to a height of 15,355 ft – 3000 ft short of the summit. But, as always with the hard-driving type of African explorer, he sustained huge casualties, mainly through starvation. He later told Jackson: 'It was very bad. You know I do not like the black man, I regard him as one big monkey, but when I did see my men dying on the road, sometimes three or four, sometimes six in a day, then I did begin to pity them.' His own portly form took punishment. He weighed 238 lb at the beginning of the expedition, but was down to 141 lb by the end.

The early 1890s marked a definite watershed between the era of the explorers and that of colonialism. In 1890 Frederick Courtenay Selous led a column of pioneers into Matabeleland to found Rhodesia. Thomson took service with Cecil Rhodes. In the wake of the 'Stanley craze' after his return from the Emin Pasha expedition, conscious imperialism became the order of the day in Britain. In 1893 the British annexed Uganda and overthrew Kabbarega, though they had to contend with his stubborn guerrilla resistance for nearly a decade. In the same year the armies of the Belgian Free State defeated the descendants of Tippu Tip to establish Leopold's hegemony on the Congo once and for all. The decade of the 1890s ended with the defeat of the *mahdiya* at Khartoum and the narrow avoidance of a Franco-British war over the Fashoda crisis. In every part of Africa the great powers brought the indigenous peoples under their sway and carved out spheres of influence. Most of the great African explorers were dead by the turn of the century, even those from the 'last wave': not just Burton and Baker but also Cameron, Thomson, Junker, Emin; of the big names only Schweinfurth and Johnston survived the First World War. The era of the explorers was over. They had acted as the handmaidens for imperialism, and had ensured that Africa's destiny would ever afterwards be intertwined with the economic power of the West.

II
THE PROCESS

6

Transport and Porterage

The tsetse fly did not bar the way to the interior only because it spread sleeping-sickness. Its deadly effect on animals meant that Central Africa was virtually closed to domesticated beasts of burden. This in turn meant that all transport of the explorers' effects and trade goods had to be by human porterage. As a result the African porter was a member of an 'aristocracy of labour', able to earn sums beyond the dreams of the average African villager.

In the Nile valley as far as Khartoum, in the Sahara, the Lake Chad area and parts of West Africa the camel could be used. But the 'ship of the desert' varied greatly in its ability to adapt to an alien environment, its carrying capacity and even in its legendary ability to go without water. Joseph Thomson suggested that, although camels did not thrive in the area of Tanzania between Mpwapwa and the coast, they ought to be useful on the vast arid plains of Ugogo. Nobody took up the idea. The attempt to introduce the camel into the deserts of the American West just before the American Civil War had been a dismal failure, and no one relished the idea of attempting to repeat the experiment in Central Africa.

Samuel Baker used camels until he reached the Upper Nile, when the terrain was no longer suitable. Travel in the Horn of Africa was also mainly by camel. But the two breeds of dromedary had differential requirements. Ideally a camel needed a daily meal if it had to carry weight. The Somali animal could not last beyond one day without food, but with daily food could go thirteen days without water. The Sudanese camel could carry 400 lb of loads for several days without food or water, but its maximum span without water was six days. The uncertainties of water and food supplies made the use of camels a risky business. During the Denham/Clapperton expedition, on one occasion their camels went without water for eight days. When the explorers finally reached a well, the animals had to wait for hours while tons of sand were removed from the surface to reveal the liquid beneath. Needless to say, the dromedaries became fractious, rebellious and desperate. Even when they had drunk their fill, the problem did not end. Oudney reported that camels would overdo their drinking then eat dates. The result was intoxication: Oudney thought the dates acted chemically with the water to set up fermentation in their stomachs.

The use of camels for porterage was restricted to the northern areas of Africa. In the far south (roughly modern South Africa and parts of Zimbabwe) the ox-waggon was the preferred mode of transport. As far north as Matabeleland and Mashonaland larger ox-waggons could transport 4000–7000 lb of goods, which would otherwise require 100 porters. In the period 1840–80 the average cost of an ox-waggon was £100; a span of four oxen cost another £100. Thereafter expenses were slight. A team of oxen, travelling at 2 mph, could be managed by a crew of three; the only other requirements were an abundant supply of water, the wherewithal for repairs to the wheels, and the care taken to see that the animals were not worked hard under the hot sun. In cool weather oxen in good condition could trek through sand for ninety-six hours without water. The Portuguese explorer Serpa Pinto, who crossed Africa from Angola to South Africa in a south-easterly direction in the late 1870s, switched from human porterage to ox-waggon as soon as practicable.

A further refinement was added by the tribes who lived between Portuguese south-west Africa and Tanganyika, on the route taken by Verney Cameron in 1874–5. Here there was a centuries-old tradition of training oxen as riding animals. Yet the animals were never completely tamed. Sometimes they became obstinate and refused to cross swamps or rivers. In such cases, on expeditions, they were immediately killed for meat.

Schweinfurth toyed with the idea of trying to introduce ox-carts into the heart of Africa. But a careful study convinced him that the idea was chimerical. Apart from the initial capital expense of the waggons, there seemed no easy way of getting the conveyances from the coast to the inner plains. It was uncertain whether there existed animals of sufficient strength and stamina to breed in tropical, rather than sub-tropical climates. Drivers would have to be trained from scratch. Doubtless with enough money and willpower *these* obstacles could be surmounted. But climate and the tsetse fly could not. The evidence was overwhelming that all domesticated animals, whether oxen, camels, mules, horses or camels, succumbed very soon to the effects of climate and disease once taken north of 5°N. Schweinfurth then suggested handcarts on the Chinese or Mormon model; these would run on a single large wheel, which would be spanned like a bridge by a framework carrying the goods. Two men, one in front, one behind, would push and pull along poles run diagonally through the barrows. Schweinfurth thought it should be possible to devise carts suitable for all terrain, whether swamp, mountain or open plain.

But Alfred Swann, who made the mistake of transporting boat sections by waggon, exposed the fallacy of Schweinfurth's hopes:

> It is all very well marching along a narrow path, but to draw wheeled vehicles is another matter. Every rock and tree-stump was a vexatious hindrance, and it required a company of axe-men to clear away obstacles. The men pulled, perspired and 'said things'. A broken trace, a capsize, up to the axle in mud, wheel off, etc, would be a fair summary of the daily life and pin-pricks one had to endure for three months. But those black fellows never gave up. Had they known what was before them, it is certain none would have chosen to be yoked as 'donkeys' in those boat sections. In order that the reader may quite understand what these men had to do, I may here explain that two boat sections weighed 300 lb each, and four others 230 lb each, besides the carts on which they were lashed. The pathway seldom exceeded two feet in width, with trees and tall grasses growing close up to its edges. If you picture these men dragging such burdens under a broiling sun, along that path for 825 miles . . . you will probably join with me in calling them a brave set of black men.

Many explorers set out for the interior with mules and donkeys, but soon regretted it. Joseph Thomson solemnly warned any would-be traveller in Africa against the folly of taking such animals either to ride or as pack animals. He had bitter experience to draw on. On his first expedition, to the great lakes of East Africa, he had five donkeys. Each could carry two men's loads, but each needed a driver to control it, so that even on paper the advantages cancelled out. Even worse was the trouble they caused. Invariably the donkey boys lost control. Every morning it would take ten men to load each beast, which kicked and struggled all the while. The donkeys would then dash off into the thorn scrub and try to rub off their loads. It would then take a further quarter of an hour to release them from the tangle. For a time it looked as though the animals would accept their fate. But no sooner was vigilance relaxed than the beasts would smash against a tree trunk, shivering girth and saddlebags and scattering the loads on the pathway. Another half-hour would then be wasted in mending the saddlebags and reloading. Crossing streams meant loads had to be taken off and carried across. On the other side there would ensue another struggle to reload the donkeys. Some travellers reported that their mules expected to be carried in hammocks whenever they got stuck in mud and would deliberately 'malinger' to have themselves thus relieved. As Thomson remarked: 'It was with a genuine sense of relief we saw these creatures die off from some mysterious malady . . . in the low swampy regions, covered with dense jungle-grass, neither bullock, horse nor ass seems to thrive.'

The sisyphean business of loading and reloading pack animals was bad enough. Even worse than the recalcitrance of the dumb beasts was the stupidity of their human drivers. On their expedition to Lake Rudolph Teleki and von Höhnel came across a driver taking a siesta in the shade. 'The donkey ran away and lost the saddle,' he protested, as if the matter had nothing whatever to do with him. Von Hohnel told the man he could do as he pleased, but he had better not show his face in camp that night without the donkey and saddle. The draconian policy worked: both items were recovered.

On his last expedition Livingstone made the egregious mistake of taking along Indian sepoys as well as baggage animals (six camels, four donkeys and two mules). The sepoys overloaded the animals, drove them too hard, left them standing loaded in the sun at resting places, and generally flogged, goaded and stabbed them with such ferocity that Livingstone felt sure they were deliberately trying to kill them. All twelve beasts were soon dead, and it was impossible to tell whether the sepoys or tsetse flies had done more damage. In cold fury Livingstone then dismissed the feckless sepoys.

In an effort to find a beast of burden that could withstand the rigours of Africa and thus make possible enlarged commercial endeavours, King Leopold's advisers in 1879 had the bright idea of using elephants. After all, were not elephants indigenous to Africa and thus resistant to the tsetse fly that had mown down horses, donkeys, mules, camels and bullocks? Captain Carter of Leopold's spurious International African Association (a front organisation for his own plans for a personal empire in Africa) brought four elephants over from India to East Africa. Hopes ran very high. It was estimated that an elephant could carry the equivalent of fifteen human loads; in one year, therefore, the cost of buying the animal would be offset by the saving on porters' wages.

In June 1879 Carter landed in Msasani Bay, just north of Dar es Salaam with a quartet of Indian elephants and thirteen mahouts. There were two males (Mahonghi and Naderbux) and two females (Sosankalli and Pulmalla). Carter's expedition set off inland with 700 porters. The elephants found the going tough and were forever sinking into the soft ground. Mahonghi got no farther than Mpwapwa before expiring of heat apoplexy; Naderbux followed him into extinction in September. Shortly afterwards the two females made an impressive entry into Tabora. But on the way to Karema, in December, Sosankalli joined the roll of fatalities. The last elephant, Pulmalla, pined away and died at Karema in April 1880. In the enthusiasm for the imagined breakthrough in transport,

Carter and his associates forgot that the domesticated Indian elephant was a very different animal from its untamable African cousin. The Indian species lived in a country of cheap and abundant food; the African inhabited a continent where life was an uphill struggle even for adapted species. In any case, Leopold's minions had not thought through the implications of their innovation. The desertion of porters was a remediable ill; the death of a single elephant on an expedition without porters could paralyse the entire enterprise.

Marine transport was an obvious answer on Africa's lakes and rivers. Livingstone used the *Ma-Robert* and the *Pioneer* on the Zambezi, Stanley took a boat in sections (the *Lady Alice*) on his 1874–7 expedition and accomplished his epic journey down the river Congo in it. In the 1880s the role of the steamers *Peace* and *Henry Reed* was crucial for the further exploration of the Congo river basin. But river transport was rarely available and the configuration of Africa's rivers worked against it even when it was. Above Khartoum the Nile became a choking river of reeds, bullrushes, ambatch and *sudd*. The lower Congo was not navigable between Isangila and Manyanga, where there was a stretch of boiling, impassable rapids. On the upper Congo the seven cataracts of Stanley Falls meant that boats had to portage on to the Lualaba. The Zambezi and the Shire provided a waterway to Lake Nyasa but it was far from ideal. The river lacked depth, had shifting sandbanks at the mouth, while above Tete there was the daunting barrier of the Kebrabasa rapids and a 40-mile detour at the Murchison cataracts. Even on the open river Livingstone found that steamboats were problematical. The currents were difficult, there was frequent need for refuelling (in this case chopping down timber), and other fuels such as coal took up an inordinate amount of space, thus reducing the craft's cargo-carrying capacity. Indeed Livingstone's enthusiasm for steamboats was predicated on other grounds than their efficiency: he wished to assert the technological superiority of Christian Europe over Islam and so win African hearts and minds.

During the golden age of the explorers, then, there remained no realistic alternative to human porterage in the continent's heartland. Some idea of the stupendous contribution made by the porters can be gained from an examination of the equipment and trade goods travellers took with them into the interior.

Arguably the first properly equipped African expedition was Lander's 1830 venture. The Colonial Office spent £350 on stores and gifts, including tent, mattresses, sheets, blankets, cooking equipment, tinned food, opium, calomel, carbonate of soda, Epsom salts, Seidlitz powders, tartar emetic, citric acid, laxative pills, cloth, fifty razors, 100 combs, 100

Dutch pipes, 110 mirrors, 50,000 needles and two silver medals. To this inventory later explorers added sodium bicarbonate, blue pills, Easton syrup, patent medicines, Collis Browne's chlorodyne, packets of Dr James's powders to encourage sweating, Carter's little liver pills, Cockle's antibilious pills and Beecham's powders. Some favoured zinc sulphate drops for conjunctivitis and millboard for emergency splinting. Others took vast quantities of purges and diachylon plasters for lumbago, which the tribes very soon discovered were also efficacious abortifacients.

For the care of wounds and as nostrums against disease there was again a wide repertoire. Explorers suffering from toothache were advised simply to pry the tooth loose and pull it out. Haemorrhage from this and other wounds could be staunched with a red-hot ramrod; for snakebite gunpowder was exploded on the wound to stop the venom spreading. Gunpowder, in a cup of warm water, was also used as an emetic. Ulcers were washed out and the cavity filled with power iodoform, then bandaged with a strip of antiseptic gauze, over which was tightly tied a piece of goat's or sheep's hide; left without redressing for several days, the ulcer usually healed and presented a wholesome surface. Swollen and blistered feet were treated with hot water (when available) or grease. The emulsion of the male fern – usually found growing at the mouth of ant-eaters' lairs – was known to remedy stomach upsets. Silver wire could be used to suture wounds. Francis Galton advised all explorers to carry their drugs in zinc pill boxes with names embossed on both top and bottom in case the lids were accidentally changed.

Alcohol divided the explorers. Some agreed with Stanley that strong liquor and Africa did not mix and advised against indulgence, certainly before sundown. Stanley, it is true, took champagne with him on his expeditions, but only for the purpose of toasting a coup, such as the 'finding' of Livingstone or Emin Pasha. But not everyone was prepared simply to drink coffee and tea, as Stanley recommended. Many old Africa hands swore that whisky kept fever at bay. Gordon, whose partiality for a 'b and s' was notorious, got the best of both worlds by lacing his coffee with brandy. Harry Johnston, always markedly fond of champagne, managed to incorporate the drink in his blackwater fever febrifuge.

By the 1860s a kind of African explorer 'uniform' had made its appearance. Norfolk jackets became *de rigueur*. Flannel shirts were worn next to the skin, and the outfit was completed by long trousers and socks tucked into heavy boots, a size too large to allow for swollen feet. On the open grasslands a few eccentrics would exchange trousers for cut off shorts below the knees. Umbrellas were popular, as were dark glasses – Livingstone ordered a pair in London as early as 1848. Much of the equipment was designed to ward off fever – such was the fear that explorers were even exhorted to sleep between two fires at night to prevent chills. Citronella oil and mosquito nets were brought as deterrents to mosquitoes. Cholera belts were worn by some; others opted for spine pads. Above all else, ranking above even the beloved Crosse & Blackwell products, the explorers prized quinine and took plentiful supplies. After 1870, in the light of medical discoveries, they made a point of boiling their drinking water and took with them the newly invented porcelain filters and thermos flasks.

Sunstroke was something of a phobia for Europeans. The remedy was thought to be a coal-scuttle helmet made of white rubber or cork with a puggaree round the crown to make it appear stylish. This absurd contraption was a staple of music-hall parodies of the African explorer. Livingstone preferred a peaked cap, and Stanley a high-crowned hat with a ring of brass-lined holes to allow the circulation of air round the head. Neither of these caught on, so that later travellers who disdained the helmet opted for a felt hat with a double brim. But the fear of the sun's rays impinging on the bare head remained acute. Even during the 1930s Albert Schweitzer was warning his disciples that a ray of sunlight passing through a chink in the roof might cause haemorrhage if it touched their heads.

Most essential of all, in a continent where fever was common and the traveller was subject to pelting rains and burning suns, where the temperature could change 30°F within an hour, was a large tent. Thomson explained why the tent had to be large: 'To be shut up ill in your tent, with your face close to the roof and your hands touching both sides, means an addition to your tortures of no mean account.'

Case studies from two contrasting expeditions – one departing from the Indian Ocean westwards, the other from the Atlantic eastwards – underscore the general propositions about equipment. For the 1857–9 expedition to Lake Tanganyika Burton and Speke took a Rowtie tent, mosquito netting, beds, chairs, portable tables, cooking pots, books, carpenters' tools, fishing rods and nets, journals, chronometers, two prismatic compasses, three thermometers, sundial, rain-gauge, sextants, barometer and pedometer. To cut down on the loads, they took simply the clothes they stood up in. For his 1878–80 expedition south-east across Africa Serpa Pinto carried with him a complete toilet service: large mirror, basin and ewer, soap dishes, dinner and tea service, and kitchen utensils (all this occupied one trunk). In three other trunks he took four bottles of quinine, three sextants, an artificial horizon, chronometers, log tables, two Pistor's circles, three astronomical telescopes, three aneroids, four pedometers, six algebraic compasses, three azimuths, two circular needles, six hypsometers, twelve thermometers, one barometer, one anemometer, one theodolite, fifty cartridges for each firearm, a suit of clothes, three changes of linen, tinder, flint and steel and other personal effects. Additionally his baggage contained a tent (9 ft 11 in. wide by 6 ft 3 in.), iron bedstead and a folding table.

A female traveller in the late 1880s, Mrs French-Sheldon, took the following: pots, pans, calabashes, tent, poles, chairs, folding tables, waterproof cloth and canvases, boxes of candles, soap, cartridges, matches, flints, cotton waste for cleaning guns, coconut oil, kerosene (in a large square tin), water cans, coffee, lanterns, water-bottles, photographic apparatus, tools, medicine cases, large tin buckets, hammocks, sleeping mats and cloth turbans with which the bearers could ease the loads from their heads and which they could barter in an emergency.

All expeditions took provisions for the first ten days or so of their travel, until they could barter with the tribes. The commonest form of the *posho* or daily ration was rice, usually carried in a *kanda*, a long narrow matting bag broadest at the bottom. The customary dole was a tumblerful of rice from a brass measure called a *karaba*. The number of doles received per diem depended on one's place in the caravan's hierarchy. Often the porters carrying the heaviest loads received the smallest *posho* while a headman, who would not even have to carry his own mat, might receive a fivefold allowance. Water was always a problem. Porters carried this in calabashes but, averse to the extra weight, would usually empty them as soon as they reached a pool or stream, only to lament later when there were water shortages or what was available was brackish. The short-sightedness of the 'dark companions' was a constant lament of the African traveller. Harry Johnston, who once called for his water-bottle, only to find that his 'boy' had already drunk it all himself, described his men as creatures of the moment, who would start out with a good supply of water, then squander it or over-indulge, so that on long waterless treks they staggered along with dry, swollen tongues, parched lips and bloodshot eyes.

But far more important than the explorer's personal effects and the supplies of food and water were the trade goods carried by the caravan, to be bartered for food *en route* or used to pay *hongo* or tribute. The importance of trade goods emerges from one eloquent statistic relating to Thomson's journey through Masailand in 1883–4. Out of 123 porters on his caravan, fifteen were entrusted with his personal stores; ten carried the tents, tent furniture and cooking gear; nine clothes, boots and books; and six carried scientific instruments and photographic equipment. Apart from five bearers with ammunition, the gun-bearer and the donkey boy, the remaining seventy-seven carried trade goods.

Cloth, beads and wire were the staples of African commerce and thus indispensable to every explorer venturing into the interior. The cloth consisted of unbleached cotton sheeting from the United States (*merikani*); indigo-dyed cloth from India (*kaniki*); red and blue check cloth (*kisuto*); coloured blankets (*blanketi*); and various patterned fabrics, including *laissoes*, coloured cloth worn by women, and *kekois* (coloured cloth worn by men). These would all be made up into bolsters about 5 ft long and 18–24 in. across, strengthened with branches. Count Teleki's 1887–8 expedition to Lake Rudolph, for instance, took 600 pieces of *merikani*, each 30–40 yds long, 250 pieces of dark-blue calico 8 yds long, and 100 pieces of a stuff of a fine deep red colour called *bendera assilia*, 32 yds long. It was a fallacy that Africans were absurdly partial to gaudy colours, as in the received wisdom of the white man's clubs in early twentieth-century Nairobi. Their taste ran to black and white, or blue and white check, blue with a white stripe, plain blue or polka dot. Africans *were* fond of red, but it had to be of a good, fast, red colour; red damask was particularly prized. Along the Congo Fred Puleston, one of Stanley's Congo pioneers, found that the tribes would not accept yellow cloth even as a gift. Payment of tribute or for food was measured in units of cloth. A *doti* was 4 yds of cloth. A sheep would cost 2½ *doti* (10 yds), an ox 6–10 *doti*, a pig 4–5 *doti*.

There were more than 400 varieties of beads used as a medium of exchange. These were packed in long bags which were inflexible and unwieldy and therefore limited to 50 lb in weight. Very popular were glass beads from $\frac{1}{12}$ in. to $\frac{1}{8}$ in. in diameter. There were the *sami-sami* (red), *mad schibahari* (blue) and *aschanga meupe* (white). Also in demand were *ukuta* – a blue glass Paris bead the size of a pea, large white opaque beads, *murtinaroh*, green, blue or light brown glass rings, ½ in. diameter. If these were unacceptable, the explorers could always fall back on the *sambai* or common white bead, or stocks of large mixed beads known as *mboro*. Towards the end of the exploration era the house of Alonardi began to introduce into Africa some very fine pale brown, blue and white beads, which they sold as 'oriental beads.'

Fashion was a problem when dealing with African tribes, for each one demanded its own brand of cloth, its own tint, colour and size of beads. The people of Kilimanjaro, for example, favoured very tiny, red and turquoise beads. Absence of the required variety could spell disaster to a caravan, which would then be in effect penniless. On the advice of his headman Chuma, Thomson took beads on his first expedition, to Lake Tanganyika, only to find that the people there required cloth. Even worse, fashions changed, so that an explorer could arrive in a tribal area well-stocked with the tribe's 'favourite' goods, only to find that his goods were outmoded.

Beads were also used as a unit of currency, usually for the smaller transactions. A *kete* was the distance from the end of the forefinger to the hollow of the thumb. So for a *kete* of beads, enough to make a necklace, one could buy three eggs, or five roots of manioc, or 2 lb of cereal, for 2–3 *kete* a hen, and so on.

Wire was usually brass (*masango n'eupe*, brass wire No 6), used for making bracelets and carried at each end of a pole. Africans were fond of brass wire as it could be coiled into bracelets and anklets, and the finer sort used with much ingenuity to adorn gun-sticks, the hafts of knives and the rods of spears. But as the epoch progressed, copper wire (*masango*) and iron wire (*seninge*), increasingly came into the picture. The Teleki expedition, for example, took 100 loads of iron wire, $\frac{1}{5}$ in. thick and just fifteen loads of the strong brass and copper wire.

Other trade goods in demand were European hats, red umbrellas, horns, clocks, matches, razors, metal belts, jewelled weapons, tops, kites, dolls, clay pipes, tobacco, paintboxes, gunpowder, salt, dried fish, pocket-knives, needles, thread, buttons, small bells, fish-hooks, dinner plates, soup-plates, silverware, tumblers, padlocks, butchers' knives, mousetraps, musical instruments, mirrors, brass leg-rings, caps and shirts. For special chiefs the explorers might take superior guns, music boxes, accordions, playing-cards, lavishly illustrated picture books or fine snuff. But it was a fallacy that ivory could be bought for a few mirrors or beads. Africans were immensely shrewd traders, and this was all the more impressive as all calculations had to be done in the head. Toughest of all traders were the women. Men could be wheedled more easily by the promise of the most prized trade goods of all: guns, gunpowder, gin, or rum. In Africa rum was principally a currency not, as the missionaries asserted, a sign of the native love of inebriation. The missionary canard was false for two main reasons. In the first place, as a unit of currency rum was subdivided so many times among so many tribesmen that each individual received no more than a naval tot. Secondly, the rum in circulation was doctored and diluted to make it go further, so that even if there was a chief wealthy enough to lay in a great store, he could probably drink a gallon with impunity.

Packing trade goods for the journey was always a headache. The cloth was packed in bales. Each bale was made up of separate cloths, varied so that no more than one needed to be opened at any one time. *Merikani* would be packed in a bale alongside highly coloured cloths from India, and gold and silk cloths for the chiefs, all folded into the required shape. These bales were passed to other men who wrapped the whole in a sheet of *merikani*. The parcel was then firmly bound with a rope until it became as hard as wood, though retaining some elasticity – the operation of roping was assisted by a thorough beating with a wooden club. Next the bale was passed on to a fourth party, who sewed it up in rough matting to protect it against rain and rough usage. The contents were then noted down in a book and the bale assigned a number. This allowed the caravan leader to locate all items on the march. Each load was 60 lb in weight and had the form of a cylinder, 3½ ft long and 1 ft in diameter. The porter had to carry this load on his head and shoulders for anything up to eight hours a day. In addition he had to carry gun, mat, cooking pot and other effects, which would often bring the total load up to 80 lb.

Beads were put into bags properly marked, and copper and brass wire were tied in coils at the extremity of a pole 6 ft long and carried on the bare shoulder. Miscellaneous articles, stores, personal effects, journals etc were packed in boxes which, from their angular unyielding character, were hated by porters. Rojab, one of Stanley's bearers, fell foul of the 'little master' on the return journey from Tabora to the coast, after he had bade farewell to Livingstone in April 1872. Crossing a swollen river by tree bridge, Rojab, carrying the box which contained Livingstone's journals and letters, lost his balance and fell into the river. Miraculously, Rojab managed to retain his footing but his only thanks from Stanley was an angry roar: 'Look out! Drop that box and I'll shoot you.'

Wilhelm Junker recommended stout basketwork covered with canvas for the boxes – iron boxes were too heavy and tin ones too fragile and friable. His solution for personal stores and indispensable articles was to divide them into ten equal parts, with each load made up of exactly the same quantity of pens, stationery, food, medicines, etc. If every box contained the bare minimum a traveller needed, Junker estimated that he could, at the limit, lose nine out of ten and still survive.

The loads were then distributed to the porters. Invariably each man pretended to be too weak to carry the load assigned to him. As Thomson reported: 'The distribution of loads was not such a simple affair. Every man struggled to get the lightest and easiest. None were satisfied with anything allotted to them, and all had endless excuses to make, so that an indescribable scene of noise and confusion arose. Each one tried to avoid the boxes, as being the most unpleasant to carry, from their want of elasticity.' But once the loads were reluctantly accepted, each man carried his off to have a distinctive mark put on it. Many struck a forked stick into the load, so as to get it more easily on to the shoulders. The quality of porters could be instantly gauged by the way they tied up their loads. A good workman left nothing to chance and spared neither cord nor rope; if the rope was deficient he would make his own from bark or *sapsavera* fibre. The explorer and the caravan's headman had to keep a strict record of where each load went, because of desertions and attempts by the porters to displace the contents of their loads.

Who were these men who crossed the continent with Livingstone and Stanley and plunged into the unknown with Burton, Speke and Baker? No single answer will suffice. Livingstone relied heavily on the Makololo whom he compared to the Argonauts, Stanley on the Swahili-speaking Zanzibaris. Those who conducted round-trip expeditions like those of Burton and Speke in 1857-9, Thomson in 1879-80 and 1883-4, Johnston in 1885 and Teleki in 1887-8 could make use of the greatest of all technicians in African porterage: the Nyamwezi. Also, the longer the expedition, the greater the loss through desertion and disease, so that by the end of Stanley's 1874-7 epic, few remained of those who had departed with him from Bagamoyo. As the original porters dropped out, fresh ones were recruited from the tribal territories through which the caravan passed. Explorers routinely referred to their supporters as the *wangwana* – literally the sons of the free and strictly speaking a term relating only to the Afro-Arabian freedmen on the island of Zanzibar. But the *wangwana* in practice often denoted both Zanzibaris who were slaves and loaned out to the explorers for the duration *and* porters and soldiers who were not Zanzibari at all; for example, a number of Ganda tribesmen enlisted with Stanley in 1875 and went with him down the Congo in 1877.

Yet undoubtedly the most striking of all the tribes who acted as porters were the Nyamwezi. Occupying the tableland south of Lake Victoria, the Nyamwezi were great traders in iron and salt; their elephant-hunters also travelled outside their own tribal areas in quest of ivory and built up an impressive trade in tusks. Thomson declared that wherever the Nyamwezi settled, they were sure to make their mark, on account of their superior intelligence, mechanical skill and love of trade. In addition, they built up a tradition of caravan organisation, with special expertise in carrying heavy loads. A Nyamwezi male was not allowed to marry until he had carried a load of ivory to the coast and brought back a load of calico or brass wire. This was the tribal stamp of manhood, turning a youth into man and warrior.

The Nyamwezi had evolved specialised methods for carrying heavy loads. Whereas some portering tribes, such as the Manyema and Wateita, carried their loads by a strap around the forehead, with the load resting on the back, the Nyamwezi (as also the Swahili from Zanzibar) carried their burdens on the head and shoulders. They were capable of carrying 90 lb dead-weight (a 60-lb load and 30 lb of rifle, ammunition and personal effects as well as the 2 yds of unbleached calico allowed each man per day to buy food) during two marches a day for weeks at a stretch, often on short commons and sometimes with no food at all. Alfred Swann was one of many to marvel at them: 'It is astonishing how they do it day after day –

plodding on apparently without undue exhaustion under the tropical sun.'
It was observed that they had large, highly developed and conspicuous
muscles on the top of each shoulder as a consequence. They could
transfer a load from one shoulder to another with remarkable dexterity by
ducking the head downwards and then upwards with a sideways swoop.
This manoeuvre was sometimes executed by up to eighty men simultaneously while singing a song.

In the early days the Nyamwezi used to carry 70-lb loads, a huge
burden especially when porters had to stop to scrape from their feet the
accumulated mud and grass of a long trek. But as time went on, a kind of
primitive union consciousness made them unwilling to accept loads
greater than 60 lb (by the 1890s this was down to 50 lb). The explorers
acquiesced in these improved conditions of service. The more intelligent
among them could see that it was self-defeating in terms of morale,
discipline and desertion to expect men to carry more than 60 lb in
addition to a Snider carbine, belt, pouch, ten rounds of ammunition,
water-bottle and up to ten days' rations. Besides, the Nyamwezi knew so
much about African travel that they habitually carried along stout staffs
which they leant on when ascending or descending mountains and used to
probe the depth of streams. At night this staff served as one of the props
on which they stretched their tent cloth. They never placed their loads on
the ground while on the march, but thrust a pole through the cords of
their pack, which they then stuck in the earth and propped against a tree as
support.

The Nyamwezi were superior to their only real rivals as porters, the
Swahili and the Wakamba. Some tribes, like the Masai, considered it
beneath their dignity to act as human beasts of burden. Their neighbours
the Kikuyu, by contrast, often became almost as good as the Nyamwezi
when they took to the life of the porter. Frederick Jackson recorded that
five Kikuyu women once carried full donkey loads of 150 lb *each* for a
whole day. But apart from the occasional Kavirondo and Kikuyu, the
Nyamwezi, Swahili and Wakamba had the field to themselves.

Where the Nyamwezi specialised in travel on the open plain, the
Wakamba's speciality was the jungle. Their method of carrying loads was
quite different. They used the neck and the back rather than the
shoulders. They would tie up a load with a long, broad strip of hide,
leaving a large loop, which was passed round the forehead from behind,
thus supporting the load, which rested on the back of the neck. When the
strain on the back of the neck became too great, they would lean forward,
which provided relief by throwing the burden onto the back. But the
Wakamba were notoriously undisciplined and specialised in stealing food
from the villages they passed through, thus souring the explorers'

relations with the locals. The Swahili from Zanzibar, who in Stanley's descriptions often sound like Kipling's Bandar-Log, were highly strung, quarrelsome, disputatious and vociferous. The Nyamwezi, by contrast, had a greater sense of group solidarity and, if troubled by some aspect of the expedition or its leadership, would form a deputation and send it to the white man, where their grievances would be put firmly but quietly.

Another advantage of the Nyamwezi was their forethought. It was not uncommon to see one of them with a thick pad of cloth, perhaps half a *gora*, or 15 yds of *merikani* wrapped around his stomach, or a couple of coils of brass wire dangling from his belt, or a neatly made sausage-like bag of selected beads in a leather bag slung around his shoulders. This enabled him to buy extra food when his thoughtless Swahili companions were on short commons.

But most crucial of all considerations to the African explorer was the rate of march. The distance a caravan covered in a day was limited by loads; with an average 60-lb load 10 miles a day was a fair average. This depended on reliable water supplies. If there was no water for 30 miles, it was better for the caravan to march that distance non-stop in a single day or, better still, a single night. If the loads were only 30 lb a man, a rate of 20 miles a day for six days a week could be achieved without difficulty. Heavier loads could be carried by two men on a pole, but then diminishing returns set in: men who could carry 30 lb apiece could carry a maximum of 50 lb between them; for 60 lb apiece the corresponding joint figure was 95 lb. And it sometimes happened that there were loads that could not be broken down into the customary 60 lb. Here the Nyamwezi truly came into their own, as they could carry heavier single and double loads than any other tribe. In an emergency, and if appealed to in the right way, a Nyamwezi would even consent to carry the *madala* on his own – two 30-lb loads slung one at each end of the pole. As Harry Johnston remarked: 'What other race would be content to trudge 20 miles a day with a burden of 60 lb, and be regaled on nothing but maize and beans?'

The catalogue of Nyamwezi virtues did not end there. They were the most musical of the porters – not an insignificant consideration given the number of 'land shanties' sung by the *wangwana*. And they were the most skilled at carrying a sick or ailing white man in a hammock. Those carried thus by other tribes testified to the extreme discomfort of being borne on the heads of porters; the poor invalid would swing crazily in the air as a Wakamba loped along, but would have a much smoother ride on the shoulders of the Nyamwezi.

For all these reasons, expeditions using miscellaneous porterage made a point of dividing the loads by tribe if possible. The least reliable, the Wakamba, got the trade goods: wire, beads and cloths; the Swahili from

Zanzibar got the personal equipment, tents, blankets and utensils. The most reliable of all, the Nyamwezi got the most basic means of survival: the food and ammunition. In addition, explorers started to distribute their loads scientifically instead of allowing a devil-take-the-hindmost free-for-all. At the start of his second expedition, in 1874, Stanley made sure the heaviest loads (60 lb of cloth) were given to the most muscular men; the short of stature were given the 50-lb sacks of beads; the young men 40-lb boxes of stores, ammunition and miscellaneous items. Older men were chosen to take charge of the instruments, books and photographic equipment. The chronometers were given to a porter specially chosen for his steady cautious tread. The major problem was the sections of the boat *Lady Alice* which Stanley intended to launch on Lake Victoria. Since the original sections brought out from England were too heavy, Stanley engaged a carpenter to subdivide each section further. Two pairs of boat-bearers then took it in turn to carry the sections; there were two pairs to each section. To sweeten the pill Stanley paid the boatmen more than anyone else except his headman and allowed them the rare privilege of bringing their wives.

Rates of pay for porters were subject to special inflationary pressures, since the bearers operated in a seller's market. On Burton and Speke's expedition the caravan leader Said bin Salim received 500 dollars a year; Bombay, Baraka and Rahan, his lieutenants, received 60 dollars each, while the rest of the porters got 25 dollars each. At least that was what they were promised, but Burton on his return to Zanzibar refused to pay, alleging that his men had been insolent, mutinous and had forfeited all moral and legal rights. Burton's dubious action set back the cause of African exploration, and the particular tangle arising from his high-handed action took years to unravel. Its immediate consequence was that porters would no longer start for the interior without receiving a year's pay in advance.

By the time of Stanley's expedition to relieve Livingstone, in 1871, the rate for ordinary porters was 2½ dollars a month. When he returned for his trans-Africa expedition three years later, he found that this had inflated to 5 dollars or even 7–8 dollars, a situation he angrily attributed to Cameron's generosity the year before. But inflation levelled out in the late 1870s. On Thomson's first expedition (1879–80) the going rate was 5 dollars a month for an ordinary porter, 6 dollars for the five headmen and 10 dollars for the caravan leader. In the 1880s, as soon as King Leopold's grip on the Congo tightened, a uniform system of payment for porters was introduced. One *brasse* (2 m) of cloth a week was the standard rate – a *brasse* had a monetary value of 1 franc 50 centimes. Additionally, the Congo porter was paid a daily ration of beads worth 15 centimes. A wage of 3 francs a week compared favourably with the average in Uganda under the British of 4 rupees (equivalent to 6½ francs) a month, but it has to be remembered that the atrocities associated with the Congo Free State created a shortage of porters from a very early date.

One of the reasons Europe was so tardy in penetrating the Dark Continent was that it was extremely difficult to make a profit. The Royal Geographical Society spent more than £11,000 on Cameron's 1873–5 expedition. In 1890 it was estimated that it cost £130 a ton to transport goods from the coast to Lake Victoria and £250–300 a ton for the Uganda/Mombasa journey. This was why expeditions were mounted on a non-commercial basis. The Royal Geographical Society and the British government sponsored Livingstone, Speke, Burton, Cameron, Thomson, Johnston and many others. Some explorations were carried out by missionaries, whose London-based societies were not run on a strict profit-and-loss financial basis. Stanley had the wealth of James Gordon Bennett and the *New York Herald* behind him on his first two expeditions. Thereafter, it was left to wealthy individuals to finance their own expeditions: the best-known names in this category were those of Samuel Baker and Count Teleki.

A principal reason for the commercial non-viability of expeditions was that, apart from the wages of porters and the cost of food and necessary equipment, a large part of the trade goods taken into the interior had to be spent on *hongo*. *Hongo*, the tribute demanded by tribes for passage through their territory, always provoked strong emotions among explorers. Emotive terms like 'blackmail' were frequently heard; some die-hards argued that the Africans had a right to charge such fees only if they cultivated all their lands; fallow land or open savannah was therefore in the public domain. There were the penny-pinchers like Burton and the men of blood such as Carl Peters who itched for the use of force to chastise the tribes for their 'contumacity'. Few travellers reflected, or would have been swayed by the reflection, that most African societies subsisted on a knife-edge, so that there was simply no surplus to share with whatever stranger happened their way. But more reasonable observers thought that *hongo*, levied in a rough-and-ready way on the nature and quantity of goods passing through, could be construed as a primitive form of customs duty and was therefore justifiable. Apologists pointed out that the traveller had to pay no other rates, taxes, rents or customs dues, and that in return for the levy he was protected by the locals and supplied with water, even where it was scarce. *Hongo* was above all a return for the labour expended in sinking wells, often the only way to get at water. As one sympathetic missionary put it: 'The natives having the trouble of sinking these wells, it is only fair that passing caravans should pay for the privilege of using water.'

The successful African explorer had to be a master diplomat in knowing exactly how far he could push a tribal chief in moderating a demand for *hongo*. If the explorer made the mistake of trying to bribe the chief with a lavish present, like a musical box, he might find the chief so intrigued by the imagined treasures of the strangers that he refused to allow passage at all and instead detained the caravan in an attempt to extort all his goods.

The battle over *hongo* was power politics at its most stark; the greater the water shortage, the greater the *hongo*. Samuel Baker, travelling in Equatoria province, nominally under the suzerainty of the Khedive of Egypt, found that the Egyptian writ simply did not run there, and that the usual passage dues were expected. The traveller F.L. James, attempting to retrace Burton's footsteps in Somaliland in the 1880s, got a taste of the excessive tribute levied in the desert there. While conferring with a local 'sultan' on the fee to be paid, thirty of the sultan's retainers rode into camp and demanded to be fed. When they had eaten their fill, their master then asked James if he could 'borrow' two of his sheep. Advised by his Aden men that he would never get through the desert country unless he acceded, James reluctantly bowed his head. The missionary Edward Coode Hore took 5½ hours in 1878 to cross the Malagarazi river in 14 bark canoes. Passage had to be paid to the canoeman for each passage in addition to normal *hongo*. To get across the river Hore spent 48 yds of calico and 6 lb of beads.

Two particularly powerful tribes stood athwart the traditional caravan route from Bagamoyo on the Indian Ocean (opposite Zanzibar) to Tabora and Lake Tanganyika. The Gogo, a powerful confederation of tribes spanning the flat plains of Ugogo, commanded a nodal area, strategically placed between the warlike Masai and Hehe tribes and, more importantly, controlling the scarce water supplies of the area. Their 'insolence' often irked explorers: there are frustrated tirades against them in the works of Burton and Stanley. But even Stanley, no pacifist, deemed it expedient to pay *hongo* on the return from the Emin Pasha Relief Expedition 1889, although in military terms (with 500-odd armed men and a Maxim gun) he could have blasted his way through Ugogo. The German Carl Peters, was furious that the 'weak' Stanley had not taught the contumacious Gogo the lesson of superior European technology, and, in the 1890s, achieved his dearest wish when he was able to set up a Krupps gun in Ugogo and slaughter the tribesmen in hundreds.

The other confederation was arguably even more fearsome. On the approaches to Lake Tanganyika, just south of the main caravan routes, lay the six independent chiefdoms of the Ha tribe. The Ha detested Arabs, thought of white men as Arabs, and therefore swindled them with a vengeance. Compelled by the war between the Arabs and the Nyamwezi chief Mirambo to take a southerly approach to Ujiji in October 1871, when on the point of meeting Livingstone, Stanley almost came to grief in the Luguru chiefdom of the Ha. In two days among the Ha Stanley was compelled to surrender half his goods in *hongo* to chief Mionvu and his brother. Mionvu began the extortion by extracting 83 *doti* from Stanley after four hours of gruelling bargaining; in return Stanley was given a promise that no more tribute would be levied. But next day Mionvu's brother stopped the caravan on the road and demanded a further *hongo* of 26 *doti*. When Stanley protested and cited Mionvu's promise, his brother said that Mionvu had no authority to bind his fellow chiefs in that way.

That night Stanley's party rested in the Ha village. Ever the fire-eater, Stanley wanted to settle the issue by force. His men counselled against such folly; they were fifty against thousands. But Stanley was desperate, as there were four more Ha chiefdoms on his proposed line of march to Ujiji, and it was mathematically certain that he would appear at Lake Tanganyika to 'relieve' Livingstone with not a yard of cloth nor string of beads. Stanley decided to make a break at nightfall. He bribed a slave 12 *doti* to guide his party over uninhabited territory to Ujiji. At dead of night he and his men stole from the village in detachments. They then marched night and day at the double for thirty-six hours until they were clear of Ha territory.

Unless one had overwhelming force to hand and was prepared to spill a great deal of blood as Peters did, wisdom always dictated the payment of *hongo*. An Arab in a powerful party once refused to pay and defied the tribe to do anything about it. The tribesmen retaliated by closing all the wells along the line of march and opening new, unknown ones. The result was predictable: just three members of the caravan survived; the rest died of thirst.

There were other complications about *hongo*. If one of an explorer's men fell ill while the guest of a tribe, he could find himself liable to an extra payment, for such an event was held to be 'bad medicine' for the village. The porters' insistence on travelling with loaded guns could also lead to undesired consequences. On one occasion a gun went off by accident and killed another porter. The local ruler, hearing of the accident, then demanded extra *hongo* for the 'crime' committed in his territory. One explorer had to pay an extra fine because he had his hair cut at a time when this was a local taboo, out of fear of harming the harvest; another was mulcted because he took a bath in his tent at a time when bathing was prohibited, for fear it would discourage the rains.

The traveller Mrs French-Sheldon encountered a quaint tribute custom in Masailand in 1891. The Masai formally forbade passage to travellers by placing a bullet in the middle of the path likely to be traversed by a caravan. Over the bullet they placed two crossed twigs, stripped of foliage except for a tasselled brush at the top. Traditionally the first person trespassing beyond this 'barrier' was speared or shot by a 'warden' in ambush. Mrs French-Sheldon may have owed her survival to being a white woman. Inadvertently, she kicked such a totem aside. In consternation her headman cried out to her not to move a muscle. Suddenly thirty Masai warriors appeared brandishing spears. In high excitement they demanded 'blood-money' for the white woman's depredation. Mrs French-Sheldon placated them with some lumps of bluestone, among the Masai prized as highly as donkeys or cattle.

Explorers expended a lot of ingenuity trying to 'beat the system'. Some reckoned that *hongo* increased geometrically with a caravan's size, so travelled in detachments which linked up only in the wilderness, so as to give the appearance of poverty. Others sought the protective camouflage of Arab caravans, on the theory that the Arabs knew to the last inch how far they could beat the locals down. But travelling with Arabs could have its own drawbacks. Sometimes Arabs negotiated favourable *hongo* for themselves in return for information about the real wealth of the white man. And it could be a disadvantage if an Arab had travelled with Europeans before. The Arab Janja infuriated Livingstone on his last expedition. He had served with Burton and Speke and tipped off a Chambeze ruler about the going rate for *hongo* on that expedition, which was both more than Livingstone could afford and well above the market rate anyway, because of the inexperience of the two earlier travellers.

Human porterage was essential to African exploration and became even more important in the age of colonialism after 1890. In the last decade of the century the supply of porters in British East Africa began to dry up. This was because the Nyamwezi were incorporated in German East Africa (later Tanganyika) after the 1885 agreement. Naturally, the Germans were keen to retain such a priceless economic asset and would not permit Nyamwezi migration into the British territories. With the exception of a handful of Kikuyu, the Kenya races were useless as porters. Moreover, in the Masai Highlands, where it was often necessary to march 25 days before finding food, adequate provisions had to be carried by the porters. But food for 25 days meant a load of 37 lb. Given the customary maximum load of 65 lb, this meant that the porters could carry just 28 lb of equipment and trade goods.

Even after the building of the railways, human porterage was necessary. The First World War, which solved the British porterage problem by removing the German piece from the African chessboard, also produced a huge demand for labour. Hundreds of thousands of porters were used in the armies on both sides, and casualties were huge. Only in the 1920s, with the coming of tarmacked roads, cars and lorries did human porterage finally become obsolete. But not before the necessities of transport had finally made Europeans appreciate *some* Africans at least as human beings and led to the dubious accolade 'dark companions'.

7

'Dark Companions'

One of Stanley's most admirable attributes was a warm appreciation of Africans and their talents. In 1871 he paid this tribute to the *pagazi* or porter:

> This useful person is the camel, the horse, the mule, the ass, the train, the wagon and the cart of East and Central Africa. Without him Salem would not obtain her ivory, Boston and New York their African ebony, their frankincense, myrrh and gum copal. He travels regions where the camel could not enter and where the horse and the ass could not live. He carries the maximum weight of seventy pounds on his shoulders from Bagamoyo to Unyanyembe, where he belongs for which he charges from 15 to 25 *doti* of American sheeting or Indian calico, dyed blue, called *kaniki*, mixed with other cloths, imported from Muscat and Cutch, equal to from 7.50 to 12.50 dollars. He is therefore very expensive to a traveller.

Among native Africans, the *wangwana* – a generic term embracing Swahili Zanzibaris, Nyamwezis, Wakambas and many others – formed a self-conscious élite. After a year with Thomson or three with Stanley, the genuine *wangwana* – that is, those who had not been hired as slaves from an Arab master – could return to Zanzibar with accumulated wages which in local terms made them rich men. As veterans of dozens of battles and owners of their Snider rifles they were military heroes and commanded the deference of the more timid Zanzibaris. In their own tales of derring-do they portrayed themselves as both the equal and the saviour of their white overlords. In a word they had their fingers on all the indices of middle-level power in Zanzibar; only rich Arabs, exceptional entrepreneurs, or the Sultan and his entourage had greater wealth and higher status. Nor was their gratification merely deferred, since they enjoyed the favours of women in the villages through which they passed, and enjoyed a high standard of diet when their employer was generous with meat or successful at hunting. Against this they had to weigh up the fact that they had no better than a fifty-fifty chance of survival. Death in battle, from the explorers' whip or noose, from wild animals, from starvation and, most of all, from smallpox and other dread diseases, meant that the status they enjoyed as heroes on their return home was by no means a self-assigned one. A single statistic is eloquent: of 708 *wangwana* who left Zanzibar with Stanley in February 1887 on the Emin Pasha expedition, only 210 returned in December 1889.

Complete with camp followers, most major Central African expeditions, certainly until the taming of the Congo in the mid-1880s, started from Bagamoyo, the mainland town across the strait from Zanzibar. Livingstone, Stanley, Burton, Speke, Thomson, Johnston, Teleki: the list of those who travelled this route is almost endless. In this respect the Europeans acknowledged a debt to the Arabs who had blazed the trail to the interior and the great African lakes. The Arab presence in Africa began with Seyyid Said bin Sultan, ruler of Oman, who claimed suzerainty over Zanzibar and the nearby coast in 1804. In 1840 he moved his court to the island of Zanzibar and controlled the East African coast from the Juba river to Cape Delgado, though his authority never extended far inland. The typical *petit Arabe*, or Zanzibari *wangwana* was a product of intermarriage between the Arabs and the aboriginal inhabitants of the island.

It was the alliance between Arab trader and Nyamwezi porter that first opened the door to the Central African lakes. In 1840 Unyanyembe became a centre of the Arab world to rival Zanzibar. An entrepôt trade was established at Tabora (Kazeh); this trade route into the interior became a source of great profit as the world demand for ivory rocketed. From Tabora the Arabs fanned out farther into the interior. A large colony was established at Nyangwe in the Manyema country west of Lake Tanganyika; this was to be the base of operations of the most famous Arab slaver of all, Tippu Tip. Meanwhile the merchant Ahmed bin Ibrahim penetrated as far north as Buganda on the north-western shores of Lake Victoria; other Arabs pushed south to Lake Nyasa.

Bagamoyo became *the* departure point for caravans to the interior. To the north, Mombasa served the Swahili-based trade with the Chagas of Mt Kilimanjaro and the Nyika and Kamba. To the south Kilwa was the main outlet for the slave trade drawing on the Yaos of the Lake Nyasa area. Zanzibar itself became a polygot, cosmopolitan centre. Said encouraged European, American and Asian traders to settle there. The Maria Teresa dollar, roughly equal to the US dollar or four shillings sterling, became the standard currency; the rupee (ten to the pound) was also accepted everywhere. Indians provided the capital for inland ventures and took over the customs administration. Zanzibar became a magnet for American merchants from Salem. Quicker than the Europeans to discern the commercial possibilities, the United States appointed its first consul there in 1836; the British responded with the appointment in 1841 of Atkins Hamerton, the man who did so much to help Burton and Speke in 1856.

The departure of Burton and Speke from Bagamoyo, on the first major Zanzibar-based expedition, produced the first account of the daily life of the *wangwana* in the interior. Burton, taking his cue from the Arabs in this and in so many matters, did not press the pace as later hard drivers like Stanley did, but proceeded at a leisurely step. At 4 a.m. the caravan would rise at cockcrow – literally, since cockerels had been brought along. Fires were lit and the meal eaten. Burton then assembled his porters and assigned the loads. The men then sorted themselves out into groups or *kambi*, choosing friends and fellow tribesmen. Each was given a cooking pot and axe, rations, sleeping-mat, three-legged stool and a rifle and thereafter expected to be self-sufficient. Porters usually wore their shabbiest clothes while on the march, but were often gaudily apparelled with stripes of animal skin or bunches of feathers; some even had bells tied below their knees.

Eventually the serpentine file got under way. In the van was the caravan's guide or *kilangozi*, usually cutting a figure in scarlet robe or flamboyant head-dress; in his hand was the blood-red flag of Zanzibar, habitually carried on all expeditions in territories claimed by the Sultan. Behind came a drummer or *hortator*. Counterpointing the rhythmic beat of the drum were the raspings of the kudu horn, the tinkling of bells and a melange of animal and bird calls uttered by the porters, who would often break into song or shanty when they were tired of chattering. The pace varied from a low of 2 mph on winding uphill paths to 4 mph on flat ground. Burton made a point of bringing up the rear to chivvy stragglers and prevent desertion.

A short halt at 8 a.m. for a meal was followed by further trekking until midday, when the heat of the ground on bare feet became insupportable. The overnight halt would be either in a village or an improvised camp. In the latter case, the more responsible *wangwana* would erect tents while the rest chopped trees or gathered firewood. While the men smoked cannabis or *bhang* (Indian hemp), the explorers wrote up their journals. Dinner would be at 4 p.m., after which it was time to stack loads and secure the pack animals. If they were in a village, there might be dancing. This was the time when the *wangwana* would sing their most elaborate shanties and ballads, in which they would query the strange motivation of the white-skinned aliens as in the following example:

Solo: *Wasungu kwenda wapi?*
Omnes: *Kwenda kwa Rendili?*
Solo: *Kwani kwenda kwa Rendili?*
Omnes: *Kwa sabaru ya n'gamia. Wasungu wa'ntaka n'gamia. Wasungu wa'nta ka kondo ya mafuta. Huko kwa Rendili n'yama tele-tele.*

Solo: Where are the white men going?
Omnes: They are going to the place of Rendili.
Solo: Why do they go to the place of Rendili?
Omnes: Because of the camels. The white men want camels. The white men want fat-tailed sheep. There in the place of Rendili is very much meat.

The *wangwana* fixed in their minds the places where the caravan halted by reference to local natural features. Thus *mikwajuni* would mean 'near the tamarinds', *mibuyuni* 'near the baobabs', *miwirimi* 'near the medlars', *mtoni* 'near the stream', *massimani* 'near the waterhole' while *malago kanga* meant 'the home of the guinea fowl', *malago tembos* meant 'the elephant camp' and *malago faru* 'the rhino haunt'. These names would be retained even after the local fauna were exterminated.

Altogether the evenings in camp were usually memorable. Speke's companion James Augustus Grant testified: 'Nothing can exceed the noise and jollity of an African camp at night. We the masters were often unable to hear ourselves talk for the merry song and laughter, the rattle of drums, jingling of bells, beating of old iron, and discordant talk going on round our tents. No Hindoo dare be so rude in your hearing, but an African only wonders that you don't enjoy the fun.' But at least, usually around 8 p.m., the men lapsed into exhausted sleep; occasionally the women in the party went on talking later.

It was important to keep different tribal and racial groups apart on the march. On Stanley's Emin Pasha expedition there were frequent armed clashes between the Somalis and Sudanese on one hand and the Zanzibaris on the other. On Speke's 1860–3 expedition he took care to keep four distinct groups well apart. In the van were the Nyamwezi, bearing the cloth and beads; in the centre were ten companies of Zanzibaris under his headman Baraka, carrying miscellaneous goods and equipment; in the rear came a handful of blacks from the Cape, professional soldiers who doubled as cooks; finally came his treasurer Said and the men of Beluchistan, together with twenty goats and a handful of women and stragglers.

Without question the most vexed areas in the relations between the white explorers and the *wangwana* were those of discipline and desertion. Partly this was a question of non-communication between cultures. Africans had little understanding of the moral and legal meanings of a contract; it was simply that which the explorer could enforce. The African social and ideological system had no *economic* view of labour as a factor in production, sold in a market according to the laws of supply and demand. For Africans labour's role was primarily *social*: that of strengthening a kinship group by shared experiences or consolidating a hierarchy for reasons of social system. In general in Africa before the colonial period it would be a fair generalisation to say that economic activity was directed towards social and political ends; the market and the laws of supply and demand were unimportant. Even less entertained were capitalistic ideas of profit, a market price for labour or a value attached to time spent on travelling while trading.

For these and other reasons the cosy Victorian notion of the 'faithful porter' – an extrapolation from the untypical behaviour of Susi and Chuma after Livingstone's death – was a myth. The most successful in their relationships with the *wangwana* were those who combined a genuine sympathy for Africans with natural granite-like qualities of leadership, men who could enter cheerfully into the world of the 'dark companions' while still displaying powerful, dogged will, indomitable courage and keeping the necessary distance to maintain authority. Livingstone, Thomson and Johnston are examples of men who possessed the former attribute but not the latter; Speke and Baker had the latter but not the former. Burton had neither. Of the major explorers, only Stanley, in this as in so many other matters, proved himself the complete African traveller.

Stanley had an uncanny instinct for when to prove his toughness and when to temper justice with mercy. During the nightmare journey through the Ituri forest in 1887 he made a point of going after deserters and bringing them back. He hanged the first two to show he meant business, but then staged an elaborate charade in which he 'allowed himself to be persuaded' by the headmen that he should pardon a third. The cunning of this ploy was that Stanley extracted concessions on behaviour from the headmen and their charges in return for a 'magnanimity' that expediency dictated was anyway the only sensible course.

As for discipline, Stanley flogged and beat his recalcitrant followers with gusto. In 1871 on the journey from Simbawenni to Rehenekko, Stanley recorded laconically: 'The virtue of a good whip was well tested by me on this day . . . and I was compelled to observe that when mud and wet sapped the physical energy of the lazily inclined, a dog-whip became their backs, restoring them to a sound – sometimes to an extravagant – activity.' Stanley would not even allow his porters to stagger away into the jungle to die of smallpox; he insisted that they carried their loads until they dropped dead.

On every African expedition there occurred a mutiny or rebellion. Stanley's way with such outbreaks was characteristically brisk and no-nonsense. One morning in October 1871 he confronted armed insubordination by Mabruki and his brother Asmani, a 6ft 4in. giant. At riflepoint Stanley barked at Asmani to lead his men out on the day's march. Asmani hesitated and seemed about to draw a bead on his white employer. Unblinkingly, Stanley defied him to do his worst. Some instinct told Mabruki that, powerful as he was, his massive brother would come off second-best in a shoot-out with this fearsome white veteran of Shiloh, Abyssinia, Indian wars and Spanish insurrections. He rushed in and knocked his brother's weapon to the ground. Mabruki, knowing how unforgiving Stanley could be, pleaded and begged for forgiveness for Asmani. Stanley concluded 'Solomonically' that the real villain of the piece was his headman Bombay, so flogged him instead. He ripped the shirt from his back and 'I at once proceeded about it with such vigour that Bombay's back will for as long a time bear the traces of the punishment which I administered to him as his front teeth do to that which Speke rightfully bestowed on him some eleven years ago. And here I may as well interpolate by way of parenthesis that I am not at all obliged to Captain Burton for a recommendation of a man who so ill deserved it as Bombay.'

It might be thought that Stanley's routine recourse to brutality would have alienated his black followers. But we have to see his actions in a nineteenth-century context. Africans were used to brutal corporal punishment in a continent where the death penalty was ordained for relatively trivial offences, there were no prisons, and the whole nexus of crime and punishment rested heavily on the use of force. Moreover, brutality was at the time routinely used in Britain itself, not just in the workhouses where Stanley grew up, but in the Armed Services and the public schools. And there must have been many North American Indians who would have preferred a brutal flogging to the genocidal fury heaped on them by General Sheridan and Colonels Custer and Chivington.

Stanley's brutal actions were also counterbalanced in African minds by his leadership qualities, his dogged, triumphal will and his infinite ingenuity and resourcefulness in a crisis. They knew that, however great the peril, if there was one man who could pull them through, it was Stanley, 'the little master'. On the Congo the missionary Bentley noticed how the work-rate of the *wangwana* always improved immeasurably when Stanley was around. They feared him, but they also respected him. Many ex-jailbirds in Zanzibar joined Stanley's service and became dedicated professionals, experts in the art of survival and proud of their membership of an élite corps. On one occasion after a shipwreck off the African coast, the survivors were found huddled on the shore in a pitiable condition.

The only man in a reasonable state of morale and in good mental condition turned out to be a Zanzibari veteran of Stanley's 1874–7 monumental journey. He was found sleeping soundly in the folds of a thick blanket, having learned the hard way how to make the best of things.

Why was Stanley so successful in his relations with the *wangwana* and why did he have such an intuitive understanding of them? This was not a linguistic or cultural matter. Stanley never got inside the idiom of Swahili manners, morals and folkways in the way the outstandingly gifted Burton did. Yet Burton's was the knowledge of the dry, dispassionate scholar. The man himself hated and despised all blacks. But Stanley uniquely understood when to use force and when cajolery in his dealings with his black followers. Those who know the details of Stanley's dreadful early years in a Welsh workhouse may be inclined to speculate that perhaps he was closer to the *wangwana* in temperament and world-view than he cared to admit. The view of life as 'the survival of the fittest' and of nature as 'red in tooth and claw' came naturally to Stanley.

The tenor of Stanley's relations with the *wangwana*, and his intuitive knowledge of how to manipulate them, emerges from an exchange he had with them while recruiting for his 'Through the Dark Continent' epic:

Two or three days after my arrival a deputation of the 'Faithfuls' came to me to learn my intentions and purposes. I informed them that I was about to make a much longer journey into Africa than formerly, and into very different countries from any that I had ever been into before, and I proceeded to sketch out to the astonished men an outline of the prospective journey. They were all seated on the ground before me, tailor fashion, eyes and ears interested, and keen to see and hear every word of my broken Kiswahili. As country after country was mentioned, of which they had hitherto but dimly heard, and river after river, lake after lake named, all of which I hoped, with their aid, to explore carefully and thoroughly, various ejaculations, expressive of emotions of wonder, joy and a little alarm, broke from their lips, but when I concluded each man drew a long breath, and almost simultaneously they uttered, in their own language, 'Ah, fellows, this is a journey worthy to be called a journey!'

'But, master,' said they with some anxiety, 'this long journey will take years to travel – six, nine or ten years.'

'Nonsense,' said I. 'Six, nine or ten years! What can you be thinking of? It takes the Arabs nearly three years to go to Ujiji, it is true, but I was only sixteen months from Zanzibar to Ujiji and back to the sea. Is it not true?'

'Ay, true,' answered they.

'Very well. And I tell you, further, that there is not enough money in this world to pay me for stopping in Africa ten, nine, or six years. I have not come here to live in Africa. I have come here simply to see these rivers and lakes, and after I have seen them to return home.'

'Ah, but you know the big master (Livingstone) said he was only going for two years, and you know that he was altogether nine years.'

'That is true enough. Nevertheless, you know what I did before, and what I am likely to do again, if all goes well.'

'Yes, we remember that you are very hot, and you did drive us until our feet were sore and we were ready to drop from fatigue. Wallah! but there never was such a journey as that from Unyanyembe home! No Arab or white man came from Unyanyembe in so short a time as you did. It was nothing but throw away this thing and that, and go on, go on, go on, all the time. Aye, master, that is true.'

'Well, is it likely, then, when I marched so quick before that I am likely to be slow now? Am I much older now than I was then? Am I less strong? Do I not know what a journey is now? When I first started from Zanzibar to Ujiji I allowed the guide to show me the way; but when we came back who showed you the way? Was it not I, by means of that little compass which could not lie like the guide?'

'Aye, true, master; true, every word.'

'Very well, then, finish these foolish words of yours and go and get me 300 good men like yourselves, and when we get away from Bagamoyo I will show you whether I have forgotten to travel.'

'Ay, Wallah, my master;' and, in the words of the Old Testament, they forthwith arose, and went as they were commanded.

Stanley's judicious oscillation between diplomacy and brutality, which allowed him to play on the *wangwana* as a great conductor plays on an orchestra, was one of the things that made him the greatest of all African explorers. He was not as great a man of Africa as Livingstone, for Livingstone was fuelled by optimism, idealism and a genuine altruistic Christian vision of a liberated Africa, where Stanley was powered by pessimism, cynicism and a sense of original sin and Old Testament doom; his many references to Christianity were largely self-serving humbug. But it has to be conceded that Livingstone was nowhere near as good a handler of the 'dark companions'. This is a truth that has been obscured by the Susi/Chuma journey across Africa with 'Dr David's' body, which in many ways was the exception that proved the rule. The recent researches of Dorothy Helly into the sections excised by Horace Waller from Livingstone's last journals provide the sober truth about Livingstone and the *wangwana*, and a gloomy truth it proves to be.

Livingstone was far less able to retain 'faithful followers' than his legend suggests. He often flogged disobedient or impudent porters. But because this did not square with the image of the 'saintly' Dr Livingstone, his editor Waller cut out all references in his edition of the *Last Journals*. Livingstone often broke his word to his *askaris* and *pagazis* In 1866 he explicitly promised his Indian marines in Bombay that their luggage would be carried for them. Once his donkeys had been killed off – either by the tsetse fly or the incompetence of the sepoys – Livingstone angrily went back on his promise and insisted that to draw pay they must act as porters. The result was mutiny and a death threat to Livingstone – both of which were suppressed in Waller's edition.

Moreover, within a few months of his sepoys' departure, Livingstone's Comoran porters left him as well. The ensuing years saw little change. Waller was obliged to suppress further passages which showed Living-stone flogging his porters, docking their pay and threatening to shoot them, as well as those in which Livingstone accused the *wangwana* of being as bad as Arabs in that they took African women as slaves.

Harry Johnston was another who very quickly learned what it was like to be on the sharp end of Zanzibari intransigence. On his very first day's march from Mombasa to Kilimanjaro in 1884, his men refused to go the planned 30 miles:

> Now was the crisis in which my authority was to be asserted or for ever to be subordinated to the men's caprices. The Zanzibaris were waiting to see how I would act, and would gauge my disposition by the way in which I met my first difficulties . . . I called on one man to pick up his burden and take the road. He promptly and curtly refused, and as quickly my Indian servant had him by the heels, whilst I soundly trounced him with his own walking stick . . . Whilst the recalcitrant porter was still screaming abjectly for pardon, and I was still gravely counting the strokes of the wand – eight! nine! ten! eleven! – the other men had hoisted their loads on their bullet heads, and were falling into line along the narrow path, leaving my servant and myself alone with the victim of our wrath.

Joseph Thomson's experience was instructive. With youthful idealism he resolved to establish an equal relationship with his men, to take the porters into his confidence and to replace floggings with fines. Such a failure to exert authoritarian leadership confused and bewildered the *wangwana*. Chuma, one of the heroes of the epic trek that brought Livingstone's body back to the coast, but more usually an uneasy ally of white explorers, determined to test Thomson's mettle. No more than a couple of days into his first expedition, to Lake Tanganyika, Thomson asked Chuma casually where he had got the load of beads he was carrying. Chuma at once ran off and told his comrades that Thomson had accused his porters of stealing. There followed the sounding of conches and the blowing of kudu horns. Into the camp the *wangwana* came storming, and asked for their discharge papers. Thomson protested that he had not actually accused anyone of stealing. There was a sullen silence. He then tried another tack. He claimed to be a mere boy (he was in fact only twenty-one) and put it to them that they should act as fathers to him and not rush off to the coast the moment he put a foot wrong. This harangue had an immediate effect, the *wangwana* put on a dance of universal goodwill, and all was smoothed over.

But even worse trouble occurred when Thomson tried to replace floggings with his new 'liberal' regime of fines. The *wangwana* could endure corporal punishment; what was completely unacceptable was the prospect of a penniless return to Zanzibar. The moment of truth came one morning when Thomson gave the order to march and nobody moved. He jumped up and swung his empty vulcanite hot waterbottle at anyone he could reach. His followers dispersed, preparatory to a march back to the coast. Furious, Thomson yelled that he would fine them all.

After a day's standoff, the porters came to him in the evening to say they would not desert if Thomson remitted the fine. In dudgeon he refused. Next morning, as good as their word, his men packed and departed. In despair Thomson sent Chuma after them to remonstrate. Realising that they now had the white man on the ropes, the porters ignored his pleas. Thomson was reduced to running after them and giving a solemn promise that he would never fine them again, no matter what transpired. The *wangwana* returned in triumph to the camp. After that Thomson did not spare the whip. On his second expedition, through Masailand, he flogged vigorously from the outset and justified his action to his tender-minded readers by asserting that such 'proofs of toughness' reduced the necessity for harshness later on.

Yet undoubtedly the explorers who enjoyed the worst relations with their followers were those who hated and despised Africans. Here the two obvious figures are Burton and Baker. Burton conducted a running feud with his men; one of the reasons he allowed Speke to make the side trip to Lake Victoria from Tabora, which led to all the later conflict about the sources of the Nile, was that he preferred the company of the Arabs in Unyanyembe to the task of flogging recalcitrant porters. And Burton set back the cause of African exploration by refusing to pay his men at the end of the journey. But Burton considered himself justified in withholding payment whenever anyone or any group annoyed him; he repeated the gesture of refusing to pay porters in Brazil, on a trip to the Paulo Affonso Falls.

Baker, who loathed Africans without having Burton's compensatory skills as linguist and anthropologist – which at least enabled him to understand what he hated – fared even worse with his men. At Gondokoro in 1862 discontent among his porters built up to crisis. They came to him with a complaint that they did not have enough meat and must therefore be allowed to raid the local villages. When Baker refused this request, his men dispersed, muttering sullenly. Next morning Baker got them fell in and delivered a pep talk, but they continued to be insolent. Baker then identified the leader as an Arab called Eesur and prescribed him twenty-five lashes. But when his personal bodyguard advanced to seize Eesur, a general mutiny erupted. Forty men rushed on the praetorians with sticks while Eesur hurled himself at Baker. The massively built Baker knocked his assailant back into the crowd, then seized him by the throat and called to his servant Saati to fetch a rope. An angry crowd surged around Baker. Things looked very ugly. Suddenly Baker's wife, still ill with fever, rushed out from the boat tethered on the Nile, where she had been recuperating. Her unexpected appearance had a calming effect. Taking advantage of the fractional indecision of the men, Baker called to the drummer to beat 'fall in'. It was just the right psychological moment. Two-thirds fell in; the rest stayed with Eesur.

Baker now insisted that Eesur be brought forward. With a wonderful sense of drama, Mrs Baker then began to plead for forgiveness for the ringleader, if he would just kiss Baker's hand and ask pardon. This was quickly done, for both Baker and the mutineers wished to get themselves out of the impasse into which they had backed.

Later, at Latooka, there was yet another mutiny when the men refused to load the camels. This time the ringleader was a man called Bellaal, who faced Baker with a loaded gun, but made the mistake of getting too close to him. 'The Beard' lashed out with a right hook and laid Bellaal out. He then bellowed out a repeat order to load the camels and waded in among the mutineers, hitting and clubbing them. Cowed and with sore heads, his men reluctantly loaded the camels. But Baker's tough action led to significant desertion. Some of the Latooka deserters were sheltered by an Arab named Muhammad Her. Eighteen months later in Khartoum Baker ran across Her, brought charges against him of incitement to mutiny and harbouring deserters, and secured conviction. On conviction he browbeat the Egyptian authorities into flogging Muhammad Her. There is something sadistic in the way Baker describes his gloating presence while Her received 150 lashes across his back.

Fully to enter the world of the *wangwana* is impossible at this distance, especially since we lack significant oral data from the porters themselves. Reconstructing individual Africans in a period dominated by European sources is difficult even in the case of the major African rulers (Mutesa, Lobengula, Mzilikazi, Kabbarega); Mirambo has, however, been the subject of a significant biography. Perhaps the only non-European in nineteenth-century Africa for whom we possess adequate source material (including his own autobiography) is Tippu Tip. Yet some kind of picture can be formed of the most important *wangwana* 'dark companions' by collating the various explorers' accounts. Such a method yields significant data in three cases; those of Bombay, Susi and Chuma.

Bombay, a Yao from the Lake Nyasa region, first swam into the explorers' ken in 1856, at the beginning of the Burton and Speke expedition. At the age of twelve he was seized by a raiding party of Swahilis as compensation for the unpaid debts of his village. From Kilwa he was shipped to Zanzibar, where he became the property of an Arab merchant who took him to Bombay. It was from that city that Sidi Mubarak took the name by which he was always known thereafter. Freed from servitude by his master's death, he returned to Zanzibar and enlisted as a soldier.

Bombay accompanied Burton and Speke on their reconnaissance trip to Mombasa and environs in January 1857, before they set out for the interior proper. He very soon won over Speke by making a 30-mile round-trip detour to retrieve Speke's mislaid surveying compass. He spoke a few words of English picked up in India, but had fluent Hindustani. Speke, surely the worst linguist ever to venture into the Dark Continent, had a smattering of Hindustani, so he used Bombay as a conversationalist to relieve the feelings of boredom and inadequacy he experienced when Burton jabbered away at machine-gun pace to the Arabs. As Livingstone, who despised Speke, later commented, 'He lifted Speke out of the disagreeable position of being a silent onlooker in all Burton's conversations. Speke naturally felt very grateful to him. Before getting him Speke sat on his bottom only.' Bombay gave Speke details of his early life and told amusing tales about the exotic birds and animals they encountered. He seemed indefatigable, as fresh and light-hearted at the end of a long march as at the beginning. His fluent Hindustani also, albeit temporarily, made an impression on Burton, who hailed him as 'the gem of the party' and contrasted him with the usual contemptible 'jungly nigger'. Certainly Bombay seemed a cut above the other headman Mabruki, whom Speke thought a sulky, dogged, pudding- headed brute, at once very ugly and very vain, with a crafty habit of maintaining a respectful appearance to cloak his impertinent manner.

Mabruki also fell foul of Burton. Sullen and morose, he wore out Burton's donkey by dragging it carelessly over rough ground. Burton had a higher opinion of Bombay, even though he thought his performance deteriorated during the expedition. Burton's judgement was that although Bombay did nothing well, he rarely did anything badly, doubtless having in mind the time Bombay and Mabruki manhauled the violently sick Speke in an improvised sledge (and sometimes carried him in a hammock) when the other porters had refused to help. The one black mark against Bombay, in Burton's book, was that he exacerbated the tension between the two explorers after Speke's return from Lake Victoria, when Burton categorically refused to accept that his companion had discovered the source of the Nile. 'Bombay, after misunderstanding his master's ill-expressed Hindustani, probably translated the words into Kiswahili to some travelled African, who in turn passed on the question in a wilder dialect to the barbarian or barbarians under examination. During such a journey to and fro words must be liable to severe accidents.'

But on Speke's second (1860–3) expedition, Bombay lost caste in his master's eyes. On this journey he had a more serious rival than Mabruki, in the form of Baraka. Baraka considered himself a cut above Bombay. He had served with the Royal Navy at the taking of Multan in 1849, and later outranked Bombay in Consul Atkins Hamerton's boat crew in Zanzibar. He therefore deeply resented being on the same footing as Bombay as a mere headman, and despised Speke's caravan leader, Said. The result was continual quarrelling. To appease Baraka, Speke took him aside and explained Indian 'dyarchy': Bombay might be commander-in-chief but Baraka was governor-general. It is not recorded how Speke managed to retain this fiction at Tabora, when he sacked Said and appointed Bombay as caravan leader. Nor is this appointment compatible with Speke's judgement that 'Bombay with all his honesty and kind fellow feeling has not half the power of command that Baraka possesses.' But perhaps the reason for Speke's volte-face is that Baraka, pessimistic, blunt and tactless, told Speke the facts as they were, while Bombay told his master what he thought he wanted to hear. At Tabora it looked as though the war between the Arabs and the Nyamwezi might delay the expedition's northward progress, much as it actually did impair Stanley's progress in 1871. Baraka expressed his apprehensions, while Bombay uttered the optimistic sentiments Speke liked to hear: 'A man has but one life and God is the director of everything.' Speke instinctively sided with Bombay when he heard the two opinions and poured scorn on Baraka's timidity: 'Bombay would never be frightened in this silly way.'

At Usui in October 1861 the Bombay/Baraka rivalry reached its climax. Bombay complained bitterly that his authority was being eroded by a whispering campaign among the *wangwana* initiated by Baraka's glib tongue. But Baraka soon proved himself no Iago. He told Speke that Bombay had obtained a concubine with wire stolen from the caravan's general store. An examination of the stores showed that Bombay was in the clear, and his story – that he bought the woman with a 'kickback' from a chief with whom he had arranged *hongo* – was true.

Speke's attempts to reconcile the warring duo were vain. At Rumanika's in Karagwe in 1861 Baraka further lost caste by provoking a fight and beating up a woman. Seizing the moment, Bombay warned Speke that although the majority of the men were loyal to the white man, there was a disloyal faction headed by Baraka. In December Baraka hit back by accusing Bombay of trying to kill him by magic. In despair at finding a resolution, Speke despatched Baraka to find the explorer Petherick, who was supposed to be linking up with him at Gondokoro.

But no sooner was his rival out of the picture than Bombay himself fell foul of Speke. On the journey to Buganda Bombay refused to strike camp on the grounds that there was no adequate guide for the road ahead. At this Speke flew into a rage, and punched Bombay three times in the mouth, knocking his teeth out. Bombay stormed off but was reinstated after his replacement Nasib, an old man, advised Speke to compose his differences with the fractious Yao. Bombay expunged his conduct by some skilful interpreting at the court of Mutesa. But in Bunyoro Speke's evil genius returned to plague him. Unable to proceed through Kamurasi's territories to find Petherick, Baraka returned and at once whipped up a mutiny. Desertion would have been wholesale had not Bombay and Mabruki held firm for Speke's cause. In recognition of this service, Speke put in a glowing report on Bombay; the Royal Geographical Society responded in 1864 by awarding him a silver medal – the first of the 'dark companions' to be so honoured. It seems that Speke's praise rebounded somewhat, for in February 1864 we find Speke writing from England to Zanzibar that he was 'extremely sorry to hear that Bombay's head had been turned by his elevation. On the journey I had often occasion to wig him for getting drunk, but always made it up again, as he was the life and success of the expedition.'

As already recounted, Bombay served with Stanley on the 1871–2 expedition to find Livingstone, but did not impress the 'little master'. On one occasion Bombay was reduced to the ranks for failing to get stragglers into camp before midnight. He lost his nerve at Tabora when it looked as though Mirambo would attack Stanley's *tembe*. While exploring the Rusizi river with Livingstone in December 1871, Stanley put Bombay in charge of a canoe containing 500 rounds of cartridges, ninety musket bullets, the expedition's sounding line, a bag of flour and all Livingstone's sugar. A local chief gulled Bombay and his opposite number in Livingstone's party, Susi, by sending them a 3-gallon jar of local mead. The two got riotously drunk and collapsed comatose. The locals absconded with the goods. As Stanley angrily recorded: 'It was only the natural cowardice of ignorant thieves that prevented the savages from taking the boat ... together with Bombay and Susi as slaves.'

A number of severe beatings from Stanley seemed to make no impression on Bombay. Stanley complained bitterly to Livingstone about the 'incorrigible' Yao. Bombay, for his part, was profoundly afraid of Stanley, as he had never been of Speke. The two parted on the worst of terms. Stanley spoke of him with contempt at the discharge ceremony:

'Stupid Bombay, though he had more than once expressed his scorn of dirty money, was glad to take a present of 50 dollars besides his pay.'

When Stanley returned to Africa in 1874 he re-engaged most of his old 'faithfuls' but was spared the necessity of snubbing his old enemy, since Bombay had already departed for the interior with Verney Cameron. Cameron considered that Bombay had lost much of the energy he was said to have displayed on previous expeditions and was inclined to trade on his reputation. Possessing little natural authority, he always preferred to take the line of least resistance. He drank too much, lacked drive, and got muddled over routes and *hongo* negotiations. At Tabora Cameron asked Bombay to inform the rest of the *wangwana* that if they did not obey their orders, they would be dismissed. Bombay translated this by telling the men to decamp immediately. At Ujiji Bombay failed to guard the stores and there was much pilfering. His one talent seemed to be the ability to build a serviceable hut.

Yet, like Speke, Cameron could never quite make up his mind about Bombay. On Lake Tanganyika he oscillated between two different perceptions: on the one hand, Bombay seemed the only one interested in the expedition; on the other, he seemed unable to give proper orders to the men, and everyone knew that a headman without authority was worse than useless. Cameron's final judgement was 'Neither the "Angel" of Colonel Grant nor the "Devil" of Mr Stanley.' Yet Bombay was the occasion of some humorous sallies from Cameron. At journey's end Bombay told him that Speke's and Stanley's *wangwana* had been of far higher calibre. 'I hope so, for the sake of the African races,' Cameron replied caustically.

Bombay died, at an advanced age for an African of that era, in 1886. Two years earlier his great rival Baraka, who had served with Stanley on the 1874–7 expedition, died on service in the Congo, where he had followed Stanley.

Susi and Chuma, the Castor and Pollux of the *wangwana* luminaries, are the two most famous of the 'dark companions', as a result of their epic walk across Africa in 1873 with Livingstone's body. Their finest hour was in many ways a surprise, for they had by no means enjoyed uniformly good relations with their Scottish employer.

Chuma, like Bombay a Yao, was, like him, taken as a slave in childhood and sold to Portuguese slave traders. Later he was educated at Bishop Mackenzie's mission school and became the Revd Henry Rowley's servant. In this capacity Chuma urged on Rowley the delights of whole-fried rats. In 1864 Chuma went to India and for a year was at the mission school of Sharanpur, 100 miles north-east of Bombay. This was where

Livingstone found him, was impressed, and took him on as his personal servant. Livingstone's early estimate of Chuma made him out to be an ingénue.

Baptised on 10 December 1865 as James Chuma, Livingstone's Yao servant at first gave satisfaction. But by August the next year, a note of exasperation is beginning to creep into Livingstone's journals:

> Chuma and Wekotani are very good boys but still boys utterly . . . I had them about me personally till I was reduced to the last fork and spoon . . . They showed an inveterate tendency to lose my things and preserve their own. If I did not shout for breakfast I got it sometime between eleven and two o'clock. I had to relieve them of all charge of my domestic affairs.

The pattern of Livingstone's relations with Chuma shows an oscillation between sympathetic forgiveness and exasperation. Livingstone thought that as a boisterous, laughing, modest, studious boy Chuma had the most character and was likely to be the most influential of all the freedmen. He forgave him when he heard him boasting to the other *wangwana* about having stolen, lied to and otherwise bamboozled the missionaries in India: 'It is just what boys will do. If I had the means of educating him I would prefer him to all the others.'

Yet Chuma was scarcely the angel Livingstone portrays. Even his patron noted that he was simply too lazy to keep a woman, and that he hoarded meal when food was short. Livingstone caught him red-handed while baking himself cakes from the meal over hot coals and rebuked him sternly. Chuma 'blushed if a black man can blush'.

Chuma was one of those who took part in the great mutiny of 13 April 1868 when Livingstone's men refused to go on. Chuma revealed his dark side by telling his master that, in addition to the fear of penetrating the lands of Cazembe which all the men shared, he himself also had a particular grudge dating from an incident in Bombay in 1865 when the good doctor docked his pay.

The third reason Chuma advanced for refusing to go farther was the most interesting. He said he could not leave Susi. Susi was a Zanzibari who entered Livingstone's service on the Zambezi in 1861, accompanied Livingstone to India in 1864 and re-enlisted in his service when the doctor returned to Africa in 1866. Susi first comes dramatically alive in Livingstone's narrative on the fateful day of 13 April 1868 when the explorer decided to leave the Arabs' protective shield and strike alone across the dangerous country south of Lake Mweru. This precipitated a general revolt, in which Susi was one of the ringleaders; he told Livingstone he had no intention of risking his life needlessly when he had all the comforts of home and a woman who fed him. Livingstone, in a passage later suppressed by Horace Waller, who wished to conceal the fact that the doctor's relations with Susi and Chuma were at times as bad as those with his other Africans, exploded:

Susi for no confessed reason but he has got a black women who feeds him, Chuma for the same reason . . . came with their eyes shot out by *bange* [sic] . . . He could not leave Susi . . . and Abraham had brought up some old grievance as a justification for his absconding. James (Chuma) said . . . he was tired of working. Abraham apologised and was forgiven. Susi stood like a mule. I put my hand on his arm . . . he seized my hand and refused to let it go. When he did I fired a pistol at him, but missed. There being no law or magistrate higher than myself, I would not be thwarted if I could help it. The fact is, they are all tired . . . They would like me to remain here and pay them for smoking the *bange* and deck their prostitutes with the beads which I give regularly for their food.

From April to November 1868 Susi and Chuma were out of Livingstone's service. When he returned to Kabwabata on 1 November, he received a deputation from his men asking to be reinstated. But Livingstone's anger with the 'ingrates' had not yet run its course:

I resolved to reinstate two. I reject the thief Susi for he is quite inveterate, and Chuma who ran away 'to be with Susi' and I who rescued him from slavery, and had been at the expense of feeding and clothing him for years was nobody in his eyes. *Bange* [sic] and black women overcame him, and I feel no inclination to be at further expense and trouble for him.

Yet shortly afterwards he relented. On 13 November he wrote:

I have taken all the runaways back again – after trying the independent life they will behave better. Much of their ill conduct may be ascribed to seeing that after the fight of the Johanna men I was entirely dependent on them – more enlightened people often take advantage of men in similar circumstances, though I have seen pure Africans come out generously to aid one abandoned to their care. Have faults myself.

He later told Stanley that Susi and Chuma had turned over a new leaf and completely rehabilitated themselves. Crossing the river Lofunso on 22 December 1869 Susi proved himself a hero by saving two Zanzibaris from drowning. Also, at this stage Livingstone was prepared to overlook peccadilloes in his two favourites since he had a genuine bad apple in his barrel in the shape of one Simon Price. Murderer, thief and incorrigible liar, Price hated Livingstone and managed to shoot dead two of the local Africans who had befriended the doctor.

Susi and Chuma justified Livingstone's faith in them by their amazing decision to take his body to the coast after his death at Ilala in May 1873. Susi and Chuma could easily have buried him at Chitambo's and then taken employment with an Arab caravan. Instead they took out Livingstone's heart and internal organs, buried them, then embalmed his body and made it ready for the long trek to the Indian Ocean. First they returned to Lake Tanganyika, beset all the way by wild animals and hostile tribesmen. At Tabora they met Verney Cameron, who again provided them with the perfect excuse to relinquish their burden; he warned them of trouble ahead in Ugogo and advised them to bury the body right there in Unyanyembe. Susi and Chuma demurred and pressed on. Nine months after starting from Ilala, in February 1874, they reached the coast, having travelled 1400 miles. In recognition of their outstanding feat Susi and Chuma were taken to England at the expense of Livingstone's friends. They helped Horace Waller in his edition of the *Last Journals*, the heavily edited and doctored work which made Livingstone *the* Victorian hero and inspiration. It was noticed that Chuma, though more intelligent, deferred to the older, taller Susi. Their visit to England was also the occasion of a public disagreement between Stanley and Horace Waller, who detested each other on quite different grounds. Waller had singled out Chuma for praise, but Stanley wrote to *The Times* to assure the world that Livingstone's real favourite was Susi.

At the end of 1874 Susi and Chuma returned to Zanzibar and worked for nearly five years as guides to the missionaries who wished to establish stations in East Africa. But early in 1879 Susi was discharged ignominiously. He was then rejected for employment by Joseph Thomson, who found him destitute through drink and debauchery. Despite Susi's fervent pleas, Thomson refused to take him with him to the Central African lakes, on the grounds that he would be a bad influence on Chuma (whom he had already signed on) and would refuse to take orders from him. 'He was, perhaps, even a more able man than Chuma in some respects, and but for his prominent failing, he might have been at least equally successful.' Susi was rescued from this anathema into which he had been cast by Stanley, who arrived in Zanzibar in 1879 to recruit porters for his mission to open up the Congo for King Leopold. Susi was present at the founding of the Belgian stations of Vivi, Isangila, Manyanga, Leopoldville and Mswata.

Chuma meanwhile accompanied Thomson to the lakes. Thomson left an extended description of him:

Among the guild of Zanzibar porters there is certainly none to equal Chuma as a caravan leader, especially for white men. His long experience under

Livingstone as an interpreter of the geographical questions so necessary to be asked, gave him a very fair notion regarding these things, so that he is able at once to pick up a European's meaning when an ordinary native would only look at him in blank perplexity. He is well acquainted with English, and about a dozen native dialects . . . Full of anecdote, and fun, and jollity, he was an immense favourite with the men, and yet he preserved such an authority over them that no one presumed to disobey his orders. If any one was rash enough to do so, woe betide the offender! Chuma went straight at him; and though not tall or muscular himself, he speedily humbled the strongest . . . His off-hand statements required to be accepted with judicious reserve. Lies came natural to him, not indeed from any premeditated purpose, or from desire of gaining profit or pleasure to himself, but simply because they seemed to be always nearer his tongue than the truth. Yet it was almost impossible to catch him tripping – a fact which often made matters extremely exasperating when we knew that, however plausible his story, it was untrue. Chuma was also extremely fond of acting the big man, and right well he could do it. To keep up his dignity he deemed it necessary to be somewhat lavish in his expenditure, so that we required to be continually on the look-out, and to keep a firm hand upon him to check his extravagance.

Thomson was amused to hear himself described, in Liendwe in April 1880, as 'Chuma's white man'. There were many translation problems on the expedition, but Thomson realised that no blame attached to Chuma. Among the Henge, Thomson's words had to be translated into Swahili, another interpreter then repeated them in the local tongue to the chief's son, and the son then relayed the message to the chief. The whole process then went on in reverse. The only fault Thomson could find with Chuma was that he had bought the favours of Liendwe damsels with bales of the finest cloth.

Yet Chuma's trip with Thomson proved to be his last hurrah. When Susi returned to Zanzibar from the Congo in 1882, he found his old friend dying of tuberculosis. Chuma made a will, dated 25 September 1882, in which he distributed his meagre possessions to his wife and friends. Shortly afterwards he died, still in his thirties. Susi then became active with the Universities Mission to Central Africa and led monthly caravans on their behalf to upcountry stations, especially in Nyasaland and the Shire. Susi died on 5 May 1891 after a long illness involving creeping paralysis.

Arguably, however, neither he nor Chuma (and still less Bombay) was the greatest of the black assistants to the African explorers. That honour probably belongs to Dualla Idris, the mainstay of Frederick Lugard's expeditions. He knew English, Arabic, Somali, Swahili, Masai and other tongues. Lugard liked to talk to him over tea or coffee and sound his opinion on a host of matters. Indeed, Lugard wanted to put him in an

administrative post in Buganda, but illness forced Dualla to accompany
Lugard back to the east coast in summer 1892.

By common consent, without help from Africans there would have
been no significant exploration of Africa by Europeans. The judgement of
a recent scholar on the first crossing of Africa underscores the point:

> Livingstone's great march to the west was as much an African as a European
> venture . . . largely managed by two Kololo . . . and . . . equipped by Sekeletu
> with cattle, as gifts for chiefs, and ivory for sale to the Portuguese.

It was altogether appropriate that the first dramatic demonstration of
this collaboration should have been on a Livingstone exploration, for the
great Scotsman spoke as follows on relations between the races:

> Genuine sympathy with human beings obliterates the distinction of race and
> clime, rank and religion, and even of intellect. It is evidence of brutal vulgarity
> of mind to treat all natives as 'niggers'. Avoid this unhappy form of slang and
> without falling into unreal sentiment endeavour to return to that chivalry
> which regards with especial forbearance and consideration the inferior and
> the helpless.

In opening up the Dark Continent the *wangwana* played a crucial role.
Their great merit was their adaptability. They had a happy knack of
picking up languages, and could turn their hands to needlework, tree-
felling, canoeing or fighting, though by and large they were poor shots.
They were inadequate as cooks, knew little of hygiene and became
seriously demoralised when ill. Yet they elicited a plethora of compli-
ments from their European masters. Mounteney-Jephson, Stanley's
right-hand man on the Emin Pasha expedition said:

> The Zanzibaris are thieves and liars but they are hard-working and have that
> joyousness and childlike simplicity which redeems their bad qualities and one
> is forced to like them, though one swears at them often . . . a noisy, rollicking
> lot, excellent fellows.

A similar opinion was recorded by Thomson:

> I cannot express, in too appreciative terms, the honesty and faithfulness which
> characterized my men, and the really genuine character which lies at the
> bottom of their semi-savage nature . . . The Zanzibar porter is infinitely better
> than he has been usually represented . . . we hear frequently about their
> troublesome conduct, desertions, obstinacy, etc. But we are never told how
> much they have to bear from their masters.

We may leave the last word to Harry Johnston, imperialist, man of the Right, light years away from a *bien-pensant*:

As a rule the Zanzibar porters are faithful, trustworthy men – I have always found them so, and have even discovered very fine qualities in their nature too. At any rate, if they fall out with a white man it is generally his fault; a very little discipline, together with a kind and quiet manner, will always keep them in order.

8

Guns and Ivory

The conquest of Africa by European nations, whose witting or unwitting vanguard the explorers were, was made possible by two nineteenth-century developments. The first was when man began to get the upper hand in the fight against tropical disease. The second was when Europe began to deploy its massive technological superiority. In the era of the explorers that technological superiority meant one thing above all: the awesome power of the gun. As Stanley's *wangwana* expressed it so graphically: '*Bunduki sultani ya bara bara*' ('The gun is the Sultan of Africa.') It is of the utmost significance that the missionary Robert Moffat, Livingstone's father-in-law, owed his prestige among the Matabele to two factors: his medical skill and his willingness to mend the Matabele guns.

The nineteenth century witnessed a spectacular advance in the technological development of mankind. At the time of Waterloo armies fought with muzzle-loading muskets, navies were still at the mercy of the winds, kings and queens travelled in stagecoaches, while the mounted courier was yet the most rapid means of communication. Fifty years later a cable had been laid under the oceans around the world, men communicated by telegraph, travelled in steamships through fantastic man-made canals and hurtled across continents on railways. Nowhere was this technological breakthrough more dramatically evinced than in the realm of firearms.

In the era of the explorers the technological revolution largely passed Africa by. Railways began on a small scale at the Cape in 1859–64 but it was not until 1867, with the discovery of the Griqualand West diamond deposits, that there was full-scale railway building in South Africa. Elsewhere in Africa railways did not make a dent in human porterage until well after the last recess of the Dark Continent had been thoroughly explored. The impact of technology on Africa and its exploration was indirect. The steamship made the continent more accessible, since there was no longer any need to make the westerly detour in the Atlantic from Europe to the coast of South America to pick up the prevailing winds. But, within a generation of the opening up of the London–Cape direct steamship line, distances between Europe and Africa were cut still further by the opening of the Suez Canal (1869). The preferred route to Africa for explorers now went through the canal to Zanzibar.

The technological revolution made its indirect impact in other ways. The widespread use of quinine removed the 'mosquito barrier' to the interior. The rapid expansion of Western industry under the impetus of power-driven machinery created a demand for tropical products. Above all, technology engendered in the explorers a feeling of cultural confidence, of effortless superiority to the benighted savage. The social control implicit in bureaucracy, the quantification of space and time and of productive capacity into 'labour-time', the understanding of scientific laws and the principle of causality all gave Europeans an enormous advantage over the African. Capitalism itself was a Frankenstein's monster of astonishing power. As Marx pointed out in the *Communist Manifesto*, the bourgeoisie 'had been the first to show what man's activity can bring about. It has accomplished wonders far surpassing Egyptian pyramids, Roman aqueducts and Gothic cathedrals; it has conducted expeditions that put in the shade all former Exoduses of nations and crusades.'

However, the dreams of Livingstone and others that, dazzled by European techniques and know-how, the heathen would convert *en masse* to the God that made such superiority possible, remained just that: dreams. Visionary projects to transform the East African lakes into a kind of Mediterranean for steamers, to create inland seas in Tunisia, or to send trains hurtling across Africa at 100 mph on a transcontinental line, came to nothing.

In its direct manifestations, European technological superiority in Africa meant its firepower. The point is a relative one. Europe as a whole never waged war on Africa as a whole; in such a conflict, where one side was unable to produce machine-guns or bombs, there could have been only one outcome. European engagement in Africa was partial only. Only a tiny proportion of Europe's strength was deployed in Africa even at the height of the colonial era; for colonialism to have survived at all was a sign of the fissiparous tendencies innate in African tribalism and the skill of the imperial powers in dividing and ruling. The supremacy of the colonial powers rested on credibility – the idea that behind its tiny handful of administrators, commissioners and missionaries was a military behemoth that one called forth at one's peril. This was why a serious military defeat, such as that inflicted by the Zulus at Isandhlwana in 1879, obliged the

British to mobilise such force as was necessary to defeat Cetewayo, even though the empire at that time held no significant interests in that part of Africa. The defeat of Cetewayo at Ulundi was necessary for the sake of *prestige*. The only true military success gained by Africans against Europeans in the colonial era (Adowa, 1896) was, significantly, achieved by the strongest African ruler, Menilek II of Ethiopia, against the weakest European nation, Italy.

It is only a slight exaggeration to say that what Africans admired most about the explorers was their firepower. We have already seen what Stanley and Baker were able to achieve against vastly superior armies by use of Sniders and other repeaters. In theory it was open to African tribes to import their own guns, but the almost geometrical progression made in weapons technology in the nineteenth century meant that the Africans were always at least a generation behind in the weapons they could lay hands on.

The high summer of the era of the explorers (1870–90) saw the most dramatic progress in armaments technology in history. Breech-loading rifles first came into general use during the American Civil War. The switch from muzzle-loading rifles to breech-loaders – the key to Prussian victory over the Austrians at Sadowa in 1866 – widened the military gap between Europe (and America) and the rest of the world. Flintlock muskets and percussion guns – the only ones then in the possession of Africans – became obsolete overnight. The results were dramatic and instant. Where the British had fought two unsuccessful wars to humble the might of the Ashanti in West Africa, they were able to achieve complete military victory in Wolseley's 1873–4 campaign. The turbulent Indian frontier was closed both in the American West and in Argentina. Maoris, Zulus, Afghans, Ethiopians, all were 'brought to heel'. The breech-loading rifles most involved in this world-wide pacification were the French Chassepot (first used extensively in the Franco-Prussian war), the American Martini-Henry and the Peabody-Martinis and the Sniders used to such devastating effect by Stanley in 1874–7. All these used metallic cartridge cases and steel barrels instead of iron as in the older weapons, and could be quickly reloaded from a prone position.

But the breech-loader was scarcely perfected when the first repeating or magazine rifle was introduced. The first, the Winchester, was used by the Turks in the war against Russia in 1877–8. Then came the Mauser (1884), the Mannlicher (1885), the Lee-Metford (1888) and the French Leber. In all these small-bore magazine rifles the use of smokeless powder became the norm. The discarded breech-loaders then entered Africa in large numbers, with the Europeans able to maintain the technological gap. The collision between Europe and Africa came at a time when European self-confidence, based on the wonders of science, was at a peak, and African social conditions were at their worst.

African chiefs, eager to extend their territory, clamoured for the new weapons. They bought them in large numbers, trading ivory, timber, gum, palm oil, hides, beeswax and gold in return. During Johnston's Kilimanjaro expedition, the chief of Maranu asked him for thirty barrels of gunpowder, 100 Sniders with cartridges and 100 muzzle-loaders. The entry of modern firearms into the continent exacerbated Africa's social problems. The pre-existing structural instability of Bantu tribalism, with raiding, looting and tribal war a way of life, and a world-view that exalted power over all attributes and held human life cheap, were all part of an essential indiscipline likely to be made worse when the rifle arrived. The endemic tribal wars multiplied. Never was a prophet more mistaken than when Livingstone pronounced: 'The universal effect of the more potent instruments of warfare in Africa is the same as among ourselves. Firearms render wars less frequent and less bloody.'

Guns also broke up the African social system in more subtle ways. Since their possession was the key to real power, traditional modes of authority, based on kinship and the hereditary principle, were supplanted by the personal magnetism of the leaders of Africa's notorious armed bands, the *ruga-ruga*. Tippu Tip and Mirambo became the exemplars of the new leadership, characterised by nomadism, reliance on the gun and charismatic leadership, as against the relatively stable village life based on hereditary chiefs. In short, traditional tribal morality was unable to withstand the destructive possibilities unleashed by an arms trade that flooded the interior with European guns and powder. But the colonial powers were right to be anxious about the arms trade. Although, measured by agricultural indices, Africa by the end of the nineteenth century had declined from its former glory, in military terms it was at its strongest yet.

The final stage in the firearms revolution came with the introduction of the machine-gun to the Dark Continent. This formidable weapon made its début with the Gatling in the American Civil War. Stanley took a Krupps variant of this to the Congo in 1883. But the real breakthrough came in 1884 with the first machine-gun to be operated by propellant gases instead of a handcrank. This gun, patented by Hiram S. Maxim in 1884 and adopted by the British Army in 1889, contained only one barrel. Since smokeless cartridges were consistent in their energy output, the loading could be done by gas pressure or by recoil instead of with a crank. The Maxim, unlike the Gatling and its derivatives, was light enough for infantry to carry, it could be set up inconspicuously, and it spat out bullets at a rate of eleven per second; its sole drawback on paper was that it could really be used only as a defensive weapon.

The explorer most associated with advanced weaponry in Africa was Stanley, and it is therefore no surprise to learn that he was the man who first took the Maxim to Africa. But the Maxim was merely one advanced component of the formidable arsenal Stanley took with him on the Emin Pasha Relief Expedition. Altogether there were 510 Remington rifles with 100,000 rounds, 50 Winchester repeaters with 50,000 cartridges, 2 tons of gunpowder, 350,000 percussion caps, 30,00 Gatling cartridges and 35,000 special Remington cartridges. Hiram Maxim himself donated one of his machine-guns. At Maxim's residence at Thurlow Lodge, Norwood, Stanley satisfied himself that the gun really could spray out 600 rounds a minute as against a maximum of 200 by any other machine-gun. He declared himself delighted with the gun's performance and announced that it 'would be of valuable service in helping civilisation to overcome barbarism'. This motif was taken up with avidity by imperialists who increasingly appreciated the growing military gulf between European and black man and summed it up in the slogan: 'Whatever happens we have got the Maxim gun and they have not.'

The performance of the Maxim on the expedition itself did not quite match expectations. It was unreliable and did not work to the manufacturer's specifications. One obvious defect was that the canvas-belt contracted when wet, making it difficult to introduce cartridges. Another was that the tin which contained the water for keeping the barrel cool was detachable and could be lost. If this one item was lost through theft or accident, the entire gun was useless. The Maxim's one great advantage was that it was very light and could be carried by just four men even during a forced march. It received its baptism of fire on the plains of Usukuma on 24 September 1889. After a three-day running fight with the Sukuma people, Stanley decided to bring matters to a head. When three regiments of the enemy approached him in a 'horn' formation, he formed a square, got his non-combatants inside, and opened up with the Maxim from a range of 300 yds. The resulting slaughter was an uncanny pre-echo, though on a smaller scale, of the holocaust visited on the Khalifa's men at Omdurman nine years later.

How many guns entered Africa in the last quarter of the nineteenth century? Lugard estimated that there were 6000–9000 in Uganda in 1890. Stanley on the Emin Pasha Relief Expedition found Emin's troops armed with breech-loaders and the still dangerous Kabbarega in possession of 2000 of them. The most careful estimate finds that between 1885 and 1902 a million firearms and four million pounds of gunpowder, plus millions of caps and rounds of ammunition, entered the British and German spheres of influence in East Africa. Farther south the arms trade particularly throve. By 1875 about 2300 guns had already reached the hands of the Barotse and the Maputo possessed 15,000 ancient muskets.

This development was especially alarming to the European pro-consuls and proto-imperialists, who saw clearly that the Indian Empire technique of using a handful of whites to hold down tens of millions of 'natives' would not work if potential rebels had easy access to firearms. The British Consul at Zanzibar, C. Euan-Smith, told Lord Rosebery in 1888 that if a large-scale trade in breech-loaders developed in East Africa, pacification of the indigenous inhabitants would be impossible. Yet all attempts to halt the trade foundered on one or other reef. A Portuguese decree of 1888 halted the import of guns and ammunition through Quilimane. It then transpired that the blockade hurt the British war then being waged against the Swahili at the north end of Lake Nyasa. The British interpreted the interdiction on arms by Portugal as a hostile act directed at themselves, and Anglo-Portuguese relations plummeted.

Other thoughtful observers doubted that an arms embargo would work in Africa. The hunter Frederick Courtenay Selous argued that the British could defeat the Portuguese slave trade only by importing to Africa a superior class of gun and ammunition together with other species of first-class trade goods. In this way they could squeeze the Portuguese out of the market and thus do more to end the slave trade than all the Exeter Hall abolitionists combined. If the import of guns was stopped, British traders would be ruined; total suppression of the arms trade in the interior would merely allow the Portuguese traders a new lease of life. There was much truth in this. Livingstone had found that in their lust for guns the Makololo sold slaves indiscriminately: to the Mambari, to Portuguese traders from the west coast and to the Arabs of Zanzibar. Selous also pointed out the distinction between selling guns in areas where game was plentiful and where it was not; he argued against a trade in the latter case on the grounds of 'the devil finding work'. Finally, he argued, there was an intimate connection between the arms trade and porterage. As the supply of porters dried up, it was increasingly hard to hire them for cloth or beads, but a payment in guns or powder would always attract takers.

The role of the explorers in all this was as a kind of transmission belt. They introduced tribal chiefs to the wonders of European firearms technology and at the same time opened up previously inaccessible areas to the arms trade. Whether their aim was to impress, overawe or evangelise the local peoples, a demonstration of firepower was always a very good way to break the ice. Explorers were often in high demand as miracle-workers who could rid a village of a man-eating lion or a predatory crocodile or who could solve the local meat shortage by bagging a hippo or two. A local chief once asked Selous to do him the favour of killing all the hippos in the Umfule river. Selous did so, 'knowing that the slaughter of these creatures would being more joy to the hearts of these poor but voracious heathen than all the tracts and bibles ever published for their benefit'.

The European trail-blazers took full advantage of the opportunity to increase their wizard-like status. Stanley impressed Mutesa by a lucky shot that killed a basking crocodile; likewise Speke, a big-game-hunting fanatic, entertained the kabaka to a demonstration of his slaughterous skills. Explorers like Baker, who had guns aplenty, were offered alliances. Missionaries, too, could be sure of a warm welcome if they brought guns to a village. John Petherick's experience among the Azande was typical:

> I seized a fowling piece . . . and pointing to a vulture hovering over us, I fired; but before the bird touched the ground, the crowd was prostrate and grovelling in the dust, as if every man of them had been shot. The old man's head, with his hands on his ears, was at my feet; and when I raised him, his appearance was ghastly, and his eyes were fixed on me with a meaningless expression.

The importance of guns, for defence, for hunting, and for impressing the tribes with European superiority, meant that every written account by a traveller or explorer in Africa inevitably contained a section detailing the firepower available to the hero. Apart from the Sniders available to his well-armed host in the descent on Bunyoro in 1872, Baker had an array of No 10 guns made by the well-known firms of Tatham, Reilly, Manton, Purdey and Beattie. His favourite personal weapons were a Ceylon No 10 double rifle and a Fletcher Double No. 24. In addition he carried a double-barrelled breech-loader called a 'Dutchman' weighing only 10 lb yet accurate at 300 yds; he used this to carry on his private war against crocodiles. He also utilised an elephant-gun so powerful that it could kill the firer if he used fine-grain powder; even when using coarse-grain, an Arab hunter had his collar-bone smashed by the gun's recoil.

Thomson, the self-proclaimed man of peace, took no chances when it came to weaponry. He supplied his men with 30 Sniders and 20 Enfields over and above the flintlocks in the personal possession of the *wangwana*. He and his companion had a first-class Express rifle, a shotgun and a small revolver. Count Teleki distributed to his men 200 muzzle-loaders, 80 breech-loading Werndl carbines, 12 colt-repeating rifles and revolvers. In his personal armoury he had a number of Holland & Holland double-barrelled 8-bore rifles, firing solid bullets of hardened lead and a charge of ten drachms of powder; a .557 Express rifle, powder charge six drachms, for explosive and ordinary bullets; one 10-bore rifle; two 500-bore Express rifles with a powder charge of five drachms; and two Paradox guns which could fire either shot or bullets.

The ivory trader A. Arkell-Hardwick provided the most complete personal inventory of an African traveller. He took an 8-bore Paradox, a .557 Express and a single-barrelled .450 Express, all made by Holland & Holland. The 8-bore was a magnificent weapon for camp defence when loaded with slugs. The .557 was the best all-round weapon for hunting big-game like elephant, rhino or buffalo. The .450 Express performed a similar role, except that it burned smokeless powder where the .557 burned black powder. The .557 Express was in some ways the most impressive of all the 'personal' guns. It was a single-barrelled top-lever hammer gun, with a flat top rib. The sights were set very low down on the rib – a great advantage as it minimised the chances of accidental canting. Its penetrative power with hardened lead bullets could drop a rhino in full charge yet also bring down small antelopes like Grant's or Weller's gazelles without mangling them or leaving a huge exit wound, thereby spoiling the skin – which had been the big complaint against the previous generation's big-game rifle, the Rigby's .303 with expanding bullets. The advantage of the .303, mainly used against elephants, had been that it could take either solid or exploding bullets. Hunters employed a 'horses for courses' approach to their rifles. Thus some favoured a Martini-Henry military rifle against rhino, buffalo or giraffe, and a 20-bore shotgun against small game, guinea fowl, etc. Each traveller had his own quirks and predilections. Selous used a .450 Metford Express, made by George Gibbs of Bristol, to kill lions, rhino and hippo. Frederick Jackson used a 4-bore against elephants, an 8-bore against rhino and buffalo, a .500 Express against hertebeeste and waterbuck, and a .360 Express against Grant's gazelle and impala.

There was an intimate connection between guns and ivory in nineteenth-century Africa, and not simply in the sense that the ivory and arms trades were second only to slavery itself as economic factors. On the open market the principal item bartered for ivory was the gun. A tusk which on the western shores of Lake Victoria could be bought for a Snider rifle and 100 cartridges would sell on the east coast for £20–50. If slavery entered the scene as well, slaves would provide the porterage so there would be no carriage charges. Nor would any expense be involved in bringing the guns upcountry in the first place, since the porters were glad to carry them for their own protection. So close was the association of ideas between firearms and ivory that the principal unit of currency used in ivory barter was the 'gun'. A 'gun' might comprise coarse grey cotton cloth, salt, brass wire, hoop-iron, crockery, rum or a brass pan, 18 in. in diameter. The final cost of a tusk was a complicated matter. In some areas payment was in blue, hexagonal pipe beads, 1/4 in. in length and diameter, exchanged in bunches of thousands. These came close to being a sort of 'legal tender'. A 'gun' was roughly equivalent to 8 gallons of rum. A good ivory tusk cost 12½ guns, or 100 gallons of rum, the equivalent of £20 at coast prices. Glave once bought 4000 lb of tusks at an average of two cents a pound. Trading started at very high prices. Then the serious barter started, and items such as forty brass rods, 2 yards of handkerchief, forks and spoons were mentioned before a reasonable price was reached and a bargain struck.

Why was there such a demand for African ivory in the nineteenth century? East African ivory, and later that of the Congo, was soft, ideal for carving, and in great demand in Europe for knife handles, piano keys, billiard balls and to satisfy the Victorian love of ornate décor and furnishing. Ivory inlay work ranged from ivory-handled umbrellas to snuffboxes and chessmen. In Latin countries ivory was used in a plethora of articles; fans, fingerboards for Spanish guitars, keys of Italian accordions, carved boudoir articles. There were flourishing ivory-carving centres at Dieppe, St Claude in the Jura, Geislingen in Württemberg and Erbach in Hesse, specialising in the production of miniature ornaments, statuettes, crucifixes, mathematical instruments, book covers, combs and serviette rings. Ivory was also used for false teeth until porcelain came in in the latter half of the nineteenth century. In the United States ivory was particularly favoured for piano and organ keys and especially for billiard and bagatelle balls, to the point where the US took 80 per cent of the soft ivory exported from Zanzibar in 1894. Even India, where the elephant could be put to better uses, imported 'elephants' teeth' were used for women's bangles and ornaments. Because ivory is elastic and flexible and can be cut into almost any shape, nothing was wasted from the tusks. Scraps and even dust would be used for Indian ink and ivory jelly.

A large elephant might be 11 ft high and measure 14 ft from the forehead to the root of the tail. Its girth might be 19 ft and the circumference of each foot 5 ft in length. From such an animal tusks weighing 75 lb and 65 lb might be extracted, for a pair of tusks was never of identical weight. Anything above 90 lb each for tusks was considered a marvellous 'bag'. The largest recorded pair is mentioned by Frederick Jackson as being 151 lb (right tusk) and 129 lb (left tusk). These were 'gross' figures, relating to the dimensions of tusks when measured on a newly killed animal. Tusks lost weight as they dried out: so an 84-lb tusk 'gross' would become a 74-lb item 'net' after drying. The problems of porterage for the ivory-hunter were therefore considerable. Stokes, the trader, who was judicially murdered in the Belgian Congo in 1895 after a kangaroo court, perfected a differential system. The *kilangozi* or head porter carried the largest tusk. Then came the strongest men bearing single tusks. Finally came weaker porters carrying large bundles of cow tusks – to small bundles attached to each end of a strong 5-ft-long shoulder stick, known as an *abdalla*. On one of Stokes's expeditions a *kilangozi* who had carried a 115-lb tusk 22 miles, retraced his steps from the night's halt and *danced* back a whole mile to the main column to tell them camp was near.

The explorer who devoted most attention to the ivory question was Wilhelm Junker. He explained that tusks were sorted according to size, since the emphasis was on weight, not quality. In the parts of north Central Africa where Junker travelled there were six main types of ivory: *damir* – the largest tusks, up to 10 ft in length, carried by alternate squads of 4–6 carriers; *brinji-ahl* – perfectly pure ivory, always carried by the strongest men; *dahar-brinji* – small tusks of good quality, each weighing about 15lb; *bahr* – tusks weighing 5–10 lb, usually 2–3 a load; *klinjeh* – the smallest tusks, in bundles of 7–9 a load; and *mashmush* – bad ivory that had been long in the ground or water, or else damaged by sun and rain, and mostly calcined, though still possessing a market value.

Three main groups were in competition for ivory, which meant the business of slaughtering elephants. In ascending order of importance these were the Arab slavers, the tribal chiefs and the European elephant-hunters and ivory-traders. Tippu Tip and his associates traded ivory only when they had to. Their normal practice was to visit a village and sniff out if there were any ivory caches there. If there were, Tippu and his men would depart, then return a few days later with sufficient force to uplift it. They achieved this by a raid which netted a large number of captives; these would then be ransomed for ivory. If there was not enough ivory in the village to redeem all the prisoners, the Arabs would take their new slaves off to be sold elsewhere. As Glave put it, 'Slavery and its attendant cruelties play a part subservient to ivory.'

Certainly the slaves were subservient in one sense: they were lucky to reach their destination, but the ivory never failed to do so. Only about a third of the ivory-carrying slaves leaving Stanley Falls could hope to reach the east coast, 3000 miles away. The gleaming tusks could be depended on to turn up in the auction rooms of London or Brussels. Harry Johnston, later to be a novelist (albeit a mediocre one) once exercised his creative faculties to imagine the differential routes whereby a single pair of tusks could be united at the salerooms of the London docks. He postulated a pair of tusks extracted by an African hunter after killing an elephant with poisoned arrows. Tusk A might by sold to a native trader for brass collars; it could then be traded away at Stanley Pool, taken downriver to the Atlantic coast and thence to Europe. Meanwhile Arabs might raid the original hunter's village and take his wife prisoner; he in turn would redeem her from the Arabs with Tusk B. The tusk would then be taken to Zanzibar and on to London.

One of the most curious aspects of the Arab ivory trade was the symbiosis that arose between slaver and the missionaries, whose official ideology should have made them the Arabs' deadliest enemies. Sometimes the Arabs, lacking sufficient porters for the entire haul, would leave a cache of ivory behind at a mission station. A missionary might have 3000–4000 lb of ivory in his cellar, having given the Arab a verbal assurance. Since the missionaries' word was as good as their bond, the European reputation for probity grew; Arabs would accept explorers' cheques and IOUs in the wilderness, knowing they would be honoured. Hence the peculiar animus engendered when Stanley gave Tippu Tip a verbal pledge at Vianja-Niara in 1876 and later failed to redeem it.

Ivory-hunting was big business among the tribes, and it called for considerable skills. Ivory tribute was also an important source of revenue for chiefs as well as recognition of their secular and spiritual authority. One tusk from every elephant killed belonged *de jure* to the local chief, and he also had the right to *buy* the other one. In the case of a powerful ruler, like the kabaka of Buganda, he would probably not exercise his secondary right but instead grow rich on a progressive capitation tax on lower chiefs: the wealthier they were, the wealthier he became. It was a sure sign of the decline in authority of a chief if he ceased to receive the customary tribute. A chief's ability to sell ivory tribute for goods that he could redistribute to his followers was an important source of his traditional authority. When the Arab and European elephant-hunters followed the explorers into previously unknown areas, they quickly diminished the elephant stocks through their lust for ivory for export. In this way they lessened the tribal chiefs' traditional stores of wealth and thus caused political instability. Once again guns and ivory can be observed joining causal hands. As the traditional sources of political authority faded, roving bands of warrior traders like the *ruga-ruga*, owing loyalty to a charismatic leader, became more common. This is a process already identified as being triggered (almost literally) by the spread of firearms. Nineteenth-century East and Central Africa in particular witnessed an almost textbook Weberian transformation in types of leadership.

The situation was similar in West Africa, where monopoly and middlemen positions in the ivory trade were jealously guarded. Du Chaillu noted:

Each of these tribes assumes to itself the privilege of acting as go-between or middlemen to those next to it, and charges a heavy percentage for this office and no infraction of this rule is permitted under penalty of war. Thus a piece of

1. Sir James Bruce 'discovering' the source of the Blue Nile and drinking the health of George III

2. Zanzibar from the sea

3. Henry Morton Stanley

4. Verney Lovett Cameron

5. Sir Samuel Baker

6. David Livingstone

7. John Hanning Speke

8. Tippu Tip

9. Speke and Grant at the Royal Geographical Society

10. Grant catching up with his reading

11. Sir Samuel Baker addressing the Royal Geographical Society

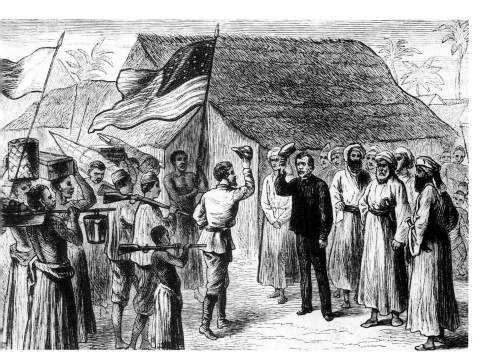

12. The meeting of Livingstone and Stanley (from a sketch by Stanley)

13. Stanley leaving Matadi, on the Congo, with Tippu Tip

14. Stanley with a Maxim gun

15. Livingstone attacked by a lion. 'Growling horribly, he shook me as a terrier dog does a rat'

16. A hippopotamus attacks Livingstone's canoe

17. The discomforts of African travel: the Makata swamp

18. Captives on their way to Tette

ivory or ebony may belong originally to a negro in the far interior, and if he wants to barter it for 'white man's trade' he dares not take it to the market himself. If he should be rash enough to attempt such a piece of enterprise his goods would be confiscated, and he, if caught, fined by one whose monopoly he sought to break down, or most likely, sold into slavery.

The greatest worry to the African chiefs in the nineteenth century was the competition from European elephant-hunters who moved into the previously virgin territory uncovered by the explorers. Chief Mwase of Kasungu, whom Livingstone met in 1863, told the doctor he did not want him to travel north-west because he had a great trade in ivory there. He was naturally afraid that if explorers got into elephant country, they would relieve him of the ivory which he currently got at very cheap rates and sold to slavers as they passed Kasungu to the east. Because European elephant-hunters had to pay hefty fees to the chiefs for permission to hunt on their lands, they required exceptionally large returns to show a profit. Apart from heavy expenses in lost horses and cattle if they hunted in tsetse country, they had to compete with indigenous hunters whose chiefs gave them the plum areas as soon as they acquired guns. Elephant-hunters had to possess superlative skills to succeed, especially in tsetse country where all hunting had to be on foot.

With so many groups chasing Africa's elephants, it was no surprise that the herds dwindled as surely as the buffalo on the great plains of North America in the same period. Between 1856 and 1876 alone Africa supplied Europe with an average of 1½ million lb of ivory annually and sent about 150,000 lb to North America. This represented a slaughter of at least 51,000 elephants. After the Franco-Prussian war the price of ivory rose to peak heights, and the search for it extended ever farther inland. When the international market for ivory became fully established in the last quarter of the nineteenth century, and large bands of indigenous hunters competed ruthlessly with Europeans such as Selous and Stokes, the massacre became even more concentrated. This was self-destructive madness of a kind only too familiar in our own century. Each year the elephants retreated further and further into the interior. No slow-breeding animal could withstand such indiscriminate destruction. Hunting on horseback also became next to impossible, as elephants were increasingly found only in tsetse country. By 1878 Selous, who had contributed so much to the slaughter, wrote despairingly that elephants were a thing of the past in Matabeleland. By the 1890s in the Congo all the elephants had been 'shot out': the only ivory that remained was old teeth that had long lain in store; in despair Leopold turned to wild rubber, with all the atrocities that search unleashed.

All the great explorers noted this holocaust they had unwittingly done so much to promote. Only the boneheaded Baker wholly endorsed the massacre, licking his lips as he mentioned possible 2000 per cent profits on the ivory trade. Livingstone was never one for the gratuitous slaughter of animals, particularly those that might be useful. After witnessing the Makololo spearing a cow-elephant and its calf, he wrote: 'I turned from the spectacle of the destruction of noble animals, which might be so useful in Africa, with a feeling of sickness.' Livingstone was adamant that the supposedly 'untamable' African elephant really could be domesticated. He argued that coins struck by Septimius Severus early in the third century AD showed clearly an *African* elephant dancing and walking on ropes in the circus. This proved, he thought, that the Romans had once possessed the secret of domesticating the African elephant – and the distinctive ears of the pachyderm on the coin showed clearly that it was an African elephant and not its more biddable Indian cousin.

Cameron, too, during his crossing of Africa, regretted the inroads on the herds made by ivory-hunters: 'Ivory is not likely to last for ever (or for long) as the main export from Africa; indeed the ruthless manner in which the elephants are destroyed and harassed has already begun to show its effects. In places where elephants were by no means uncommon a few years ago, their wanton destruction has had its natural effect and they are now rarely encountered.'

Schweinfurth, having witnessed the demise of the elephant in Buganda, warned his readers that similar attrition was going on in Bunyoro, where the great beasts were being progressively 'shot out'. Joseph Thomson in the early 1880s reported that he had not seen a single elephant in fourteen months around the Lake Regions and reflected sadly on the fact that twenty years earlier Livingstone had reported a positive abundance of the beasts at the southern end of Lake Tanganyika. The saturation of Africa with ivory-hunters was the cause:

> The traders from East Africa have overrun the country till they have met those from the Cape, the Zambezi and Benguela. They have joined hands with those from Loanda and the Congo, and interchanged courtesies with traders from North Africa and the Nile region. Not one great area can now be pointed out where the elephant can be said to roam unmolested. The ivory trade has certainly reached its turning point. Each year less ivory will be got, and the date is not far distant when hardly a tusk will find its way to the coast . . . This ruthless destruction of elephants cannot continue long. They cannot be bred in a year or two, and when once destroyed in any region can never be replaced. The area in which they are still found is being gradually reduced. An iron band of ruthless destroyers is drawing around it; and it may be safely predicted that in twenty years the noble African elephant will be a rare animal.

Some of the explorers did not merely lament the loss to their own perceptions of the absence of elephants but expressed compassion for the sufferings of the noble animals and those of the slaves compelled to manhaul the tusks to the coast. Junker said: 'What unspeakable miseries of every kind are inflicted on millions of wretched natives directly or indirectly through the ivory trade itself! If only the moans and groans of heartfelt agony could be heard that have been caused by a single tusk in its wanderings for thousands of miles before it reaches our workshops!'

Stanley wrote to his successor as Governor of the Congo Free State in 1884 to congratulate him on a ban on European elephant-hunting in the Congo. Even though the ban was purely prudential – for until he had consolidated his power Leopold wanted to conciliate the tribes by withdrawing the competition from European ivory-hunters – Stanley declared: 'Stop the shooting of the elephants, do not murder any more for the sheer pity of the noble beasts. Let the ground of the Association be sacred to the elephants. We do not yet know, but we may have use for them.'

Elsewhere in his writings Stanley scornfully compared the lust for ivory to the Australian and Californian gold-rushes, the mining boom in Colorado, Idaho and Montana and the diamond-fever of Cape Colony. But his own work had contributed substantially to this get-rich-quick mentality. He had already alerted Europe to the fortunes to be made from ivory on the east coast route. What cost a cent in Manyema, where ivory was so common that it was used for doorposts and eave stanchions, retailed for a dollar or two in Tabora and in Zanzibar.

The gruesome reality of elephant-hunting emerges from the account given by the hunter Gordon Cumming to Mark Twain:

Having planted a bullet in the shoulder bone of an elephant, and caused the agonised creature to lean for support against a tree, I proceeded to brew some coffee. Having so refreshed myself, taking observations of the elephant's spasm and writhings between the sips, I resolved to make experiments on vulnerable points, and approaching near, I fired several bullets at different parts of its enormous skull. He only acknowledged the shots by a salaam-like movement of his trunk, with the point of which he gently touched the wounds with a striking and peculiar action. Surprised and shocked to find I was only prolonging the suffering of the noble beast, which bore its trials with such dignified composure, I resolved to finish the proceedings with all possible despatch, and accordingly opened fire on him from the left side. Aiming at the shoulder I fired six shots with the two-grooved rifle, which must have eventually proved mortal, after which I fired six shots at the same point with the Dutch six-pounder. Large tears now trickled down from his eyes, which he slowly shut and opened, his colossal frame quivering convulsively, and falling on his side he expired.

Even more horrific was the Sudanese scene described by Schwein-furth, when hunters fired the grass and drove herds into the inferno. Thousands of huntsmen and drovers with drums and conches frightened the elephants into the jaws of death. Schweinfurth described their fate:

No resource for escape is left to the poor brutes. Driven by the flames into masses, they huddle together young and old, they cover their bodies with grass, on which they pump water from their trunks as long as they can, but all in vain. They are ultimately either suffocated by the clouds of smoke or overpowered by the heat, or are so miserably burnt that at last and ere long they succumb to the fate that has been designed for them by ungrateful man. The *coup de grâce* may now and then be given them by the blow of some ready lance, but too often, as may be seen from the tusks that are bought, the miserable beasts must have perished in agonies of a death by fire. A war of annihilation is this, in which neither young nor old, neither male nor female, is spared, and in its indiscriminate slaughter it compels us sorrowfully to ask and answer the question: *cui bono?* No other reply seems possible but what is given by the handles of our walking sticks, our billiard balls, our pianoforte keys, our combs and our fans, and other unimportant articles of this kind. No wonder, therefore, if this noble creature, whose services might be so invaluable to man, should even, perhaps some time during our own generation, be permitted to rank in the category of things that *have been*, and, to be as extinct as the ure-ox, the sea-cow, or the dodo.

Some elephant hunters acknowledged the pathos and misery involved in elephant-hunting but pleaded the *force majeure* of financial necessity. Selous's apologia was along these lines: 'It seems dreadful to slaughter so many of these huge creatures merely for their tusks; for, if there are no Bushmen or other natives about, the carcasses are abandoned to the hyenas and vultures. But *il faut vivre*. Ivory is the only thing obtainable in this country with which to defray the heavy expenses of hunting; and if you depend on your gun for a living, as was my case, it behoves you to do your best when you get a chance.'

What Selous did not mention was that his 'bags' were excessive by any reckoning. He did not just kill elephants to make a living, as his specious logic suggests, even if we accept his premise that he had been 'compelled' by some unknown agency to make his living in just that way and no other. He lamented the steep decline in the numbers of giraffes encountered in his lifetime without mentioning his own role in their decline. His own statistics are eloquent. In ten weeks (Sept.-Nov. 1874) he killed ten elephants. In 1878 he surpassed himself by massacring twenty-two in a single day. Yet elephants were merely the jewel in his slaughterous crown. In the four years 1877–80 he shot 548 animals, including 229 in 1879 and 112 in 1880. Between 5 June and 5 December 1874 Selous shot 93 big-game animals, comprising 24 elephants, 19 buffalo, 7 zebra, 5 black rhino, 4 white rhino, 4 warthog, 2 giraffe, 1 hippo, 1 lion and assorted antelope as follows: 7 puku, 5 impala, 3 tsessebe, 3 lechwe, 3 kudu, 1 sable, 1 eland, 1 steinbok, 1 waterbuck, 1 roan.

One day the psychodynamics of this kind of restless slaughter by Europeans in Africa will have to be examined at length. In Selous's defence it must be recorded that he was by no means alone in his proclivities. Something will be said later about Speke's insatiable desire for killing. But Selous was just one of many 'gentlemen' or players among European travellers in Africa whose principal distinction seems to have been the big-game tallies they amassed. Of Richard Meinertzhagen, the twentieth-century 'sportsman' Elspeth Huxley has this to say: 'The tally of slaughtered animals, then present in such astonishing abundance, seems nauseating . . . he had only to see an animal, provided he was reasonably sure it was a male, to shoot it.' The hunter W. Buckley, who often killed eight bull elephants in a single year, commented jejunely after twenty years of butchery: 'I have an uncomfortable feeling that if elephants had not been so ruthlessly and persistently hunted . . . (they) would have been turned into useful domestic animals.' In the 1930s in the Sudan the explorer Wilfred Thesiger shot 70 lions in five years, on the grounds that they were 'deemed' vermin. 'Gentleman' Jim Corbett and Laurens van der Post were other well-known twentieth-century travellers with a passion for killing game. Often, as with Speke, deep psychological urges were being satisfied by the slaughter. One hesitates to use the overworked word 'sadism' but after reading a distasteful story like the one by Count Teleki, when he related how he had shot a male and female rhino while they were mating, it is difficult not to see a twisted and transmogrified sexuality at play.

It is sometimes alleged that it is anachronistic to expect late twentieth-century attitudes to animal conservation to have obtained among nineteenth-century African explorers or even early twentieth-century travellers in the continent. This argument is the product either of ignorance or disingenuousness. A close study of African explorers reveals a very clear dichotomy between the 'sport' fetishists like Baker and Speke and those with a genuine feeling for animals, like Livingstone, Burton, Stanley, Emin Pasha and Schweinfurth. Burton despised Speke for his lust to kill, while Stanley severely reprimanded Glave for big-game hunting mania, on the grounds that this was not an occupation to satisfy serious or intelligent minds. There is a very clear inverse relationship between intellectual calibre and enthusiasm for the hunting of big game. The intellectually impressive, like Livingstone, Burton and Stanley, despised the pursuit. The intellectually deficient, like Speke and Baker, revelled in it. The 'anachronistic' argument will not hold on other grounds. Late nineteenth-century literature of travel in Africa is full of swingeing attacks on the devotees of 'sport' and the widespread destruction of game animals; there is a very good example in H.A. Bryden's book. As for the 'defence' mounted by the Meinertzhagens, Thesigers and others, there is an obvious refutation in the work and life of Apsley Cherry-Garrard and Cherry Kearton, men a generation older than these egregious 'sportsmen'.

9

Slavery and the Slave Trade

Slavery was a fact of life in nineteenth-century Africa, and the explorers came to terms with it in different ways. Fundamentally their attitude was ambivalent: on the one hand they hated the 'peculiar institution' and used it as unique evidence that Africa was a benighted country, in need of deliverance by European capital, institutions and religion; on the other hand, it was something they could at the very least coexist with in their daily lives, and it was often something from which they could derive considerable advantage. This ambivalence in the explorers' attitude was made more complex by a fundamental ambiguity within slavery itself. African slavery was subdivided into domestic thraldom and the trade in human flesh for export. These two were as distinct as the Papal Inquisition and the much more sinister Spanish Inquisition, yet were often confused, sometimes by the explorers themselves. It is one of the sources of the many conflicting reports on African slavery. The different accounts by the explorers reflect a differential experience of domestic slavery and slavery for export.

Yet even this neat division of slavery into two types masks all kinds of nuances. The missionary-explorer Edward Coode Hoore, one of the great pioneers in Tanganyika, said that slavery was 'a most complicated system, the details of which require years to understand'. At its deepest level slavery involved a complex symbiosis of the African and Arab types. Whereas slavery for export was overwhelmingly an Arab affair, domestic slavery had been a feature of Africa from time immemorial. As Lugard scathingly remarked: 'Slavery has been an African institution for a thousand years . . . you could not send three men on a mission, or two would combine to enslave the third.' Lugard was inclined to regard the domestic kind of slavery as merely a sort of feudal system, or a natural stage in the evolution from savagery to civilisation. From the viewpoint of the colonial ruler (which Lugard was) slavery even had certain advantages: it enforced respect for rank and thus facilitated administration and government.

Livingstone, who had seen something of the horrors of slum life in the industrial cities of Britain, entered another argument for condoning domestic slavery: that the saving grace of the 'no growth' pre-capitalist African economy was its prevention of extremes of inequality and class hatred:

> The Arabs are said to treat their slaves kindly, and this may also be said of native masters; the reason is, master and slave partake of the general indolence, but the lot of the slave does not improve with the general progress in civilisation. While no great disparity of rank exists, his energies are little tasked, but when society advances, wants multiply; and to supply these the slave's lot grows harder. The distance between man and master increases as the lust of gain is developed, hence we can hope for no improvement in the slave's condition, unless the master returns to or remains in barbarism.

There were many different contexts which could act as the genesis of domestic slavery. The most common was war, when prisoners were enslaved. British conflict with Bunyoro came to a head in the 1890s when Lugard tried to extinguish the practice of making slaves out of prisoners of war. It was Kabbarega's refusal to toe this line which, more than anything, precipitated British occupation of his country. Slaves featured too as part of the quasifeudal tithe paid to a superior ruler. They were also used as a medium of exchange in economies based on barter, so that many slaves were bought on the open market from neighbouring tribes. The persons most at risk were women and children. Children were often offered as compensation or 'blood price' for homicide or other serious crimes; they were also bartered for grain in time of famine and made easy targets for kidnappers. Such was the prejudice in favour of women and children as slaves that Verney Cameron reported from Ujiji that 90 per cent of the slaves there fell into those two categories; most of the men taken were simply put to the sword. A female slave had much better prospects in the arena of domestic serfdom. In Ugogo or Unyamwezi she had a chance of becoming the wife of the man who bought her, and if she bore him children she was kindly treated. If a woman was sold to Arabs or itinerant traders, on the other hand, she was handed from one man to another on the whim of the moment. Yet, paradoxically, the Nyamwezi had the reputation of being much crueller masters than the Arabs; the inference must be that this judgement applied to *male* slaves.

In all such cases slaves were bought to expand the master's kin groups, to till his fields, become retainers and soldiers, servants or canoe paddlers or, in the most gruesome context, to act as victims in human sacrifice. E.J.

Glave on the Congo reported cases where slaves had been bought to be eaten. The German explorer, Dr Buttner, who explored the lands due east of Stanley Pool, between the lower Kwango and the Congo, in 1885, witnessed the despatch of two slaves who were then cooked in a cannibal feast. Buttner recorded with wonderment that the two men were not even bound, but submitted to their execution like dumb, senseless brutes.

Generalisations about domestic slavery are therefore difficult. Slaves were sold not just for export or for work on plantations as, say, in Portuguese East Africa but were traded within tribes. The resale of slaves was influenced solely by market considerations, such as the relative price of slaves and ivory. Moreover, different African tribes had different approaches. The Ngoni raided for slaves but kept them inside their tribal state and did not sell for export. The Nyamwezi diversified from porterage into slavery, showing a diversity of entrepreneurial skills, as did the Manyema. In 1881 a quarter of the population of Unyanyembe was estimated to be slaves. Slaves could be 'outsiders' or they could be integrated into the kinship system of the tribe that bought them. They could become wives, daughters, sisters, fathers, sons or brothers to the 'free' of the new society. In time they could acquire wealth and even own their own slaves. In one bizarre case reported by the traveller Duff MacDonald, an African sold himself to a Portuguese master for three pieces of calico, and with the proceeds bought himself a wife and a boy. There were many cases of a man entering slavery voluntarily to get a wife from a master who owned many nubile females. Amazing as it may seem, slavery was often a preferable option for a woman. Harry Johnston told a story that even suggests a dash of feminism:

> One of the mission girls at Stanley Falls was sold to three or four different men one after the other, but refused to be the wife of anybody who could not read and write like herself. She was beaten, put in stocks, and tied up several times, but was absolute mistress of the situation as far as getting married was concerned and the money had to be returned. Now she is married to the lad of her choice. She said she was not going to be one of a crowd; she wanted a husband of her own.

The complexities of the indigenous African system of servitude never ceased to bemuse and puzzle the explorers. Livingstone, famous as a doughty opponent of the *Arab* slave trade, was inclined to make light of domestic slavery. When among the Makololo in 1855 he remarked:

> The servitude rendered from time immemorial by the poorer to the richer classes cannot be called slavery, though akin to it. The poor man is called the child of the rich man, and their intercourse is on a sort of equality . . . the poor

man has his own gardens, hut, etc. and eats his own produce, having the advantage of recourse to his master in case of need. The services rendered are assistance in sewing and preparing skins, in erecting cattle pens, in service in case of going to other towns, or in war as squires. The wife assists the mistress in the same way. The arrangement is absolutely necessary for the poor who cannot conveniently be independent. It is like slavery only in no specified wages being paid, but the obligations are well understood.

Duff MacDonald agreed that the principal reason an African chief acquired slaves was to sell them in the export trade, for use in expanding their kinship structures and for purposes of home economies:

An old person he (the village chief) obtains for a single skin, but a young slave costs two; and women cost much more than men. The female slaves thus bought are his junior wives, and he keeps them busy in hoeing the farm, and all such female duties. The male slaves he employs in farming, building, making baskets, sewing garments and such masculine pursuits. He keeps all these persons strictly at their duties, and at the same time welcomes an opportunity of selling them at a profit. The gains thus realised he lays out in purchasing more people. If his daughters were unmarried, he would give them slave husbands.

Domestic slavery did not necessarily mean a fixed and rigid hierarchy; it did not correspond to the relationship between Arabs and *their* slaves, where superior firepower gave the Arabs virtually permanent superiority. E.J. Glave in the Congo recounted a story which illustrated the whirligig of fortune in a tribal context. Ndobo, the ferocious and tyrannical chief of the Ikengo, came to a sad end through his mania for the game of *lobesi*. In *lobesi* pieces of pottery were chipped into wheels about the size of an American quarter dollar; one side was whitened and the other burnt black. A player would take an odd number of these pieces in his hand and throw them on a mat, first betting on either the black or the white. The winner was the man guessing the majority colour. Usually the game was played for brass wire, beads or cloth but Ndobo lashed himself into a gambling frenzy and decided to stake all. One by one he gambled his slaves and lost. Finally, when all his ivory and slaves were exhausted, he staked himself. He got into a game with a man called Molumbe, who had once been his slave. He bet on white and threw seven *lobesi*. They came down three white and four black. Ndobo was taken, handcuffed and shackled amid the slaves he had brought downstream; now he too was a slave. Molumbe at once extracted his pound of flesh.
  'My slave, Ndobo! Tender me homage!'
  '*Lusaku, Nkulu,*' replied Ndobo meekly ('I am your slave, master.')
  That slavery could break down ties of kinship as well as consolidate

them was graphically illustrated by Brazza, who used this example to show that the West Africans were in need of French suzerainty:

> One of my slaves saw approaching the elder brother who had already sold him twice, for the first time he managed to escape. This fond relative was now coming to take possession of his junior to sell him a third time; and with such effrontery that he was wearing the red bonnet and cloth he had bought when he made the second sale. The younger brother tried to hide himself, but the other, turning to the Adoumas, said, 'Look, he doesn't recognise his own brother.' I was on the point of exploding when two of my Senegalese, no less disgusted than I was, jumped on the rascal, shoved his head in the sand and spat in his face before chasing him off.

Whatever the explorers' experience of domestic slavery, there were usually no two opinions about the slave trade for export. West Africa, as is well known, had long felt the lash of the trade. Fortunes had been made in England from the exploitation of human misery, and the triangular trade route Bristol–West Africa–North America – Bristol. An estimated 14 million Africans were transported across the Atlantic by slavery and an even larger number uprooted. The population loss thus sustained by the continent was offset by an improvement in African diet. Slavers planted maize and other New World crops near the embarkation points on the slave coast of West Africa, to feed captives during the Atlantic crossing; maize proved to be a more nourishing crop than millet and cassava.

When Britain decreed against the slave trade and slavery, and in the United States the 'peculiar institution' was confined to the South, fomenting Northern anxieties that were resolved only by the Civil War, Brazil alone remained as a magnet for the Atlantic slave trade. For the first four decades of the nineteenth century the Portuguese supplied their colonial cousins liberally, even though this meant running an Atlantic blockade by Royal Navy cruisers. At the beginning of the nineteenth century 10,000 slaves a year were exported to all parts: the Indian Ocean as well as South America. In 1817–18 twelve ships with 4000 slaves on board sailed from Mozambique for Rio. During the years 1815–30 an average of 10,000 slaves a year left Portuguese East Africa for Brazil and a further 7000 for the French islands in the Indian Ocean. By 1830 Quilimane was probably the most important slave port in Africa, exporting about 10,000 slaves annually. In 1837, the last year for which good figures on the old Portuguese trade are available, the export of slaves from Mozambique to Brazil and Cuba reached 15,000. Many other slaves were employed on the *prazeros* or great estates of Mozambique.

The Quintuple Treaty of 1841 bound Britain, France, Austria, Prussia and Russia to seize all ships fitted out for slave trading. The Portuguese were browbeaten into agreeing to the right of search in 1842, but the United States held out against this infringement of its sovereign rights, and in practice France would never agree to the right of search either. So an effective anti-slave trade campaign was prevented. In 1848 it was reported that there was no significant abatement in the slave trade from Mozambique to Rio.

Thereafter events moved rapidly on the Atlantic front. British warships entered Brazilian ports to enforce the abolition of the slave trade, even as Brazil was engaged in warfare with its Argentine rival to the south. Public opinion in Brazil was also changing. An epidemic of yellow fever in 1849–50 was attributed to the incoming slaves and there arose an outcry against their continued importation. In 1850 about 60,000 slaves entered Brazil but this number was down to a trickle of 2,000 in 1853. The Brazilian slave trade was dead. Slavery itself was abolished by the Rio Branco bill of 1871, applying to all children of slaves, and finally in 1888 to the slaves themselves. But the trade in slaves from Mozambique to the Indian Ocean continued. Livingstone, who travelled through the Portuguese territories in the 1850s, reported that the Lisbon government was sincere in its desire to abolish the trade but was let down by venal and corrupt officials in post at Mozambique: 'The Portuguese government has not generally received the credit for sincerity in suppressing the slave trade which I conceive to be its due.'

But it was the *Arab* slave trade with which the explorers mainly came in contact. This trade gained momentum both from the abolition of the Atlantic trade and from the Arabs' occupation of Zanzibar when Omani Said, Sultan of Muscat, transferred his court there in 1833. The island, two-thirds of whose 200,000 population was slave, was ideal as a holding depot for the human cargo. The slave business soon moved inland. Bagamoyo, facing Zanzibar on the mainland, was the main outlet, with Kilwa farther south augmenting the flow. By 1840 the Arabs were established at Tabora and by the late 1840s had reached Lake Tanganyika. An Arab trader was at the court of Buna, ruler of Buganda, by 1843. Atkins Hamerton, the British consul in Zanzibar, estimated in 1841 that 40,000 slaves were imported into the island annually, of which about half were shipped north. In 1844 he made these figures 20,000 and 10,000, basing them on the highly unreliable customs returns (i.e. ignoring the illegal trade in slaves). His original figure of 40,000 was endorsed by two of the best observers, Richard Burton in 1856 and by the consul, Rigby, in 1858.

Half-hearted pressure from the British on Said to halt this trade was ineffective. In the mid-1860s the Zanzibar slave market was still one of Africa's scandals. Livingstone wrote in 1866:

This is now almost the only spot in the world where 100 to 300 slaves are daily exposed for sale in open market. This disgraceful scene I several times personally witnessed, and the purchasers were Arabs or Persians, whose dhows lay anchored in the harbour, and these men were daily at their occupation, examining the teeth, gait and limbs of the slaves, as openly as horse-dealers engage in their business in England.

In 1868 30,000 slaves arrived from the Nyasa area at Kilwa: at least another 30,000 had perished *en route*. About two-thirds of the survivors went to Zanzibar, and the rest to Madagascar, the Comoro Islands and the Persian Gulf. The worst part of the journey was the 24-hour run to Zanzibar: 1000 slaves would be packed into a space scarcely large enough to take as many bags of rice. Under the fierce sun they died and were thrown overboard; if their bloated corpses drifted ashore they were pushed back to sea with a long pole, and so on to successive landfalls until they disintegrated. Those who lived were taken to the Zanzibar slave market and examined minutely for physical defects. The microscopic and degrading physical examination of the female slaves particularly disgusted European visitors. Once the slaves were bought they were dressed in a distinctive loincloth and could look forward to reasonably good treatment.

In 1865, while provisioning in Zanzibar, Livingstone noted that the northern Arabs were chiefly to blame for the Zanzibar slave market. Though willing to co-operate with the British, the Sultan of Zanzibar could not coerce the Omani Arabs, since to abolish the trade in his dominions would start a social revolution which might end in his expulsion or death. Livingstone's estimate was that 3000 slaves were imported annually into Zanzibar on the ruling family's account and another 12,000 by wealthy merchants on the island. There were 100,000 slaves on the whole island and the institution pervaded Greater Zanzibar (including the Pemba Islands).

The Great Powers met in conclave in Paris in 1867 to decide what to do about slavery. The meeting produced fine sentiments but no concrete results. Two years later the opening of the Suez Canal brought East Africa within the British sphere of influence. Public opinion in Britain demanded that the price for carrying on legitimate trade with African peoples should be the abolition of the slave trade.

But first Nature took a hand. The cholera epidemic of 1869–70 which ravaged the western Indian Ocean created a demand for slaves in Arabia to replace those who had died, but in Zanzibar it caused a glut of slaves; the market price plummeted as slaves were now considered carriers of the dreaded disease. Large numbers of Zanzibari slaves were therefore assembled for shipment northwards. Then the great hurricane of 1872 convulsed Zanzibar, ruined Arab plantations on the island, and made slaves a burden on their owners.

In this context the Sultan's resolve to resist British demands for abolition weakened. In 1873 Sir Bartle Frere arrived in the island and delivered a virtual ultimatum to Sultan Barghash. An agreement was signed, abolishing the notorious slave market and the export of slaves to Zanzibar. But this 'triumph' of British imperial power did not halt the East African slave market. Slaves from inland were taken north or smuggled across the strait to the Pemba Islands. Chaillé-Long contemptuously referred to the Bartle Frere agreement as 'a papal bull against the comet'. A blockade to stop the trade would have needed to stretch three-quarters of the way round Africa and the only effective blockade ever mounted on the east coast was the Anglo-German effort of the first half of 1889, achieved at enormous cost.

How did the slaves reach the coast? A typical slaving scenario would go like this. An Arab entrepreneur would borrow money, typically from the Hindu moneylenders of Zanzibar. The contract would stipulate repayment of the capital on the basis of an amount of ivory worth twice the advance. The slaver would then hire 100–300 men for his vile business, usually the riff-raff of jails and the *canaille* of waterfront stews. The next task was to purchase guns and ammunition and hundreds of pounds of glass beads. The slaver's men were usually paid five months' wages in advance at, say, nine shillings a month, with a promise to pay at the rate of sixteen shillings a month for any period exceeding five months. This advance would be paid partly in cash and partly in cloth.

Once in the interior, the slaver had to make friends with his target chief. He would begin by subtly insinuating himself into the local life of the tribe, trading beads and cloth for ivory. But it was the Arabs' firearms that were the particular object of desire; these the Arabs would trade only in exchange for concubines. Thus, ever so gently, began the trade in human flesh. More and more guns were released for more and more slaves. After 3–4 months the Arabs might have enough slaves to send a caravan back to the coast.

The next stage was when the Arab trader became a power-broker in local politics. Usually, the chief would seize the opportunity to steal a march on a local rival and would agree to join forces with the Arabs for a raid on his neighbours. Typically the combined band of cut-throats would reach the unsuspecting village before dawn. The raiders then surrounded the village, fired the huts and poured volleys of musketry into the flaming thatch. As the panic-stricken victims rushed out of their blazing homes, the men would be shot down 'like pheasants in a battue'. The women and children would be kidnapped and the cattle driven off as booty.

The women were then secured in an instrument called a *sheba*, made of a forked pole, secured by a cross-piece lashed behind, and fashioned so that the neck of the prisoner fitted into the fork. The wrists were tied together on the pole in front of the body. Children were fastened by their necks with a rope attached to the women so as to form a living chain. Cameron reported that slaves were often gagged by having a piece of wood, like a snaffle, tied into their months. In the Manyema region heavy slave forks around the neck were combined with hands tied behind backs. The slaves were next attached by a cord to the vendor's waist. Together with the cattle they were then taken to the slaver's headquarters, ready for the march to the coast. The slaver's men received one-third of the stolen animals as booty; the slaver two-thirds plus the slaves. The slaves were then put up for sale at public auction. To avoid retaliation from Europeans, the deed of sale was made out for soap, shoes or cloth. The only hope for the women and children was if a husband redeemed them with ivory. The end of the story in the interior usually involved a quarrel between the Arab entrepreneur and his tribal ally. This chief would then be murdered and his people in turn enslaved.

E.J. Glave once questioned a slave woman in Masankusu village about her fate. He was touched by the way the woman clutched her starving little child to her shrunken breast. She told the following tale:

> I was living with my husband and three children in an inland village, not many miles from here. My husband was a hunter. Ten days ago the Lufembe raiders attacked our settlement; my husband defended himself, but was overpowered and speared to death with several of the other villagers. I was brought here with my three children, two of whom have already been purchased by the slave traders. I shall never see them any more. Perhaps they will sacrifice them on the death of some chief, or perhaps kill them for food. My remaining child, you see, is ill, dying from starvation; they give us nothing to eat. I expect even this one will be taken from me today, as the chief, fearing lest it should die and become a total loss, has offered it for a very small price. As for myself, they will sell me to one of the neighbouring tribes to toil in the plantations, and when I become too old and unfit for work I shall be killed to celebrate the death of a free man.

Further additions would be made to the slave manpower of a caravan as it made its way slowly to the coast. A chief might sell a job-lot of criminals and no-goods from his village. In times of famine or scarcity parents would sell their children to passing caravans for food. Sometimes an entire village would be enticed to join the procession on the promise of food a day's march away, only to find themselves prisoners. More usually, people would simply be inveigled into a caravan by the prospects of a bulk sale of food only to find themselves in chains.

Slaves, when conveyed by canoe along rivers, were temporarily relieved of the weight of the heavy shackles. Slave traders always carried light handcuffs, of cord and cane, hanging from the sheath of their knives. The slave was packed on the floor of a canoe in a crouching posture, with hands bound in front by handcuffs. When the canoe was tethered to the bank at night, further precautions were taken. The position of the bound hands was changed; they were pinioned behind the back so that the wretched slaves could not attempt to loose their bonds by gnawing through the strands. If the party was a small one, to make escape impossible, the slave's wrist was bound to that of the master, so that any movement would arouse him. A river or lake journey on a large caravan was bound to produce huge casualties. On the 200-mile journey across Lake Tanganyika to Ujiji, slaves sat doubled up in the bottoms of canoes, so tightly packed that on average 25 per cent were found to be dead on arrival at Ujiji.

The German explorer Wissmann once met a caravan 200 miles from the coast and 1000 miles from its starting point on the upper Congo. Hundreds of slaves were fastened together with long chains and neck-yokes, in sets of 10–20. Women and children who were not expected to escape were tied with ropes only or left unfettered. The men were walking two by two in the *mukongwa* or slave-fork, in which the head was fastened. They were in a miserable and lamentable state, their arms and legs almost fleshless, their bodies shrivelled, their heads bent and looks heavy. Wissmann noticed that the slaves were bound together according to their powers of marching, without regard to sex. A.J. Swann noted that on many slave caravans the fettering system was haphazard. Some slaves were chained together by the neck. Others had their necks fastened into the forks of 6-ft poles, the ends of which were supported by the men who preceded them. The women carried babies on their backs, in addition to a tusk of ivory on their heads.

The tribulations endured by slaves on the march to the coast were harrowing. Wissmann reckoned that the life expectancy of a working slave, as opposed to a harem female, was about one year. Cameron estimated that in order to deliver 5000 slaves to the coast, a slaver would have to devastate a hundred villages. Human deaths during the raids and on the march to the coast would amount to at least 30,000. In a 'micro-study' of the problem, he demonstrated that, to obtain a haul of fifty-two female prisoners, the slavers destroyed ten villages, each with a population of 200–1500 souls. Most of the inhabitants were incinerated when their huts were burned down around their heads, shot as they struggled out through the smoke with wives and families, or later perished of starvation in the jungle. At Mtowa village Thomson found a slave caravan which had set out from Manyema with 3000 slaves; 2000 had already fallen victim to famine, murder and disease. Thomson thought a survival rate of one in three was a reasonable average. Livingstone put the figure even lower: 'It is our deliberate opinion, from what we knew and have seen, that not one-fifth of the victims of the slave-trade ever become slaves. Taking the Shire valley as an average, we should say not even one-tenth arrive at their destination.'

On the trek to the coast slaves suffered continuously from starvation. The subsistence allowed was a cowrie shell a day. With this one could buy a single potato or a maize cob. Slaves were supposed to exist on this for a march of 10–15 miles a day. Meanwhile their filthy bodies were scarred by lashes from the *chikote* – a piece of hide used as a whip. A swarm of flies followed the column everywhere, feeding off the blood that ran from the open sores on the slaves' feet and shoulders. Death followed quickly from starvation or from eating poisonous fungi in a desperate attempt to supplement the diet. In their weakened state the slaves were an easy prey for disease. A 1000-strong caravan was once virtually wiped out by smallpox.

Sometimes stragglers on the road would have their throats cut, *pour encourager les autres*. If a slave was ill and unable to continue the journey, he was killed. The Arabs reasoned that if they showed any mercy, the entire caravan would at once 'go sick'. It was clearly illogical, as intelligent Europeans saw, to condemn the slave trade as evil but somehow to expect that the said evil could be carried out in a humanitarian way. As one of them remarked: 'The system of slavery is diabolical. You cannot carry it out on *couleur de rose* principles.'

Slave caravans from the west usually made for Ujiji first, where they did not loiter, as the town was notorious for its unhealthy climate. Then they pressed on to Tabora. Not all slaves were taken to the coast. Tippu Tip used to ship some to the Zambezi, where they were sold to the Portuguese. Others were traded along the way for food, particularly oxen: the going rate in the heyday of the slave trade was an adult male for one ox. Other slavers lay in wait along the route of the caravan, picking up stragglers or inducing slaves to desert, to increase their life expectancy by being sold in Ujiji or Tabora rather than Bagamoyo or Zanzibar.

Next stop on the trek east was Tabora, and then Mpwapwa, the 'Clapham Junction' of Africa, where other trade routes from the north and south converged. In a single year 200 caravans would pass through Mpwapwa, bearing maybe 30,000 slaves. On reaching the coast the problem was to run the British blockade and get the slaves to Zanzibar. There were three main ways to circumvent the British. One was to wait until the monsoon season drove the British squadron off station. Another was to keep the slaves at the coast until they could speak Swahili fluently, then ship them over to Zanzibar openly in detachments, with documents claiming them as natives of the island returning from the mainland. A third way was to run up the French flag; French resistance to the right to search seriously impaired British efforts to end the slave trade. Livingstone testified to the way the French tricolour was cynically used as cover by Arab traders in the Mozambique channel, who sneeringly challenged Britain to do something about it.

Explorers who felt passionately about the slave trade fumed at the impotence of the British blockade. Cameron proposed a police cordon through Nyasaland, across the country between lakes Nyasa and Tanganyika and on to Lake Victoria and the Albert Nyasa, but even if this could have been financed and manned, it would merely have altered and diverted the slave routes, not abolished them. The only way the scheme could be made practicable was if the cordon was one of traders, who by their enterprise were able to persuade the tribes that the products of labour were more profitable than those of slavery. Even so, that would still leave unguarded the routes from the centre of Africa to Morocco and to Portuguese Angola. There was also a fear that total abolition of slavery overnight might lead to a bloodbath. The Arabs would be unwilling to feed and clothe slaves over whom they had no control, but on the other hand to release them would be to create an explosive revolutionary situation. The destruction of their former possessions might be the preferred solution.

From Bagamoyo, or from Kilwa, the centre for slave-exporting from the Nyasa and Zambezi area, slaves were exported to three main areas. Large numbers went to Zanzibar as household servants; the majority of Zanzibaris were slaves, even the *wangwana* – the so-called 'free men'. Even greater numbers went to Pemba, the world centre of the clove industry, which depended on slavery. A third detachment went to Muscat, centre for the re-export trade to Arabia, Persia, Syria and Turkey.

In time the people of Manyema, who intermarried with the Arabs, outdid their mentors in the sale of human flesh. When the Arabs first came to Manyema, the people were terrified of their guns and thought the Arabs had stolen lightning. But they learned quickly. Lugard thought the Manyema were *tabula rasa*. Originally brave, loyal, trustworthy and the best porters in Africa, they had the bad luck to encounter the Arabs before they met Europeans. They then became so addicted to slavery that Harry Johnston swore they must have had Arab blood in their veins to begin with. Their country became Arabised and resembled Zanzibar in its half-caste population. Cruel, pitiless and formidable, the Manyema could put 2000 men armed with breech-loaders into the field. They were a notable thorn in the side of Livingstone, and later of Stanley. Their depredations completely ruined the plans of the German explorer Stuhlmann, as they laid waste the lands to the north-east by which he had hoped to travel to the savannah country.

The two explorers who saw most of the slave traders were Livingstone and Baker. Livingstone first encountered the slave trade in 1851–2 when he penetrated north into the territory of the Makololo chief Sebebwane and found the Portuguese from Angola there. The Makololo told him that until the coming of the Portuguese the idea of buying and selling human beings had never occurred to them. But Livingstone did concede that among some Central African tribes slave trading was customary. In 1853 Livingstone met his first Arab slavers, who had just reached Makololo territory, having been held at bay before by the falls that barred passage on the Zambezi. Said bin Habib offered to put his men at Livingstone's disposal, but the doctor felt he could not compromise his principles just to discover another lake.

During his journey to Loanda on the west coast (Nov. 1853-June 1854), Livingstone met many slave gangs. He reported that slavery impeded exploration, since wherever the slavers had been the locals thereafter made no distinction between them and genuine explorers, and because the tribes were more exorbitant in their demands; the spread of the slave trade had inflationary effects. As Livingstone commented wearily: 'There is a universal curse in slavery.' When he reached Mozambique in 1856 after his great trans-Africa journey, Livingstone found that the Portuguese regularly sold slaves to the Transvaal Boers in exchange for ivory; even worse, from Livingstone's point of view, was that the principal traders were half-castes. It was this that aroused the doctor's ire and led to his famous contrast between the good intentions of the Lisbon government and the corruption and venality of its men on the spot.

On his second expedition, in the Zambezi valley, Livingstone frequently drew attention to the rapid spread of slavery since his first visit. He thought there had been a significant increase in the trade in the Zambezi region and attributed this to the drive by the Portuguese and Arabs to acquire more slaves for export; later scholarly work has confirmed his impressions. In Livingstone's writings there are many descriptions of the horror and devastation caused by slavers in the Nyasa region, where the Arabs were particularly active. He estimated that some 20,000 slaves a year were being taken out of the Lake Nyasa area. On one notable occasion he met a long line of manacled men, women and children. Lashing them on were black drivers armed with muskets and dressed in various articles of finery, marching jauntily in front and at the rear of the line, blowing exultant notes on long tin horns as if engaged on some noble task. At sight of Livingstone, the caravan leaders bolted. Livingstone liberated the slaves. They knelt down and thanked him. All the adults had their necks in the fork of a stout stick, 6–7ft long, kept in by an iron rod, riveted at both ends across the throat. When the women were told to take the meal they were carrying and cook it for breakfast, they thought it too good to be true. One little boy said to Livingstone's men: 'The others tied and starved us; you cut our ropes and tell us to eat. What sort of people are you? Where did you come from?' Then they told their harrowing tales. Two women had been shot the day before for trying to untie thongs. One man who collapsed with fatigue was cut down with an axe. Another woman had her child's brains dashed out because she complained she could not carry it *and* the load.

Livingstone's most sustained experience of the slave trade was on his last expedition, between 1866 and 1873. When he ascended the Rovuma river, he found the terrain littered with dead slaves, abandoned slaves and slave sticks. The Arabs had been forced across Lake Nyasa by the local tribes, but the Mazitu slavers had laid waste an area 100 miles broad and depopulated it. What had previously been a populous, fertile, well-watered land was now a desert which took eight days' hard marching to cross. He deplored the Arabs' consistent use of force to gain their ends, fearing that the end of the line would be a continent-wide war of Arab against African. That in turn would make things even worse, as the Arabs, unable to obtain supplies of ivory, would invest even more heavily in slaves. 'Slavery is a great evil wherever I have seen it . . . even in its best phases, I would not be a slave-dealer for all the world.'

In 1867 Livingstone was obliged to travel for protection with Central Africa's most famous slaver, Tippu Tip. This was an example of the curious symbiosis of explorers and slave traders that was a marked feature of the second half of the century and which drew so much critical fire from England. Livingstone had already been censured by the *bien-pensants* of Exeter Hall for the alliance of convenience he formed in 1858 with the Portuguese slaver Marianno. Tippu Tip later travelled with Cameron and Stanley and gave them invaluable help. Yet the explorers were thereby drawn into morally ambiguous domains. Livingstone chafed at his dependence, but his own ill-health and lack of food made co-existence with the Arabs a necessity. Whenever Livingstone expostulated with tribal elders on their connivance and collaboration with the Arabs, they retorted with the oldest excuse in the book: we'll give up when everyone else does. But the doctor was severe with those of his followers who dared to buy children as slaves. Towards Tippu Tip, as towards his other Arab friends, Said bin Habib and Muhammad bin Gharib, he was tolerant; he regarded them as the acceptable, or least objectionable face, of the slave trade.

Livingstone hated his time in Ujiji because of his dependence on the Arabs. In his *Journals* he railed at them: 'This is a den of the worst kind of slave-traders; those whom I met in Urungu and Itawa were gentlemen traders: the Ujiji slavers, like the Kilwa and the Portuguese, are the vilest of the vile.' His former liberal attitude towards Arab slavers began to harden, especially after witnessing many atrocities in Ujiji and meeting Arabs who freely confessed that they regarded African lives as of no account.

But nothing Livingstone experienced in Ujiji had prepared him for the dreadful, traumatic holocaust he witnessed in Nyangwe in July 1871. On the morning of 15 July Livingstone paid his customary visit to the market, hoping to forget his troubles in the hurly-burly of the crowd. It was a hot, sultry day, and about 1500 people, mainly women, thronged the market. After a while, finding the heat oppressive, he began to walk back towards his house. He had not walked more than thirty yards when two guns went off almost at once. Immediately there was pandemonium in the market. Stalls were knocked over as hucksters and buyers fled in panic. The crowd split into two, one section making for the upper end of the market-place, another for the river. Livingstone saw three gunmen pouring volley after volley into the market fugitives. But an even more terrible fate awaited those who had rushed for their canoes beached in a narrow inlet of the Lualaba. A much larger party of gunmen was waiting in ambush here. Most of the panic-stricken refugees got to the canoes without being hit. But then they discovered that in their terror they had forgotten to bring their paddles with them. Unable to shove off into the river, they could only sit impotently while fresh arrivals poured into the overloaded canoes. Soon the creek was jammed with sinking, overladen and unwieldy canoes. Into this mêlée of jostling, shrieking humanity and capsizing canoes the Arab gunmen directed a devastating fire. Their victims were sitting ducks.

Seeing that the canoes were a death-trap, others ran along the bank past the creek and plunged into the open river. Livingstone could soon see a long line of heads making for an island about a mile offshore. Yet in their panic and crazed desire to get out of range of the guns, the fugitives had forgotten the formidable strength of the Lualaba current. Almost to a man, the swimmers were swept downstream. Some did not have the strength to keep swimming and quietly sank beneath the water. Others were taken by crocodiles. There were about a hundred people in the river but one by one their heads disappeared.

Meanwhile three canoes had finally managed to break out from the killing grounds in the creek onto the open river, their occupants paddling with hands and arms. But the three canoes were soon overwhelmed as desperate swimmers tried to clamber on board. All three craft were swamped and capsized, and their human freight pitched into the river to die with the other unfortunates. A mere handful of those who took to the water survived, and only then because they had the presence of mind to swim back towards the sound of the guns.

From the other side of the river came the sound of shooting and the sight of columns of smoke. It was abundantly clear that what had happened in Nyangwe market was no spontaneous combustion. The massacre was premeditated. It later transpired to have been fomented by Dugumbe, the most powerful Arab in Nyangwe, for reasons of 'credibility', since the locals had begun trading with an upstart slave of Said bin-Habib's, and Dugumbe feared that his power over them might be slipping away. He therefore decided to teach them a dreadful lesson. The same Dugumbe appeared at Livingstone's side as he stood shaking with rage, uncertain whether to draw his pistol and attack the three gunmen. Dugumbe calmed Livingstone and persuaded him that it would be a mistake to become embroiled in local vendettas. As a sop to the white man Dugumbe spared the lives of all who sought Livingstone's personal protection.

Over the next few days Livingstone took stock of the situation. Between 330 and 400 Nyangwe people, most of them market women, had been killed. Twenty-seven villages had been put to the torch. His mind was in agony, and he was plagued by recurrent nightmares in which he relived the terrible events of 15 July.

Livingstone detested the sin more than the sinner. He liked many individual Arabs but hated what they had done to Africa. By diffusing guns and powder through the Continent, the Arabs increased the ferocity of tribal wars by augmenting the destructive capability of these subsistence-level societies. Their readiness to buy slaves *increased* pre-existing internal stability; *pace* the propaganda of the missionaries it did not cause it. Slavery, after all, was not an alien imposition but a co-operative endeavour between Arab and African. The comparative absence of *general* African hostility towards the Arabs was precisely because buying and selling human beings was a culture already widespread in the Dark Continent. Finally, it should be said that it was consummate humbug for Europeans to blame Arabs exclusively for the slave trade, when they themselves did not eschew the products of its ultimate motor, the ivory trade.

Though he was never a witness to a transcendent horror like the Nyangwe massacre, Baker in many ways saw even more of the slave trade, since his travels and explorations took place in the very eye of the flesh-trading hurricane. Slavery was entrenched in Equatoria almost as soon as the physical barrier of the *sudd* was breached. Petherick reported that in many areas of the upper Nile the most enthusiastic slavers were Europeans: the Frenchman Dolphin Bartholémy, the Austrian Michael Luftolla, the Maltese Andrea de Bono and the Belgians Ambrose and Jules Poncet. These men worked hand-in-glove with venal Sudanese and Nubian officials of the Cairo government.

Schweinfurth was another explorer who pointed up the contrast between official Egyptian condemnation of the slave trade and the behaviour of its men in the field: 'Nowhere in the world can more inveterate slave-dealers be found than the commanders of the small detachments of Egyptian troops.' He instanced Darfur as the nucleus of the Central African slave traffic. It was a frontier boom town which afforded a refuge to every type of criminal in the Sudan. Schweinfurth reported that it was common for Sudanese in the course of a quarrel to utter the threat: 'I will murder you and escape to Darfur.' Overlaying all was the 'spendacious mendacity' of the Islamic Nubians: 'Untruthfulness has become to them a second nature, and most of them will tell lies by habit, even when it is not of the smallest advantage to conceal the truth.' Schweinfurth estimated that by the late 1860s 3000–4000 slaves a year were imported from the Bahr-el-Ghazal to Egypt; in addition, between 12,000–15,000 slaves a year were exported overland from the Azande and Mangbetu country. Speke's and Grant's reports also showed clearly that the slave trade was increasing on the upper Nile in the 1860s.

This was the situation Baker found when in 1861–2 he got his first taste of slave merchants at Gallabah on the Blue Nile in 1861–2. Soon afterwards, in 1863, he came very close to an armed clash with slavers. Baker placated his 'rival' by swearing that he was not interested in ivory; once calmed down, the slaver admitted that all his fellow traders had watched Baker's approach with alarm, as they suspected him of being a consul in disguise.

Baker soon learned the 'wrinkles' of slavery. He reported that in a good season 150 men on a slaving expedition could emerge with 20,000 lb of ivory, valued in Khartoum at £4000, as well as 400–500 unredeemed slaves worth £5–6 each. Since the slaver's men were paid in slaves, his wages bill was nil. He did, however, point out that slaving expeditions carried no cast-iron guarantees of success. One Muhammad Her with 110 Nubians, Sudanese and Arabs and 300 local allies were massacred to the last man by the Latookas after an unsuccessful attempt at ambush. With his typical disdain for the African, Baker could not resist gilding the lily by adding that the Latookas acquiesced in the capture of their women and children, but counterattacked ferociously only when the raiders tried to seize their cattle.

It was not long before Baker had fallen into cosy coexistence with slavers. His jaundiced comments on his fellow travellers were made from the peaceful security of a secluded courtyard. Outside the walls the slavers' men made a corn still and spent the day drinking, fighting and gambling: 'The natives were ill treated, their female slaves and children brutally ill used, and the entire camp was a mere slice from the infernal regions.' One of Baker's stories conveys very well the sickening atmosphere of routine brutality. On one raid a pretty girl of fifteen had been captured. Soon afterwards a man arrived from the plundered village with ivory for her ransom. 'Hardly had he entered the gateway when the girl, who was sitting at the door of her owner's hut, caught sight of him, and springing to her feet, she ran as fast as her chained ankles would allow her, and threw herself in his arms, exclaiming, "My father!" It was her father who had thus risked his life in the enemy's camp to ransom his child.' The sequel was almost predictable. The slavers, realising the situation, set on the man, bound him to a tree, and shot him dead without more ado. The incident hardened Baker, who objected to anybody but himself using force. Shortly afterwards a woman and her daughter escaped from the slavers and were recaptured. The slavers sentenced them to a flogging. Baker intervened to oppose the punishment. He warned the slavers that not only would he oppose any flogging by force but having defeated the floggers he would take them to Khartoum and denounce them as murderers. Even an Arab cut-throat knew better than to oppose 'the Beard' when he was in this mood. The slavers acquiesced in their humiliation.

On another occasion Baker faced down a party of slavers who intended to attack Kamurasi, by showing the British flag and declaring Bunyoro a British protectorate. But his larger boasts, when governor of Equatoria in the early 1870s, to have suppressed the slave trade were so much hot air. All Baker did was to stir up the slave traders without achieving any concrete results. He himself virtually admitted that his bombast was worse than useless. In 1863, on reaching Gondokoro, he found a populous region teeming with vast herds of cattle. On his second journey in 1872, he found the area denuded of people; the slave trade had wiped the land of milk and honey off the face of the earth. On the marchlands of Bunyoro the situation was even worse:

> It is impossible to describe the change that had taken place since I last visited this country. It was then a perfect garden, thickly populated and producing all that man could desire . . . all is wilderness! The population has fled! Not a village is to be seen! This is the certain result of the settlement of the Khartoum traders. They kidnap the women and children for slaves, and plunder and destroy wherever they set foot.

But Baker's rhetoric boomeranged. His *Albert Nyanza* had made a big impact on readers in Britain when published in 1866. But when he brought out *Ismailia*, dealing with the second expedition, Baker found that his reputation had dimmed. Critics roasted him on the fork of either humbug or naïveté for his claim to have led a large military force south merely to extirpate the slave trade:

> That a tried traveller . . . a man who had already spent years in those regions of Central Africa where the slave trade is indigenous . . . should be so credulous as to suppose that even the Khedive would be ready to organise such an expedition for philanthropy alone, quite passes our belief.

The plain truth was that there was nothing the explorers could do to alter or mitigate the slave trade. It was purely a choice between realism and posturing, between pacific methods and self-destructive sabre-rattling. Some reviewers noticed that on the slave trade, as on so many other issues, Baker and Livingstone were polar opposites. Livingstone believed in peace, Baker in war; Livingstone loved the black man, Baker hated and despised him; Livingstone believed that missionary endeavour had to precede trade in Africa; Baker believed the reverse. There is no question but that Livingstone largely won the battle for public opinion in Britain. One critic wrote: 'Compare the bloody march to Gondokoro with the "death scene" in Livingstone's *Last Journals*, and the heroic march to the coast, and you have a fair key to what the two methods are likely to accomplish for the regeneration of the African race.'

The experiences of Livingstone, Baker and other explorers also enable us to offer some generalisations on the relationship of the ivory trade to the slave trade. Clearly there was a close connection between the two: Livingstone stated that 'black ivory carried white ivory'. But the correlations have to be stated with care. Obviously, the ivory trade was more lucrative when the porters were slaves and there were fewer overheads. It did not need a superlative economist to work this out. A tusk which in Buganda could be bought for a Snider rifle and a hundred cartridges would sell at the coast for up to £50. If slaves carried the tusks, there were no porterage charges, and the sale of the slaves themselves in Bagamoyo brought in a welcome bonus. Nor was any expense involved in bringing guns and ammunition upcountry, as porters were glad to carry them for their own protection. This was one good reason why, *pace* the missionaries, legitimate trade did not at once drive out the slave trade. The ivory trade was 'legitimate' but the cheapest way to supply it was by slave porterage. Thomson, who thought that the missionaries really had dealt a death-blow to the trade in the Shire and Nyasa areas, testified that after the 1873 Bartle Frere treaty the principal object of slavery was to obtain unpaid carriers for ivory. Thomson further reported that the traffic in slaves alone would never repay the slavers. Slaves were also taken to force tribes to disgorge their caches of ivory, since villagers, fearing raiders, never stored tusks in their huts but buried them in the ground outside the village perimeter.

But the interlock of slaves and ivory should not be pushed too far. It was ivory and ivory solely that drove the Arabs across half the continent; they would not have penetrated the dark forests of the upper Congo for slaves alone, since there were tens of thousands of these available much nearer the east coast. Livingstone himself admitted that the slave trade was a *pis aller* for those Arabs who could not make the grade as ivory hunters. Cameron reported that Tippu Tip actually preferred to hire regular porters to carry his tusks rather then use slaves: 'Tippu Tip and many Arab traders asserted that they would be glad to find other means of transport for their goods instead of trusting to slaves; but not regarding slave-dealing as a sin in the abstract, they availed themselves of the means at their disposal.'

On the other hand, those primarily interested in slaves did not acquire them to carry ivory. The bulk of slaves consisted of women and children – scarcely ideal carriers for huge tusks; the adult males, moreover, were usually in chains or slave sticks so could not act as bearers. On his way inland in 1871 Stanley met a slave gang and drew attention to this aspect: 'The chains were ponderous – they might have held elephants captive: but as the slaves carried nothing but themselves, their weight could not have been insupportable.' On the Ituri river in 1889 Stanley saw an even more striking demonstration of the proposition that slaves and ivory were things apart. He met a flotilla of fifty-seven canoes laden with helpless women and children slaves plus professional porters bearing 15 tons of ivory, who had been hired at the coast and points inland.

A symbiosis developed between explorer and slave trader, most notably the help that Tippu Tip gave Livingstone, Cameron and Stanley – and there are many other examples. This mutual tolerance became part of the pattern of African life in the frontier era and struck deep roots. Even the settled missionaries were prepared to follow Livingstone's example and were not so antagonistic to the slavers as might have been expected. To some extent this was simple realism. The missionary knew he had no power to release slaves from Arab settlements or caravans. Even if he had had the power to release those who wanted freedom, he would have been unable to feed them. Both the Arabs and the slaves knew this, and therefore desertions to the mission stations were rare, except at the coast. On the other hand, the missions were a great help to the Arabs, who were able to obtain medical supplies and leave their sick slaves there. It was the custom of the missionaries to accept on condition they could allow the slaves to escape; the Arabs assented willingly, knowing there was no place for them to escape to.

The symbiosis was also often unwitting on the explorers' part. By the late 1880s and early 1890s some 20,000 porters a month were leaving Bagamoyo for the interior. Slave owners signed on their slaves as porters on European expeditions without revealing their servile status. While the slave was away, the master looked after the slave's family; on his return, the slave would make over three-quarters of his accumulated pay to his master. All unknowingly, therefore, the explorers used slaves. Three-quarters of Stanley's 680 porters on the Emin Pasha expedition were slaves. The Uganda railway survey party in the 1890s consisted largely of slaves, as did Sir Gerald Portal's 1893 mission to Uganda. In the same period the British East Africa Company had 1300 *wangwana* in its service, and most were slaves. The ultimate absurdity was that the Royal Navy vessels on the anti-slave trade patrol were coaled and bunkered at Zanzibar by slave labour. For all that, the slavers took a risk in allowing their vassals to act as porters on European expeditions. Such slaves experienced a form of 'consciousness raising' as they imbibed European culture and values and learned the ways of the white man.

Slave traders also acted as a transmission belt between the Europeans and the Africans. Harry Johnston reported that the truculent Chief Mandara knew of Mirambo and Mutesa, had heard of Sultan Barghash and the consul, Kirk, and even Queen Victoria. Though he had never travelled more than fifty miles from his birthplace, Mandara knew of the British conquest of India, the French occupation of Madagascar, and the German descent on coastal East Africa. He greatly dreaded the coming of the French and the Germans for, as Johnston noted: 'Curiously enough the European power most liked and respected by the Zanzibar traders is England, though for half a century we have tried our hardest to ruin the slave trade.'

However, it would be a mistake to imagine that all was sweetness and light in the relationship between slavers and explorers. Without any doubt, as Arab tentacles reached farther and farther inland, to the Congo, Buganda and Burundi, the difficulties of the explorers were compounded. Quite apart from the price inflation the traders engendered, and the perennial problem of being mistaken for slavers and thus incurring the backlash owing to their earlier raids, explorers suffered in two main ways from Arab inroads. Where the Arabs had been worsted in battle by the tribes, the locals had gained confidence, were no longer afraid of guns and thus could not be browbeaten by European travellers. Where the Arabs had won, the result was usually the abomination of desolation. Raids could transform an area almost overnight. Cameron, travelling in an area where Livingstone had reported plentiful food and a thriving population just sixteen months earlier, found a charred wilderness where a carrion crow overflying would have to carry its own provisions. Only the most heavily stockaded villages, full of armed warriors, were safe from marauders. The result was the destruction of normal agricultural life. The threat from slave raiders reduced many tribes to starvation. They dared not send their women into the plantations to work, lest they be carried off by slavers; they were thus reduced to eating roots, flies, caterpillars and crickets. Clearly there was no relief there for any expedition that did not carry a full complement of rations. Guy Burrows once asked the Mabode of the Welle for a translation of a doleful lament they were singing. It turned out to be a dire comment on the Arabs as 'wrath of God':

> They kill us all with the gun
> They killed my father with the gun.
> They killed my mother with the gun
> They killed my brother with the gun.
> They kill us all with the gun.

The worst part of it was that in many cases it was the endeavours of the explorers that opened up previously inaccessible areas to the Arabs. Livingstone was the first major culprit. When he used a show of force to browbeat chief Tengani into opening up the Shire river, he unwittingly opened the door to the slavers. Stanley prised open the upper Congo beyond Stanley Falls to Tippu Tip and his marauders by his 1876–7 epic voyage down the Congo. Unlocking this door was all the more serious, since Tippu Tip had earlier declared the Lualaba/Congo passage impenetrable and for that very reason had pulled out of his joint venture with Stanley. It was with a feeling of horror and guilt that Stanley, on returning to the upper Congo in 1883 and finding the slavers there, realised that he was fount and origin for the misery visited on the tribes around Stanley Falls. Stanley achieved a dismal double in this regard on the Emin Pasha expedition by opening the Ituri forest, Lake Albert and southern Equatoria to the Arab manhunters. The pattern was everywhere the same. The traveller W.A. Chanler, the next European to visit the remote Lake Rudolph area in northern Kenya after Count Teleki's pioneering expedition, reported that the consequence of the Teleki expedition was to unlock the area to Arab and Swahili marauders.

The explorers often rationalised their guilt for these unintended consequences by claiming that African slavery was not so terrible after all. It was a favourite sport of Richard Burton to dilate on the theme of happy and lazy slaves lounging in the sun while their free masters toiled. Here he cynically took advantage of the inability of one European in a million to differentiate between the relatively innocuous domestic slavery and the calamitous trade for export. The naïve Charles New endorsed this view: 'A slave here is not in worse condition than the free.'

Joseph Thomson, animated as ever by the spirit of contradiction or the imp of the perverse, also rounded vociferously on British *bien pensants*. He scouted the common view in England that slaves were left to starve or subsist on roots and grass. On the contrary, he argued, Arab slave-owners were gentle, humane and kindly; their charges grew up lazy and pampered and spoke to their masters with great licence and even impertinence: 'Of the horrors of the slave trade I saw no sign, beyond meeting an occasional delinquent in chains. In every settlement I visited I saw only contented, well-fed people, leading an idle lazy life . . . During my residence in Africa I never saw an Arab cruelly ill-using any of his slaves.' It was a common argument used by Arab apologists that the Arabs regarded the Dark Continent much as a stupid squire in England might regard his estates. Thomson put his own gloss on the bucolic analogy. If there was a fault in the Arabs, he said, it was that of their culture, which made them look on their slaves as a European would look on a pig. 'If the latter was unable to give his animals food, he would naturally regret to see them die of starvation, but would feel the loss to his pocket more. And so it was with these Arabs. They regretted to see their slaves perish of hunger; but as food proved to be so dear, they could not afford to buy them any as it would have absorbed more than their money value. Hence they were left to starve, without the slightest idea that an inhuman act was being committed.'

Many other explorers rationalised the unwitting role they had played in worsening the lot of the indigenous peoples by exposing them to the slavers. They argued 'once a slave, always a slave'. In other words, it was held that the insecurity and uncertainty of slavery marked a person from birth or from the moment of captivity, in such a way that manumission was actually cruelty masquerading as kindness. Slavery produced people who were liars, cheats, skrimshankers and work-shy barrack-room lawyers. A manumitted slave was invariably therefore an idler and a burden to himself and others; the problem called for extensive retraining and re-education of freedmen.

The Great Powers were slow to respond to the challenge thrown down by the explorers. Despite an overwhelming consensus of public opinion in Europe in favour of suppressing the slave trade, statesmen usually found more pressing business to attend to. It is true that Article 9 of the Treaty of Berlin, which established the Congo Free State as Leopold's personal fief, insisted as a *quid pro quo* for the grant that the monarch abolish slavery in the territory. This Leopold was only too pleased to do, and he accomplished it in a military campaign in 1893, for he had in mind the substitution of one form of slavery for another. On the east coast meanwhile the Portuguese did next to nothing to help the missionaries in their campaign against the slave trade. The British made their perennial mistake of thinking that great issues can be solved by private companies. Frederick Lugard's attempt to crush the slavers of Lake Nyasa in 1888, using the forces of the African Lakes Company, was a humiliating failure. Lugard had to return to England to drum up additional military support.

It took the might of Germany to put a spoke in the revolving wheel of the slave trade. In East Africa the Germans condoned domestic slavery as a necessary social cement but harried the slave trade ruthlessly. At last the Arabs came up against a people prepared to be as merciless as themselves. This was sometimes counter-productive. German efforts to suppress the slave trade were bedevilled by some of their own explorers. It was left to Wissmann to save his country's honour. He took decisive military action against the slavers in 1892 in the area between lakes Nyasa and Tanganyika and then joined forces with Harry Johnston for a thorough extirpation of the Arabs in the Lake Nyasa area itself. Johnston was by then British consul in Mozambique and a committed agent of Cecil Rhodes, but his co-operation with Wissmann in 1893–5 was in some ways his finest hour. It was the German juggernaut advance from Bagamoyo to Tabora and Ujiji that ended the slave trade there and diverted it south-east to Dar es Salaam and its hinterland. The Arabs were caught in a vice, for meanwhile in 1893 Leopold launched his great campaign against Tippu Tip's successors on the upper Congo. By now the slavers were everywhere in retreat, though it took until 1900 for the Germans to wipe out the last traces of the trade in Tanganyika.

Domestic slavery, however, was still thought useful for inculcating models of hierarchial deference. A tug-of-war between reformers in Berlin and administrators pleading expediency in East Africa meant that there were still 50,000 slaves in German East Africa in 1914. Even under the British mandate extirpation of slavery was difficult, and it was 1939 before the last vestiges were cleared out.

The story of the explorers' relationship with the slave trade is not an entirely happy one. Nor did their proselytising endeavours for legitimate trade end by helping Africa very much. The Europeans outwitted the Africans at every turn. The main effect of getting European trade goods in exchange for slaves and ivory was to make tiny élites even richer and more powerful: this phenomenon was observed especially among the Yao, Masari and Makwa chiefs. The goods Africans exchanged for slaves were in no way equal to the ivory extracted from Africa by the West. And what the Africans received in advanced technology did not make up for what they lost in labour power through the ending of slavery.

10

An Object Lesson in Obstacles

The best way to illustrate the manifold hurdles that lay in the explorers'
path is to provide a case study. In order not to make the argument
tendentious, I have selected a relatively obscure part of Stanley's 1874–7
expedition. His three-month crossing of modern Tanzania to Lake
Victoria lacks the high drama of his later time on the lake and his epic
descent of the Congo. It has neither the colour of the meeting with
Livingstone at Ujiji nor the uniquely nightmarish hues of his triple
crossing of the Ituri forest in 1887–8. But for this reason it is a much more
reliable guide to the kinds of obstacles that routinely beset all African
explorers.

After being financed in 1874 by the *Daily Telegraph* and the *New York
Herald* for an expedition to complete Livingstone's work, Stanley arrived
in Zanzibar in September 1874 with three white companions, all very
young men. Frederick Barker was a former hotel clerk and the brothers
Pocock (Frank and Edward) were Medway fishermen. He took four dogs
and six riding asses into the interior with him, but more importantly, he
had 300 porters and 18,000 lb of trade goods and arms. His first objective
was Lake Victoria, but first he took his white men on a reconnaissance of
the Rufiji to acclimatise them. Finally, on 17 November 1874, he gave the
order to march.

The start of what was to be Stanley's greatest exploit in Africa was not
auspicious. The march from Bagamoyo began in great heat under a
dazzling sun which became overpowering as they descended into the
Kingani valley:

The ranks become broken and disordered; stragglers are many; the men
complain of the terrible heat, the dogs pant in agony. Even we ourselves under
our solar topees, with flushed faces and perspiring brows, with handkerchiefs
ever in use to wipe away the drops which almost blind us, and our heavy

woollens giving us a feeling of semi-asphyxiation, would fain rest, were it not that the sun-bleached levels of tawny thirsty valley offer no inducements.

The men cried out for water and some lay on the ground and bemoaned their fate in leaving Zanzibar. Conditions were so bad that by the time they reached Kingani the mastiff Castor had died of a heart-attack, while the other dogs were already in a bad way, Jack the bull-terrier being much bothered by the swarms of grasshoppers he met on the route. At the Kingani river and on the hills between Bagamoyo and Kingani plain Stanley posted his most trusted men as guards to prevent desertions.

At Kikoka on 18 November Stanley reluctantly ordered a day of rest. He was inclined to attribute the excessive exhaustion of the *wangwana* not just to the heat but to the use of drugs, especially opium. His reluctance to halt was borne out when a letter arrived from the troublesome Arab governor of Bagamoyo, asking Stanley's men to return the women they had 'abducted'. When Stanley gave the order for the women to be returned, the *wangwana* sprang to their Sniders. An incipient mutiny was suppressed only with difficulty with the help of the Pococks and his 'faithfuls' from 1871–2. The Zanzibaris then decided they would like to return to Bagamoyo for a final binge but 'they were bodily driven on by the armed guard, not without considerable violence'. The incident brought to the surface all of Stanley's dislike for alcohol. His men had been drunk in Zanzibar, drunk again in Bagamoyo, and if they could get their hands on liquor, would be so again. Stanley tried to set an example by making all his meals teetotal, but his men simply regarded this as an amiable eccentricity. It was now more than ever necessary to put space between his expedition and the troublesome governor.

But if the expedition had got off to an unpropitious start, Stanley still had some grounds for guarded optimisim. He was already developing a warm feeling for the Pococks, especially Frank, who wrote to his parents: 'Mr Stanley is much pleased with us in the way we handle the boat. He is a good man to be away with. We share just as he does in everything.' The boat was a clue to Stanley's optimism. After Ferris the carpenter had cut the boat down by six inches and subdivided each section to make it portable, *Lady Alice* could be carried any distance over any terrain and launched almost at a moment's notice with twelve men (with ten oars and two short paddles). At the Kingani river they screwed together the sections and made a most successful crossing. Stanley's scientific instrumentation was far superior to what he had carried in 1871. He had 224 men in his party (347 souls all told) and twenty-three boxes of ammunition.

What were Stanley's intentions when he set out from Bagamoyo? In following the established caravan route at first he was partly trying to build up his men's confidence and partly trying to avoid the territory of the Masai, for whom he had an exaggerated respect. Once beyond the orbit of the Masai, he intended to strike north-westward to Lake Victoria to establish who was right about this great stretch of waterway. Speke thought Lake Victoria was just one vast lake, Burton thought it was a cluster of several smaller lakes, while Samuel Baker thought that lakes Albert and Tanganyika were one and the same. The way to solve all this was to circumnavigate Lake Victoria and Lake Albert, visiting the great king Mutesa on the way, and possibly to end with a visit to Gordon in Equatoria – Gordon who had no interest in exploration as such. Finally 'beyond this point the whole appears to me so vague and vast that it is impossible to state at this period what I shall try to do next'.

From Kikoka and Rosako they entered the Usigwa country. The going was much easier now. They marched through beautiful parkland, which dipped into lovely vales and rose into gentle ridges. There was plenty of water and grass and the soil was a fat, rich sandstone. They entered Nguru, a luxuriant country as green as an English lawn, and began a steady climb to 1100 ft, despite the fact that some of the porters were already ill from sores, blisters and swollen legs and a few were coughing blood from their lungs.

They pressed on through Mfuteh to the Wami river, home of the timid and suspicious Ngulu people, who gave them a wide berth. Along the Wami river there was abundant game and the banks of the Wami were fringed with tall trees, but beyond these extended grassy plains with patches of thin forest, where the baobab and date palm were most in evidence. This was lion country, and the expedition very soon lost two of its goats to the big cats. But it was the crocodiles (invariably called 'alligators' by the Pococks) who always irritated Stanley most, and he spent much time shooting at them in the river.

On 29 November they hacked their way through a riverside grove of palm, gum, dwarf ebony and stunted copal to reach the Rubuti ford and cross the Wami river. The locals used a caricature Niagara suspension bridge to make the crossing, but the ford was only about 2½ ft deep across the 40-yd-wide river. After traversing the Wami, the expedition continued across its tributaries and after five more river crossings came to Simbamwenni, well known from the 1871 journey. On 3 December they crossed the Mkundi river into Usagara.

The rains had now begun, the trees had a more autumnal aspect, the country was more open. There followed a long, fatiguing march on short water ration through impressive hill scenery to Makubika. Peaks and knolls rose around them in all directions, for they reached an altitude of

4500 ft in Usagara before dropping down to 3500 ft at Mpwapwa. On most of these heights was a village, for this was a land rich in goats and often raided by the Masai for that reason. The locals were jittery and nervous at the passage of such a large expedition.

By 9 December they were at the highest point of Usagara in a plain dotted with dense thorn scrub and teeming with game. Stanley set out to bag some animals for the communal pot. He stalked and shot two fine zebra, then sent his boy Billali back to camp to fetch men to carry the meat. He settled down to guard the kill with only Jack the bull-terrier as company. Just as the sun began to set, he saw a lion coming towards him unsuspectingly, following the scent of the dead zebras. Stanley whistled to warn the carnivore of his presence; the lion bounded off. Ten minutes later the big cat returned with nine others from his pride. Stanley reached for his cartridges, only to realise to his horror that Billali had accidently taken the cartridge bag back to camp with him. Stanley had just three shots left. When the lions were about 150 yds away, Stanley fired at the leader. The lions retreated a bit, then regrouped for another attempt. Stanley began to edge away from the spot, resolved to leave the meat to the pride. Just then a babel of voices was heard and Billali returned with forty well-armed men. A charge through the darkness with guns blazing dispersed the lions and enabled the men to get possession of the meat and bear it off in triumph.

Three days later they reached Mpwapwa. The day before, at Tubugwe, they encountered fourteen human skulls strewn on the plain, relics of a caravan ambushed by Masai raiders. They were making remarkable progress, having been out from Bagamoyo just twenty-five days. This compared with fifty-seven days on the 1871 Livingstone expedition and four months by Cameron, and was achieved while bearing both *Lady Alice* and the pontoon *Livingstone*. But already there was a toll. Fifty bearers had deserted and Edward Pocock had been dreadfully ill with fever during the march through unhealthy coastal flats, marshes and brakes. Yet Stanley scarcely broke step at Mpwapwa. Not even a slight attack of fever detained him. After taking the precaution of bringing 100 gallons of fresh water with them, he insisted on pressing on across the forbidding desert called *Marenga Mkali* (Bitter Water), a flat jungle-covered plain 30–40 miles wide, without a single drop of water or a single human dwelling place. The heat was intense, the earth foetid, the exhalations from the swamps nauseous, the thorn bushes a constant impediment. This was ideal terrain for an ambush: 'Had an enemy lurked in the jungle of sufficient audacity and power to withstand a few Sniders, the expedition might have been ruined there and then.'

So far they had trekked through plains interspersed with groves of tamarisks, sycamore, cottonwood and baobab but as they crossed from Usagara into Ugogo on 16 December there was nothing to break the monotony of the broad bleak plain but the occasional solitary baobab. Both Stanley and Frank Pocock now began to suffer from fever, in addition to heat and thirst. And the Wagogo were their usual extortionate selves. Gourds of water for the expedition now cost two yards of cloth. Stanley had to remain in camp at Chikombo while he recovered from fever. He recuperated much faster than the Pococks, but as soon as he was well he ordered the advance; the reality of illness was always judged by Stanley strictly in accordance with his own sensations. The advance killed off the Newfoundland Nero who was already blind and weak from disease.

They were now edging northward through Ugogo. Stanley found that the advantages of this northern route did not outweigh those of the southern itinerary he had followed in 1871; *hongo* was not quite so high on a per capita basis, but there were more chiefs, so things balanced out. He grew weary of the everlasting demand for *doti* every morning before the expedition could even get under way.

But there was worse in store. As they proceeded farther into Ugogo, they found the whole country in the grip of famine. Soon there was no question of eating meat. Stanley survived on boiled rice, tea and coffee but by the end of the month his rice had run out and he was reduced to eating the local porridge. His weight shrank from the 180 lb at which he had topped the scales earlier in the year at Windsor with his short-term fiancée Alice Pike, to 134 lb. This brought on another attack of fever. At least as bad as the famine was the rain. It had rained intermittently every day since Rosako, but on 23 December when they were half-way across Ugogo, the monsoon season began in earnest. The temperature plummeted from 96 to 69°F, thunder and lightning crashed around them, and the dry riverbeds became raging torrents.

Christmas Day 1874 was the most miserable any of the four white men could remember. They sat huddled in their tents in wet clothes and blankets while the downpour outside produced a flood in no more than fifteen minutes. A third dog died. Next day Stanley decided to cut through the jungle to avoid paying tribute. They slogged through a thorny bush of acacias, tamarisks, mimosa and blue gum, crisscrossed with elephant tracks. On 28 December they emerged at the village of Masumami, the first Gogo chief to impress Stanley. In return for 13 *doti* he gave him an ox and 2 gallons of milk. He went on to ask Stanley to stop the rain from falling on his lands and was disconcerted when Stanley revealed that he had no power to do so.

Next day they marched across the sterile desert of Salina, level as a sea, but containing not a drop of water. When the predictable torrent rained down on them, it transformed the desert into a quagmire within an hour. Frank Pocock remembered this storm as being every bit as ferocious as the one that engulfed them over Christmas. They had to slurp and slosh up to their waists in mud and water. As if this was not enough, when they approached the village of Mukonduku, the Wagogo approached in warpaint with spears raised. It transpired fortunately that they were doing nothing more than putting on a show.

But Stanley faced serious problems in Mukonduku. He found the chief, Chalula, to be crafty, hostile, insolent and extortionate: 24 *doti* was demanded and paid. This stuck in Stanley's craw but the chief had 2000 well-armed warriors at his call; it would require no less than 500 *wangwana* with Sniders to see them off effectively. A difficult situation was made worse by a conspiracy of fifty of his men. When Stanley detected it, he clapped the ringleaders in irons and had them flogged; this provoked a spate of desertions. On his last day in Ugogo Stanley faced serious problems: desertion, a lengthening sick-list, hostility from Chalula, famine and torrential storms. For a day he was *hors de combat* with fever while Barker and the Pococks deputised. Then on New Year's Day 1875, with guides from Chalula, he struck north off the road to Unyanyembe, skirting the eastern base of the upland plateau wall or hilly range.

They were now in Ukimbu, where no white man had been before, and as such were the object of especial curiosity from the locals. To assuage their anxieties, the travellers went through blood-brotherhood ceremonies with them. On the second day of January their Gogo guides deserted them and one of the expedition's donkeys was taken by a hyena. There was more cover for predators in the hills. On the Gogo plain there were only the acacias, gums and euphorbias; on the plateau there were many groves of the *myombo* or African ash.

But there was worse to come. On 4 January they suffered six inches of rainfall in an hour. They were able to look down over a lake that used to be the Gogo plain. Their own camp took severe damage: 'Hearing cries outside, I lit a candle and my astonishment was great when I perceived that my bed was an island, with the water threatening to carry me off south with the flood.' An investigation of the damage revealed that large quantities of tea, sugar, rice, and gunpowder and the harmonium that Stanley was taking as a present for Mutesa had been destroyed. It was only at noon, when the sun had come out and dried up part of the 'lake', that they were able to start the day's march.

As they climbed the plateau of Uyanzi, Stanley took his last look back at Ugogo, ever a thorn in his side:

Farewell to it, a lasting farewell to it, until some generous and opulent philanthropist shall permit me or some other to lead a force for the suppression of this stumbling block to commerce with Central Africa. This pleasant task and none other could ever induce me to return to Ugogo.

But saying farewell to Ugogo brought no change of fortune. The expedition lurched to the very edge of disaster in Ukimbu. The bad omens were there early. First Stanley had to compel a local chief at gunpoint to accept a lower *hongo* than he demanded. Then they collided with a column of refugees from the war between Nyungu and Mirambo. They hired guides and began to ascend ridges studded with iron ore. Then they had to cut their way through dense scrub, carpets of thick bushes, tall enough to permit them to battle their way through the lower branches but almost impenetrable by reason of the interwoven and impacted foliage. As they hacked their way through a labyrinth of elephant and rhino trails, Stanley described the going thus:

> The day brought us into a dense jungle of acacias and euphorbia, through which we had literally to push our way by scrambling, crawling along the ground under natural tunnels of embracing shrubbery, cutting the convolvuli and creepers, thrusting aside stout, thorny bushes, and, by various detours, taking advantage of every slight opening the jungle afforded, which naturally lengthened our journey and protracted our stay in the wilderness.

It soon became clear that their guides had lost their way. Stanley ordered one of his men to shin up a tree. From the bearings he took from landmarks, it dawned on Stanley that the guides had been leading them east. Hearing that his lookout could see a village called Uriveri, he sent volunteers to fetch food. Shortage of rations was by now reducing the expedition to a pitiable state. Men were staggering under their loads and, crazy with hunger and thirst, lagging far behind the vanguard. Stanley camped that night at a large pool and sent Manwa Sera out with a party to round up stragglers. Three were found dead on the trail. Two donkey boys, together with the donkey Simba, loaded with coffee, had evidently wandered off into the jungle, for they were never seen again.

The foraging parties came back with dreary news. The villages in the environs did not have a grain of food to spare. The situation was desperate. A party of twenty men was sent out on a 30-mile circular sweep to locate eatables while the men who remained grubbed for roots and Stanley vainly sought game. He shot two lion whelps, which were skinned and hastily devoured. Others in his party found a putrid elephant corpse on which they gorged themselves until they were sick.

With his people now in extremity, Stanley opened his medicine chest and found within 10 lb of oatmeal. Mixing this in an iron trunk with 25 gallons of water, he was able to make a thin gruel. Two cupfuls each were then distributed to his starving followers. This, plus the faint sound of a Snider bullet, encouraged them to think that the worst might be over. Next morning the foraging party returned from Urimi with just enough millet to provide a square meal for everyone in the camp.

Stanley decided to follow his foragers back to Urimi (Suna). They climbed a wooded ridge and camped on a hill at over 5000 ft. Stanley shot a duck and a wild boar but, maddeningly, several of the *wangwana* refused to touch the pork on the ground that they were strict Muslims. Skirting around a quagmire covered with thousands of elephant tracks, the expedition plunged into another jungle and marched 20 miles before emerging in the cultivated fields of Suna, exhausted and famished.

Though there was food in Suna, they were greeted with sullenness and hostility. It transpired that the foraging party had simply pillaged and looted to get the millet. Stanley made amends by flogging the culprits in the villagers' presence. Good relations were established and it was agreed that the expedition be allowed to halt for three days. Stanley was much taken with the physical beauty of the Warimi, especially the women. All the men were circumcised and went naked; one of the warriors was 7 ft tall. 'The Warimi are the finest natives we have encountered between here and the sea.'

The main reason Stanley needed an extensive breathing-space at Suna was that he had a rapidly lengthening sick-list. Of the 347 souls who had left Bagamoyo with him, twenty were already dead, eight left behind sick, and eighty-nine had deserted. Thirty men hovered near death, from dysentery, bronchitis and pneumonia. Others were prostrated with sore feet and diarrhoea. Worst of all was Edward Pocock, whose raging fever daily gave cause for concern. On their final day in Suna Stanley diagnosed it either as typhoid fever or as the killer exanthematic typhus. It was clearly fatal to move him, but by the fourth day the Warimi were becoming sullen and peevish, as their 'guests' bade fair to overstay their welcome. Stanley reluctantly gave the order to move on, slowly, and with Pocock in a hammock.

The expedition cut a sorry figure as it moved out of Suna. They were at such a low ebb that if attacked they would have been able to put up very little resistance. Frank Pocock and Barker were in constant attendance on the hammock and at first Edward seemed to have drawn a second wind. But the jolting journey soon sent his health on a downward spiral. He weakened rapidly and at 10 a.m. on 17 January he died. His last words were: 'The Master has hit the right place.' He was buried at night under a stunted *myombo* tree, which his brother Frank etched deeply with a cross. Stanley conducted the burial service.

The dejected exploration party continued its trek, still at an altitude of 5000 ft above sea-level, another 36 miles to Ituru, where the locals spoke a language unlike any hitherto encountered. By now Stanley's debilitated men were dropping like flies. The list of illnesses was legion: dysentery, opththalmia, rheumatism, sciatica, asthma, chest complaints, skin diseases, swollen legs. The men's poor condition was aggravated by lack of water. Since Mpwapwa they had not crossed a single stream and were obliged to collect all their drinking water from rain pools. Yet as they entered Ituru, conditions seemed to improve. The clammy temperatures of around 78°F fell to between 63 and 66°F. Streams became more numerous. There was a plethora of birds: geese, ducks, plovers, snipe, cranes, herons, spoonbills, jays. Ominously, though, all the cattle, sheep, goats and even the dogs they encountered were skeletal and cadaverous.

But if they thought they had come safely through the shadow of death, they soon found themselves in an even deeper vale of tears at the town of Vinyata. Stanley spread out the cloths that had been sodden in Ugogo to dry in the sun while he received a visit from the witch-doctor. The visit left him with an uncomfortable feeling that the Vinyata people might be contemplating treachery; the impression was reinforced when Manwa Sera came in with the news that Kaif Halleck, one of the Zanzibaris who had accompanied Stanley to Ujiji in 1871, had been mysteriously murdered. The Waturu seemed to have been inflamed by the inadvertent display of the wares bleaching in the sun. Stanley ordered a close guard set on his camp and waited for the Vinyata men to make the next move.

Next came a demand for 'reparations' for alleged pillaging by Stanley's men. In conciliatory style Stanley conceded the principle, then recoiled at the scale of compensation desired. Suddenly the initiative was snatched from him. Two of his men were attacked while on a wood-cutting party; one was speared to death, the other wounded. The next instant a shower of arrows fell on the camp. Stanley at once implemented his contingency plans. He ordered his men to form square behind the sections of *Lady Alice*, which formed a kind of citadel. Frank Pocock distributed twenty rounds each. When the enemy made a frontal assault, they were beaten off with losses of fifteen dead and many more wounded. Some of the fighting was hand-to-hand, and the sole surviving dog distinguished himself: 'Bull, my British bulldog, had seized one of the Waturu by the leg, and had given him a taste of the power of the sharp canines of his breed before the poor savage was mercifully despatched by a Snider bullet.'

Having beaten off the first Waturu attack, Stanley ordered Frank Pocock and sixty axemen to construct a proper stockade and clear the ground to within 200 yds of the camp. The enemy responded by assembling even larger forces against them. Stanley realised that if he simply stood his ground inside the stockade, the odds would favour the Waturu in a war of attrition. Sterner measures were called for. He divided his seventy effectives into four detachments to form moving squares that were to stay in constant contact with each other.

But Fayallah Christie, leader of one of the squares, failed to follow orders in his enthusiasm for the fray. His detachment was lured out of range of the others' support, then surrounded by the Waturu and slaughtered to a man. Only quick thinking by Stanley, who sent up Manwa Sera and the reserve in the nick of time, prevented the second square from being overwhelmed. Even though it contained all the best shots, the second company was in mortal danger, completely surrounded, holding out defiantly in a hut. The advent of Manwa Sera permitted a sortie and the enemy were caught between two fires. The third square also took heavy losses and lost six dead. Only the fourth body performed as Stanley had hoped, fired a number of villages, and returned laden with oxen, goats and grain. But with twenty-two men killed, the second day of the battle had been grim and all but disastrous.

On the third day, Stanley took to heart the lesson of wrongful dispersal of forces. Forming his men into one square, drafting in porters to fill the gaps left by the fallen, he advanced in a bristling formation on the entrenched village on a rocky spur where the shaken Waturu had now taken refuge. The compact mass of fighting men bore all before it. The enemy were routed, the palisaded village put to the torch. At last Stanley clearly had the upper hand. They were safe to continue their journey. But he could ill afford the further losses in manpower. In a mood close to despair he wrote:

> You can better imagine our perils, our novel and strange fortunes if you reflect on the loss of 120 men out of a force so limited. Such a reduction even in a strong regiment would be deemed almost a catastrophe. What name will you give it when you cannot recruit your numbers, when every man that dies is a loss that cannot be repaired; when your work, which is to last years, is but commencing; when each morning you say to yourself, 'This day may be your last.'

On 26 January they resumed their march, alternately along the banks of the Leewumbu river and through forests of *myombo*. There were 240 of them now – three Europeans, 206 *wangwana*, twenty-five women and six boys, but thanks to the raid on the Waturu they had six days' ample provisions. They took to travelling by the light of the moon and pressing on until noon, then resting and forming a stockade camp. They crossed the river Mwaru – the boundary between Mgongo Tembo and Ituru – using the boat and a strong rope. On 29 January they arrived at the principal town of Mgongo Tembo, making a point of heralding themselves as a peaceful caravan.

The chief of Mgongo Tembo proved as friendly as the Waturu had been hostile. He had met Burton and Speke eighteen years before on their way to Unyanyembe. His dislike of violence had much to do with his daily fear of assassination, which led him to change his sleeping place every night. He advised Stanley that it had been a great mistake to have offered the heart of a sacrificial ox to the Vinyata witch-doctor, as the Waturu believed that the loss of a heart from one of their flocks would weaken them and make them easy prey for enemies; 'The Wanyaturu are robbers and sons of robbers,' Chief Marewa remarked contemptuously.

Stanley held a review of his people during his two days with Marewa and found that only 173 out of 347 were left – seventy-seven having already perished from disease or battle. On 1 February he led them out on to the magnificent Luwamberri plain, which teemed with game. They could see myriad rhino, buffalo, giraffe, zebra, gnu, springbok, waterbuck, kudu, hartebeeste, wild boar and birds of every stripe: ibises, fieldlarks, fish-hawks, kingfishers, spur-winged geese, ducks, vultures, flamingoes, spoonbills and cranes. They were now able to feast on the abundant fauna, but even the lavish choice of meats did not deter deserters. On 6 February Stanley was obliged to summon a court-martial to sentence a deserter who had decamped with a box of ammunition. A sentence of flogging and chaining was narrowly carried against a large minority who opted for the death sentence.

They now crossed a succession of rivers – Itawa, Gogo, Seligwa and Luwamberri – into the rich territory of Usukuma. As they virtually stumbled over game in the low hills and baobab and mimosa thickets, the *wangwana* decided to give a new title to the man who brought them such a wealth of chickens, goats, melons and vegetables by guiding them into this land of milk and honey: *huyu msungu n'ufungua mikono* ('the white man with the open hand'). Leaving the plains, they ascended to Mombiti at 4000 ft above the sea, where again there was abundant cheap grain, chickens, millet, potatoes, sesamum, tobacco, pot herbs, goats and honey. After spending three days in high spirits at Mombiti, they entered the jungle to avoid Mirambo's guerrillas, said to be rampaging in the neighbourhood. The only cloud over these days was the death of Gardner, Livingstone's faithful follower over nine years.

They crossed another plain to the Monangah river. All around were giraffe, but the country was too open for a successful stalk. Stanley did manage to down a springbok near Usiha, as they struck across a pathless country full of elephant tracks and rhino wallows, but it was an animal of another kind that brought them close to an eleventh-hour disaster. The braying of a donkey brought out the people of Usiha in full warpaint. After shooting had been narrowly averted, Stanley learned that the expedition had been mistaken for Mirambo, since Mirambo had a donkey whose braying was the inevitable prelude for an attack.

At Usiha they managed to hire an additional twenty porters for the easy passage through beautiful pastoral country to Lake Victoria. They threaded their way through a picturesque plateau, then across a monkey-infested forest. They remained on good terms with the peoples they met, though still once or twice being taken for Mirambo's warriors. Usukuma impressed them all as a blessed land. The only casualty sustained was by the bull-terrier Jack who lost an eye when he chased a mongoose into a hedge of euphorbia or milk-weed and got the poisonous juices in his eye.

They began a gradual descent through a series of rock-like hills. Monkeys lined the tops of the hills and watched them curiously. A long march brought them to Kagehyi, within sight of the lake. Frank Pocock was the first to spy the distant glistening waters, thus becoming the fourth white man to see Lake Victoria, after Speke, Grant and Chaillé-Long. The porters burst into songs of joy at sight of the lake; universal joy was constrained only by the knowledge that Barker was now very ill with fever. A day later brought them to the small conical huts of the village of Kaduma on the lakeside, where they rented quarters. Euphoria was general at the thought of a long well-earned rest. In 103 days they had come 720 miles from Bagamoyo – an average of seven miles a day. It was now 27 February 1875.

It had been a great feat of marching, but the human cost was extraordinarily high. Out of 347 persons with whom he had started, Stanley had lost 181 through battle, famine and desertion. One white man was dead and another seemed likely to die, and did, shortly afterwards. Such were the everyday realities of the European exploration of Africa.

III

OBSTACLES

11

The Impact of Disease

Mungo Park, the first of many physicians in the ranks of African explorers, left a valuable account of the tropical diseases he encountered in West Africa in the last decade of the eighteenth century. With his information as 'control' we can monitor the impact of sickness on Africa and its explorers during the golden age of discovery in the following century. Any discussion of this topic has to start from the realisation that not all the killer diseases that make the journals and diaries of travellers in Africa such grim and depressing reading were native to the continent. Those who penetrated the Dark Continent in the nineteenth century did not virtually destroy the indigenous civilisations overnight by the introduction of alien bacteria and viruses, as the *conquistadores* had done in South America, but they did aggravate an already grievous situation.

Let us begin then with a consideration of the diseases caused by small animal parasites – those native to Africa – some of which were potential killers: malaria, sleeping sickness (trypanosomiasis), bilharzia, filariasis, hookworm infestation (ankylostomiasis) and river blindness (onchocerciasis). Others were rarely fatal but merely drained vitality, diminished agricultural output and lowered life expectancy: amoebic and bacillic dysentery, skin ulcerations, worm infestations (other than ankylostomiasis), yaws and leprosy.

For the most part the African was helpless in the face of these dreadful maladies. The black man clung to faith in the healing power of fetishes: the name of the most powerful one worshipped in West Africa was Mumbo-Jumbo – a name Park introduced into the English language. Native surgery was skilled enough as far as it went, but it went only as far as the cure of minor ailments. Park described how Africans lanced abscesses with a cautery in the form of a red-hot spearhead. And he was impressed by their cupping methods of dealing with inflammation.

Typically, the large end of a bullock horn was placed over the affected area. The severed point would be partially sealed with beeswax; the air within the horn was then sharply inhaled by the nurse so as to create a near-vacuum. After that the nurse sealed a tiny aperture in the wax with a skilful movement of the tongue.

Many of the most terrifying parasite-borne diseases make an appearance in Park's pages. He recorded cases of yaws, elephantiasis (filarial infection), guinea-worm infestation, yellow fever and advanced forms of leprosy. He noticed that dysentery, which struck down many whites, was uncommon among Africans. But most of all he noticed malaria, the most dreaded scourge in West Africa.

By far the greatest European fatality in Africa was from malaria. The statistics are chilling. Of the 40 men who accompanied Mungo Park's second expedition to the Niger in 1805, not one returned to England. Six were killed in battle, the rest died of malaria or dysentery. Another Niger expedition in the same year, under Captain Peddie, lost a third of its men before he cut his losses and returned to the coast. Captain Tuckey, who got as far as Isangila on the lower Congo in 1816, left half his crew behind, dead from fever. Explorers were merely the most dramatic casualties. Those two bastions of Imperial Britain, the Church and the Army, lost men in droves on the west coast of Africa. During 1804–25, over 60 per cent of the men sent out by the Church Missionary Society died of the disease. The Wesleyan Missionary Society recorded fatalities of 65 out of 275 between 1835 and 1907. More than half the members of the Baptist Missionary Society perished in the decade 1878–88. Out of 80 missionaries of the Free Church of Scotland, including wives, 24 died and 27 were invalided out between 1875 and 1900. Of 197 who joined the Universities Mission to Central Africa during 1860–90, 37 died and 45 resigned or were invalided home within five years.

Even worse was the record of the armed services. A tour of duty in the 'White Man's Grave' was traditionally loathed and feared in the Royal Navy, where the high mortality led sailors into gallows humour about the 'coffin squadron' and where Bathurst was known as 'Half Die'. In the eighteenth century it was estimated that between 25 and 75 per cent of the military died in their first year on the Guinea coast. In one garrison with a muster of 1568 soldiers, during 1822–30 no less than 1298 died. Of the survivors 125 were mortally stricken with fever during the voyage home, and 50 per cent of the remainder died from delayed effects in Britain; only 57 were finally discharged as fit.

The Guinea coast was the worst spot in West Africa for the white man, with a death-rate higher than that in India or the West Indies. Early statistics are muddied because this location boasted sleeping sickness and yellow fever in addition to malaria. There were no salubrious nearby sanatoria; the nearest was Ascension Island, where many men went just to die. Apparent African immunity to the disease led to speculation that the black man was better adapted to a tropical environment or that he threw off the fever because he sweated so copiously. But all facile theories based on pigmentation collapsed when escaped slaves from the Americas were settled in Sierra Leone and sustained the same death rate as Europeans. It was the *indigenous* Africans whose resistance was developed. During the official British Niger expedition to found a settlement at Lokosa in 1841, 42 out of 145 white men died from malaria. But of the 158 Africans also on board the three boats not a man perished; 11 contracted fever but all survived.

Every single European explorer and traveller in nineteenth-century Africa sustained at least one attack of fever. Many were its terminal victims, among them some of the very finest pioneers, like E.J. Glave, who served with Stanley in the Congo. Glave went out to Africa in 1883 at the age of twenty. He served six years (two tours) in the service of the Congo Free State, returned to England in 1889 and then travelled in Alaska and the Yukon until 1893. That year he returned to Africa, crossed the continent, and explored the still little-known area around Lake Bangweolo, where Livingstone had perished. Glave died of fever in 1896 on the eve of sailing from the Congo for Europe.

In the nineteenth century science wrestled in vain with this disease. Not until the turn of the century was it finally appreciated that malaria is caused by a blood parasite of man, carried by the anopheles mosquito. Of the 3000 species in the genus mosquito, about a hundred are anopheline, and it is among these that the transmitters of human malaria are found. The parasites are passed on by the female anopheles mosquito, which needs to feed on human blood before it can lay its fertilised eggs.

Malaria has existed since the dawn of human civilisation. Hippocrates wrote about it in Ancient Greece. Alexander the Great is usually thought to have died from it (though some opt for assassination by poison), as also the Roman emperors Vespasian, Titus and Hadrian. Dea Febris, the goddess of fever, was worshipped in Rome. Some historians have seen the dramatic decline in population of the Empire caused by the disease as a major factor in Rome's decline and fall.

Malaria was also common in medieval Europe until reduced by land reclamation, street lighting, ventilation and improved drainage. Some medical historians have speculated that animal husbandry played a part, in that the mosquito switched its attention to cows' blood and away from humans'. In England it was common in fenlands and in the marshy grounds of the Thames Valley. Some 5 per cent of admissions to St

Thomas's hospital were attributed to the disease. Among its famous victims in English history were James I and Oliver Cromwell.

In the Middle Ages malaria was thought to be due to the action of planets and comets, to electrical storms or rains of 'fever poison'. By the nineteenth century the correlation of the disease with marshy ground was too clear to be gainsaid, so science returned, in effect, to Hippocrates, who had claimed that the cause was drinking stagnant water or inhaling the vapours from marshy ground. The so-called 'miasmatic theory' postulated that swamp air contained chemical poisons which had been freed from rotting wood. Miasma had a good innings as bogeyman. In the 1880s missionary houses were still being constructed on two storeys and so as to face inland, away from lakes and rivers, on the grounds that 'miasmata' could not rise far above the ground or turn corners.

The impact of this theory of the genesis of malaria can be seen everywhere in the work of the great explorers. Mungo Park thought the prime cause was exposure to night dew. Winwood Reade in the 1850s asserted that when dew fell on ships' decks before sunrise, it produced small insects that carried the fever. He added a further layer of Victorian 'science' by alleging that these insects were particularly fond of fair-complexioned humans, drunkards and those of lethargic or 'strumous' dispositions. Some of Reade's pontifications make hilarious reading today, even if the comedy was in his day of the black variety:

> There can be no doubt, therefore, that malaria is contained in rain, which the natives allege to be pernicious if it falls on the naked skin . . . It has been proved that malaria perishes at sea, about three miles distant from the shore . . . Rains, dews, winds blowing from malarious localities, marsh exhalations, and possibly infection by the human breath may therefore be considered as the proximate causes of fever.

Reade's friend Burton was not much wiser: he thought the cause of malaria was sleeping out in moonlight. For Stanley the cause was a substance in the air called ozone. As late as the 1880s the Scottish traveller, John Buchanan, in the Shire highlands confidently told his readers that fever was brought on by over-exertion, sweating and sleeping in clothes wet with perspiration: 'The same proceeding in Scotland would almost ensure a cold, and in Africa it brings on fever.' David Livingstone was the sole explorer to guess that there was a connection between malaria and mosquitoes.

Livingstone suffered his first bout of African fever in 1853, but his most severe attack began on 20 February 1867, during his last African journey. He recorded in his journal: 'Every step I take jars in the chest and I am very weak; I can scarcely keep up the march, though formerly I was always first . . . I have a constant singing in my ears and can scarcely hear the loud tick of the chronometer.'

Other explorers told a similar story. Clapperton and Oudney endured a nightmarish experience of what can only be termed 'aggravated fever' at Kouka in the summer of 1823. All day and all night they lay tossing and sweating in their tent, often delirious. While they suffered thus, flies, mosquitoes and scorpions tormented them; black ants bit them and raised red weals on their bodies; white ants meanwhile consumed their clothes and bedding; rain poured through the leaky roof; while outside they could hear the coughing of hyenas, which prowled through the streets of Kouka at night, having entered through the rickety gates in the walls, seeking all ill and defenceless creatures that they might devour.

What always amazed the explorers was how quickly fever could strike. While crossing the Kafu river during his 1864 probe of Lake Albert, Samuel Baker looked back to see his wife 'standing in one spot and sinking gradually through the weeds . . . her face distorted and perfectly purple, she fell, as though shot dead'. Baker thought it was sunstroke, but it is virtually certain she was suffering from cerebral malaria. She was carried unconscious in a litter for three days and, having regained consciousness, was in delirium for seven more, with convulsions as a complication. Then she recovered, rested for two days and continued the journey. Her convalescence was not helped by the fact that at that juncture lack of provisions made it impossible for the Bakers to stay long in any one spot.

Du Chaillu, who believed implicitly in miasmata as the cause of fever, suffered fifty attacks of fever in four years. He reported the usual symptoms to be initially loss of appetite, irritability, heaviness in the head, languor, aching limbs, unpleasant tastes in the mouth, yawning and stretching, prostration. Then came the chill, followed by the fever proper. But sometimes the fever skipped the initial stages and began without warning, except for acute headache, nausea and pains in the back and limbs. Du Chaillu noted that his pulse increased in frequency, ranging from 80 to 130 beats per minute. The most serious fevers led to enlargement of the spleen or the liver; the complexion was sallowed and the whites of the eyes became yellow. The worst fever du Chaillu experienced was preceded by a fortnight's loss of appetite and weariness. His body was hot and dry, he perspired profusely, suffered rushes of blood to the head, a high and irregular pulse and general prostration. Thirst gnawed at him urgently, but the stomach rejected whatever he swallowed.

In the very worst cases, when the fever was fatal, the patient became insensible. There was violent vomiting and regurgitation of ingested food, which was seen to be mixed with green and yellow fluids. The patient's urine became dark red or black. The pulse was irregular, the breathing slow. Finally the victim sank into coma and died without a struggle. Another symptom of fatal fever was when there was no yellowness but instead the face became pale with a peculiar ghastliness. The patient's skin was cold to touch, but he did not complain of cold. The pulse was small and frequent. Sometimes the patient would sink away without a reaction setting in. Sometimes in the terminal stages deafness and blindness would occur. Occasionally there was raving delirium and the patient would have to be held in bed by main force. The inevitable end in such a case was stupor and death.

Even those who survived bore the scars for years and sometimes for life. There was a particular irony here, since many travellers in Africa stated as a motive for their journeys to the Dark Continent a desire to escape from the high level of sickness and disease in the overcrowded European cities, and the unhealthy valetudinarian or hypochondriacal attitudes there. Burton's return to England in 1859 after repeated bouts of fever drew cries of alarm from those who had known him before his expedition to Lake Tanganyika. His fiancée Isabel Arundell, who married him the following year, reported: 'I shall never forget Richard Burton as he was then. He had had twenty-one attacks of fever, was partially paralysed, and partially blind, he was a mere skeleton, with brown-yellow skin, hanging in bags, his eyes protruding, and his lips drawn away from his teeth. I used to support him about the Botanical Gardens for fresh air, and sometimes convey him away almost fainting in a cab.' Burton's return to England in this condition in 1859 was particularly interesting, since in that very year the building of the Thames Embankment banished malaria from London.

How could Europeans protect themselves? Traditional remedies were lying in steam baths, taking cold dips in the sea, applying blisters or swallowing doses of strychnine, arsenic and calomel. The missionary Felkin recommended spreading the gospel only at high altitudes, on the grounds that malarial fever was not found higher than 4000 ft; this ignored the fact that comparative cold could sometimes bring out a *latent* fever. In the days when the bleeding of a patient was considered a panacea, leeches would be applied to the fever victim or blood let – sometimes up to 100 oz (2800 ml) of blood, or half the blood content of an adult. But the first real breakthrough in the fight against malaria came with quinine. In Peru the Indians had known for centuries about the beneficial use of the bark of the *Myroxlon* tree. It was said they got the idea from observing pumas chewing the bark when they were ill. Calling it *kina-kina*, the Indians stripped it from trees, soaked it in water to make an infusion, then took the mixture by mouth. After the Spanish conquest they passed the secret on to the Jesuits; it became known as 'Jesuit bark'.

The Jesuits in turn introduced *kina-kina* into Europe. Their practice was to give it freely to the sick who were poor but to charge the rich. But Protestants tended to suspect the remedy of being Jesuitical witchcraft, which was why Cromwell was denied the 'Jesuit bark'. Thereafter there were ups and downs in the bark's popularity, because each sample varied in potency and hence efficacy. Also, the mixture had an unpleasing bitter taste, so that many at risk from fever tried to avoid drinking it. The use of cinchona alkaloids was placed on a more rational basis when two French pharmacists succeeded in isolating the alkaloids of quinine from the bark, by distillation and crystallisation. After 1820 it was possible to prescribe quinine powder in determined strength, and it became generally available after 1854, when Dutch settlers established cinchona plantations in Java and exported it.

The immediate results were dramatic. Dr W.B. Baikie lost not a single man during the 1854 British Niger Expedition as a result of taking quinine. But Baikie himself died during the voyage home because he stopped taking the quinine tablets once he left the African coast; the dormant fever then killed him.

Even more triumphant were the results of Livingstone's 1858–64 Zambezi expedition. Livingstone had been experimenting with quinine since 1850. He treated his own son and daughter with it when they lay ill with fever at Lake Ngami, and in 1851 on the Zonga river he repeated the prescription with his son Thomas. He took his family back to Cape Town then set off north again. From Kuruman he wrote:

One of the chief objects of my present expedition is to investigate the character of that disease which is the main obstacle to Africa being opened to beneficial intercourse with the rest of the world. If I can only discover a healthy range of country and means to foil that terrible plague, I shall be content to let the unicorn sleep in everlasting oblivion.

Livingstone always realised that if Central Africa was to have a future, it was necessary to overcome fever. In 1853 he wrote:

I would like to devote a portion of my life to the discovery of a remedy for that terrible disease, the African fever. I would go into the parts where it prevails most and try to discover if the natives have a remedy for it . . . What an unspeakable mercy it is to be permitted to engage in this most honourable and holy work.

It seemed particularly important to Livingstone that missionaries should be medically qualified and thus able to make an impact on the indigenous peoples they encountered.

After his first attack from fever on 30 May 1853, Livingstone tried a remedy with quinine, then decided that the most effective treatment was its combination with purgatives. He noticed that with the first bowel movement the perspiration burst forth from the skin and the headache vanished. Thus were born 'Livingstone's Pills' or the 'Zambezi rouser.' This consisted of three grains of calomel, three grains of quinine, ten grains of rhubarb, four grains of essence of jalop, mixed with a little opium. Livingstone was convinced that he had found a panacea for malaria proper. He knew that the autopsies on fatalities in the first British Niger Expedition had revealed that in every case the gall bladder was distended with black bile, with the consistency of tar. His remedies relieved the symptoms in 5–6 hours by causing the bile to be discharged.

Livingstone's 'rousers' were a signal success on the 1858–64 Zambezi expedition. Among the seven Europeans on the *Ma Robert* from 1858 to 1860 there were no deaths; on the *Pioneer* only three out of eighteen died. The expedition proved that Europeans could now compete on an equal footing with the Arabs in the heart of Africa. The Arabs had proved resistant to fever partly because they had inherited African immunity through mixed blood and partly because their flowing robes and headgear limited mosquitoes' access to their bodies. Indeed it has been speculated that what truly gave the white man the confidence to conquer Africa was the coincidence of the discovery of the efficacy of quinine with the introduction of breech-loading rifles.

But there were still problems in the use of quinine. No one really knew *how* it worked, it tasted bitter, deafness often followed prolonged use, and secondary side-effects often included nausea and vomiting. Livingstone's wife Mary died because she could not hold down her tablets. Also Livingstone noticed in the Shire highlands that one type of fever seemed proof against quinine: 'The limited experience we have had seems to indicate that the type once established had a constant tendency to recur.' For all that, quinine was a tremendous breakthrough in the battle against African fevers. When Livingstone's medical box was stolen on his last expedition, and he was thus deprived of quinine, he lay dangerously ill for weeks, and thereafter was intermittently ill for two years, suffering particularly from dizziness and tinnitus. His life was saved by the intervention of the Arab Muhammad Bogharib, who took him to Ujiji in March 1869.

Many of the explorers left detailed accounts of their sensations during malaria; some even laid bare the secrets of the unconscious during delirium. Harry Johnston, who claimed incidentally to have been close to making the connection between mosquitoes and malaria as early as 1882, was forced to rush from the presence of King Leopold of the Belgians in 1883 when seized by a delayed attack of the sickness; he ended up vomiting out of an open window of the palace at Laeken. Burton, ever the scientific observer, recorded the course of the fever from the onset of general languor to delirium itself. It began with a heaviness and a lassitude in his limbs; there followed nausea, a sensation as of a weight in the head, dull pains in the shoulders and a frigid feeling creeping towards the centre from the extremities. Then came a spasm of shivering cold, splitting headache, high blood pressure, vomiting and collapse. Burton found he could eat nothing for a week but was plagued by an unquenchable thirst – unassuagable since he vomited up whatever he drank. During the fever he had a sensation of divided identity, of being two people who constantly fought and opposed each other. In his delirium, which occurred with predictable regularity, twice a day, at 2.a.m. and 2.p.m., he thought he had wings and could fly. Burton was meticulous about dosing himself with quinine at the midway point between the two daily fits, since he believed that the drug, taken at the wrong time or in the wrong amounts, could lead to apoplexy.

But if Burton's delirium revealed something of his self-destructive side and a high level of soaring creativity, the fits experienced by his companion on the 1857–9 expedition, John Hanning Speke, revealed something altogether more morbid and sinister. His fever

> began with a burning sensation, as by a branding-iron, above the right breast, and then extended to the heart with sharp twinges. After ranging round the spleen, it attacked the upper part of the right lung, and finally it settled in the region of the liver. On the 10th October, suddenly waking about dawn from a horrible dream, in which a close pack of tigers, leopards, and other beasts, harnessed with a network of iron hooks, were dragging him like the rush of a whirlwind over the ground, he found himself sitting up on the side of his bedding, forcibly clasping both sides with his hands. Half-stupefied by pain, he called Bombay, who having formerly suffered from the *Kichyoma-Chyoma* ('little irons'), raised his master's right arm, placed him in a sitting position, as lying down was impossible, and directed him to hold the left ear behind the head, thus relieving the excruciating and torturing twinges, by lifting the lung from the liver. The next spasm was less severe, but the sufferer's mind had begun to wander, and he again clasped his sides, a proceeding with which Bombay interfered.

The following morning Speke suffered an epileptic fit, with symptoms like hydrophobia:

> He was once more haunted by a crowd of hideous devils, giants and lion-

headed demons, who were wrenching with super-human force, and stripping the sinews and tendons of his legs down to the ankles. [At the climax of the fit] sitting, or rather, lying upon the chair, with limbs racked by cramps, features drawn and ghastly, frame fixed and rigid, eyes glazed and glassy, he began to utter a barking noise, and a peculiar chopping motion of the mouth and tongue, with lips protruding – the effect of difficulty of breathing – which so altered his appearance that he was hardly recognisable.

Stanley, who boasted that he had survived more than 200 fevers in Africa, came closest to death in May 1881. Later, horrified, he recalled his delirium:

The mind drifted away and carried me to a world whose atmosphere was crowded with the most hideous wriggling things imaginable. When these became too hideous to be borne and swarmed about my face and seemed about to enter my nostrils – I made an effort to recover myself and they fled . . . presently I am at the entrance of a very lengthy tunnel, and a light as of a twinkling star is seen an immeasurable length away. There is a sensible increase in the glow, the twinkling ceases, it has become an incandescent globe. It grows large and it advances and I fancy I hear the distant roar. It is a train and it is approaching and the sound of its rush is appalling – and the light grows blinding. It is no more a star, nor a globe but a wide circle of expanding flames, and the roar is now so overwhelming that I fear I shall be caught in the tunnel – and in this fear I wake up again to hear once more the increasing loud drumming in the head. It is the drumming and the wriggling creatures in the atmosphere of the strange world – and that glowing light and appalling roar that will revert to my memory when I think of this fever.

Exact diagnosis of the fevers from which the African explorers suffered is difficult. By dosing themselves with quinine and sleeping under mosquito curtains, Speke and Burton certainly took preventive action against malaria, even though they were ignorant of its aetiology. It has been suggested recently that some of the delirium incidents suggest relapsing fever, caused by ticks rather than mosquitoes. The netting would have warded off the mosquitoes but not the noisome ticks, who lived in the mud roofs and walls of the rude huts where the explorers slept, emerging at night to feast on human blood. Feeding on humans, they passed on the spirochaete of relapsing fever. Here, too, Livingstone's intuitions were later to prove well founded. He was the first to notice a possible connection between tickbite and relapsing fever after being bitten in 1854 by a 'Tampan' tick about the size of a pin-head at Ambaca in north-west Angola. This was a disease that spread east–west, from the Zambezi to the Atlantic seaboard. Africans were highly resistant in their own villages but when they travelled they were vulnerable to unfamiliar strains of the spirochaete. The common antidote, before the discovery of penicillin, was arsenic.

Again, the fever Livingstone found resistant to his 'rousers' and from which Captain Ferger of the *Pioneer* died in 1861 was almost certainly blackwater fever. This was a type of fever whose origins long baffled doctors; even in the 1920s there were those who thought it a secondary disease, caused by overdoses of quinine. First diagnosed as a distinct illness in Africa, the fever was widespread in two continents: there were outbreaks in Florida, Panama, Venezuela and Trinidad, as well as in East Africa (including the then territories of Nyasaland, Barotseland, Rhodesia and South-East Africa), Madagascar, the Sudan and West Africa (especially Angola, Nigeria and the Congo). One explorer who certainly suffered grievously from this strain, and left a detailed description, was Harry Johnston. The peculiarity of this disease was its sudden onset: there were no advance symptoms or warnings of ill-health other than a slight feeling of feverish sprightliness. The first real evidence of the fever's presence was in the passing of urine. First it became the colour of stout, then black, finally it acquired a reddish tinge, until it was the colour of port wine. There followed a deadly nausea, debility, and three days of constant vomiting. In all instances the skin turned a bright yellow or yellow-brown, and for that reason the disease was often confused with yellow fever. In fatal cases the patient's temperature would rise to 107°F; he would then lapse into a coma and die. Johnston concocted a 'remedy' for blackwater fever which had more in common with the nostrums of Hardy's 'Conjuror Trendle' than with medical science. His recipe was champagne, lemonade, limes and lemons, beef tea, chicken broth and a moderate dose of quinine.

Malaria did not affect the African explorers only through death or debilitation. Many of the notorious feuds and conflicts between white comrades in the Dark Continent can also be laid at its door. Malaria was known to produce abnormal sensitivity and the feeling that comrades were plotting against one another. When an attack of malaria was coming on, 'things look black and gloomy, the actions of companions are sure to appear distorted, and their motives apt to be misconstrued'. How serious the consequences could be is evident from the remark by Dr Parke, physician on the Emin Pasha Relief Expedition, who recalled: 'I think each European on Mr Stanley's staff, seven in number, who crossed Africa, had fever probably 150 or 200 times.'

Petty hatreds, personal animosities and suspicions did not just affect the working relationships of Europeans on expeditions. Such paranoia spilled over into relations between the races and could lead to serious miscalculations. It has been speculated that Mungo Park's tragic death was an effect of dysentery. Suffering badly from this, Park took massive doses of calomel (mercurious chloride) as a purgative. Consequently he could neither speak nor sleep for six days. It is possible that this unbalanced his mind and led him to shoot at Africans first and ask questions afterwards during his 1805–6 expedition – in contrast to his enlightened and sympathetic attitude to Africans on his first Niger journey.

Those best placed to resist these secondary effects of malaria and the other fevers were European explorers who genuinely loved Africa and Africans. Such was Paul du Chaillu, who left a touching memoir of the way African women nursed him through malaria:

> They tried to cook nice food for me; they sat by me to fan me; they brought more mats for my bed; brought me water, got me refreshing fruits from the woods; at night, when I waked up from a feverish dream, I used to hear their voices as they sat around in the darkness, and pitied me and devised ways for my cure.

It must be stressed that the immunity of Africans to malaria was always a relative thing. What happened was that over the generations resistance to local strains built up. Where Africans themselves went in for long-range travel, they tended to be as vulnerable as the European explorers. The best known case is that of the Makololo. Under Zulu pressure they fled from their homeland in the Orange Free State to the Zambezi valley; there they enslaved the more numerous Barotse. But because the Barotse were immune to the local strains of fever, and the Makololo were not, the power of the conquerors declined and the Barotse were able to regain control. In Africa the truism held good: conquerors either subjugated peoples in part by introducing new diseases; or they were themselves laid low by the new diseases they encountered in the conquered areas.

If fever was the disease most dreaded by the European explorers, it was sleeping sickness or trypanosomiasis that caused the greatest ravages among Africa's indigenous population – a fact chillingly conveyed in Conrad's *Heart of Darkness*. This was the one deadly disease that could wipe out whole communities at a stroke. In 1901 360,000 people died of it in Buganda and a further half-million in the Congo. Here the impact of the explorers was crucial, for in thirty years they carried into the heart of Africa a disease hitherto known only on the 'White Man's Grave.' In 1880 sleeping sickness was confined to Senegal, The Gambia, Sierra Leone, Ivory Coast and the Gold Coast. In the next three decades it spread to Nigeria, Cameroon, Portuguese and Spanish Guinea, French Equatorial Africa, the Congo, Uganda, Tanganyika, Nyasaland and the Rhodesias, Bechuanaland and Mozambique. In a word, during the 'golden age' of the great explorers this disease was unknown in Central and East Africa; the medically shrewdest of all travellers, Dr Livingstone, never mentions it. The initial symptoms were fever, swelling of the lymphatic glands, severe irritability and mood swings. Later came inflammation of the brain and lethargy combined with extreme sensitivity to cold and a strange mania for meat. Victims craving flesh eat dead bodies, set fire to their own huts or even attempt to devour themselves. So dreaded was trypanosomiasis among the indigenous tribes that Glave and his comrade Herbert Ward both reported that on the Congo in the 1880s the most dire insult you could utter to an enemy was *Owa Na Ntolo* ('May you die of sleeping sickness').

Sleeping sickness, highly contagious once contracted, was initiated by the parasitic trypanosomes conveyed in the bite of the tsetse fly. The preferred prey of the tsetse fly is wild game, which over many millennia had evolved immunity to the trypanosomes. It was the very success of human civilisation in West Africa and the higher levels of tribal organisation there that allowed sleeping sickness to become endemic. More advanced social and political systems than elsewhere in Africa in turn engendered higher populations. These killed off the game or created scarcity. Since game was scarcer in West Africa than in the rest of the continent, the tsetse flies and parasites preyed on humans instead. This pattern was proved conclusively when rinderpest swept through East Africa in the 1890s. Introduced by the cattle imported for food, rinderpest roared through the continent, scything down both game and cattle in large numbers. The incidence of sleeping sickness then increased dramatically, as the tsetse flies, seeking alternative hosts, began to prey on man instead and inject him with trypanosomiasis.

The tsetse fly, which is mentioned in the Book of Isaiah (Vll:18–25), is about the same size as a common horsefly, of a dull greyish colour, with bars of a pinky tinge across the body. Its wings are like those of a British house fly only longer. The proboscis protrudes in a horizontal direction, not downwards as with other flies; ⅛ in. long, it penetrates the skin through a thick flannel shirt without difficulty. The fly was frequently heard by the explorers giving vent to the high-pitched buzzing noise which gave it its name. But when advancing to attack, the fly makes for its target noiselessly, without all the preparatory fuss made by others of its genus. As late as 9 p.m. tsetses would burst into a tent to feed; explorers noted that they often drowned in pitchers of wine.

It was discovered that animals bitten during the dry season usually survived until the beginning of the rains but rarely lived past the first shower. Most donkeys could spend an entire season in fly country without visible effects, but succumbed as soon as the rainy season reactivated their bites. A horse if bitten would die within twenty-four hours of being ridden through a river. Common symptoms were a starving coat, swellings under the jaw, loss of appetite and progressively poor condition. To test if a horse had been bitten, it was customary to pour buckets of water over the nag. If it had been 'stuck' (to use the hunter's terminology), the animal's coat would stand on end, like that of a lung-sick ox. After death the animal's blood was usually found to have lost its liquidity and become gelatinous.

It was the tsetse that had barred passage to black Africa by killing off the Arabs' horses and camels. The fly also kept the technology of black Africa primitive, since, deprived of animals, the African could hand-plough only small plots of land, had no transport, and incidentally lacked a source of first-class protein. Livingstone knew the effect tsetses had on animals but was unaware of their killer potential for humans even though bitten several times. He puzzled also over other aspects of the fly: the fact that it could be present on one bank of a river but not on the other, the fact that some big-game areas contained no tsetses, and that game seemed anyway immune. His famous intuition enabled him to assert in 1849 that the fly was *the* barrier to progress in the continent. But he based this on the tsetses' impact on beasts of burden; he was unaware of the trypanosome factor. He thought the flies injected venom like snakes. It was left to Dr David Bruce much later to demonstrate how sleeping sickness was caused by the parasites transmitted in the insect's bite and to explain some of the 'mysteries' about human survival. Each time the fly bites, between 350 and 400 trypanosomes are injected. Now the human body can destroy about 400 trypanosomes at a time but is overwhelmed by a larger number. So for sleeping sickness to be contracted, it was necessary for a human to be bitten at least *twice*.

Livingstone was also the first to make a detailed study of the worm that wandered around Africans' eyes – the disease now known to medical science as filariasis. Another cruel illness, bilharzia, still the most general cause of debility in Africa today, is carried by human parasitic blood flukes such as worms. The most common symptom is bleeding during urination, a symptom Livingstone noted though he did not connect it with a specific disease. Europeans first encountered bilharzia during Napoleon's 1798 campaign in Egypt, but it took Emin Pasha in the 1880s to point out the correlation between the disease and freshwater snails; the blood parasites are in fact carried by waterborne snails. No effective remedy was discovered until 1918, with the introduction of tartar emetic injections, but although these were found very effective in killing adult flukes, treatment was expensive. A prolonged course of intravenous injections, with associated side-effects, was necessary; also, because the drug was toxic, only highly trained staff could handle and administer it.

River blindness, or onchoocerciasis, was often noted by Richard Burton during his period as consul in the Bights of Benin and Biafra in 1861–4. It occurs between two bands of latitude: the northern boundary is marked by an invisible line from Senegal to Ethiopia, while the southern limit runs from Angola to Tanzania. Still acute in upper Volta, where ferrymen used to have an average working life of two years before they went blind, onchooceriasis is a cousin of elephantiasis, in that a blood fluke is spread by a small, black, humped-back fly.

Guinea-worm infestation, the first parasite on man to be recognised in history, occurs in the Bible as the 'fiery serpents' that tormented the Israelites in the 21st Book of Numbers. Capable of raising powerful blisters on the leg, this disease was one of those studied by Emin Pasha. Schweinfurth reported it unknown north of Lat. 3°N in the 1870s, but ubiquitous south of that line. The traveller John Petherick, who met Speke, Grant and Baker at Gondokoro in 1863, was struck down with this shortly after recovering from fever. His wife wrote home as follows:

> The wounds on Petherick's legs, which I wrote to you about, have now been recognised as caused by the horrible guinea worms: one is partially drawn out. The head, when it first protruded from the flesh, was turned on a straw, and gradually, as you would wind silk on a reel. When resistance is offered, the straw is placed on the leg, there to remain a few hours, we awaiting the opportunity to wind up perhaps an inch or more. To extract the worm entire may take days; if broken it burrows again, and months may elapse ere it protrudes, and always in a different place. I need not tell you how much pain my good husband is compelled to endure.

Another endemic pest, which attacked Park and Livingstone, caused dysentery. Dysentery is of two kinds; bacillic and amoebic. Amoebas, a product of bacteria, lodge in the lower bowel, causing diarrhoea, weight loss, chronic sickness, dyspepsia and anaemia. Livingstone noticed that amoebic dysentery was common in the rainy season. But the more common African variety, bacillic dysentery, was transmitted by flies. Once again, nineteenth-century explorers lacked modern antidotes such as sulphonamides. Tropical ulcers struck at explorers and Africans alike. Livingstone once suffered from these for eight consecutive months and cured himself only by taking advice from Arab traders and applying powdered malachite. Hookworm infestation was confined largely to slaves on the West Africa coast but there its symptoms entered the language. 'The vice' was the disease itself; 'dry belly ache' was the abdominal pain without diarrhoea which resulted from the slave remedy of doses of white lead.

Leprosy was another dreaded scourge of nineteenth-century Africa;

the notorious Robben Island was then a leper colony. Famous sufferers in history, apart from the self-inflicted case of Damien of Molokai, include Edward the Confessor and Robert Bruce, who died of it. Widespread in Europe during the early Middle Ages, it is said to have been overtaken by the Black Death, which exterminated all lepers – or at least not quite all, since the last case in England was reported in 1798. Leprosy is spread by a large bacillus; where the host's immunity reactions are ineffective, so-called lepromatous leprosy occurs. Massive destruction of the nerves leads to foot-drop, wrist-drop, deformity of the feet, chronic ulceration of the limbs, loss of toes and fingers. The patient's face often takes on a leonine appearance from the thickened skin. Blindness and obstructions to breathing may follow. Leprosy is not inherited or carried by victims, and is transmitted only after prolonged contact. Encouraged by unclean clothes, inadequate nutrition and dirty living quarters, leprosy was not finally halted in its tracks until the introduction of the sulphone drugs in the 1940s which, however, merely suppress the symptoms and do not cure the underlying condition. Henry Savage Landor, travelling at the end of the nineteenth century, found leprosy common in Addis Ababa and among the Yamba and Galla tribes, but scarce in areas where the inhabitants ate millet.

Yaws is a skin disease which forms deep open sores on the body and was widely reported by the explorers. Africans treated it by applying lime paste and blacksmith's filings to the sores, whereas Europeans used mercury salts. Yaws often produced the appearance of syphilis, and is a near relation, though, curiously, and as if by a kind of sympathetic magic, childhood illness from yaws produced lifetime immunity to syphilis. The difference between the two diseases is that yaws is transmitted by skin contact among children, whereas syphilis is transferred during sexual intercourse to the mucous membranes of the genitalia.

Yet another parasitic pest introduced into Africa by the explorers was the jigger flea. It arrived at Ambriz on the west coast in 1872, brought there from Brazil by a British ship. By 1879 the jigger had reached the Cameroons. The missionary Bentley reported it widespread on the Congo in the 1880s, and by the end of that decade it had entered Uganda. By 1899 its seaborne conquests had taken it to India. Lionel Decle, writing in the 1890s, found the jigger ubiquitous in the Dark Continent.

The female jigger flea burrows into the toenails and the skin between the toes. Swelling up to the size of a small pea and causing great irritation, the flea is expelled but leaves behind a septic ulcer. Africans grew skilled at removing jiggers with needles; the favourite extractor in Brazil had been the lighted cigarette end. Subsequent infection could lead to the loss of toes and legs. In 1897 Baden-Powell was plagued by jiggers while campaigning in Southern Rhodesia. The Europeans on the Emin Pasha Relief Expedition saw people on the shores of Lake Victoria in 1889 whose entire legs had rotted off. Sometimes these unfortunates were also in the terminal stages of sleeping sickness.

Victims of trypanosomiasis were a particular favourite as targets for jiggers, since such people were too weak and apathetic to extract them. The missionary Bentley reported that in some such cases a person's foot would be invaded by hundreds of jiggers; the resulting sores and swellings and associated anaemia could sometimes finish off the victim before the sleeping sickness had finished its dreadful work. It was not just humans who suffered. Dogs and pigs were customary victims, but the jigger was indiscriminate in its targets. The traveller Gibbons reported that a hunter encountered a leopard which seemed disinclined to move either forwards or backwards. After he shot the (literally) sitting target, the hunter discovered that the big cat's feet had been almost eaten away by jiggers. This illustrates a general proposition: disease struck at animals as well as humans. Thus monkeys had toothache, abscesses on their feet, worms in their stomachs, headaches and tumours; lions suffered from fleas, tapeworms, ingrowing toenails.

Yellow fever was another dreaded disease borne by insects, this time by the aedes mosquito. Symptoms were headaches and agonising pains followed by the vomiting of large amounts of blood, made greasy and black by the action of the gastric juices. About half the fever's victims vomited themselves to death in a few days; those who survived had immunity for life.

Yellow fever is commonly thought of as a disease of the Caribbean, and it is true that its most dramatic interventions in history were staged there. A British attempt to colonise Puerto Rico in 1598 after seizure from the Spanish was defeated by 'yellow jack' (so called by sailors from the quarantine flag flown on infected ships). It also killed two-thirds of Admiral Vernon's force besieging Cartagena in 1741. The Louisiana purchase by Thomas Jefferson was an effect of the disease, since Napoleon abandoned his pretensions in the western hemisphere after 29,000 (out of 33,000) of his army invading Santo Domingo in 1801 were wiped out. These disasters sustained by foreign invaders encouraged the use of the name 'patriotic fever' in Latin America. In the nineteenth century yellow fever crossed from Cuba to the mainland of the United States. New York and Philadelphia felt its lash, while 25,000 souls perished from it in the southern states. The death-toll among rich tourists in Florida produced the soubriquet 'society fever'. The opening of the Panama Canal in 1914, after the earlier French fiasco involving de Lesseps, was a tribute to medical science's identification of the aedes mosquito as the carrier of the disease: not only were Cuba and the United States cleared of the scourge, but the canal was built in the dead centre of what had previously been the yellow fever heartland.

The prevalence of yellow fever in America long encouraged the idea that this was an American disease which had spread to Africa. In fact, Africa was the true home of 'yellow jack'; it had been taken to America by Columbus and the early discoverers. It never spread to Asia because, it is thought, Asian mosquitoes were already saturated with parasites and viruses and could accept no more. In Africa there was a wide belt of yellow fever immunity that stretched from Angola to the Rift Valley. There were many reasons for this. Because monkeys were riddled with yellow fever, Africans living in an endemic area became infected with mild doses as children and thereafter were immune. The disease was not contagious, Africans were highly resistant to it, and only occasionally did the disease break through to affect Africans who lived outside an endemic area and thus lacked immunity.

Yellow fever, like malaria, was overwhelmingly a white man's disease. Like malaria, too, during the golden age of African explorers it was thought to be caused by miasmata. It baffled white administrators by its vicissitudes. Though known not to be contagious, it seemed unstoppable once it took a hold; fumigation and cremation of corpses had no effect. The main febrifuge used was mercury in the form of calomel. Yet though mysterious, its effects were palpable. Accounts of fatal epidemics among Europeans date back to The Gambia in 1455. After the British occupation of that territory in 1816, 74 men out of 105 in the Bathurst garrison died of it. Twenty years later half the European population of the town was wiped out in another outbreak. There were other serious epidemics in 1842, 1859, 1866 and 1878.

All these illnesses were the effects of small animal parasites carried by insects. Yet, even before the white man came, Africa was also prey to a long list of epidemic scourges caused by bacteria and viruses. Pre-eminent was smallpox, second only to sleeping sickness as a threat to the indigenous population. The Africans called it *Ki-Ngongo* ('the great suffering') or *Ki-Beta* ('the great punishment'). It was possibly, in terms of routine fatalities, *the* major killer of the native peoples in the nineteenth century. Symptoms were high temperatures followed by purulent blisters after three days. Many victims succumbed at that stage. In the case of sur-vivors, the sores dried up and formed scabs which finally dropped off, leaving disfiguring scars. The disease was spread by direct contact with a patient, or his clothes, bed linen and eating utensils.

Smallpox was an ancient ravager, known in the Egypt of the Pharaohs. Its most celebrated appearance in the Ancient World was in Athens in

431–429 BC at the beginning of the Peloponnesian War, as described by Thucydides. Famous historical victims include Marcus Aurelius, Mary II of England and Louis XV of France. In the New World it wiped out the Incas and the Aztecs in the wake of the *conquistadores* and carried off 60 million in Europe during the Thirty Years' War (1618–48).

First reported in Africa in the eight century AD, it was said to have originated in Asia and reached Europe by means of the returning Crusaders. It was certainly well established in England by the thirteenth century. Meanwhile it gradually spread its tentacles across Africa. By the eleventh century it was firmly established in the Niger Valley, and by the fourteenth century it had reached the east coast of Africa. The Portuguese carried it from the east coast to Angola, whence it began to penetrate into Central Africa in the early nineteenth century. To make matters worse, a more virulent strain – *variola major* – appeared in Angola in 1864, said to have been associated with an increasing export trade in wax and ivory. Luanda experienced 40,000 fatalities and a 60 per cent mortality.

There were particularly terrible epidemics in Tanzania and Uganda when the German and British colonial masters moved in in the early 1890s. But even in the high era of the explorers there was no shortage of horror. Stanley's journals on all four of his African journeys are full of instances of smallpox, usually sustained by his Zanzibar bearers or *wangwana*. Stanley was always impatient with the disease, and on one notorious occasion, in September 1871, brutally beat his servant Selim for stealing sugar, even though Selim was at the time suffering grievously from 'the great punishment'. Mortality from smallpox among the *wangwana* on Stanley's expeditions was always high, mainly because he would allow no stopping for rest, recuperation or convalescence.

Fred Puleston, the Congo traveller, described even more loathsome scenes at villages decimated by the disease. At one of them he found vultures so gorged with rotting flesh that they were too heavy to take off and fly. At another deserted village he found a Golgotha of skeletons, with a 15-ft boa feasting on one of the cadavers. Du Chaillu's friend, chief Ngoma, suffered so badly that the Frenchman feared he might be accused of having caused the smallpox and thus of compassing Ngoma's death through witchcraft: 'Ngoma, especially, was a great sufferer, for the skin sloughed off his body in large patches, his face was swollen up, and the putrid smell that came from his body was dreadful.' But it was the same throughout Ashangoland:

Each village was a charnel house. Wherever I walked, the most heartrending sights met my view. The poor victims of the loathsome disease in all its worst stages lay about in sheds and huts. There were hideous sores filled with maggots and swarms of carrion flies buzzed about the living but putrid carcasses. The stench in the neighbourhood of the huts was insupportable. Some of the sick were raving, and others emaciated with sunken eyes, victims of hunger as well as of disease. Many wretched creatures from other villages were abandoned to die in the bush.

Missionaries had the same story to tell as the explorers. In Uganda in 1887 C.J. Wilson of the Church Missionary Society declared that smallpox regularly decimated the Ganda. In Unyamwezi in 1887, Dr E.J. Southon of the London Missionary Society reported that the average life expectancy among native males was 20–25 years; those who did not fall in battle or to famine succumbed to smallpox. Summing it all up in 1876, Dr James Christie, the great nineteenth-century expert on African disease, concluded, 'There is no disease in East Africa so fatal in its ravages as smallpox.'

This was one disease that local doctors tried hard to combat. Thomas Bonditch reported from the Ashanti in 1815 that 'ingrafting', or setting a thief to catch a thief, was popular. The local witchdoctor would puncture the inflamed leg and pour in pus. Other African quacks prescribed ointments and the burning of cloves. Arabs and black Islamics wrote verses from the Koran on a parchment, washed the ink into a cup and drank its contents. They also practised variolation similar to the Ashanti method – inoculating with pus from the pock of a victim. This could result in a generally mild attack of smallpox and lifelong immunity.

The last two decades of the nineteenth century in Africa saw smallpox at its apogee. Out of 260 porters left behind at Yambuya with the rear column (1887–8) on Stanley's Emin Pasha Expedition, only sixty survived the ravages of the disease. Harry Johnston later described the native peoples of Africa as no more than a 'hive of gangrenous germs'. A true breakthrough in the treatment of this disease came only when in England Edward Jenner discovered that an inoculation of cowpox prevented smallpox. Smallpox has since featured as one of mankind's rare success stories – the first killer disease eradicated by man.

Plague occurred less often in Africa than the other killer diseases, largely because the continent supports a huge population of rats, on which the plague-bearing fleas are parasitic. The plague bacillus is spread by fleas as they feast on human blood, but in normal circumstances there is no occasion for them to prey on man. Only when extremes of temperature kill off large numbers of rats do the fleas transfer to humans, with catastrophic results. In the nineteenth century, before the advent of modern drugs, bubonic plague occasioned an average 50 per cent mortality during an epidemic, while the more deadly pneumonic plague boasted a 100 per cent killing rate.

The explorer who saw most of plague was Samuel Baker. On his return journey from discovering Lake Albert, at the junction of the Nile with the river Sobat, plague fell upon his party. Men bled copiously from the nose, lying helplessly in delirium about the decks of river-craft, their eyes yellow as orange-peel. The Bakers' 15-year-old servant Saat was raving and threw himself into the river to cool the burning fever that consumed him: 'His eyes were suffused with blood, which, blended with a yellow as deep as the yolk of egg, gave a horrible appearance to his face, that was already so drawn and changed as to be hardly recognised.' Soon after Saat's death, when Baker staggered into Khartoum, he found the capital of the Sudan reeling under a triple blow. Malignant typhus had carried off 3600 out of 4000 black troops in the garrison; a two-year drought had caused famine; and a cattle and camel murrain had destroyed so many animals that commerce was at a standstill. Baker was as ignorant as to the causes of plague as anyone else: he speculated that overcrowded cities and places of pilgrimage such as Mecca produced typhus and plague because of overcrowding and poor ventilation; here he probably confused plague with cholera, which *did* start among the Mecca pilgrims in 1836 and 1858 and spread along the trade routes of Africa.

Another virus-based disease was trachoma, which still afflicts 30 million black Africans today. Famous historical sufferers include Cicero, Horace, St Paul, Pliny the Younger and St Francis of Assisi. A chronic inflammation of the eye behind the upper eyelid, caused by a virus-like organism, trachoma in Africa was essentially a children's disease, related to shortage of protein intake and abundance of dust, dirt and flies.

Yet another group of diseases caused by bacteria and viruses was introduced into Africa from outside. The most horrific of these was cholera. Endemic in India, especially the Ganges basin, cholera spread to tropical Africa in the early nineteenth century for reasons still not entirely clear. It is thought that the disease was carried to Zanzibar and the east coast by ships from India, and in 1816 was limited to the coastal hinterland of Tanzania. Cholera epidemics thereafter came in waves, with peaks in 1816–23, 1826–37, 1842–62 and 1865–75. The last of these produced a total mortality in East Africa well into six figures. The effect of these epidemics was to carry cholera to the coastal regions of Kenya and Somaliland in 1826; inland from Kenya and Tanzania to the great lakes by the 1840s; and by 1865 to Morocco and West Africa, where the disease established a stronghold in that heartland of all diseases, The Gambia. An estimated 20,000 people died of cholera on Zanzibar Island within a four-month period in 1858, 7000–8000 of them in the town of Zanzibar itself. Burton, who had never seen such ravages from the disease, even in India, noted: 'The soil and air seemed saturated with poison, the blood appeared predisposed to receive the influence, and people died like flies.' But even worse was to come in 1869. In November that year cholera broke out again in Zanzibar and spread with rapidity through its narrow, feculent streets. For weeks it raged unchecked. It died down in February, only to revive in March. Not until July 1870 did it abate, leaving 12,000–15,000 dead in Zanzibar town and 25,000–30,000 on the island as a whole.

Cholera was no less destructive than bubonic plague but even more terrifying with its threat of swift, inescapable, agonising death. Its germs are bacteria of curved shape called vibrios. Symptoms of the disease are agonising cramps, runaway diarrhoea and frantic thirst. A toxin is released which sheds the layer of the outer bowel; death may occur within two hours of onset. Drought, famine, high humidity and heat increase the risk of occurrence. Those not attacked probably owe survival to the high acid content of their gastric juices, which destroys the germs before they reach the intestines; however, survivors can still be carriers. One macabre aspect of cholera is that the corpse maintains a high temperature for some time after death; post-mortem muscular contractions can suggest that the body is still alive. In early 1859 Burton on his return from the Lakes made a diversion to the slave port of Kilwa, to find it prostrated by cholera:

> There were hideous sights about Kilwa at the time. Corpses lay in the ravines, and a dead negro rested against the walls of the Customs House. The poor victims were dragged by the leg along the sand, to be thrown into the ebbing waters of the bay; those better off were sewn up in matting, and were carried down like hammocks to the same general depot. The smooth oily water was dotted with remnants and fragments of humanity, black and brown when freshly thrown in, patched, mottled, and part-coloured when in a state of half pickle, and ghastly white, like scalded pig, when the pigmentum nigrum had become thoroughly macerated. The males lay prone upon the surface, diving as it were, head downwards, when the retiring swell left them in the hollow water; the women floated prostrate with puffed and swollen breasts.

Cholera was a waterborne disease, never found in mountainous country. Its appearance struck a peculiar terror into African tribes, since there was no record of such a malady in their oral traditions and it thus seemed like a punishment from the dark gods. Mutesa, kabaka of Buganda, anxiously questioned Speke in 1862: 'What brought the scourge? What could cure it?' In 1876 Stanley reported that the rulers of Rwanda sealed off their frontiers to Arab traders, believing them to be the principal carriers of the disease.

Africans fled in panic from the disease, thus spreading it. Among many other consequences of cholera for the explorers was that Livingstone on his last expedition was trapped in Central Africa until 'found' by Stanley. Because of the dreadful events in Zanzibar no relief caravans could be sent to his assistance in the interior.

There were few defences against cholera until the twentieth century, when antibiotics, safe water and quarantine regulations combined to defeat it. In the United States sodium potassium permanganate was peddled as a quack remedy. Burton reported that the Arabs dosed themselves with opium and locally distilled spirits.

Yet another disease introduced into Africa from Asia was beri-beri. Generally presenting dropsical symptoms, with paralytic weakness of the legs, beri-beri travelled across the Pacific from Japan, made inroads in tropical America and the West Indies and thence to West Africa. Meanwhile, in the second prong of a two-horned attack, it island-hopped from Ceylon, Mauritius and Madagascar to East Africa, though it did not reach the heart of Africa until the 1890s. By the turn of the century travellers such as Landor found it common in the Sahara area.

Syphilis and gonorrhoea were also unknown in Africa until introduced by the Dutch and Portuguese in the sixteenth and seventeenth centuries. Livingstone found these venereal diseases almost unknown, except among half-castes, but remarked on the very similar symptoms in yaws. It was the Arabs who brought syphilis to the Lake Tanganyika area about 1860, but it did not take a grip in the heart of Africa until Stanley's *wangwana* spread it on the Lualaba–Congo in 1876–7. Furthermore, by unwittingly opening the unknown upper Congo to the Arab slavers, Stanley also ushered in a further strain of venereal disease. By the 1880s Fred Puleston was reporting the familiar horrors of tertiary syphilis and general paralysis of the insane: bodies full of sores, nails lost, noses dropping off, deformed babies.

Other diseases suffered by Africans included elephantiasis, goitre, scrofula, scarlet fever, malarial ulcers, impetigo, hydrocele, inflammation of the bladder, piles, sciatica, asthma, bronchitis, dropsy, mumps, epilepsy, hernia, paralysis, whooping cough and ophthalmia (from which Speke suffered grievously in 1857–8). There were also a few local specialities such as ainhum, a Gold Coast ailment that led to amputation of the toes, and leucoderma: a whitening of the skin of the hands, lips, etc. Finally, at the end of the nineteenth century, came a wave of European maladies – influenza, measles, pneumonia – brought in by the colonial administrators.

Consequently the illnesses suffered by the explorers and encountered during their travels present a variegated and heterogeneous picture. At the beginning of the century Mungo Park encountered smallpox but no measles, gonorrhoea but no syphilis, leprosy, yellow fever, yaws, guinea worm infestation and elephantiasis. At the turn of the century Landor reported the full gamut of all categories of illnesses among the Tuareg: fever, smallpox, guinea worm, rheumatism and, especially, ophthalmia. Cameron reported smallpox and leprosy and himself suffered from scurvy. Stanley diced with death in March 1871 at the start of his expedition to find Livingstone by allowing himself to be bitten by a tsetse fly, unaware of the aetiology of sleeping sickness. In addition to his careful jottings on the great killer diseases, Livingstone wrote about tropical ulcers, scurvy, the dimness of vision of people who lived on a pre-dominantly cereal diet, and the absence of stones in the bladders of Africans.

Livingstone's views on mental illness are particularly interesting in the light of the oft-repeated proposition that the European explorers must themselves have suffered from a form of madness to venture into the horrors of the Dark Continent in the first place. The neurosis of the explorers themselves is dealt with later in chapter 16. Of neurosis among Africans, even allowing for their differential perceptions of reality, Livingstone saw much, but he declared that he had never encountered a clear-cut case of what we would now call psychosis.

This survey of African diseases also held good in the areas of the continent that lay outside the ambit of exploration proper. In a journey across the widest part of Africa, from Somaliland to Senegal, Landor found leprosy, venereal disease, dropsy, ophthalmia, yellow fever, smallpox, guinea worm, elephantiasis and herpes. Burchell, travelling among the Hottentots, encountered ophthalmia, smallpox, jaundice and measles. Only in South Africa was there a strain of cattle-fever not found elsewhere. This was Texan or redwater fever, caused by a protozoon carried by the blue tick. In its acute form it killed cattle within a week. Redwater fever caused great havoc in the lower and hotter regions of the South African subcontinent after its introduction in 1870. As with other diseases, altitude and low temperatures were deterrents; it was discovered that the tick was infective only when the temperature was above 85°F.

The explorers' impact altered the pattern of disease in Africa in a number of ways. Directly, they and their men spread new illnesses. Indirectly, they opened a path for slavers and ivory-hunters, who brought in fresh strains. And since the explorers were the trail-blazers for the later wave of prospectors, imperialists, soldiers and colonial administrators, who brought in fresh ailments, the causal chain must ultimately stretch back to the pioneers. Quinine, the saviour of so many explorers, indirectly spelt death to tens of thousands of Africans, as it was only with an effective febrifuge that Europeans could penetrate the Dark Continent.

Before the coming of the white man, most diseases in Africa were endemic rather than epidemic. The population density of Africa was much lower than in Europe or Asia. Most of Africa's people lived in small communities, isolated by vast forests and lack of communications. There was neither motive nor opportunity for the outside world to make contact with them. Consequently, an equilibrium obtained between the indigenous peoples and their diseases. Since so few people lived in an African village, they could not sustain the bacterial and viral infections of more densely populated communities, simply because the bacteria and viruses require rapid passage from human to human if they are to survive. Similarly, there was an equilibrium between villagers and animal parasites. What occurred was a selective survival of the more resistant men and women because they were protected against the diseases either by chance genetic qualities or by accidental possession of overlapping immunities, derived from related infections. The equilibrium between debilitated hosts and parasitic clients was destroyed by the irruption of Europeans into the Dark Continent. So too was the symbiosis between man and virus.

In the age of imperialism, the natural consequence of the explorers' endeavours, the effects of the breakdown of African seclusion were dramatically evident. The Emin Pasha Expedition, at once the last of the great exploration journeys and the first of the large-scale imperialistic forays, broadcast disease from the Atlantic to the Indian Oceans. Later, resettlement programmes, labour migration and the building of roads and dams were all agents of sickness dispersal. Germs were spread by the recruitment of labourers in the Congo and migratory labour in the South African mines. Men from present-day Mozambique, Malawi and Zimbabwe took their diseases to the distant gold mines of Johannesburg and in turn brought back new organisms to their homeland. Inhabitants of the malaria-free Kenya Highlands were conveyed to Mombasa, where they died in droves. Fresh parasites came in with the Senegalese labourers drafted for work on distant groundnut plantations and from migrant Tanzanian pickers on distant sisal farms.

Other manifestations of colonial rule compounded the process. Warfare following risings by the native peoples proved an entering wedge for epidemics. This process was observed in the aftermath of the plethora of risings between 1890 and 1910: in Zimbabwe (Matabele risings); Tanzania ('Maji Maji' outbreaks), Uganda (Kabbarega's guerrilla war), Namibia (Herero rising), and in Somaliland, Sierra Leone and Nigeria. White colonial rule also spread disease through the infrastructure of road and rail links and by the administrative conveniences of District Commissioners, such as concentrating heterogeneous populations into large villages. The rinderpest epidemic, already mentioned as a consequence of the colonial import of cattle, decimated the herds of the pastoral peoples of East Africa; the resultant malnutrition made them more than ever susceptible to disease.

In the worst cases of colonial exploitation, a process not unlike genocide took place. The population of the Congo declined from an estimated 40 million in 1879 just before the coming of Stanley and the other architects of Leopold's Congo State, to 15.5 million in 1910 and 9.25 million in 1933. Parts of French West Africa experienced a 90 per cent population loss during 1911–31. Devotees of 'historical inevitability' may well speculate that contact with the outer world had to come sooner or later, so the moral responsibility of explorers for the spread of disease was not great. But it was fortunate indeed that over the centuries Africa had had fleeting contacts with Europeans. Otherwise, the near-annihilation that occurred among American Indians and the peoples of the Pacific after the 'fatal impact' with the white man might have occurred.

Without question the advent of the Europeans devastated the native peoples. But the epidemic scourges of Africa, like smallpox and the plague, had ravaged the continent long before. And even though Africans had evolved a symbiosis with animal parasites, the sapping effects of fevers, dysentery, leprosy, bilharzia and ulcers meant that they operated at very much less than full energy or efficiency. Secondary consequences were a smaller crop production, reduced calorie intake and hence malnutrition and apathy. Malnutrition in turn later made the African an easy prey to the non-tropical infections like pneumonia, bronchitis and tuberculosis.

It would therefore be a mistake to postulate a golden age of disease-free Africa, ruined by the coming of the explorers. As in any historical analysis, compassion should not stand in the way of realism.

12

Armed Clashes

Ever since Mungo Park lost his life on the Niger in 1806 fighting hostile tribesmen, a primary concern for the European explorer was how to placate or conciliate the tribes encountered on the march or, if it came to it, how to overcome them with superior firepower. The conventional view is that there were just two ways to cross Africa: the Livingstone way and the Stanley way. The Livingstone way was to take the bare minimum of firearms, for protection against highwaymen and casual brigands, to travel only by permitted routes and to make no difficulties over *hongo*. The Stanley way was the method of deterrence: assemble a huge caravan, heavily armed with the very latest repeating rifles, and be ready to use force; at the limit blasting a passage by force was the preferred option.

These pure paradigms of African travel never obtained in reality. Stanley was not so warlike as this stereotype suggests, nor was Livingstone so pacific. Even at the microcosm, it was only the image-making of Horace Waller and other Livingstone admirers that obscured the truth that the doctor was prepared to beat and flog with the best of them. And Savorgnan de Brazza, who built up a persona round his self-proclaimed pacifism, in fact flogged his porters and treated harshly those who threatened him; he once shot and killed two men who were attacking his canoe.

Violence was not the result only of individual actions by men who had come to Africa in the first place to be free of the restraints of 'civilisation'. Deeper social currents came into the picture. The use of force was endemic to Africa; the most admired human beings were warriors and conquerors. On the other hand, the explorers came to the continent in an era that was the most violent of the nineteenth century. Between Burton's arrival at Zanzibar in 1857 and Stanley's fourteen years later the following bloody conflicts had taken place on the world periphery: the Indian Mutiny, the Maori wars, the French intervention in Mexico, the

American Civil War and the Paraguayan war. Europe had witnessed the Franco-Austrian war over Italy, the Austro-Prussian war of 1866, the Spanish Civil War of 1868 and the Franco-Prussian war of 1870–1. This is to say nothing of innumerable frontier wars and imperial campaigns, like that of the British against Emperor Theodore in 1868.

Armed clashes were anyway almost inevitable given the 'contradiction' between the subsistence level at which most African tribes operated and the European explorers' demands for food and water from the villages; the general collision of cultures and expectations; and – a barrier exacerbated by polyglot Africa – the overall failure to communicate meanings and intentions. For all these reasons it was not surprising that explorers' accounts are full of armed encounters with hostile tribes. So Brazza, who boasted that he was a man of peace as opposed to Stanley's man of force, fought a running river battle with the Abfourus in 1877; du Chaillu, who prided himself on his good relations with Africans, was forced to fight a fierce action against the Ashangos; Chaillé-Long killed eighty-two of Kabbarega's warriors in a ferocious action at Mruli; Teleki's expedition experienced some bruising skirmishes with the Kikuyu; Serpa Pinto was attacked in the Lui country where, out-numbered 100 to 1, he and his men were able to fight off an attack thanks to a servant who happened to load an elephant-gun with nitro-glycerine and frightened the attackers with a tremendous explosion.

Despite their desire to travel to unknown regions without let or hindrance, the explorers generally evinced a grudging admiration for the tribes who were powerful enough to oppose them. Among the most admired tribes were the Matabele, Galla, Barotse, Yao, Zulu, Ngoni, Makololo and Ganda. A myth grew up around the Masai that they were uniquely fearsome. This exaggerated idea of Masai ferocity was probably fostered by Arab traders who wished to keep Europeans out of their own areas of profitable activity. The myth was swallowed whole by Stanley who, despite his cynicism, had a gullible side, and was accepted as gospel until Thomson revealed the 'emperor's clothes' in 1883–4. Even missionaries suffered from the disease of 'big battalion worship' and tended to despise the lesser tribes they preyed on. Europeans were most at home when dealing with the massively powerful military tribes like the Ganda. Not even a Stanley-type caravan, 1000 strong and armed to the teeth with Sniders and Remingtons, could hope to survive all-out war with a chief like Mutesa. For this reason early relations with the Ganda always saw diplomatic skills at their most finely honed. The Europeans rationalised their military impotence by praising the Ganda state for its 'civilisation'; in other words, they insinuated that because of the high level of technology, social structure, agriculture, hygiene, roads etc. the Ganda were already primitive Europeans, and thus it was not necessary to use force against them. So it was that most of the explorers' armed clashes were with lesser tribes; only Baker was foolhardy enough to take on a first-rank military nation.

Violence in Africa was unpredictable, likely to occur when least expected, usually because the explorer involved had not read the warning signs. A classic example was Burton's experience at Berbera in 1855. Burton had served right through one of the most violent decades in Indian history without seeing a minute's front-line action. Before setting off in late 1854 for the 'forbidden' city of Harar he had been given dire warnings that he would never return alive. 'The human head once struck off does not regrow like the rose' was one of the more striking minatory oracles he received. Yet he reached Harar and returned unscathed. After going so signally in harm's way, Burton could not have imagined that the angel of death was flapping its wings at the coastal town of Berbera, where no attacks on Europeans had previously occurred. But this was where Burton had his one and only taste of combat and came closest to a violent death.

On 19 April 1855 a complacent Burton, together with lieutenants Stroyan, Herne and Speke and forty-two porters – Nubians, Egyptians and Arabs – were encamped on a rocky ridge overlooking the Red Sea near Berbera. Normally, Burton's camp was under covering fire from a British gunboat, but the *Mahi* was suddenly withdrawn to Aden for blockading duties. This provided a 'window of vulnerability' which the Eesa tribe of Somalis proceeded to exploit. Out of overweening self-confidence Burton neither fortified his camp nor placed extra sentries at the camp perimeter, even though an Eesa probe had earlier been reported, and such probes in Africa were the inevitable prelude to an assault in force.

At 2 a.m. on the 19th Burton was aroused from his slumbers by panic-stricken ululations. Like a hurricane some 350 warriors swept into the camp. Burton improvised his defences hurriedly. He told off Herne to rally his men at the rear; Herne found no one there but the enemy and was lucky to escape with his life. Burton meanwhile roused Stroyan and Speke from their tents and formed a defensive ring around the entrance to the giant Rowtie tent. Stroyan was cut down before he got there. Herne, Burton and Speke blazed away with Colts until their ammunition was spent, then made a run for it just as the Eesa cut down the tent from behind.

Outside in the darkness the three men became separated. Slashing with his sabre at anything that moved, Burton took the full force of a javelin through his cheek. It smashed four back teeth and part of his palate and emerged through the other cheek. Semi-conscious from pain and loss of blood, Burton was carried by his men to the shore where they signalled to a dhow captain, an old friend, to take them off. On board the captain extracted the lance and staunched the haemorrhage.

Next morning the search for survivors began. Herne had found a hiding place after no more than a few bruises from a war-club. Speke, however, had had an amazing brush with death. Taken captive early in the fighting, he was bound with thongs and forced to watch a war dance. He sustained threats of castration and immediate death if he would not abjure Christianity. When the Eesa grew tired of his obstinacy, they moved off, whispering orders to a single guard left behind. The guard then drove a lance right through his thigh. 'Smelling death' Speke knocked out his assailant with a two-fisted smash with his bound hands. He then dashed off over the shingly beach towards the surf. The Eesa gave chase, but Speke by zigzagging in the darkness threw them off the scent. He then spent the rest of the night gnawing through his bonds. At dawn the rescue party from the dhow arrived. Suffering from spear wounds in eleven places, Speke hovered near death for a week. Both he and Burton convalesced in Aden, where they were warned that survival dictated a return to England after convalescence. So ended Burton's 'first footsteps' in East Africa.

The Burton experience shows that it would be naïve to assume that Africans never attacked white men without compelling reason. Schweinfurth also discovered this fundamental truth. On his return journey from Mangbetu, in company with a Nubian ivory merchant called Muhammad Aboo Sammat, he was ambushed without any warning or provocation by the Abanga tribe. Muhammad took a spear thrust in the thigh and two of his porters were cut to pieces. Rapid gunfire beat off the attackers but, seeing them regrouping, Schweinfurth and Muhammad retreated into the nearest village and made a fortified camp by pulling down huts and setting them up as barricades. The Abanga then attacked again, firing showers of arrows into the village and yelling 'Meat! Meat!' For much of the day they stayed out of rifleshot but towards dusk came within range. They then took heavy casualties from Muhammad's well-drilled Nubians who were loaded with heavy shot. The tide of battle turned. In retaliation for the attack Muhammad's men burned down all the Abanga huts, destroyed their maize crops, raped and enslaved their women and bayoneted all the village dogs.

Unwarranted attacks *did* sometimes take place on Europeans whose expeditions had an obvious scientific character. But in general the avowed pacifists like Thomson and Brazza or the missionary explorers like Livingstone, whose finance and sponsorship came from learned or religious bodies like the Royal Geographical Society and the missionary societies, fared better than the exploring buccaneers who were self-financing, like Baker and Teleki, or those with massive resources to draw on like Stanley, financed as he was by the wealth of the *New York Herald* on his first two journeys. When self-financing combined with individual arrogance, high levels of armament and detestation of the African, as in the case of Baker, the results were catastrophic.

The two stormy incursions of Baker into Bunyoro have already been related (see pp. 72–80). But a bare recital of the facts leaves unanswered many questions – questions which arise from the conflict of evidence. Basically, there are three sources for Baker in Bunyoro, all differing markedly. First, there is Baker's own account; secondly, the oral traditions collected by European missionaries and their wives, especially Ruth Fisher; thirdly, oral traditions utilised in the twentieth century by African historians. Each of these accounts has its built-in bias, and the historian who tries to tease out the truth is likely at the end to take Pilate's attitude to the veridical.

Baker's violent antipathy to Kamurasi in 1864 may be explained in part by the fact that until that time his experience had been confined to the comparatively minor headmen of the segmentary Nilotic societies of the north. The deviousness of an African court and the evasive yet autocratic manner of the *mukama* of Bunyoro, ruler of an area almost as large as England, were something new. In a word, Baker may have been disconcerted that Kamurasi did not conform to his idea of an African chief; his reaction would probably have been very different if he had first visited the autocratic Ganda court, as Speke and Grant did.

Kamurasi had good reason to be suspicious of the white man. Shortly after Speke and Grant's visit, a party of Sudanese arrived in Bunyoro, claiming to be the explorers' friends. In collusion with Kamurasi's sworn enemy Ruyonga they repaid the lavish hospitality of the Unyoro by suddenly turning on them and massacring 300 of them. Kamurasi was also aware that Baker (admittedly through necessity rather than choice) was associated with Sudanese slave and ivory gangs, whose guns gave them local superiority and who slaughtered without regard for race, sex or rank; their treachery extended to their own allies, whose cattle and women they would seize when the fancy took them. So far from taking Kamurasi's very real anxieties into account, Baker acted truculently and threatened to unleash these human locusts on Bunyoro if he did not get his way.

On one occasion the *mukama* complained that one of the Sudanese had been insolent to him and even threatened to shoot him. Kamurasi pointed out that such behaviour in normal circumstances would have been the man's death-warrant; he had spared him solely out of consideration for the white man. Instead of accepting this graciously, apologising and promising to look into the matter, Baker 'advised Kamurasi not to talk too big as . . . he might imagine the results that would occur should he even hint at hostility, as the large parties of Ibrahim and the men of Muhammad Wat-el-Mek [two of Baker's Sudanese associates] would immediately unite and destroy both him and his country . . . the gallant Kamurasi turned almost green at the bare suggestion of this possibility.' This was typical both of Baker's hectoring arrogance and his luck: he would scarcely have got away with this bluster with Mutesa.

African oral tradition provides other reasons for the tension between Kamurasi and Baker. The Nyoro people had never seen a white man before, so Kamurasi called a council to discuss who the strangers were and what to do about them. His councillors were of the unanimous opinion that the white man and his even stranger wife were the ancient inhabitants of the land, the Bacwezi, returned to claim their own. Several convincing 'proofs' were adduced. In the first place, the strangers knew their way around the country and did not need guides. They showed no respect to the country's chiefs, strengthening the inference that they regarded themselves as its owners. To a people content with the fire of twigs at night, the Bakers' lamps appeared like stars; the cook who busied himself four times a day with mysterious objects like kettles and pots must surely be a witchdoctor mixing potions.

Kamurasi invited his unwelcome guests to his court, spread leopard-skins on the ground and provided two stools for them. The Bunyoro oral tradition takes up the story:

> When they were seated, the king cast furtive glances, and concluded in his mind that they were father and son; the elder man with the fierce beard he called the 'Beard,' while the young man he called the 'Little Star'. But the Beard explained to him that his companion was not a man, but his wife, and they had taken this very long journey out from England to look for a large lake which his friends had heard lay somewhere near to Bunyoro and he wanted the king to give him sufficient porters to take him there. Then Kamurasi knew that the stranger was speaking lies, for no man would leave his own country and people, and face danger and fatigue, merely to look at water. He saw at once that the white man had come to wrest him from his kingdom. Had he not brought fearful implements that spat out fire and killed birds and beasts; was he not asking for men with whom he could form the nucleus of an army; had he not brought with him a wife, who should bear him sons to succeed him? So Kamurasi determined within himself that he would not allow these strangers out of his sight, to wander about his country sowing rebellion in the hearts of his subjects; he would make them prisoners and try to kill them with hunger.

Tension between Kamurasi and Baker increased when the king

delayed finding porters and tried to stop food supplies. Baker browbeat him into submission with a threat that white men could compass his death and that of his sons at a distance by using 'bad fetish'. As if to prove the point Baker shook the ashes from his pipe on to the head of the king's son. Some of the ashes fell into a bowl of milk the lad was holding; to Kamurasi this was clear proof that the 'Beard' had bewitched his son.

Angrily he summoned his councillors and spoke of war. But Baker had successfully broken their spirits. 'Can you kill a man that has forty soldiers armed with fire?' they asked. 'We beseech you save us and our children by sending these people out of your country.' So it was done. Baker's parting gift to the king, a pistol, was interpreted as further 'bad medicine' when Kamurasi started practising and with his first shot blew off his own forefinger. It was considered a bad omen for the Nyoro to be ruled by a 'disfigured' man; Kamurasi owed his very survival and avoidance of the 'king must die' ritual to the skill of his surgeons, who fixed him up with a new finger made from a goat's bone.

Eight years later Baker returned to Bunyoro. On 22 March 1872 a lavishly equipped and well-organised expedition reached the Victoria Nile from Fatiko. With Baker this time were his wife and his nephew, Lieutenant Baker. The ostensible reason for Baker's presence south of Gondokoro was suppression of the slave trade. To add to his natural arrogance, Baker now had a knighthood and the Khedive's commission as Governor-General of Equatoria. The stage was set for confrontation with the new *mukama*. Kamurasi had died in 1870. His three sons fought for the succession in the traditional Bunyoro way, which glorified survival of the fittest. Each of the three, Kabbarega, Kabka Miro and Ruyonga, called in the slave traders as allies. The slaver Abou Saud played one off against another and eventually installed Kabbarega after killing Kabka Miro; Ruyonga, however, he kept alive and 'on ice' as pretender in case he ever needed to depose Kabbarega.

Into this simmering cauldron came Baker, as ever with all the hubris of ignorance. Unaware that the time-honoured method of establishing the Bunyoro succession was to fight for it, Baker sanctimoniously stigmatised Kabbarega for his treachery in securing his position as king by murdering a royal brother.

Arriving at Masindi on 25 April, Baker next day had an interview with the twenty-year-old light-complexioned Kabbarega, an imposing man 5 ft. 10 in. tall. Baker started to talk about European 'improvement': agriculture, commerce, good government. Kabbarega cut him short and demanded help for a campaign against Ruyonga. Baker curtly refused.

Disappointed, Kabbarega broke off contact. Oral tradition maintains that he still remembered the time Baker had tapped ash on his head and feared the 'Beard' would bewitch him if he got inside the royal kraal. Grudgingly he allowed Baker to begin an agricultural settlement. The first man to sow cotton in Bunyoro, Baker also planted cucumbers, melons and pumpkins. Trade was opened with the Nyoro, and large stores of ivory obtained by barter. But on 14 May he did something that panicked the jittery Kabbarega. He took formal possession of Bunyoro in the Khedive's name and hoisted the Egyptian flag. Baker claimed (improbably) that this was done with the full consent of Kabbarega; Nyoro traditions (naturally) deny this.

The friction intensified. Kabbarega went out of his way to avoid meeting Baker, on the grounds that measles and smallpox were raging through his kraal. Informed thus by Kabbarega's heralds, Baker called the king a liar. Oral tradition takes up the story:

> And Kabbarega sent back the answer, 'My servant speaks the truth. But why do you want to enter my house? A visitor stays where his host puts him, and does not seek to pry into his house.'
>
> These words made the European very angry, and the following afternoon he came down to Kabbarega's with some soldiers, without first sending to be announced. The king immediately summoned his chiefs, and plotted with them to kill the stranger. He said to them, 'Let us go and meet him in the open courtyard, and the moment I raise my spear, all of you fall upon him and spear him to death. Are we not an army against a few?'
>
> So Kabbarega went forth to meet the white man followed by all his chiefs armed with spears. The European greeted him, and said, 'I have brought my soldiers to show you how we teach them to drill.'
>
> Kabbarega answered, 'I will also show you how I can drill my men.'
>
> Then the Beard made all his men to pass before him twice with their arms shouldered, and, as he was commanding them, Kabbarega raised his spear and sent it quivering toward the European, but it missed its mark and fell to the ground after having grazed his arm.
>
> The white man then picked it up, and, handing it back to Kabbarega, said, 'If you have anything against me say so; I have only come on a friendly visit.'
>
> Kabbarega was speechless when he saw the fearlessness of the man he had tried to kill, and he turned and went into his house, while the European returned to his fort.
>
> The king called his chiefs and said, 'You cowards and traitors to your king; did we not make a compact that when I thrust my spear you would all fall on him and kill him? You have failed me, and jeopardised my life, for I know that the white man will seek to slay me.'
>
> But on the following morning the Beard sent friendly greetings to Kabbarega, and invited him and his chiefs to visit him that evening. When they arrived they were shown many fearful and marvellous things. The Beard brought out some little bullets, and, after setting fire to them, he threw them high up in the air, and immediately the whole country became light as day,

although it was nearly midnight, and sun, moon and stars appeared in the sky, but disappeared again just as they were falling to earth.

Kabbarega was now quite sure that this stranger must be one of the Bacwezi, for no man could play with the things of heaven and be so immune from death.

Kabbarega now reverted to his father's policy of trying to starve the strangers out. Baker simply sent his men out on plundering expeditions. Kabbarega sent word that such actions were felonies. He began to send out scouting parties to observe Baker's dispositions and movements. Fearful that Baker's men might launch an all-out attack with their 'lightning sticks', Kabbarega decided to get in the first blow. On 7 June, in an apparent show of friendship, he sent Baker's troops a quantity of plantain beer which he had poisoned. The troops saved themselves only by rapidly swallowing emetics. Next morning came a treacherous attack on Baker's camp.

Thousands of armed natives now rushed from all directions upon the station ... the troops were now in open order, completely around the station, and were pouring heavy fire into the masses of the enemy within the high grass which had been left purposely uncleared by Kabbarega, in order to favour his treacherous attack. The natives kept up a steady fire upon the front behind the castor-oil bushes and densely thronged houses.

With the help of a machine-gun, Baker's men gradually gained the upper hand. Baker ordered Masindi put to the torch and pursued the enemy through the flames. The battle of Masindi merely confirmed Kabbarega in his hatred of Europeans. He sent assurances that he had not instigated the attack, but Baker did not believe him. Worried about his baggage and the flying column he had detached to Fatiko which might return and walk into a trap, Baker decided on a retreat to the Victoria Nile, there to ally himself with Ruyonga. But he was well aware of the risks. It was by now the rainy season, and the grass in this country of dense, tangled bush was 9–10 ft high, providing ideal cover for ambushes. He decided to stall and conceal his true intentions.

Kabbarega made further peace overtures, to which Baker replied emolliently with presents of a porcelain pot and a music box. But on 11 June came a barefaced attempt to assassinate Baker as he strolled round the ruins of Masindi. When this failed the Nyoro attacked his camp in force. Baker withdrew from the outer perimeter into the inner fort, then sallied out and fired all the villages in the neighbourhood. Things were now becoming desperate. He decided to make a bonfire of all surplus supplies and possessions and make a forced march to Foweira, taking only iron rations.

On 14 June the retreat began in drizzling rain. Ten miles from Marindi the enemy fell on the column. A running fight developed. Baker abandoned his cattle and some of the baggage. Next the Nyoro attempted an ambush with a regiment hidden in reeds along a riverbank abutting a swamp. Baker flushed them out by directing a terrific fusillade into the reeds before starting a crossing of the swampland. The Nyoro were reduced to flinging their spears impotently at long range. The pattern of short, sharp engagements continued. Fortunately for Baker there were no night attacks: this would have used up all his ammunition. Even without actual attacks his men were so nervous that they blazed away at shadows. The Nyoro, for their part, were angry that such a heavily outnumbered force should have given them the slip. They concocted a story, doubtless based partly on the fact of the abandoned baggage, that Baker had corrupted his pursuers by scattering cowrie shells and beads in the tall grass, thus drawing off the Nyoro warriors who proved themselves more devoted to lucre than to their king.

On 24 June Baker and his men reached Foweira to find it gutted. They set to work to build a new fort and to fashion canoes so that they could cross the Nile. Raiding parties were meanwhile sent out far and wide to commandeer all river craft and their paddlers, so that Kabbarega could not pursue them across the Nile. Baker summoned Ruyonga to meet him but the pretender, fearing capture or treachery, would not come in person but sent an envoy to make blood-brotherhood by proxy.

Once across the Nile Baker was safe. His pursuers abandoned the chase when they found the river denuded of canoes. Baker then proclaimed Ruyonga the agent of the Khedive and thus the true ruler of Bunyoro. But his planned revenge against Kabbarega had to wait until November, when the tall grass would be dry enough to burn. He therefore left Abd-el-Kader with sixty-five men to stiffen Ruyonga's levies and marched to Fatiko with the rest. The offensive against Kabbarega required reinforcements from Gondokoro. Meanwhile Ruyonga, assisted by an army sent by Mutesa of Buganda, always glad to foment mischief against his old enemy, cleared Kabbarega's forces out of northern Bunyoro. As it happened, the reinforcements from Gondokoro arrived too late for Baker to be able to campaign against Kabbarega, since his term of office as Governor expired on 1 April 1873.

What sense can we make of this stirring and violent episode? There are contradictions both between Baker's account and the oral traditions and *within* the traditions themselves. African oral histories pose problems in that the chronology is often distorted, the sequence of events confused and occurrences separated by many years telescoped. Moreover, tribes naturally played their successes up and their failures down for propaganda purposes. And the tribal bards tailored their traditions to fit the wishes of the ruling dynasty. This is hardly surprising: we do not, after all, expect to hear the historical truth about Richard III from Shakespeare, who was constrained by similar prudential motives. Nevertheless it would be a gross error to dismiss *all* oral tradition as legend, even bearing in mind that Africans did not always distinguish the ontological status of fact and myth.

With these general caveats we may proceed to examine the story of Baker and Kabbarega in the light of oral tradition. A particular problem here is that European travellers in Bunyoro–Kitara could not understand the language and so relied on interpreters. These interpreters, from personal, clan or tribal motives, may at times have misled their employers intentionally or unintentionally through lack of competence in translation; hence one obvious source for the discrepancy between the oral traditions and the explorers' accounts.

The Nyoro account of the collision of Kabbarega and the white man differs in many important respects from Baker's. There was, to begin with, a pre-existing layer of hostility in that Baker flew the Egyptian flag. The slavers who ravaged the Bugungu area of Bunyoro were known to come from Khartoum, which in Kabbarega's eyes meant from Egypt. Moreover, Baker's Sudanese, hundreds strong, were said to have inflicted revolting cruelties on the Nyoro people wherever they went, and in particular introduced sodomy, a previously unknown horror. Without consultation Baker had the Nyoro flag lowered and the Egyptian one raised. The proclamation of annexation to Egypt came as a great shock to Kabbarega, who asked plaintively. 'Are there to be two kings in Bunyoro?' Additionally, the tradition maintains that Kabbarega did not send poisoned beer to Baker; it was merely very strong and the Sudanese, unused to such potency, became horribly drunk and vomited. In the ensuing recriminations Baker executed Kabbarega's envoy Mboga. Then Baker mowed down droves of Nyoro warriors with a machine-gun and set fire to the king's enclosure and neighbouring villages.

It is quite clear that a judicious examination of the episode will tend to credit the African account more than Baker's. On his own admission Baker hated and despised Africans, would not have considered them to have any rights, and rationalised his own bullying by talk of treachery. A later remark made by Baker to Burton about Stanley rather gives the game away: he said it was quite permissible to slaughter recalcitrant Africans; the mistake Stanley made was to admit what he had done to a European audience. We may infer, then, that Baker's account in *Ismailia* was heavily doctored. The inference is strengthened by the fuliginous way Baker deals with the Mboga incident; Baker simply says that in the confusion the envoy 'disappeared' – a term that has a peculiarly sinister resonance for an audience in the late twentieth century.

The one aspect of the oral tradition that seems false and propagandistic relates to the poisoned beer. It seems clear from hints in the oral accounts that Kabbarega was prepared to use any means to be rid of the white interlopers. Significantly, there is no mention of the incident in the account given to Ruth Fisher during the colonial era of the 1890s. This seems partly a case of not wishing to offend the colonising power and partly a desire not to damage the reputation of Kabbarega, who by then was fighting a guerrilla war against the British. The story of the Sudanese, who had drunk their way from the Nile to the heart of Africa, being overcome by the potency of plantain beer, rings false. We may conclude, therefore, that Kabbarega really did try to poison his unwelcome guests, while conceding that Baker and the Sudanese by their bullying and plundering had tried the king's patience to the limit.

Fully to make sense of this, the most serious armed clash between explorer and tribal ruler in the entire era of 'Darkest Africa', we need to examine Baker's psychology and his pathological drives. The Baker family fortunes were based on large sugar plantations in Jamaica and Mauritius. Baker had imbibed from his conservative, class-conscious and racist parents a violent prejudice against do-gooders and stay-at-home philanthropists combined with a contempt for the 'lesser breeds'. Before he came to Africa he had managed the family plantations in Mauritius and Ceylon and had shown a harsh intolerance towards the native peoples, especially the backward Singalese. He consistently defended the use of force against primitive peoples and as constantly inveighed against the benighted savagery and idleness of the African. He compared the blacks of Nuer unfavourably with his pet monkey and suggested the reason suicide and insanity seemed unknown among Africans was that their brains had never become burdened by thought or study. He considered sloth and barbarism among the African irremediable because they had been caused originally by climate. The path to civilisation he thought impossibly long because the ancient Britons of Julius Caesar's time 'although savage, were far superior to any tribes of Africa'.

Baker in full flight is well illustrated by a journal entry at Latooka on 10 April 1863:

I wish the black sympathisers in England could see Africa's inmost heart as I do, much of their sympathy would subside. Human nature viewed in its crude state as pictured amongst African savages is quite on a level with that of the brute, and not to be compared with the noble character of the dog. There is neither gratitude, pity, love, nor self-denial; no idea of duty; no religion; but covetousness, ingratitude, selfishness and cruelty. All are thieves, idle, envious, and ready to plunder, and enslave their weaker brethren.

A consideration of Baker's excesses helps us to put in context the many allegations concerning Stanley's brutality – for there is no doubt that in the England of the last quarter of the nineteenth century it was Stanley, not Baker, who was considered the man of blood. In fact, Stanley, as with his *wangwana*, had a fairly shrewd idea of when to use force and when conciliation when dealing with African tribes; it was usually circumstances that drove him into armed confrontation. Baker may be said to have relished the opportunity to pour lead into the ranks of African warriors; with one notable exception Stanley did so only when he had no realistic alternative.

Stanley's first controversial armed encounter was at Bumbire Island on Lake Victoria in 1876. He had left the bulk of his party on the southeastern shore of the lake and proceeded on an anti-clockwise circumnavigation in his boat the *Lady Alice*. After a most successful meeting with Mutesa, kabaka of Buganda, Stanley headed south-west and reached Bumbire Island, 11 miles long by 2 miles wide, on 28 April. He was received very roughly. Scores of tribesmen hauled the boat on to the beach to prevent a quick getaway. Then Chief Shekka settled in for some bargaining over *hongo* before he would consent to feed his hungry visitors.

Stanley began to suspect treachery when the Bumbire people seized his oars. He feared that next time they would return for the firearms. Sure enough that afternoon Shekka appeared at the head of 300 yelling warriors. Drums beat, conches blew, warriors appeared in warpaint; there could be no mistaking Shekka's intentions. With admirable presence of mind Stanley urged his tired men to launch the *Lady Alice*. A superhuman effort of heaving by his eleven-strong crew got the boat into the water just in time. As the men of Bumbire came on at the double. Stanley discharged his elephant gun, loaded with two large conical balls. The warriors withdrew in momentary confusion. Stanley took his opportunity. It was now a question of getting the *Lady Alice* out through the narrow entrance to Bumbire bay before the enemy could seal the exit. A race for the narrows ensued. Pursued by two large canoes, Stanley let his assailants get within a hundred yards before blasting them with a further fusillade of explosive balls from his elephant gun. Both canoes sank. The enemy sheered off, having taken casualties later established as fourteen dead and wounded.

The sequel was nearly disastrous. For thirty-six hours the *Lady Alice* drifted on the open Victoria, out of sight of land, and buffeted by storms. The men were cold, hungry and thirsty; all around them voracious

crocodiles cruised. Stanley vowed vengeance. His opportunity came three
months later, when he had recruited his expedition and received powerful
reinforcements from Mutesa. On 4 August he approached the island with
470 men. In the front line in canoes and the *Lady Alice* were his
handpicked Zanzibari sharpshooters, each with twenty rounds of
ammunition.

Stanley made as though to land, at a spot where he knew the sun would
be shining in the Bumbire warriors' eyes. The warriors raced him to the
'beachhead' to contest the landing. At 100-yds range Stanley formed a
battle line, with the canoes anchored together broadside to the beach. A
crashing volley from Sniders and elephant-guns thinned the warriors'
ranks. They withdrew into long cane-grass at the water's edge. Tracking
them with his field glasses, Stanley moved his flotilla in to a range of
50 yds then raked the grass from end to end with withering volleys.
Finding that courage alone availed nothing against this fusillade, the men
of Bumbire withdrew to higher ground out of range. Stanley then feigned
a landing, tempted them back down on to the killing ground and
slaughtered another couple of dozen. By the evening forty-two Bumbire
warriors lay dead and over a hundred wounded; Stanley's men were
unscathed except for two bruised from rock-throwing. This exploit and
Mutesa's protection ensured there was no further trouble with the
peoples of Lake Victoria.

Stanley was proud of his skills as a strategist and tactician and wrote up
the battle of Bumbire at length both in his despatches to the *New York
Herald* and *Daily Telegraph* (his co-sponsors) and in his book *Through the
Dark Continent*. Naïvely, he failed to foresee the outcry that would
follow.

Even while he was in Africa the Anti-Slavery and Aborigines
Protection Societies protested to the Foreign Office about the methods of
a man who was flying the Union Jack in Central Africa. In November
1876 at a meeting of the Royal Geographical Society the socialist writer
H.M. Hyndman tried to introduce a motion of censure on Stanley, who
was one of the Society's gold medallists, but was ruled out of order. He
and another gold medallist Henry Yule further stirred the pot at the Royal
Geographical Society and kept the issue simmering in the press. Gordon
Bennett, always eager to have a go at the British, weighed in on Stanley's
side. When the explorer emerged at the Atlantic in August 1877 after his
epic journey down the Congo, the *New York Herald* commented:

This will greatly distress the philanthropists of London who will again appeal
to the British government to declare him a pirate. Their humane but rather
impractical view is that a leader in such a position should be slaughtered

himself and let discovery go to the dogs, but should never pull a trigger against this species of human vermin that puts its uncompromising savagery in the way of all progress and all increase of knowledge.

This was calculated ambiguity. Stanley's determined and slaughterous response to the *first* assault at Bumbire, in April 1875, was entirely justified by self-defence. The *second*, 4 August, attack on Bumbire could not be justified at all, except in terms of retribution and revenge. Stanley's specious 'refutations' of his critics, based on the proposition that an untamed Bumbire on his flank was a threat to his food supply and communications, was valid only for the situation in April, not that in August. Stanley knew this very well, but traded on the likelihood that the two different events would be confused and conflated as one.

The debate raged on into 1878 when Stanley returned to England. Stanley dealt firmly with his critics and the flavour of his outbursts is well conveyed by the following: 'He only wished he could get every member of Exeter Hall [the headquarters of the Evangelical Movement] to explore by the same route he had gone from the Atlantic to longitude 23. He would undertake to provide them with seven tons of bibles, any number of surplices, and a church organ into the bargain and if they reached so far as longitude 23 without chucking some of the bibles at the Negroes' heads he would . . .'

This was good knockabout stuff, but it did not address his critics' fundamental objections. This was the basis in international law for violence used by an expedition sponsored by a newspaper against the aboriginal inhabitants of a given territory. As one critic put it: 'Its black possessors have a perfect right to resist his invasion if they choose; and should they do so, we entirely deny that as a "pioneer of civilisation" he is entitled in the name of this mission, to force his way through them by the use of elephant rifles and explosive bullets.' Hyndman dubbed Stanley's methods 'a system of exploration by private war'. Here Stanley's critics were referring not just to the Bumbire episode but to the famous thirty-two battles Stanley fought on his way from the Lualaba to the mouth of the Congo in 1876–7.

The first encounters were with the Wagenya people on the Lualaba in November 1876, while Stanley and his men were still accompanied by the powerful slaver Tippu Tip. Then came battles with the even more formidable Kusu. On 8 December at Unya-Nsinge, near the junction with the Congo, Stanley directed a daring amphibious operation, which led to the utter defeat of the Mutako people and the destruction of fourteen of their canoes. Then on 18–20 December at Vinya-Nyara, 125 miles north of Nyangwe, Stanley waged a savage three-way combat against an unholy alliance of the locals and his old enemy the Kusu, who had been called in to 'eat up' the interlopers. Stanley's peril was deadly, for the expedition had split into two, and he had lost contact with the larger overland party led by Tippu Tip.

The first enemy attack, on a fortified stockade manned by Stanley and the *wangwana*, resembled the defence of Rorke's Drift two years later in another part of Africa. African dead lay in heaps on the killing ground between the stockade and the jungle. But despite heavy casualties, the enemy did not give up. Anyone venturing outside the stockade was immediately punished by arrows shot by Kusu sharpshooters in the treetops. On the second day of fighting Stanley extended his defence perimeter by making a sortie and then having the *wangwana* clear the nearest stretches of jungle; meanwhile he got his own sharpshooters to scale trees and take out the Kusu snipers. By the evening of 19 December Stanley had constructed a defence in depth, screened by sharpshooters' nests at each end of the village.

On 20 December the expected offensive began. The enemy hit them on both flanks: 800 warriors formed the riverborne assault force, in canoes; the Kusu formed the spearhead attacking from the forest. To blunt the landward attack before it developed into an unstoppable charge was the task of just twenty *wangwana* sharpshooters. Stanley and twenty others dug in to receive the assault from the river.

Stanley and his men doled out terrible punishment to the attackers but even so were on the point of being overwhelmed when demoralised whoopings from the Kusu announced that Tippu Tip and the land party had suddenly arrived. What was a desperate action a minute ago turned into a rout of the tribesmen. Stanley and the original defenders then made a nocturnal sortie and captured or destroyed all the hostiles' canoes. Resistance to the white man was over on this stretch of the river.

But grimmer battles still were yet to come. Worn out with his slow progress overland and the toll taken on his men by smallpox, Tippu Tip refused to accompany Stanley beyond Vinya-Nyara. Threats, bluster and cajolery by Stanley were to no avail. On 28 December 1876 Stanley launched into the unknown with Frank Pocock and 149 'dark companions' on the *Lady Alice* and a flotilla of canoes. Tippu Tip and his men turned back for Nyangwe.

The throbbing of drums and cries of '*Niama! Niama!* followed the explorers on to the Congo. As the river broadened out, Stanley was in hopes that hostility would lessen, but he was disappointed. On 3 January 1877 he fought a three-hour battle with a people Stanley calls the Mwana Ntaba. Next day came another river battle when a close-order barrage from the *wangwana* dispersed a fleet of canoes with a crocodilian aspect. From 5 January onwards Stanley had to fight a daily battle even as he portaged his craft around the seven cataracts of Stanley Falls. Mwana Ntaba, Baswa, Kumu, Asama, Wenya: the list of hostile tribes seemed endless. It was 28 January before Stanley's party cleared the seventh cataract of the falls, having fought all the way. Already Stanley could count twenty-four separate battles. But the worst conflict was still ahead of him.

On 1 February 1877, at the confluence of the Congo and the Aruwimi, the powerful Soko tribe barred the way; fifty-four huge canoes lay ready in battle formation, in two 'horns', half converging on the travellers from the Congo's right bank, half from the Aruwimi. With a resourcefulness that a Themistocles or an Agrippa would have admired, Stanley drew up his boats in a defensive formation in the narrows between the Aruwimi and an island, so that he could not be surrounded. The Soko canoes, containing perhaps 2000 warriors, then bore down on them:

> Down the natives came, fast and furious, but in magnificent style ... their canoes were enormous things, one especially, a monster, of eighty paddlers, forty on a side, with paddles eight feet long, spear-headed and really pointed with iron blades for close quarters, I presume. The top of each paddle shaft was adorned with an ivory ball. The chiefs pranced up and down a planking that ran from stern to stern. On a platform near the bow were choice fellows swaying their long spears at the ready. In the stern of this great war canoe stood eight steersmen, guiding her towards us.

But the Soko were funnelled into the narrows where, at close range, the Snider fire from the *wangwana* was devastating. Every single shot found its billet. The women and camp followers in Stanley's party held up huge shields in front of the *wangwana* against which Soko spears and arrows crashed impotently. For ten minutes the carnage raged unceasingly. Then the Soko broke and fled, the cream of their warriors already reddening the Aruwimi with their blood. Stanley pursued the Soko, carried the fight to the shore, sacked their village then put it to the torch. That was the twenty-eighth combat.

Even more testing of the calibre of the *wangwana* was the great battle on 13 February, the thirty-first, against the Bangala, for here for the first time Stanley and his men confronted an enemy who possessed firearms. The Bangala, occupying a massive settlement along the right bank of the Congo, were armed with blunderbusses, loaded with jagged pieces of iron and copper ore. As soon as they sighted the expedition, the Bangala sent out sixty-three canoes against it, and thereafter fought in relays, with each village in the riverine 'conurbation' sending out its force in turn. The battle lasted from noon to just before sunset, all the way along the settlement, in which time the flotilla covered just 10 miles. Stanley knew that he was in serious danger of being outgunned. His ammunition was low and he had counted 315 enemy muskets of the 'Brown Bess' type. Yet the Bangala were so wary of the deadly fire from the Sniders that they kept their distance. This was their great mistake. If they had closed the range to less than 100 yds their numbers and weapons would soon have told.

The triumphant six-hour battle against the Bangala proved to be Stanley's penultimate during his epic navigation of the Congo. A month's freedom from combat made him careless, for he was caught in an ambush by the Bolobo people on 9 March between the confluence of the Nkutu and Stanley Pool. In a grim hour-long fight he lost fourteen men wounded before gaining the upper hand. Fortunately, the peoples of the lower Congo favoured trade above warfare, so that Stanley's struggles for the rest of this journey were with Nature and the elements.

Why was hostility to Stanley so pronounced on the Congo in 1876–7? Failure to communicate intentions and mistaken identity must take most of the blame. On the Lualaba/Congo, Stanley considered himself to be 'in the public domain' so made little attempt to pay *hongo* or offer *doti*. He was also involved in a race against the clock in terms of his dwindling resources and ammunition. He was travelling too fast to be able to stop and explain his mission to every tribe he came across, especially as this would remove the element of surprise if it came to fighting and thus use up even more of the precious ammunition. Significantly, when Stanley proceeded in a leisurely way up the Congo in the opposite direction in 1883, while founding the Congo State for Leopold, and was able to trade and explain his intentions, he encountered little hostility – though, admittedly, the memory of his ferocious descent six years earlier had something to do with that. Stanley himself bore no grudges against the Congo tribes, as he was able to see their point of view:

> The natives had never heard of white men; they had never seen strangers boldly penetrating their region, neither could they possibly understand what advantage white or black men could gain by attempting an acquaintance. It is the custom of no tribe to penetrate below or above the district of any other tribe. Trade has hitherto been conducted from hand to hand, tribe to tribe, country to country.

Moreover, although the extent of cannibalism on the Congo in this era has been exaggerated, it did exist. Faced with the constant cries of *Niama! Niama!* Stanley was prudent to take no chances, to shoot first and ask questions later.

There were additional reasons for the hostility, as confirmed in the respective oral traditions. On the Lualaba as far as Vinya-Nyara, the expedition was mistaken for slavers, hardly surprisingly since Stanley was hand-in-glove with Tippu Tip. The Soko were warned by the drums, which heralded the coming of the white man all the way down the river, that a powerful tribe was on its way, led by a man with a face as pale as the moon. There was no record in Soko tradition of any tribe on the move with so many canoes, except for war. For this reason they fought at the Aruwimi.

The Bangala later explained their aggression by pointing out that they had never seen a white man before 1877, thought that such beings must be ghosts or demons, since the only figure known to have a white face was the Ibanza or Great Spirit, who never visited the Congo. That was why they fought. But the Belgian Coquilhat, who knew the Bangala well in the 1880s, thought the explanation facile because the tribe was inherently belligerent. The missionary Holman Bentley concurred: 'Anyone who knows the people can have but one opinion; being there, he [Stanley] had either to fight in self-defence, or walk quietly to their cooking pots and submit to dissection and the processes of digestion.'

The Bolobo had an even more ingenious explanation for their bellicosity. They explained that since the tribes of the upper Congo had opposed Stanley, their own credibility required that they do likewise. Otherwise the Congo legends would record that while others faced the white man's bullets, the Bolobo hid in the grass like women. 'We should be ashamed to travel or to trade, so of course we went.'

More generally, the African operated in a milieu where extreme suspicion of strangers was merely common sense. As one observer remarked:

> As for the hostility of the natives, it has to be remembered that these unfortunate people have been accustomed to find ruthless enemies in every armed company moving through their territories. It is not given to them to differentiate between one party and another: for all they could tell to the contrary, Mr Stanley might have been another and worse sort of man-hunter. That they are cannibals does not militate against their character.

In their attitudes to violence and the justifiability of force against the indigenous populations of Africa, the explorers ran a gamut from almost complete pacifism to a virtually conditioned reflex of use of firepower. The two extremes were represented, respectively, by Livingstone and Thomson and Baker and Peters. As a true Christian, Livingstone believed in moral influence and peaceful measures. 'Depend upon it,' he noted, 'a kind word or deed is never lost.' Such an attitude was of a piece with the whole man. Stanley, who had serious doubts about the Livingstone method, recorded:

In him religion exhibits its loveliest features; it governs his conduct not only towards his servants, but towards the natives, the bigoted Mohammedans, all who come in contact with him. Without it, Livingstone, with his ardent temperament, his enthusiasm, his high spirits and courage, must have become uncompanionable and a hard master. Religion has tamed him, and made him a Christian gentleman: the crude and wilful have been refined and subdued; religion has made him the most companionable of men and indulgent of masters – a man whose society is pleasurable.

There was only one context in which Livingstone thought the use of force justifiable: if white women were in danger of rape – even though there is no recorded case of rape of a white woman by blacks in the pre-colonial period.

Joseph Thomson's disposition to pacifism was prudential rather than temperamental. He did not command large enough expeditions to make the use of force a viable option, and he anyway thought violence a sign of inexperience; he pointed out that even a minor chief could raise the surrounding countryside against an expedition and that a reputation for violence spread like a forest fire and meant that the explorer was everywhere received with distrust and hostility. But Thomson's pacifism was relative only. When he found the Taita tribe taking advantage of a weak and mild-mannered CMS missionary, he dealt out a sound thrashing to a culprit to rectify matters. And he *did* believe in force as the ultimate resort. Thomson's admirer Harry Johnston summed his position up neatly: 'I am of the opinion of Mr Thomson that it is preferable to suffer many indignities sooner than to be the first to shed blood. I also agree with him that it is insanity to travel about Africa unarmed. Never anywhere was that saying truer: *si vis pacem, para bellum.*'

Johnston also regretted that, through accident, misunderstanding or sheer blunder on the part of an explorer, he often found himself caught up in violence. It was a tragedy that African exploration should ever result in the spilling of blood. On the Kilimanjaro expedition he allowed himself to be manipulated by chief Mandara into hostilities with the Kiboso, Kirua and Maranu tribes. The resulting bloodshed found Johnston at his most reflective:

It was curious to look from the bloody field of battle to the great dazzling snowy dome which rose above us to the north, immaculate, pure and freezing in its isolation, and then think that it, after all, was the cause of all this trouble. If Kilimanjaro had not drawn me hither on this quest, the people of Mosi and Kiboso would not have come to blows on my behalf, and these poor mutilated corpses might still have been live men in the prime of life, eating, drinking, laughing with their wives and children. Must it be that I should walk through blood to reach the snow?

Livingstone, Thomson and Johnston may be regarded as typical 'doves' of African exploration. No such scruples obtained with the 'hawks'. Baker believed in civilising Africa through a compulsory trading system – a *corvée* (he actually used forced labour when he was governor of Equatoria) to extirpate African 'idleness' – and tough military despotism. Loathing the very idea that a black man should be considered the equal of a white, Baker advocated war, military occupation and imperialism. His actions in Bunyoro in 1872 proved a match for his words, to the point where the Scottish chief engineer on the expedition later wrote to *The Times* to denounce the excessive use of force he had witnessed. Chaillé-Long, who followed in Baker's footsteps to Bunyoro, proved a worthy disciple, and recorded, after his riflemen had demolished Kabbarega's fleet of war canoes: 'The shells of my Reilly burst among them, tore great holes in their boats, that sunk, having nothing to stop the leaks, or bursting in their naked bodies, carried consternation and terror, where only a moment before a hellish desire for massacre animated them in their wild fiendish glee.'

Hawkish attitudes were in the ascendant during the final decade of African exploration, in the 1890s, when colonial rule was already in full swing. Lugard expressed himself a believer in 'force first, conciliation afterwards'. The egregious Carl Peters could always be guaranteed to go one better. Speaking of the Masai, he declared: 'It is quite a mistaken motto of travellers that in Africa one must learn patience . . . I have found, after all, that the one thing that would make an impression on these wild sons of the steppe was a bullet from the repeater or the double-barrelled rifle.'

Alongside Baker, Chaille-Long, Lugard or Peters, Stanley, who enjoyed the worst press in Victorian Britain for violent frontier solutions, appears a model of restraint and tolerance. There was *some* humbug in the animadversions on Stanley by Burton, Cameron, Thomson and other critics. The plain fact was that they lacked the resources to enforce their will or fight their way out of tricky situations and so lacked the range of options open to Stanley, with his much more lavishly financed caravans. Also, Stanley has, by an unfair association of ideas, been tarnished by the atrocities that occurred later in the Congo Free State he had founded. For twenty years after 1885 the scum of Europe by chance found itself in a position of power as absolute as that of the Jesuits in pre-1767 Paraguay. Where the Jesuits spread peace, industry and equality, Leopold's bloody ruffians dispensed floggings, executions, mutilations, torture, crucifixion and infanticide. It is Stanley's misfortune that we remember Leopold's Congo as the 'heart of darkness' and thus co-opt him by association into that bloody maelstrom. The true men of blood in nineteenth-century

Africa, meanwhile – Baker, Peters and others – have been conveniently forgotten.

13

Animals Dangerous to Man

An observer of the African scene comparing conditions there in 1900 with those obtaining fifty years earlier would have noticed one thing above all. Whereas the African plains and grasslands teemed and pullulated with game in 1850, half a century later there were vast areas of the Dark Continent where most distinctive species had been wiped out. By revealing a land, if not flowing with milk and honey, then certainly a paradise for Nimrods, the explorers sent wildlife in Africa into a downward spiral from which it has never recovered. But not before the beasts had taken a toll of their oppressors. Speke merely dreamt of revenge by predators and carnivores; some explorers were to experience the danger in their waking states.

The explorers discovered and named new species, opened up virgin territory for hunters and naturalists to follow, and generally exposed to the world the amazing variety and profusion of African fauna. Destruction followed swiftly. The first distinctive animal to go down before European guns was the quagga, a sub-species of zebra, of a bay colour with stripes on head, neck and shoulders, which became extinct about 1870. Count Teleki and his companion von Höhnel differentiated for their readers the four species of zebra that remained: Burchell's zebra, about the size of a horse but with no stripes on the legs; Chapman's zebra, the same size but striped all over to the hoofs; Hartman's or the mountain zebra, as big as an ass but striped all over, and Grévy's zebra, found mainly in north-east Africa, with a head rather like that of a donkey but with its stripes both bigger and closer together than the other species.

The missionary-explorer George Grenfell carried out the same careful study on the leopard, the continent's ubiquitous carnivore. He distinguished four varieties. First there was the common leopard with small rosettes, found all the way from Algeria to the Cape. Then there was the forest leopard of West Africa, Liberia and the north-western Congo; this resembled the leopards of India and Ceylon and had shorter legs and larger rosettes than its more common cousin. In addition, in the north-eastern Congo, on the Aruwimi, in the Ituri rainforests and around Ruwenzori – the exact area opened up by Stanley on the Emin Pasha expedition – there was a leopard with markings very like a jaguar. Finally, in Somaliland and the Horn of Africa there was a fourth distinctive type of *felis pardus* or *felis panthera*, closely related to the Persian strain and with large rosettes like the ounce; this too was already close to extinction by the end of the nineteenth century.

The mighty hunter Selous was the first to make a clear distinction between the white rhino *(rhinoceros simus)*, a square-mouthed grass-eating species that grazed on the open plain, and the black rhino *(rhinoceros bicornis)*, a smaller prehensile-lipped pachyderm which fed exclusively on bushes and scrub. But the most talented naturalist of all the explorers was Harry Johnston. Apart from his discovery of the rare okapi in the dense Congo forests in 1901, he pioneered the taxonomy of hyenas, differentiating the striped hyena that lived in hill country from its much more dangerous spotted cousin that prowled on the plains.

Johnston also drew European attention to the differential game wealth of the western and eastern portions of the continent. Wildlife was far more plentiful in the east, especially in the areas which are today the nation-states of Kenya, Tanzania and Uganda. In sixteen months in West Africa he saw wild monkeys only six times, whereas in East Africa he saw them daily. On the Kenyan plains near Lake Jipé Johnston saw more game than in any other part of Africa: thousands and thousands of zebra, giraffe, hartebeest, eland, sable antelope, impala, ostrich and rhino. The Congo presented a mixed and somewhat confusing picture. General scarcities coexisted with amazing local profusions. Snakes were in general very rare along the Congo, except for a concentrated pocket around Boma, 80 miles from the sea. Hippos were not seen much on the lower river but became more numerous the higher one ascended. In the 1880s elephants were still common on the upper Congo. Leopards were found everywhere but the lion, entirely absent between Sierra Leone and the Congo, began to appear after Stanley Pool and at the time of Johnston's Congo trip in 1883 was found in some numbers at Bolobo, together with leopard, striped hyena, civet and jackal. The rhinoceros was unheard of throughout the length and breadth of the Congo proper. But on the Congo tributaries Fred Puleston found plenty of rhino but no elephants, lions or leopards. By contrast Grenfell in 1886–7 found the Kwango rich in game: elephants, hippopotami, buffalo, antelope and red-riverhogs. All travellers, however, agreed that buffaloes were common. Stanley had two notable encounters with these beasts on the lower Congo. Once, between

Vivi and Isangila, he fired at one and missed; fortunately for him, the buffalo did not follow its normal pattern of charging when fired on, but turned round and trotted off. On a subsequent encounter with a buffalo, Stanley's most trusted servant was gored to death.

East Africa was the real cornucopia for big game. The buffalo, rarely found west of the Niger, was present here in teeming herds, The lion, giraffe, rhino, zebra and ostrich preferred the sparsely wooded savannah of East and South Africa; elephants, leopards and apes, the rainforests and densely wooded regions. The great African species still clung on in the great plains of East Africa even after the introduction of modern firearms had thinned their ranks almost to extinction elsewhere. The travellers Capello and Ivens reported that in Quioco (Portuguese West Africa) in 1878 buffalo, elephant and rhino were all but shot out. But A.B. Lloyd confirmed in 1894 that rhino, ostrich, buffalo and antelope were still on the plains of Ugogo in large numbers.

At this stage, as in the case of the elephants, it was only the more intelligent and thoughtful explorers and travellers who had qualms about 'sport'. Livingstone particularly condemned hunters who 'bagged' large numbers of animals, then left their bodies to be preyed on by vultures and hyenas: 'I take it to be evident that such sportsmen are pretty far gone in the hunting form of insanity.' The traveller Gibbons, on the other hand, liked killing animals for sport but 'I confess on occasions when I have been compelled to shoot animals with no other object than to feed my gluttonous carriers, to have fairly hated the sound of my own rifle.'

The explorers' accounts of their African travels were full of their encounters with and observations of the continent's fauna; this, after all, was one of the subjects that lent colour to their books and secured them a wide readership. Sometimes it is the mundane detail that sticks, as when Montagu Kerr told his readers that giraffe meat looked like the flesh of ailing salmon, as it had much the same pinky-red colour, with streaks that divided it into flakes just like the fish. Sometimes it was the wearisome grind of African travel that was uppermost: Baker's tale of how all his stores were eaten by rats; Jackson's account of a plague of millions of rats in the Elgon Andorobo country of East Africa. Occasionally, as with Harry Johnston, the traveller's tales contained acute observation on the minutiae of animal behaviour. Baker, whose usual interest in animals was restricted to slaughtering them, showed unwonted patience in compiling a detailed breakdown of the methods of birds of prey. He noticed that vultures worked entirely by sight and were unable to detect a concealed carcass or one in long grass even when very close to it. He also observed that birds of prey came to a kill in an invariable order. First came the black and white carrion crow, guided by its extraordinary sense of smell. Then came the common buzzard which, like the vulture, operated entirely by sight. Next the red-faced vulture arrived, to be closely followed by its larger cousin, the bare-throated vulture. Last of all came the marabou stork. All travellers remarked that the veldt and the high plains were always free of rotting flesh, no matter how great the execution of the hunters' guns. Contrary to legend, lions were quite happy to feed off carrion. After them came the hyenas and jackals, and then the birds of prey as noted by Baker. Any last remnants were then picked clean by ants.

Yet naturally the Victorian reader's attention fastened most of all on the collision between explorer and dangerous animal. Crocodiles apart, Johnston estimated that the chance of a fatal encounter in Africa between explorer and a dangerous species – snake, elephant, leopard, buffalo –was about 1 in 10,000 *in normal circumstances*. But that was only if the explorers left such dangerous animals alone and were not inveigled into hunting them for food, under tribal pressures or, like Baker and Speke, for psychological reasons of their own. This was asking too much. While Burton, Livingstone and Stanley despised big-game hunting, even some of the least neurotic explorers, like du Chaillu, blazed away at anything that moved. Yet even du Chaillu had the grace to admit that the native hunter killed by a 'nightmarish' gorilla had attacked the beast first.

So it was that many animals that never attack man unprovoked were sucked into the maelstrom of man versus animal. The most dramatic death in this category was that of Captain Deane on the Congo. After having narrowly escaped death during a treacherous attack by the Monongeri on the Belgian station at Stanley Falls, Deane later succumbed to the tusks of a male elephant he had tracked through the forest. Even antelopes, when provoked by hunters, could be dangerous. Two riders once recklessly rode into a herd of eland for 'sport' only to have their horses badly gored by the eland bulls. And perhaps the most bizarre death from an animal not normally considered perilous for humans was when the wife of the missionary François Coillard was attacked by a vulture. This giant bird was kept in the Limpopo village, where the Coillards preached the gospel because it was an efficient snake-killer. Apparently excited either by the colour of her dress or her umbrella, it attacked and savaged her. Some of the locals ran up and beat it off but it had no sooner been repelled than it returned to the attack with even greater vigour than before. Mme Coillard had not enjoyed good health before this and the shock seemed to affect her very badly. She died a few days later of the wounds sustained. The irony that the attack happened on a Sabbath did not in the least shake the Coillards' simple faith.

When we come to animals quite capable of attacking though

unprovoked, we have to be careful in our assessment of the likely risks. Johnston's figures seem widely at variance with impressionistic evidence from other sources. Fred Puleston suggested one reason for the skewed statistics Johnston offered:

> If a man is killed by a leopard, lion, boa constrictor, hippo or crocodile, the report is always the same, 'fever'. On more than one occasion a mother has requested me to send home flowers from her boy's grave. I would always send some, with the assurance that they were plucked from the grave of her son. A very high-born lady in France has some flowers carefully pressed and sacredly hoarded, under the fond delusion they were gathered from her boy's grave, when the only grave her boy had was a leopard's stomach.

There are many authenticated attacks on humans by the inaptly named 'king of beasts'. A pride of man-eaters attacked an Ovambo party in 1858 led by the traveller T. Green. A.B. Lloyd reported that the people of Toro were regularly attacked by lions. Usually lions became man-hunters when they were too old to hunt normally, when excessively hungry or when they swam by chance into man's ken. Charles John Andersson, greatest of the explorers of South Africa proper, mentions several such cases in Cape Colony. On one occasion a lion wandered into a church and had to be despatched. On another, one of the big cats jumped through the window of a hotel kitchen and made off with a side of beef. Andersson spent most of his journeys in contests with lions, though these were entirely of his seeking. Once again we confront the fundamental proposition that dangerous animals were usually provoked into fulfilling their potential.

Lions are lazy, tapeworm-infested, somnolent animals (up to ten of each twenty-four hours are spent in sleep) who hunt in groups, for the most part. Their famous rugose propensities are largely a myth. Montagu Kerr reported that lions never roared unless at bay or wishing to strike terror into the game they were pursuing. When prowling at night or retiring to its lair in the morning, the lion kept up a sound somewhere between a pig's grunt and a dog's growl, except that it was commonly agreed to be louder than fifty of the latter in chorus. A lion could be heard distinctly when it was several miles away, so that it was often hard to tell whether the beast was close at hand or far away.

South and East Africa were the best areas for Africa's largest carnivorous mammal. They were found but rarely on the Congo. In 1883 Stanley had a rare sighting when proceeding upriver to Stanley Falls with his flotilla. Seeing a lion acting in an agitated manner on the shore, he landed a party, to find that the lion had just killed a large buffalo but had been disturbed by the humans before he could eat or carry off his prey.

Lions were also more dangerous in regions where they were much hunted and thus used to the sounds and effects of firearms. In this way the impact of the explorers on the indigenous peoples could sometimes be to heighten the risk to them from wild animals, whose familiarity with gunfire had bred contempt. On the other hand, often the explorers performed valuable service to a local community by tracking down and killing some especially persistent predator.

Andersson apart, the explorer who had most dealings with the king of beasts was Thomson. On his first journey he was in his tent, pitched apart from his men, when he heard a lion sniffing around outside. His rifle was unloaded and he had mislaid his revolver. Thomson lay awake all night tense and anxious while the lion prowled around outside, uncertain whether or not to enter. A few hours later the same beast carried off one of Thomson's men. On his second journey, through Masailand, a pride of lions made a sustained attack on Thomson's caravan. They killed several donkeys, put the porters to flight and generally caused chaos. Many of the donkeys who survived and fled through the bush were mistaken for lions by the panic-stricken porters and shot down. As Thomson related grimly: 'The shouts and cries of men, mingled with the roaring of lions, the braying of donkeys, and an almost continuous fusillade from firearms, furnished all the elements of a night of horror.'

But all the most hair-raising encounters with lions came about because Europeans were trying to kill the big cats, whether for 'sport' or as a favour to a chief. A traveller named Kriger shot a lion and was then attacked and badly mauled by the lioness while examining the prostrate body of his quarry. His left arm was bitten through in several places. He struggled with her for several minutes, forcing his arm between her open jaws, thereby preventing her from seizing his shoulder or throat. His life was saved by a fluke. He suddenly fell backwards over a steep bank concealed by undergrowth. The lioness was so disconcerted by the sudden disappearance of her prey that, after casting a bewildered look around, she turned and fled.

The most famous of all lion stories concerns Livingstone. At Mabotsa in South Africa in 1843 Livingstone set out with a party to try to help rid the village of a particularly persistent marauder. They found a pride of lions on a small hill and tried to surround them. One lion was shot at, but the shot missed and the beast bounded out of the circle. The hunters then reformed the circle. They trapped two lions in their net but through lack of courage they allowed these lions too to break out. Returning disconsolately to the village they saw a solitary lion sitting on a rock and got off a shot from 50 yds. The cry went up that the big cat was hit. Livingstone describes the sequel.

I saw the lion's tail erected in anger behind the bush, and, turning to the people, said, 'Stop a little till I load again.' When in the act of ramming down the bullets I heard a shout. Starting, and looking half round, I saw the lion just in the act of springing upon me. I was upon a little height; he caught my shoulder as he sprang, and we both came to the ground below together. Growling horribly close to my ear, he shook me as a terrier dog does a rat. The shock produced a stupor similar to that which seems to be felt by a mouse after the first shake of the cat. It caused a sort of dreaminess, in which there was no sense of pain nor feeling of terror, though quite conscious of all that was happening. It was like what patients partially under the influence of chloroform described, who see all the operation, but feel not the knife. This singular condition was not the result of any mental process. The shake annihilated fear, and allowed no sense of horror in looking round at the beast. This peculiar state is probably produced in all animals killed by carnivora; and, if so, is a merciful provision by our benevolent Creator for lessening the pain of death. Turning round to relieve myself of the weight, as he had one paw on the back of my head, I saw his eyes directed to Mebalwe, who was trying to shoot him at a distance of ten or fifteen yards. His gun, a flint one, missed fire in both barrels. The lion immediately left me, and, attacking Mebalwe, bit his thigh. Another man, whose life I had saved after he had been tossed by a buffalo, attempted to spear the lion while he was biting Mebalwe and caught this man by the shoulder, but at that moment the bullets he had received took effect, and he fell down dead. The whole was the work of a few moments, and must have been his paroxysms of dying rage. In order to take out the charms from him, the Bakatla on the following day made a huge bonfire over the carcase, which they declared to be that of the largest lion they had ever seen. Besides crunching the bone into splinters, he left eleven teeth wounds on the upper part of my arm.

Selous was scathing about Livingstone's claims for God's beneficence. He knew several people who had been mauled by lions, and all declared the experience very painful indeed. Selous remarked sardonically: 'Since then several Kaffirs who have been bitten have told me the same thing, so that I can but conclude that this special mercy is one which Providence does not extend beyond ministers of the Gospel.'

Selous and Livingstone differed also on the potential threat to humans from lions. Livingstone claimed that unmolested lions would never attack man in daytime, but he added a rider, *provided* they are not hungry. He told the story of a man stalking a rhino who just by chance glanced over his shoulder and found a lion stalking *him*: from the emaciated appearance of the animal, it appeared to be starving. But Selous thought the nineteenth-century fashion for debunking the 'king of beasts' had gone too far; he was inclined to rate the risk from lions to the hunter above that from the elephant and the rhino. And if a lion got in among an explorer's pack animals, that was final. An intrepid donkey could fight off a leopard or a hyena but stood no chance against a powerful 600-lb male lion.

Apart from Livingstone, the explorer who came closest to death in the jaws of a lion was Andersson. A charging lion was within a hand's breadth of him when it suddenly fell dead after receiving a second musket ball. But Andersson was guilty of hubris. He was endeavouring to help a tribe in south-west Africa so deficient in hunting skills that they specialised in trying to deprive lions of their kill, with zebras an especial target.

The sole recorded case of an explorer actually being killed by a lion was noted by Baker on his first expedition. His German companion Florian was mauled to death but, again, he was hunting the beast when taken. Dangerous as the lion was, he troubled explorers far less than his smaller cousin, the leopard. All the big cats were liable to become man-eaters when humans shot out the game on which they preyed naturally, but the leopard needed no particular coaxing to sample human flesh. Emin Pasha reported that in Mangbetu he had never known of an attack on man by lions, but those by leopards were commonplace. Junker reported that leopards abounded in Zande country but lions were rare. In fact a kind of reverse symbiosis obtained between the two big cats, to the point where they even seemed to have different 'spheres of influence'. Where lions were numerous leopards were rarely seen, for the simple reason that lions attacked and killed them on sight as competing predators. But the hostility of the lion to its lesser cousin was merely the most dramatic instance of a universal hostility, particularly noted by Junker, of the entire animal kingdom, and especially birds, towards the leopard.

In the consistency of its unprovoked menace the leopard ranked second only to the crocodile as a thorn in the explorers' side. Virtually every African traveller's reminiscences contained at least one story of an encounter. Andersson in his *Notes of Travels in South Africa* filled thirty pages with his own experiences with Africa's ubiquitous big cat. Another early traveller in South Africa, James Chapman, spoke of a persistent pattern of attacks by leopards on female villagers. From Swann in the Congo to Stanley on the Malagarazi in Tanzania the tales came in of the audacity of the rosetted menace, which specialised in killing donkeys as they plodded through long grass or came to drink at waterholes.

Explorers most often confronted leopards because of the inroads made by the beasts on their herds and flocks or those of friendly chiefs. The traveller William Fitzgerald was entreated to rid the village of Witu in East Africa of these feline pests after the villagers had lost sixty hens in one night. Leopards yielded to no other animal in audacity. Capable of downing a giraffe, a leopard would often leap over high palisades to kill a sheep and goats, then perform the amazing feat of leaping back out while carrying prey as heavy as itself. They were especially fond of goats and dogs. Montagu Kerr reported that leopards demolished an entire flock of goats in Angoniland in one night. Each of the goats was killed so deftly by long fangs piercing each side of the throat that not a drop of blood could be seen on the carcasses nor the slightest sign of mangling. But the domesticated dog was the leopard's *bonne bouche*. Leopards were so fond of dogs that they were known to have jumped through windows into houses and then carried off household pets before the owner's astonished gaze.

The barefaced effrontery of the leopard often stunned the explorers. Junker once entered his bedroom at Kassala to find one of the big cats there waiting for him. Teleki shot a leopard right outside his tent in the very heart of his camp. In South Africa in 1876 a leopard entered the house of a Boer named Pit Jacobs. It was just about to carry off a child when it was surprised by Jacobs and his men. In the confusion the big cat sprang out through the door. A leopard calmly seized one of Puleston's bearers at Boma out of a moving line. Having just fed, the animal did not drag him away into the bush but proceeded to play cat and mouse with him in full view of his comrades. This was being just too audacious. Puleston came on the scene and shot the big cat dead; the young man who had played mouse survived. But perhaps the most astounding story is one told by Lloyd. A leopard walked into the chief's kraal at Toro in Uganda and padded about until it came to an unprotected house where some fifty men and boys were sleeping. It walked in deliberately, selected a young lad who was sleeping between two older men, strangled him noiselessly, then carried him off without waking the men. On its way out the leopard stepped over several sleeping men without disturbing them. All in all, there is no reason to dissent from the judgement of Samuel Baker, one of whose favourite servants was killed by a leopard at the waterside, that this animal was far more dangerous than the lion.

But some tribes, especially in South-West Africa, were more frightened of hyenas than of either of Africa's big cats. In every village he visited, Chapman heard tales of women and children being carried away and devoured. Andersson, travelling in the same areas, confirmed this and reported that in the Lake Ngami region hyenas were considered such a pest that the locals used against them 'spring-gun' traps similar to those employed against poachers in eighteenth-century England. The hyena was an unpredictable animal: when angry it would attack a large buffalo; when in cowardly mood it could be held at bay all night by a courageous donkey. But Harry Johnston confirmed that it was a deadly menace. As well as taking sheep and calves from herds, it would carry off children and sick or wounded men. Tristram Pruen, a traveller, went so far as to state that most of the injuries inflicted by animals on humans in Africa were sustained from hyena bites. Hyenas would attack a sleeping man outside the perimeter of the camp fire and tear off a mouthful of flesh. People had lost elbow bones, ears and parts of cheeks in such attacks. On one occasion a boy, lying ill from smallpox, had his ankle crushed by a bite from a hyena's powerful jaws.

The lion's traditional enemy was the buffalo, and it was a moot point among explorers which of the two was more dangerous to humans. Livingstone thought the buffalo the more formidable of the two. He found the corpses of two lions killed by buffaloes and claimed that this was the inevitable outcome of single combat, that buffaloes were only ever defeated by a plurality of lions. This was an exaggeration, as Stanley's experience on the upper Congo, among others, showed, but it was true that these two species were very evenly matched as combatants. The hunter Frank Vardon, Livingstone's friend, once intervened during a battle between two lions and a buffalo by 'bagging' all three of them at point-blank range; the enraged combatants did not even notice him approach. An even more bizarre instance of the 'war of all against all' was noted by Verney Cameron. One day early in 1874 he noticed the remains of a lion, buffalo and crocodile lying together. The locals told him the following curious story. A buffalo came to drink at the river but was attacked by a lion. The two animals rolled into the water together, where the fighting mass was seized by a crocodile. The two struggling mammals in turn used their combined weight to drag the crocodile out of the water and twenty yards inland. There the trio perished in an inextricable entanglement of mutual slaughter.

Buffaloes on their own often made dramatic entries into the explorers' world. Caravans were frequently attacked without provocation. Capello and Ivens had a narrow escape from such an assault in Quioco in 1878. And in 1874 a buffalo charged Verney Cameron's caravan and put it to flight. Puleston considered the buffalo 'a nasty devil', and it is certainly true that its horns accounted for a significant number of human fatalities. E.J. Glave's white companion at Lukolela station, Kemble Keys, was killed by a buffalo he had wounded; Glave himself was nearly killed in similar circumstances. The Prussian Baron Harnier was also gored to death, thus ending a singularly ill-starred venture in which both his European companions had previously succumbed to marsh fever. Opinions differed as to the reasons for the bufallo's aggressive behaviour. Junker thought that the buffalo was basically bad-tempered, but that it was being fired on by hunters that brought out its most lethal instincts. Glave thought the human thesis was supererogatory: he related a grim fight to the death on the Congo between an irate buffalo and an enraged hippo. Selous's theory for the many unprovoked charges on caravans by buffaloes was that such specimens had previously been wounded in fights with lions.

The explorer who most clearly felt the sharp end (literally!) of the buffalo was Joseph Thomson. During his journey through Masailand a buffalo attacked his column and gored one of his donkeys to death. It took a long time before Thomson's bullets finished him off. Thomson's explanation for the bull's 'egregious' aggression was etymologically sound. He said that it was a rogue male driven from the herd and its temper had soured in consequence.

But that incident was for Thomson a minor taste of what was to come. On the last day of 1883 he had a near-fatal encounter. His ordeal started when he went ahead of his caravan with his servant Brahim to replenish the meat supply. He shot a buffalo from 50 yds, then put another bullet into its skull. Foolishly, despite warnings from Brahim, he did not wait until the animal was finished off but went within 6 yds to give it the quietus:

The buffalo's head turned in my direction. A ferocious, blood-curdling grunt instantly apprised me of the brute's resolution to be revenged. The next moment it was on its feet. Unprepared to fire, and completely taken by surprise, I had no time for thought. Instinctively I turned my back on my infuriated enemy. As far as my recollections serve me, I had no feeling of fear while I was running away ... There was a loud crashing behind me. Then something touched me on the thigh, and I was promptly propelled skyward.

My next recollection was finding myself lying dazed and bruised, with some hazy notion that I had better take care. With this indefinite sense of something unusual I slowly and painfully raised my head, and lo! there was the brutal avenger standing three yards off, watching his victim, but apparently disdaining to hoist an inert foe ... Seeing signs of life in my hitherto inanimate body, he blew a terrible blast through his nostrils, and prepared to finish me off. Stunned and bruised as I was, I could make no fight for life. I simply dropped my head down among the grass in the vague hope that it might escape being pounded into jelly. Just at that moment a rifle-shot rang through the forest, which caused me to raise my head once more. With glad surprise I found the buffalo's tail presented to my delighted contemplation. Instinctively seizing the unexpected moment of grace, I with a terrible effort pulled myself together and staggered away a few steps. As I did so, I happened to put my hand down to my thigh, and there I felt something warm and wet; exploring further, my fingers found their way into a big hole in my thigh. As I made this discovery there was quite a volley and I saw my adversary drop dead.

Thomson had lost a considerable amount of blood. He fainted, regained consciousness, then nearly fainted again. His followers staunched the bleeding. They told him that when the bull tossed him, he went up one way, his hat another, his rifle yet another. He was bruised along the face and ribs. One horn had penetrated six inches into his thigh, grazing the bone. The wound was more a stab than a rent or rupture. As there was nothing poisonous in the horn he realised there would be no long-term effects and began reflecting on his family's gathering in Scotland for New Year's Eve, what a Hogmanay story he would be able to tell them next year! He rationalised his folly by toasting the New Year in a soup of the animal that had so nearly killed him.

> The curious thing is that I have no recollection of anything after feeling myself touched on the thigh by the buffalo's horn. I did not even feel myself fall. With regard to my unconsciousness of fear on finding myself vis-a-vis with the maddened and deadly animal, I can only imagine that I must have been in a manner mesmerised, and in the condition described by Livingstone when he found himself under a lion.

Another animal famed for its unprovoked attacks was the rhino. Such incidents were reported throughout the length and breadth of the continent: from Andersson in South Africa to Donaldson Smith in Somalia, and from Thomson in East Africa to Denham and Clapperton in the West. Livingstone's companion William Cotton Oswell had his horse gored by a rhino; the veteran elephant-hunter Hartly was seriously injured by one in Mashona country; Teleki and Von Höhnel were assailed by one on the slopes of Mt Kenya; David Jacobs, son of the Boer hunter Petrus Jacobs, had a narrow escape from goring; a certain Dr Kolb was bayoneted by a rhino's horn in Central Africa and died at once. Thomson's caravan in Masailand was assaulted in successive weeks by rhino, buffalo and lion. Donaldson Smith's party sustained three attacks by rhinos in Somaliland, in the last of which, near Lake Rudolph, one of the pachyderms gored and killed a camel. Morgan Thomas was tossed by a rhino that he accidentally awoke from sleep.

The rhino's reputation for bad-tempered aggression was legendary. It is related that the rhinoceros which Emanuel, King of Portugal, sent the Pope in 1513 flew into a paroxysm of rage at its confinement and destroyed the ship on which it was being transported. There were eyewitness accounts in Africa of fights between rhinos and elephants, in which the elephants were worsted and fled. Lions were known to avoid them. Lacking any other enemy, rhinos often fought among themselves. Once again, opinion was divided on the likely cause of the animal's behaviour. Denham and Clapperton thought there was something about mounted men that particularly enraged the beast. Selous thought attacks on humans only occurred by mistake or if the rhino was enraged by hunters; he thought it nothing like so dangerous an animal to the hunter as the lion, elephant or buffalo. Andersson disagreed, stating that it was incontrovertible that the rhino would attack in non game-hunting situations. Baker noticed that a rhino would charge objects it could smell but not see. Concealed in the long grass, it would suddenly come charging out. It was very difficult to hit when charging as the vulnerable spot, the brain, was protected by the horn. Hunters learned to aim just behind the shoulder; a bullet through the central lobes of the lung caused instantaneous death.

The explorer who had the closest encounters with the rhino was Andersson. It has to be said that he went looking for trouble. As part of his self-assigned programme for helping the tribes of South-West Africa, Andersson once shot eight rhino in five hours and boasted that he could have killed twice that number. He justified his slaughter by saying that the hapless locals would eat anything he shot, including the flesh of carnivores like leopards and hyenas.

On one occasion while pursuing a wounded rhino he was ambushed and gored; the horn ripped his right thigh from knee to hip. On another, in South-West Africa, one of Andersson's companions tried to follow a rhino's trail in an ox-waggon. After a while he stopped, made camp and started to follow the beast's trail more closely, whereupon the rhino charged him. He took refuge in the ox-waggon, but the rhino sank his horn into the bottom boards with such force as to push the waggon several paces forward, even though it was at rest in heavy sand. It was lucky that the rhino had attacked the waggon from behind, for a flank attack would certainly have overturned it. Baulked of his prey, the rhino rushed the camp fire, upset the pot and scattered the burning brands in all directions. One of the Africans hurled an assegai, but the soft iron bent like a reed against the animal's thick and almost impenetrable hide.

It often occurred that explorers in pursuit of one dangerous animal would encounter another. This happened to Count Teleki. On one occasion he had just shot an elephant, and the pachyderm was tottering in its death throes when a rhino suddenly came charging out of the bush at him. A lucky shot secured him prize specimens of Africa's two largest mammals in the same hour.

The hippopotamus was another unpredictable and bad-tempered beast and would charge river craft without warning. Since it was difficult to escape from them on a river, and to be spilled into the water meant probable death from crocodiles, it was not surprising that some travellers rated ordeal by hippo as the supreme jeopardy. Puleston said the hippo had 'no redeeming qualities': it was not a scavenger, it was destructive to native crops, and it destroyed huts and plantations in its lumbering passage through villages. Emil Holub concluded: 'Of all the larger mammalia of South Africa I am inclined to believe to an unarmed man the hippopotamus is the most dangerous.' Their aggression could be triggered by hunters who had killed their young or when females were defending their offspring, but there were also many riverine rogue males who needed no pretext for attack. Baker related the story of an Arab who tried to drive a rampaging hippo from his plantation; the hippo caught him in his huge mouth and crunched him like matchwood. A Dinka chieftain of Baker's acquaintance was also bitten in half during an unprovoked attack on his canoe. The Arab Sheikh Sofi was disembowelled after he made the mistake of harpooning a hippo without finishing it off.

The great hippo slaughterer among explorers was Speke, yet it was Baker who experienced the closest encounters with the river-horse. In 1864 during his circumnavigation of Lake Albert, his canoe was charged at the most crocodile-infested point of the lake. Just after the charge, which fortunately failed to pitch the party into the water, Baker counted eighteen large crocodile heads stippling the water all around them. What Baker feared Gibbons actually saw come to pass in the Nile. At Fajou a hippo charged a canoe with eight occupants. All were tipped into the water and all were taken by crocodiles before they could reach the bank. In 1870 Baker had two further nasty brushes with the hippo. In March one of the leviathans charged Baker's paddle-steamer and smashed holes both in the paddle and the iron-plated bottom; the steamer was in imminent danger of sinking before his men managed to plug the leaks.

Later that year Baker and party came under attack once more. This time Baker despatched the hippo before it could do significant damage but not before pumping eight shots into the beast. When they examined the body, Baker's men found that the hippo had taken three shots in the flank and shoulder, four in the head, one of which broke his lower jaw, and one through the nose which passed downwards and snapped off one of his tusks. The animal's body was also striated with frightful scars, the result of continual conflict with other bulls.

Explorers on the Congo had frequent jousts with the river behemoth. Stanley, Ward and Glave all wrote of serious and persistent attacks. Grenfell reported repeated attacks by hippos on the steamer *Peace* during his 1886 expedition on Lake Leopold. Indeed the unparalleled aggression of both hippopotami and crocodiles on the Congo in the 1880s was attested to by all Europeans in the area; the situation changed only when the giants of the river began to appreciate the potency of European firearms.

It may be an exaggeration to say that every single book of nineteenth-century African exploration and travel featured hair-raising stories about crocodiles, but not by very much. Without question this terrifying saurian was the most feared and detested of all the animals dangerous to man. The attitude was highly rational: the human toll taken by crocodiles far exceeded that of all other predators put together. Any form of life, with the single exception of a fully-grown elephant, venturing into an African river was likely to fall foul of those terrible jaws.

The casualty list of domestic animals was bad enough. Dogs, horses, mules, goats, swine, sheep, oxen and cattle all disappeared into the ravening reptilian maw. Teleki lost oxen during a river crossing; the missionary Coillard lost all his pigs and both his beloved Newfoundland watchdogs. Selous lost three of his big hunting dogs in the Umsengaisi river to the loathsome predators.

It was a widely received opinion that crocodiles, like leopards, particularly relished canine flesh. Livingstone's experience certainly bore out this thesis: on his last expedition the dog belonging to his servant Wekotani was killed by a leopard, while his own poodle was taken by a crocodile as the doctor crossed the Chimbwe river. The most dramatic encounter involving loss of animals was Stanley's. Refusing to pay the high levels of *hongo* levied to cross the Malagarazi river by ferry in 1871 Stanley decided to get his animals across unaided. Around sunset Stanley's favourite donkey, Simba, was driven into the water with a rope attached to his neck. The donkey reached the middle of the river, where the water was about 15 ft deep, when a crocodile seized him by the throat. Stanley's *wangwana* pulled frantically on the rope, trying to aid Simba in his desperate struggles. One crocodile would not have availed against so much manpower on the other end of the rope, but, as Stanley recorded laconically in his journals: 'There must have arrived other crocodiles for the poor animal suddenly sank like lead.'

Explorers related with fascinated dread how crocodiles drowned their victims, but did not eat them straightaway as their teeth were not adapted for chewing. Instead they carried them off to a subterranean 'larder' and waited until the flesh started to rot before eating. Often crocodiles would collaborate to eviscerate a particularly unwieldy victim, such as a wildebeeste. But any infringement of 'private property' rights was dealt with severely. Puleston described a Dantean scene on the Congo when two 30 ft monsters fought to the death because one had raided the other's larder.

Yet even more fearsome than the devastation wrought on man's flocks and herds were the casualties inflicted on man himself. From Egypt to the Kalahari the stories were identical. In South Africa a trader called Robinson was taken by a crocodile when he waded into a river to recover a bird he had shot. At Ujiji A.J. Swann's servant Tom was swept into the water and devoured. On the Congo a huge saurian took a Portuguese trader from his canoe just an hour after he had dined with the missionary Bentley. On the Blue Nile a man was snatched from his canoe while crossing the river Atbara. On the same river another man thought himself safe by sitting on a camel while the animal swam across, but was swept off the hump by a single lash of a scaly tail. A crocodile came within inches of carrying off Joseph Thomson and was on the point of striking when Thomson's men fired on it and scared it off. Puleston had particular reason to loathe the fearsome reptile and never concealed his hatred: 'The essence of all that is bloody, relentless, loathsome, cruel, heartless' was one of his milder descriptions. His brother was killed by one on the Ogowé river. Later his friend who commanded the Belgian post at Lutete also met a horrible end. Lutete was attacked by Kilonga-Longa and his warriors. The white men decided to evacuate. They got out canoes and pulled a short distance away from the house while the commander and his bodyguard created a diversion to convince the hostiles that they were all still inside the post. He then started to swim the short distance to the canoes. 'Suddenly he disappeared, then, springing up in the water with his face towards us, distorted in agony, he screamed "Crocodile!" I hope I never again see such a look of intense agony on a man's face.' Then the boiling waters ceased to seethe, and the commander was gone.

The death-toll from crocodiles must have been immense, to judge from impressionistic and circumstantial evidence. On the Congo Bentley shot a crocodile which pegged out at 17 ft 6 in. and was found to have killed several humans. Capello and Ivens mention a crocodile in Luanda conservatively estimated to have killed more than 100 persons, and there is good evidence from other localities to suggest that this was by no means unusual. During a short stay with the Marutse of the Zambezi, Emil Holub heard of thirty authenticated local deaths by crocodile. Africans always opened up a crocodile after they had killed it, as it was full of valuable bracelets and anklets taken from its victims. Chapman reported an apathetic fatalism among the Africans he met; they treated news of someone's being taken by a crocodile as of no more significance than the Victorian would regard a death from pneumonia. Livingstone endorsed the judgement. In May 1863, on his second expedition, a crocodile seized a Johanna man. His comrades, one of whom was the victim's brother-in-law, did nothing whatever to rescue him. On the other hand, Glave reported that on the upper Congo the imprecation '*Owi na nlorli*' ('May a crocodile eat you') was a mortal insult, which required a duel before honour could be satisfied.

Africans rarely counterattacked for human losses but were sometimes goaded to action following grievous culling of their herds. A favourite method was to leave poisoned meat at the waterside for the reptiles to devour. Another was to construct strong cages which jutted into the water, into which animals would be led to drink. But as with the modern 'sharkproof' cages used by underwater photographers, such barricades often invited frenzied attacks from the frustrated predators. In North Africa the Arabs dealt with the threat rather more cleverly. They dug holes in the sand within a few yards of the river, the holes filled with water and there their goats and sheep could drink safely. Casati reported one notable exception to the general apathy. The small tribe of Bari on the island of Bedden in Equatoria lived exclusively on the flesh and eggs of crocodiles. They specialised in lassoing the monsters, then dragging them ashore and killing them. Otherwise, the tribes were largely reduced to asking the explorers to rid them of the gruesome riverine menace. To a man they loathed crocodiles with a deep passion and missed no opportunity of revenging themselves for the losses sustained by *homo sapiens*. Even Stanley, who usually took no interest in dangerous animals, would blaze away at the reptiles at every opportunity. The explorers' hatred was raised to fever pitch by the consideration that one was not even safe out of the water. They learned to build camps at night in such a way that the fires and fortifications were placed between themselves and the river, to prevent the possibility of their being plucked out of their sleeping quarters at night and dragged to the river, as nearly happened to the German explorer Wissmann. Donaldson Smith's Somaliland diary for 25 August 1893 recorded that a mule was attacked in the centre of his camp by a crocodile, which dragged it some distance towards the water before it was shot.

Even if a crocodile failed to drag a human under the water, the victim of an attack could be left with dreadful wounds, from which death might follow later. Junker reported that the crocodiles of Lado were particularly ferocious. He was an eyewitness when a boy had his arm bitten off at the elbow by a crocodile, so neatly that Junker could not detect the least shred of a sinew projecting from the stump. Only a few drops of blood flowed from the clean cut, and all that was needed was careful bandaging. But not all victims were so fortunate. Donaldson Smith's servant Yusuf was seized by a crocodile which was then beaten off, but Yusuf's arm had to be amputated. Harry Johnston noted the curiosity that on the Congo the monsters seemed to go in more for lopping off human limbs than taking the whole person.

The mugger crocodile of the Nile was a formidable foe that often crossed Baker's path. He noticed that there were two distinct species of saurian on the White Nile: one was dark-brown, short and thick; the other was a pale greenish yellow of immense length. Local lore said that the smaller variety was the deadlier, and Baker soon had occasion to see this for himself. In 1870 around Gondokoro he found the monsters particularly ferocious. Two local sailers were taken on successive days while Baker was there. A little later one of Baker's men was seized in water only hip deep. He gouged the monster's eyes with his fingers, thus buying time until his comrades beat it off. But his leg below the knee proved to be so mashed and splintered that it had to be amputated. A few days later another of Baker's men was seized by the arm at the elbow joint. His friends caught him by the waist, and their united efforts prevented his being dragged into the water. But the crocodile, having tasted blood, would not let go and tugged and wrenched until the arm came off completely at the elbow-joint. The brute then made off with its prize. The man was brought to camp in agony, and it was found necessary to amputate another piece slightly above the lacerated joint.

The boldness and ferocity of crocodiles often amazed observers. Gibbons mentions one that charged a six and a half ton boat. It bounced off with a shock, but the assault itself was indicative of a general determination to upset river craft.

There was no such thing as a crocodile 'no go' area. Livingstone swore up and down that the saurians were not voracious on Lake Nyasa, yet in 1876 a white man, taking the doctor at his word, found his large canoe repeatedly rammed by a huge crocodile, demonstrating once again the tenacity of the brutes and the lengths they would go to to tip boats' complements into the water.

The other hardy annual in Victorian nightmares about Africa was snakes. Many explorers were inclined to dismiss the danger from serpents as negligible. Du Chaillu claimed that by and large snakes avoided human beings and would not attack unless trodden on. Obviously this proposition was in the main true; given the numbers of ophidians in Africa – Tanzania alone has 114 varieties – the continent would be uninhabitable if all snakes attacked on sight. As Harry Johnston put it: 'It is remarkable that in all books of travel relating to Africa and the experiences of all travelled "Africans" one hears next to nothing of dangers from poisonous snakes or of deaths from that cause, though there are in the Congo at least seven examples of viperine and cobra snakes whose venom is fatal.'

As with his estimate of the general danger from wild animals, Johnston rather overstated his case. There were numerous instances of 'near misses' with the herpetological reptiles. Capello and Ivens reported a completely unprovoked attack by a 6 ft viper. Andersson witnessed a case of almost literal fulfilment of Lady Macbeth's 'Look like the innocent flower, but be the serpent under't.' A botanist stooped to pick up a rare plant and found a cobra beneath his hand. He retreated backwards very fast, but the cobra came after him and began to gain on him. The botanist then by chance fell backward over an anthill and was relieved to see the enraged cobra dashing furiously past him. Even though the African cobra does not raise its head as high as its Indian cousin when about to strike – and there is of course no African equivalent of Asia's king cobra, or hamadryad – cobras were especially dangerous because of their habit of entering human dwellings in pursuit of rats. Du Chaillu shot a 10 ft specimen in such a situation, while Junker twice had to despatch a cobra with spear thrusts; on the first of these occasions he spitted the snake to the central post of his tent with a single lance thrust.

The puff-adder was another highly venomous pest, not so dangerous as the cobra because it was sluggish and had a striking range only half its own length. The danger from the puff-adder was twofold: they were reluctant to run away or move from a traveller's path, and they were well camouflaged and thus hard to spot but easy to tread on. Their thick body made them appear especially gruesome; Baker once cut up a puff-adder and found it 5 ft 4 in. in length but fully 15 in. in girth. But the reality matched the appearance. one of A.J. Swann's servants died quickly after being bitten.

Most dangerous of all were the mambas, the green and, especially, the black, which could reach a length of 10–11 ft. Between 15 March and 30 May 1861 James Chapman achieved the dubious distinction of the 'grand slam' in dangerous snake encounters: the cobra, puff-adder and green mamba. He and other travellers noted that the green mamba would not chase people, as the fearsome black mamba was known to, but that if humans were between it and its retreat it would not turn aside. Morgan Thomas was bitten on the foot by a green mamba but survived.

It was doubtless fortunate for the explorers that the dreaded black mamba was comparatively rare. Herbert Ward claimed that a black tried to attack him in the great Congo lagoon at Stanley Pool, but that the current bore him to the shore before the serpent could strike. It was Livingstone who had the clearest sighting of the black mamba. At Kolobeng an 8 ft 3 in. specimen massacred a pack of dogs before being shot. Lashing out in all directions, the mamba scored four direct hits. The first dog to be bitten died at once, the second lasted five minutes, the third an hour, while the fourth succumbed several hours later, thus demonstrating in an almost textbook fashion the diminishing virulence of the venom.

Familiarity with serpents did not lessen among the Africans ancient, primeval fears of the very symbol of evil – appearing in this guise in so many mythologies: African, Norse, Christian. Du Chaillu told a story of the panic that could be caused by the very word.

But Cameron also remarked on the vast gulf separating his men's mental world from that of the tribes in the Gombe who actually worshipped snakes. He went to shoot a 10 ft boa that had invaded a hut, but the locals prevented him and instead turned it out of the village with long sticks, on the ground that it was a spirit. The Gombe peoples were not the only ones to go in for ophiolatry. Casati recorded that the Dinka tribe of Equatoria province kept pythons as pets; the tame monsters fed on milk and would answer the calls and signs of the housewife.

Clearly no such indulgence could be extended to poisonous snakes. In this area customs and folkways were largely devoted to finding antidotes to snakebite. Hottentots imbibed small quantities of venom weekly to provide them with immunity. In the Kalahari desert the locals treated snakebite by making an incision and inserting a different sort of poison on the principle of *similia similibus curantur*. Other remedies were ligature, caustics, excision, *eau de luce* administered every five minutes. Some tribes scarified with a knife and sucked out the venom, but they had to take care that the person sucking had no mouth sores. Sweet milk, taken internally or externally, or hartshorn were also thought to be efficacious, as were white beans applied externally, dried turtle blood and 'snake stones', thought to draw poison like a sponge. Europeans favoured an immediate internal and external application of Croft's Mixture, whose principal ingredient was ammonia. The Boers made an incision in the breast of a fowl and pressed the bitten area to the fowl; if the fowl died, another was produced, and so on until finally the birds stopped dying, showing that all the venom had been absorbed. Snakebite was always a serious matter. Denham and Clapperton noticed an Arab with a distorted foot, of no use to him except when he was on horseback. It turned out he had been bitten by a snake and, even after the infected part had been cut off his foot, he was still confined to his hut for thirteen months before recovering.

The large constrictor snakes were not such a deadly menace but still formidable enough and possibly even more terrifying to the imagination. Pythons and boas were found broadcast across the continent, and nearly every African explorer's account contains some sort of story calculated to give the Victorian reader nightmares. Du Chaillu entertained his audience to a tale of how he killed a 19-ft python which became enraged when caught in an Apingi game fence; on another occasion he shot a 16-footer that slithered into his camp. Livingstone declared that in southern Africa it was commonplace to find pythons 15–20 ft long. Lloyd encountered a 20-footer which was fully a foot in diameter. The largest authenticated specimen killed was a 30 ft female boa, the size of a child in diameter, which Chaillé-Long's men killed in September 1874 after they had found it living behind his hut. 'The huge monster writhed still with life that it seemed almost impossible to extinguish, though the head and the back were crushed in several places. I confess that every night thereafter, on retiring to my bed, I felt a strange sensation of horror, as I thought of the possibility of my being "Laocooned" ere morning.'

On the night of 12 March 1875 Chaillé-Long's nightmares nearly became reality. The American explorer, who seldom slept at night, felt restless and crept away from his bivouac to have a quiet ponder in a secluded spot on a river bank. Eventually he drifted into slumber. 'I was suddenly awakened by the consciousness of the presence of something horrible. Was it my good star, or the natural repulsion that had shocked my nerves and saved me from a Laocoon-like embrace? At my feet, its ponderous jaws wet with the fatal horrible saliva, lay a huge boa. Transfixed to the spot, I called my soldiers to me, who soon despatched him and made a savoury meal of his flesh.'

The threat from the constrictors to humans was probably not so great as these fears suggested. Nevertheless there were well authenticated instances of pythons and boas taking women and children. Even adult males in some areas slept with their legs in a 'V' shape, such was their fear of being swallowed whole as they slept.

Among most tribes the killing by an explorer of a boa or a python was very welcome, for eating a snake's brains was widely held to confer cunning in the art of war, while eating the eyes was supposed to enable one to see at night. A snake's tongue stretched out and dried was the witchdoctor's favourite amulet. Even when these specific charms had been removed, the head of a boa was still considered valuable, as it could be worn round the neck as a charm against sickness or other calamity. Du Chaillu reported that a great delicacy in West Africa was snake cooked in plantain leaves, seasoned with lemon juice and cayenne pepper. In areas where the reverse of snake worship obtained, Africans liked to prove their mastery over the lesser animals by engaging the giant snakes in single combat. Puleston witnessed such a contest. First the African warrior smeared himself all over with palm oil. Then he engaged a large boa. The snake tried to wrap itself round the man's body but could get no purchase and slipped off each time. Eventually it collapsed with exhaustion and, being of no further entertainment value, was killed.

It was amazing how often the explorers encountered serpents while engaging with some other dangerous animal or, as in the case of Denham, at risk from hostile warriors. During his ill-judged raid with Barca Gana and the Arabs on the Fulani, Denham found himself fleeing the enemy as part of the general rout. He was thrown off his horse, speared and saved from death only because his clothes were too valuable to be torn. While his plunderers quarrelled over the spoils Denham, completely naked, ran away at top speed. Pursued by two men, he was almost at the end of his strength when he saw a mountain stream at the bottom of a deep ravine. He seized the branch of a large tree which overlooked the ravine, intending to let himself down gently into the water. He put his hand on a large viper, which at once uncoiled, ready to strike. In terror Denham lost his balance and tumbled headlong into the waters below. The speed of his snake-assisted disappearance was what saved him from his pursuers.

But the most dramatic of such encounters was that related by the Revd. W. Hunter at Ngangila, thirty miles north-east of Boma, the lower Congo's 'home of pythons'. He and his men had just entered the jungle after buffalo when 'a huge snake knocked one man to the ground, breaking one arm and several ribs. It then threw itself about him and reached for another man, whom it also got into its embrace before I could get to the spot. When I arrived I had to pick a shot at its head and not harm the two men, whom it held with the grip of a vice. I shot it but once. The expansive ball used blew out one half of its brain, and its motions on the ground were a sight long to be remembered. When the snake ceased to struggle I and the natives could walk along its back as easily as you could walk on a great big log. No doubt you remember that the stomach of the snake contained not less than one peck of brass, copper and iron rings such as the natives wear on the arms and legs. The stomach was taken by one of King Nsikachi's witchdoctors, and prized by him as a wonderful charm. A snake of that size could swallow an antelope as large as a cow, horns and all.' They measured the serpent and found it fully 30 ft long.

The explorers' cup was filled to overflowing by insects. For obvious reasons the airborne varieties were the greatest pests. In the country of the Shilluk, between Khartoum and Fashoda, Schweinfurth's boat was attacked by bees. Schweinfurth himself was stung so badly that he threw himself into the river to escape the insects, but they continued to sting him even under water. He clambered back on board and sought refuge under a linen sheet in which he cocooned himself, having first crushed to death the bees that still clung to him. Outside the hum and buzz of angry bees continued to be heard. Schweinfurth declared he would rather face half a score of buffaloes or a brace of lions than go through another such attack from African bees.

On the Aruwimi cataracts near the beginning of the first of his three dreadful crossings of the green hell of Ituri in 1887–8, Stanley had an experience that led him to dub the location 'Wasp Rapids'. On 25 July 1887 his party set out to negotiate a dangerous stretch of rapids. While the boats were in the most dangerous part of a narrow boiling channel, one of the men steadied himself by grasping at a branch overhead, and accidentally disturbed a wasp's nest. The angry insects at once sallied out to punish the intruders. The sequel was terrible. The churning, seething river was as wild as the sea and required the full attention of the *wangwana*, but meanwhile the wasps were inflicting grievous bites. The men had no choice but to endure stoically the most frightful wounds. With their eyes glued to the water, they were forced to allow the insects to settle and sink their jaws into skin. Stanley and Jephson, fully clothed, fared better than their dark companions. Suddenly, some 200 yards beyond the rapids, the wasps left them as abruptly as they had descended.

Things were no better in West Africa. Du Chaillu made a close study of a riverine nest-building wasp called locally the *eloway*. Generally the wasps would choose a branch full of leaves for their clay-built nests, which would thus be hidden from view. The local peoples fled from this wasp as from no other animal or insect. The hives contained thousands, and disturbed wasps would issue in great swarms from several holes to attack the intruder. Their bites were extremely painful and they left in the wounds they inflicted an acrid poison which caused agonising pains for 2–3 days. The *eloway* were particularly hard to deal with, even for men with firearms. The clay in the nests was so impacted and hard that a bullet fired from medium range made no impression; but to approach closer was to risk weeks of agony and even death.

Locusts were one of Africa's reliable scourges, then as now. Coillard related how newly hatched locusts with wings too weak to fly – for they had only just cast their skins – were trampled into the ground in their tens of thousands. Many survived and devoured fields of maize, manioc and sorghum. When they were able to fly, the cries and gestures of men and women in the fields made them take off; the wind then carried them away. But when in the first stage – that of a wingless cricket – the insects ploughed remorselessly on through the plantations. They crossed rivers in gigantic armadas and could put out a fire by a blanket of sheer numbers, taking enormous casualties as they did so. Seeing the dead still clinging to shrubs and leaves of grass, human observers would think them alive until touch revealed the desiccated, mummified state of the insect skeletons.

Mosquitoes were a menace to the explorers, even when their disease-bearing qualities were not known. Chaillé-Long, on his way to meet Mutesa, found mosquitoes so abundant and their bites so irritating and venomous that sleep was all but impossible. He took careful note of African methods of dealing with them. They surrounded themselves continuously with a circle of fire, on which cow dung was thrown, thus forming a dense smoke which by its stifling odour kept the enemy at bay. The other favoured way was to smear one's entire body with ashes or the ordure of beasts.

Yet insects did not need wings to be a thorn in the traveller's side, sometimes almost literally so. The termite or white ant attacked possessions rather than persons, and specialised in eating wood, leather and cloth. Baker noticed three different strains of white ant. The largest lived in fallen trees; the next largest commuted between trees and buildings; the smallest was found exclusively in buildings. Termites nearly finished off Barth's leather bags and mats on the shores of Lake Chad. Du Chaillu once opened his personal chest to find that all his clothes had been eaten. Denham told a story of an Arab who lay down to sleep on a mat and carpet inside a *barracan* or tent. In the morning he woke up quite naked to find that his coverings had been eaten to the last thread. Andersson's entire bed was eaten under him as he slept, even though there had been no sign of a termite when he dropped off.

If the white ants had had no natural enemies, they would soon have munched their way from one end of the continent to the other. Providentially they were preyed on by the formidable black soldier ants, a cannibal species and one of the most fearsome living organisms in Africa. Called *bashikouay* in West Africa or *litumbo* in the East, they possessed a highly developed military organisation and marched in columns 12–15 in. wide and 100 ft long. They could build a straw bridge, two yds wide, across a river. They would eat any living thing in their path. With a bite as bad as a scorpion, they could strip a rat bare in four hours or denude a newly sown field of wheat or barley seed. African lore said that the constrictor snakes, having killed, would make a careful reconnaissance of the surrounding countryside before swallowing their prey, lest there was an army of black ants on the march; lolling helplessly distended while it digested its meal, the boa would make easy pickings for the terrible soldiers. The bite of these ants was extremely painful and the creatures themselves tenacious; if one attempted to brush them off the flesh, the head would detach and bury itself under the skin, where, if not removed, it would cause a painful sore. For this reason explorers always beat a hasty retreat from their tents if ever a column of black ants invaded.

The black ant was generally considered more formidable than the red, but the red had a greater reputation as a carnivore. So fond were they of animal flesh that if a chief slaughtered a cow when they were in the vicinity, he had to keep his slaves up all night burning fires of straw around the meat to keep the ants away. Absolutely fearless, like their black cousins they would attack anything in their path.

Duff MacDonald reported a case where a half-mile long column, with a density of thirty insects to the square inch, once killed an elephant. They achieved this by entering the beast's nostrils and causing such irritation that the elephant was maddened and committed suicide by dashing itself against a tree, leaving his tormentors free to feast on the giant carcase.

Red ants lived mainly on shrubs in the forest, while the black ant was more a creature of the plain. If a traveller happened to brush against a branch containing the ants, he soon understood why the *wangwana* called the red ant *maji moto* – hot water. Like the black ant, they did not relax their hold even when the head was severed from the body.

Livingstone made the mistake of accidentally treading on one of their nests. 'Not an instant seemed to elapse, before a simultaneous attack was made on various unprotected parts, up the trousers from below, and on my neck and breast above. The bites of these furies were like sparks of fire and there was no retreat. I jumped about for a second or two, then in desperation tore off my clothing, and rubbed and picked them off seriatim as soon as possible.' This was wise. The only way to deal with red ants was to strip off all one's clothes and stand in the smoke of a fire.

There seemed literally no end to Africa's insect pests. In the Sudan Junker narrowly escaped being bitten by a huge yellow scorpion, which had crept in among his bedclothes. Ticks were so common in Abyssinia that Baker concluded that the Egyptian plague of 'lice' (Exodus 8:16–17) was really a plague of ticks.

Apart from mosquitoes, tsetse flies, sandflies. midges, the stunted fly *(simulium damnosum)*, jiggers, huge hippo flies, black and red ants, 2-in. long cockroaches, 4-in. long locusts, mason wasps and grey wasps, huge crickets and mantises, Africa also boasted *kungu* gnats, aromatic bugs and caterpillars with poisoned hairs that produced a skin disease. Yet even so the continent's catalogue of horrors was not exhausted, for the most famous insect attack on an African explorer was carried out by none of these. Sent by Burton on a boat-buying mission, Speke found himself on 8 March 1858 on the island of Kivera on Lake Tanganyika. At night his tent was invaded by a plague of black beetles. Since there were too many of them to expel, he ignored them and dropped off to sleep. He awoke just too late to prevent one of the insects entering his ear. He relates the horrific sequel thus:

> 'He began with exceeding vigour, like a rabbit at a hole, to dig violently away at my tympanum . . . what to do I knew not. Neither tobacco, oil, nor salt could be found: I therefore tried melted butter; that failing, I applied the point of a penknife to his back, which did more harm than good; for though a few thrusts kept him quiet, the point also wounded my ear so badly, that inflammation set in, severe suppuration took place, and all the facial glands extending from that point down to the point of the shoulder became contorted and drawn aside, and a string of bubos decorated the whole length of that region . . . I could not open my mouth for several days . . . For many months the tumour made me almost deaf, and ate a hole between that orifice and the nose so that when I blew it, my ear whistled so audibly that those who heard it laughed.

To face hostile tribesmen, to witness the horrors of the slave trade, and to endure Africa's diseases would have pushed to the limit the mettle of the bravest adventurer alive. When we add to this the ordeal by wild animals faced by the white pioneers in Africa, it is hard not to conclude that in their insouciant disdain for danger, the explorers were either a genuine breed of supermen or clinically insane. Or perhaps both.

IV
ATTITUDES

14

Explorers and Imperialism

The golden age of the explorers took place in the fifty years before conscious imperialism, associated in Britain with such names as Joseph Chamberlain, Lord Rosebery, Milner and Lugard, took a hold on the European mind. Imperialism, always a slippery concept, was in the era of colonial empires a *mélange* of high-minded and sometimes utopian 'improvement' mentalities, strategic considerations and economic self-interest. In some minds there existed the thought that Africa might yet prove to be to the pioneers what Latin America had been to the *conquistadores* – an Aladdin's cave of precious metals. The myth of tropical treasure – of the land of Ophir, the Queen of Sheba, King Solomon's Mines – made a powerful appeal to the Victorians. The explorers acted as a kind of collective John the Baptist to the messiah of imperialism. But unless we understand the confusion in the minds of the imperialists themselves, we cannot really follow the convolutions in the explorers' projects to bring the Dark Continent into the light.

Ever since J.A. Hobson produced his *Imperialism* in 1902, it has been a familiar notion that one impetus towards empire was the search for outlets for surplus capital from Europe and North America (what we should nowadays call the West). This idea was embraced avidly by Lenin who used it to explain his notion of 'superprofits' extracted from the colonial empires, whereby the bourgeoisie co-opted an 'aristocracy of labour' and thus headed off revolution. It then became a favourite pastime for Africanists to demonstrate that empire-building had followed no such pattern; the export of surplus capital was the least of the imperialists' concerns. It was pointed out, variously, that from 1870 to 1900 the bulk of British exports went to the Americas or the white Commonwealth; that the United States was the greatest individual borrower from Britain; that Germany invested mainly in the Americas and in central and eastern Europe; that French financiers were not interested in Africa; that

Leopold was a 'projector' of the eighteenth-century variety and had no banking capital behind him when he set up the Congo Free State; that capitalism is not monolithic, being divided into industrial, commercial and financial sectors.

But at the end of the 1960s it was suddenly realised that this division between an *a priori* Lenin dogmatising about imperialism without having done the necessary historical research on the one hand, and on the other, 'pure' empirical Africanists burrowing in archives and dealing in facts, would not do. Careful study of the work of Hobson, Lenin, Gaylord Wilshire and other 'leftist' theoreticians of imperialism showed that they were not concerned to analyse what had happened in the past (i.e. pre-1902) but to *predict* the future course of capitalism. The ideas of Lenin, Bukharin and Hilferding were *not* concerned with Victorian colonial expansion and they did *not* advance the idea that the driving force behind British and French empire-building was surplus capital in search of outlets. Establishment historians like Sir Keith Hancock proved to have been tilting at windmills.

A new synthesis became necessary to explain the events of 1870–1900. One popular idea was to postulate a caesura between the 'Imperialism of Free Trade' (1870–90) and the 'New Imperialism', annexationist and war-minded, after 1890. It was generally accepted that the surplus capital argument had little to do with Africa. Economic pressure groups did play an important part in the partition of Africa but it was fallacious to imagine that Europe was bursting with surplus funds seeking an outlet in the Dark Continent. Statesmen had many other pressure groups to consider. They manipulated bankers just as much as bankers manipulated them. Lord Salisbury was no more subservient to the Rothschilds than Bismarck was to the house of Bleichroder. The usual relationship of government to capitalist in Africa was like that of Stanley to Leopold – an uneasy alliance of convenience best summed up as like that of the apprentice to the sorcerer. Besides, direct political domination did not even imply profit maximisation, as the experience of Cecil Rhodes's British South Africa Company in the two Rhodesias showed. Finally, African trade was insignificant for the Great Powers. The only territories valuable for European capitalism at the outbreak of the First World War were Algeria, Egypt and the independent South Africa. The economic insignificance of Africa explains why, despite the Fashoda (1898) and Morocco (1906) crises, conflict in Africa never led to war between the Powers.

A problem distinct from that of imperialism, though obviously causally connected, was what sense to make of the 'scramble for Africa' – that determined carving up of the continent that received its dubious seal of legitimacy at the Berlin Conference of 1884–5. One popular idea was that

Germany under Bismark was the prime mover, that Germany's late realisation of the desirability of colonies triggered a desire for a 'place in the sun' and thus that the scramble for Africa was really the outer projection of European conflicts. The Robinson and Gallagher thesis arose to combat this. In their *Africa and the Victorians* the authors argued that Britain acquired its possessions in Africa primarily to safeguard the route to India, with British military strategy hinging on the Cape and the Suez Canal. Ironically, this view was in effect an updating of an idea by another Marxist, Kautsky, who pointed to strategic interests as being an aspect of the British 'Free Trade Empire'. Karl Kautsky argued that the joint interests of British working-class consumers and of shipowners were far more powerful in Britain than elsewhere. It was this combination that prevented the British from adopting protective tariffs and forced capitalists to find new markets with free trade methods. Africa and India thus became part of a seamless web of specific social forces.

Yet another view is that it was France, not Britain, which set off the 'scramble'. The root cause of French colonialism was not financial, but derived from the push of the Army and the bureaucracy to obtain new posts – a kind of Empire building out of 'empire building', as it were. Only later did French imperialism become a tool of industrial and financial capitalism. The key figure in French colonialism was Jules Ferry (prime minister from 1880 to 1881 and 1883 to 1885). He battled to overcome a public opinion generally hostile to colonialism. In 1870 the whole of French overseas territories contained less than five million people and were run at a loss. The Franco-Prussian War, the Commune and the early years of the Third Republic witnessed further French recoil from adventures abroad. Ferry, however, proselytised for the view that gaining overseas territory would serve a threefold end: it would compensate for the loss of Alsace-Lorraine to Germany, it would provide new markets and, most of all, it would give an expanding army a proving ground. But Ferry fought an uphill battle. Most republicans scorned the idea that an African empire could make up for Alsace-Lorraine; this was like trying to compensate a mother who had just lost two children by engaging twenty servants for her. Gautier declared that of all eras in all countries France in the 1870s was most profoundly opposed to foreign adventure.

It is in this context that the vital role of Brazza's explorations must be seen. After 1871 France seemed on the point of abandoning West Africa entirely. Her naval presence on the Gabon coast was drastically reduced, and two forts on the Ivory Coast were abandoned. Brazza's heroic efforts turned the tide. The small settlement on the Gabon coast, which in 1875 France considered ceding to Britain, was the embryo from which by 1900 was born a French equatorial empire twice the size of the motherland.

The man who explored this territory and inspired the French empire was Ferry's right-hand man Savorgnan de Brazza.

Yet some historians hold that it is a fallacy to seek an explanation for the 'scramble for Africa' in purely rational terms. Some have interpreted it as an irrational movement born of national hysteria. On this view imperialism comes to seem a national anxiety neurosis, in which an answer is sought abroad for intractable ills at home. Ronald Hyam has turned the argument about surplus capital on its head and experimented with the notion of empire as a safety valve for 'surplus sexuality'. On this view the early Victorian optimism of a Livingstone gives way to a *fin de siècle* pessimism; so we find Cecil Rhodes arguing 'If we don't, someone else will.' The sociologist Joseph Schumpeter's view was that imperialism had nothing to do with economic motives. To use Marxist terminology, it was a detached superstructure no longer corresponding to a base; to use Schumpeter's own expression, it was 'social atavism'. On this reading, imperialism was an irrational phenomenon, a backward-looking nostalgia for pre-capitalist, war-orientated forces. This is clearly problematical. It ignores not just the capitalistic element in imperialism and the philanthropic and missionary contribution but also the *rational* calculations of *some* capitalists (Rhodes, Mackinnon) and *some* statesmen (Rosebery, Salisbury, Bismarck).

To sum up, there can be no single answer to the relationship of the explorers to imperialism in Africa, simply because there was no single imperialism to begin with. 'Imperialism' can be cashed (in the William James sense, that every idea has a cash value) only in individual cases, each of which reveals a different mixture of individual motives, types of person involved and large-scale forces. British, German and French motives in the 'scramble for Africa' were all different. Leopold's acquisition of the Congo cannot even be seen as empire-building in the true sense, unless we accept the notion of 'the imperialism of one man'. It was rather an old-fashioned personal bid for plunder and spoils, with the monarch functioning as his own limited company – 'the king incorporated'. The Congo Free State was, until 1908, Leopold's personal fief; the decision of the Berlin Conference to grant him this domain must be one of the few times in history that large-scale piracy had been legalised by international concordat. By contrast Portuguese imperialism was 'uneconomic imperialism' – essentially negative, in that it was inspired by nostalgia for the past and fear that other nations would seize Portugal's possessions. Portugal presents the spectacle of a power *not* propelled by economic considerations in Africa. Her trade there was insignificant, her emigrants preferred to go to Brazil rather than Angola, and she had virtually no capital for investment abroad.

Fifty years separated Livingstone's landing at Cape Town from the first significant British annexation in Africa, of Uganda. Livingstone was a key, arguably *the* key figure, in the formation of British imperial attitudes to Africa. He promoted imperialism at three different levels: to expose the slave trade; to destroy it by the introduction of industry and technology; and to regenerate Africa spiritually through the spread of Christian missions. 'Civilisation, Christianity and Commerce'; these were the Livingstone watchwords. He wanted a highway built into the interior so that European trade could reach Africa. The combination of science, industry and free trade, he was sure, would bring the African to Christianity. Once a global market for African products was established, the production of goods for export would produce great wealth and thus bring about the euthanasia of slavery. Livingstone thought that even his favourite tribes, like the Makololo, were irredeemable without Western commodities and furthermore that without the import of such goods any missionaries sent out to Africa would simply sink to the savage level of the local people. Livingstone declared that all his explorations were secondary to this end: 'The Nile sources are valuable to me only as a means of enabling me to open my mouth with power among men. It is this power I hope to apply to remedy an enormous evil.'

The difference between Livingstone and a later imperialist like Joseph Chamberlain was that Livingstone did not imagine annexation. He thought that once Africans were brought into the ambit of Christianity and British trade, they would develop and improve autonomously. He imagined white settlements in highland locations as spurs to the African; his imagination could not have encompassed the continent as a vast agricultural estate controlled from Europe. His particular enthusiasm was the foundation of a colony of 'honest poor' whites among the Mang'anja in the Shire highlands; such people would manage large-scale food and agricultural production with African labour. So sure was he that such a colony would soon bring the Zambezi slave trade to an end that he even toyed with the idea of anonymously funding twenty or thirty families to come out to Africa as an experiment.

On 1 December 1859 he wrote ambitiously that he wished

> to make Africa north of Latitude 15° S a blessing to Africans and Englishmen. The sons of the soil need not be torn from their homes in order to contribute to the wealth of the world. There is room for them where they are, and they may be led to produce their quota, and a large one, to the circulating wealth of the world. There is room and to spare for English immigrants to settle on and work the virgin soil of the still untilled land of Ham. As the African need not be torn from his country and enslaved, no more need the English poor be crowded together in unwholesome dens, and debarred from breathing the

pure air of Heaven. There is room for all in the wide and glorious domains of
the Lord, the king of all the Earth.

Livingstone was not alone in thinking that European technology was *the*
breakthrough force in the Dark Continent. The Society of Arts, an
ameliorist organisation dedicated to expanding trade, manufactures and
agriculture (it had a membership of 3000–4000 merchants and businessmen) made ambitious – and over-optimistic – estimates of the future of
the railways in Africa, in their efforts to get investors to switch their
railway funds away from the favoured regions of India, Japan, Russia and
South America. The Society accepted Livingstone's arguments that
European technology would impress Africans by its power, make them
forget their petty squabbles, turn them into scientific cultivators of the
soil, and thus end the slave trade. Meanwhile luminaries such as Sir
Rutherford Alcock propagandised for an African telegraph, and Donald
Currie, president of the Castle Line, for steamships on the African lakes.
Sir Henry Rawlinson, president of the Royal Geographical Society,
declared in 1876 that half the battle for civilisation and Christianity would
be won if a couple of steamers were at once placed on each of the fourteen
great African lakes. Plans to put steamers on the lakes also formed part of
the plans of all five British missionary societies. Livingstone himself tried
to lead by technological example in setting up a sugar mill (which had
been brought from Glasgow in pieces) in the town of Tete – he could not
get it to Sekeletu by river.

But the Foreign Office would have none of it. They considered all such
plans for colonisation premature and stressed that the Treasury would
not pay for steamships on Lake Nyasa. As Palmerston remarked to the
Foreign Secretary: 'I am very unwilling to embark on new schemes of
British possessions. Dr Livingstone's information is valuable, but he must
not be allowed to tempt us to form colonies only to be reached by forcing
steamers up cataracts.'

Livingstone's reputation dipped after the fiasco of the Zambezi
expedition only to rise again triumphantly after his 'finding' by Stanley
and especially after his death and Waller's consummate propagandist
editing of his last journals. But by the time he departed on his last
expedition in 1865 Livingstone himself was sceptical about the viability of
white agricultural colonies. The failure of the Zambezi venture shook him
to the roots: he saw that whites had no chance of competing as tropical
labourers with blacks and that therefore they could be managers only.

Livingstone's main contribution to imperialism was his long reflection
on the part tropical colonies could play. His vision was undoubtedly
paternalistic, but as such it chimed with general Victorian imperialist

sentiment. His call to Europeans to intervene in Africa for the Africans' sake became the later justification for British intervention. Explorers, missionaries, consular agents and limited companies all marched under the twin banners 'Livingstone' and 'Civilisation, Christianity and Commerce'. Inevitably they acted as the Trojan horse for empire, as Livingstone always believed they would. The tremendous impact of the Livingstone legend after the publication of Waller's sanitised version of the *Last Journals* revolutionised British attitudes to Africa. As a recent scholar has remarked, 'Played out to its logical end ... the British antislavery impulse led to empire.'

But Livingstone's voice was far from that of a prophet's crying in the wilderness. Speke thought Africans required a government 'like ours in India' if they were not to be destroyed by the slave trade. Baker argued that only with the suzerainty of the British government could the slave trade be suppressed and legitimate trade established. To humanitarians who objected that wars of annexation cost lives he riposted that the putative casualties were as nothing alongside the annual toll taken by inter-tribal wars and the slave trade.

If Baker and Speke stressed the slave trade, Verney Cameron was one of the most eloquent advocates of the economic benefits of imperialism. He referred to the 'almost unspeakable richness', 'vast fortunes' and 'incalculable wealth' in tropical Africa. He also thought a market economy would spontaneously destroy the slave trade, just as the industrial economy of the North had destroyed the plantation society of the South in the United States, with the difference that the slavers could not mount four months' warfare in the field against European armies, let alone four years'. He recommended a port at Mombasa and a railway line to Lake Tanganyika, together with steamers on each major section of river. At impassable rapids depots should be set up and tramways or roads built so that bullock carts could carry goods around the cataracts.

> Why are not steamers flying the British colours carrying the overglut of our manufactured goods to the naked African, and receiving from him in exchange those choicest gifts of nature by which he is surrounded, and of the value of which he is at present ignorant?

Cameron also made a strong plea for British rule in Central Africa. Anglo-Saxons should direct African labour 'and employ it so as to make it of great use to the British Empire'. Africa would recede until opened up by civilisation:

> Now this country, if not taken in hand, one day or another must become simply an overgrown wilderness, and its valuable products will be lost. It will become

more difficult day by day to prevent the growth of these [slave trade] crimes, until the country is taken in hand by a strong and determined Government, or by some great company, like the East India Company, which would have the power of governing, and be able to carry on its work in a perfectly upright, independent, open manner and in a way such as would defy the cavillings and evil speakings of anybody and everybody in the world.

Cameron secured treaties placing the Congo and Zambezi basins under British control, subject to the discretion of the British government. His actions evoked no interest, and in February 1876 the Foreign Office, as with Livingstone and Lake Nyasa fourteen years earlier, repudiated Cameron's Congo protectorate. When he then tried to set up a Chartered Company for East Africa, he was told that the day for such things was past.

But Joseph Thomson, Cameron's fellow-Scot, scoffed at the idea of Africa as a second India. He questioned the optimistic projections about the fertility of African soil, the commercial exploitability of African raw materials and products, the availability of African labour for European plantations, the feasibility of building railways and pointed instead to the problems posed by African diseases. He attacked the missionaries for attempting too much too soon and contrasted them with Islam, which used simpler methods, had lower expectations and had more to offer Africans. He pointed out that profits and civilisation did not necessarily go together: a road between lakes Tanganyika and Nyasa would revolution- ise African society but could never pay its way. In sum, Christianity, commerce, civilisation, colonisation and imperialism were cant terms under whose cover all manner of evil could be practised. But Thomson was a great believer in Chartered Companies and thought that 'Downing Street' was a drag on the chain.

Harry Johnston, by contrast, who followed most closely in Thomson's exploring footsteps, was an early imperialist and by no means regarded 'Civilisation, Christianity and Commerce' as humbug or hypocrisy:

By their own unaided efforts I doubt whether the Negroes would ever advance much above the status of savagery in which they still exist in those parts of Africa where neither European nor Arab civilisation has as yet reached them. There they are still to be found leading a life which, in its essential features of culture and social organisation, is scarcely altered from what it was 4000 years ago, when the black man and their simple arts and savage surroundings were truthfully limned in Egyptian frescoes. The Negro seems to require the intervention of some superior race before he can be roused to any definite advance from the low stage of human development in which he has contentedly remained for many thousand years.

This argument on the 'Hobbesian' state of Africa was a familiar one, used to telling effect by the explorers, and thus once again adding to the eventual pressure for imperial annexation. Livingstone described a typical African scenario as follows: 'A chief of more than ordinary ability arises and, subduing all his less powerful neighbours, founds a kingdom, which he governs more or less wisely till he dies. His successor not having the talent of the conqueror cannot retain the dominion, and some of the abler under-chiefs set up for themselves, and, in a few years, the remembrance only of the empire remains. This, which may be considered as the normal state of African society, gives rise to frequent and desolating wars, and people long in vain for a power able to make all dwell in peace.'

Moreover, ran the consensus of opinion among the explorers, it was not just that war and violence were endemic among the African; he also had no culture or civilisation in any recognisable sense of those terms. Livingstone was struck by the lack of history or culture: 'the very rocks are illiterate, they contain so few fossils'. In examining African society 'we are thrown back in imagination to the infancy of the world'. Baker gleefully seized on the apparent lack of history, culture and architecture in Central Africa and said the only conclusion possible was that there had been no development on the continent since primeval times. Livingstone remarked that in Africa the human mind had stagnated, that no science had developed, and that the only curiosity was towards satisfying the wants of the stomach. He was stupefied that tribesmen living within a few miles of the Victoria Falls all their lives had never made the effort to see 'the smoke that thunders'. Harry Johnston remarked on African insensitivity to flora and fauna and the wonders of nature. A Latooka chief quizzed Baker on why he wanted to discover the Nile sources: 'Suppose you get to the great lake, what will you do with it? What will be the good of it? If you find that the large river does flow from it, what then? What's the good of it?'

From there it was but a short stop to the proposition Speke advanced, that Africans were imbeciles. 'It is strange to see how very soon, when questioning those negroes about anything relating to geography, their weak brains give way, and they can answer no questions, or they become so evasive in their replies, or so rambling, that you can make nothing out of them. It is easily discernible, at what time you should cease to ask any further questions: for their heads then roll about them like a ball upon a wire, and their eyes glaze over and look vacantly about as though vitality had fled from their bodies altogether.' Charles John Andersson, the explorer of the Okango river, concurred. 'O ye sentimentalists of the Rousseau school – for some such still remain – witness what I have witnessed, and do witness daily, and you will soon cease to envy and praise the life of savages!'

The explorers propagandised for imperialism by carrying out economic surveys of the lands through which they travelled. They stressed the two-way benefits of a partnership between African labour and European capital and technology. This economic emphasis became more pronounced in the propaganda for imperial policies in the 1880s. Africa was variously seen as an investment opportunity, a new source of raw materials, a protected market, a population safety valve and as a system of out-relief for the unemployed sons of gentlemen – a very numerous group, according to Cameron. Harry Johnston agreed: 'Great as our Indian Empire is, it can only employ a half of the intelligent well-educated British youth who are anxious to enter Government service. Africa, well-developed, can easily find employment for the remainder.'

Imperialists also justified their interventions by underlining the 'heart of darkness' aspect of Africa given prominence in the explorers' books: the insecurity engendered by tribal war and the slave trade, the cruelty, religious superstition and cultural inferiority, the barbarism, savagery and general backwardness of Africa. This made the imperialist a kind of trustee, charged with bringing the benighted primitive to the light – this was 'the white man's burden'. Speke argued for imperialism on the grounds that it would at least enable Africa to reach the level of India and raise the African from the mire:

> As his fathers ever did, so does he. He works his wife, sells his children, enslaves all he can lay hands upon, and, unless when fighting for the property of others, contents himself with drinking, singing, and dancing like a baboon, to drive dull care away. A few only make cotton cloth, or work in wood, iron, copper or salt; their rule being to do as little as possible, and to store up nothing beyond the necessities of the next season, lest their chief or neighbours should covet and take it away from them.

By their writings, then, the explorers provided the legitimation for imperialism. Thomson summed up this attitude:

> Whatever Europeans have done in Africa has been at the dictates of civilisation and for the good of the negro, while, as if not content with that, more than one leader of African enterprise on looking back over his blood and ruin-marked path, has seen the evidence of a guidance and support more than human.

The case for imperialism would have been weakened had not cruelty and social instability provided powerful arguments for amelioration, thus providing Europeans with cover for less altruistic motives. The raiding and belligerence of powerful tribes including the Masai, Matabele, Galla,

Ganda and Barotse and the inroads of the slave trade brutalised inter-tribal relationships and provided a golden pretext for imperialism. One of the pretexts for the Pioneer column which Selous led into Mashonaland in 1890 was to rescue the Mashona from the ravages of the Matabele. The missionary R.P. Ashe, describing the atrocities resulting from Mutesa's war against the neighbouring kingdom of Karagwe, reported:

> So the caravan of captive women and children went on, leaving the Kagera river behind choked with corpses of husbands and brothers who had died in their defence, the way marked by emaciated bodies and whitening bones of helpless children who died on the terrible march. This is Africa left to herself. Livingstone, Stanley and Cameron have told us what Africa is when left to the Arabs.

John Kirk, long-time British consul at Zanzibar, developed the argument from political instability at great length in his despatches to London. He pointed out that tribal onslaughts from Bechuanaland to Ethiopia, whether by Masai, Galla, Matabele, Ngoni, Landeens, Gunangwara or Maviti had consequences even more catastrophic than the slave trade and that until such movements were either broken up or kept in check by a strong hand it was useless to hope for any advance by civilisation. One of his pet projects, which he constantly dangled before a reluctant Foreign Office, was an aggressive campaign to exterminate the Masai. Naturally, in the imperial era proper it was discovered that the explorers and their auxiliaries in the press and consular office had oversold this particular bill of goods. The Masai proved not to be the holy terrors of Kirk's imagination. On the other hand, the more mendacious explorers were found out. Lugard, relying on Baker, determined to chastise Kabbarega in the 1890s, even in the face of condemnation by missionaries like R.P. Ashe. Yet even Lugard, a self-confessed man of force, later grudgingly admitted that Kabbarega was very far from the villain Baker had made him out to be. Johnston, too, later realised that *he* had been manipulated into taking tough action against Kabbarega, whose guerrilla warfare against the British in the 1890s is one of the unsung genuine wars of resistance.

Africa's endemic cruelty and suffering was an important element in the winning over of public opinion for the 'white man's burden' of imperialism. The sheer weight of evidence eventually had its effect. In time it came to be the received opinion that no major change in the conditions of Central Africa could be achieved without imperial control. The argument was reinforced by one other telling factor. The descent of Central Africa into inter-tribal anarchy was accelerated by the Arabs and Portuguese, neither of whom was capable or desirous of helping in the historical transition which the forces of social change demanded of the African.

The general arguments provided by the explorers for extending British suzerainty over Africa may be summarised as follows. In the first place there was the now familiar tenet that there was no alternative. The books of the great explorers showed a continent riven by tribal warfare and slave trade, where the only countervailing influences were the feckless Portuguese and the Arab slavers. Unless, then, all talk of taking the Gospel to the heathen and civilising the Dark Continent was claptrap, European governments *had* to intervene.

Secondly, it was clear that piecemeal measures were inadequate. Baker and Gordon had tried to annex the lands around the sources of the Nile and eliminate the slave trade in Equatoria, but their task had been made impossible by distances, logistics, administrative incompetence, corruption and a lack of sympathy among their subordinates for the anti-slavery crusade. Thirdly, post-1873 experience rammed home the lesson that a formal abolition of slavery – like that agreed between Sir Bartle Frere and the Sultan of Zanzibar – was one thing; actual abolition in the interior was quite another.

In the fourth place, it was considered unacceptable that Africans with primitive production techniques should keep out the far more advanced Europeans. Harry Johnston pointed out that the African was 'living like an animal in the midst of boundless wealth'; what was important was that European help should be given to develop this wealth for the benefit of both parties. Finally, there were those, like Burton and Baker, who stressed the alleged infantile nature of the African. His racial and cultural inferiority were as marked as was the lack of experience of the child when compared with the parent. On this 'child analogy' it followed that the guidance of a parent was needed and this parent, hardly surprisingly, turned out to be the white European.

It is important to be clear that until comparatively late in the day this 'parenting' was usually thought of as best done by a Chartered Company, not by the British government itself. The prevailing image of the empire in Britain at the time of Livingstone's death was that of a collection of white settlement colonies – what later became the Dominions: Canada, Australia, New Zealand, Cape Colony, Natal. India, taken under direct rule after the Mutiny of 1857, was the exception that was supposed to prove the rule, but it is possible that the comparatively recent demise of the East India Company on the subcontinent may explain why from 1870 to 1890 so many Africa-watchers thought the basis of British rule in Africa would be royal chartered companies rather than formal colonies. Certainly Queen Victoria's 1876 title 'Empress of India' was widely unpopular among those who considered India alien and non-imperial territory, as it was not a white-settled territory. The other insidious argument in favour of a 'white only' empire was that to rule alien races, used to despotism, was ultimately to invite despotism at home, as had happened in the Russian empire.

The minority colony view owed much to Livingstone. As his biographer has remarked: 'Events in Africa between 1874 and 1894 forced a reassessment of what the Empire really was. The addition of new African colonies, peopled not by whites but by blacks, changed the whole balance of the Empire and inevitably altered the way people in Britain viewed it. This new view was significantly influenced by Livingstone's ideas and those of his missionary successors.' The same author makes the point that Chamberlain's 'manifest destiny' speech after the annexation of Uganda in 1894 was a clear echo of Livingstone's instructions in 1858 to his Zambezi expedition. 'We come upon them as members of a superior race and servants of a God that desires to elevate the more degraded portions of the human family . . . to become harbingers of peace to a hitherto distracted and trodden down race.'

In addition to trail-blazing and propagandising, some of the explorers lived on into the era of imperialism proper and played roles of greater or less significance. Harry Johnston, Frederick Lugard and Carl Peters are examples of men who did some genuine exploring in the early part of their careers, before their more famous manifestations as imperial pro-consuls. Stanley founded the Congo Free State for Leopold II and it was his meticulous work in the Congo during 1879–84 that enabled Leopold to make good his African claims at the Berlin Conference of 1884–85. But although Leopold's Congo is yet another candidate as precipitant towards the scramble for Africa, the entire enterprise cannot even be dignified with the name of imperialism. As has been well said: 'The Congolese system was too viciously wasteful, too recklessly short-term in its conception to deserve even the term of exploitation. It was no more than a prolonged raid for plunder.'

The Emin Pasha expedition found Stanley serving two masters: Leopold, to whom he was still bound by contract, but towards whom he entertained a grudge because the king had kept him in Europe for nearly three years in 1884–6; and William Mackinnon, chairman of the Emin Pasha Relief Committee and of the Imperial British East Africa Company. The ambiguity of Stanley's intentions during this expedition later incurred for him the charge of duplicity and Machiavellianism. Scarcely less controversial was Stanley's claim to have signed treaties with powerful chiefs in Uganda, whereby they ceded sovereignty to Britain.

Later Stanley was forced to admit that what he had signed was a series of 'blood-brotherhood' or non-aggression pacts.

But by 1890 Stanley was firmly in Mackinnon's camp and that of the other imperialists. That year, when he returned to England in triumph, before any of the doubts about the darker aspects of the Emin Pasha expedition had begun to be aired, he was the lion of the hour. The 'Stanley craze' – evinced in the runaway success of his highly tendentious *In Darkest Africa* – injected a kind of high-octane fuel into the engine of imperialism. It bade fair to set Britain on a collision course with German imperialism, which had conflicting claims in the Tanganyika area of East Africa. Both Bismarck and Salisbury tried to defuse the crisis, to cries of 'betrayal' from the hawks on both sides, conveniently clustered in London and Berlin around, respectively, Stanley and Carl Peters.

Stanley set out on a speech-making tour, in which he accused the Salisbury government of letting slip a great opportunity in East Africa. Salisbury hit back at once. In a speech at the Merchant Taylors' Banquet on 22 May 1890 he poked fun at the 'African lion' then at the very height of his popularity:

> Mr Stanley has warned you that the British government is doing terrible things – that it has surrendered vast forests and tremendous mountains and great kingdoms which he has offered the British public to occupy; and he gives you mysterious hints in order that you may interfere in time or – if you do not interfere – that you may be satisfied to submit to his threat that the Company with which he is connected will abandon Africa to its fate.

In the end the threat of a war with France and Russia in Europe forced Bismarck to come to a generous accommodation with the British in East Africa. The way was clear for Mackinnon's British East Africa Company to expand. Formal empire began with the annexation of Uganda in 1894, though by this time the ageing Stanley was being elbowed off the stage by a younger, more full-bloodedly imperialist generation in Africa: men of the stamp of Johnston, Lugard and Rhodes.

The short life of Joseph Thomson (who died aged thirty-six) illustrates how even a young man coming late to African exploration could pass easily across the invisible threshold separating the era of exploration from that of imperialism. By the time Thomson returned from his successful crossing of Masailand in 1884, the Berlin Conference was carving up the continent for the convenience of the European powers. It was a happy chance for French imperialism that the conference took place while the expansionist Jules Ferry was still in power. By 1885 France had added parts of the western Sudan to its traditional toehold on the coasts and rivers of Senegal and Guinea, occupied ports on the western Slave coast and, using Brazza as its spearhead, set up stations on the Ogowé and Congo rivers, and laid claim to the Niari valley. Stanley meanwhile had set the capstone to his five years with Leopold by establishing Kinshasa on the south bank of the Congo.

The Germans had annexed South-West Africa and claimed suzerainty over the Togo and Kamerunian coasts. Most sensational of all was the German advance in East Africa which five years later brought the collision with the British. In 1883 the fire-eating Carl Peters proposed a German empire in South Africa. Six years before Cecil Rhodes received his charter for the settlement of Matabeleland and Mashonaland, however, Berlin replied coldly that the countries south of the Zambezi were regarded as a British sphere of interest. A year was a long time in the 'scramble for Africa'. In 1884 Peters led a small party into the East African interior and concluded twelve treaties in six weeks whereby the chiefs alienated land 'for all time'. After the Treaty of Berlin which ended the conference on 27 February 1885, the Kaiser issued a charter extending his 'protection' to all the Peters territory. Peters then formed a German East African Company and transferred to it the treaty rights of 1884. Sultan Barghash of Zanzibar protested vociferously to the Kaiser; in answer five German warships anchored in Zanzibar roads in August 1885. The British consul, Kirk, meanwhile had been ordered by London to encourage Barghash to accept a German protectorate; in view of the French threat to Egypt and the success of the Mahdi in the Sudan, Gladstone wanted no quarrel with Bismarck. In 1886 a joint Franco-British-German commission investigated the Sultan's claims to territories in East Africa; following German pressure the three commissioners recommended that the Sultan should be allowed to possess merely the ports on the mainland and a ten-mile coastal strip opposite Zanzibar.

Given his ambivalent attitude to colonial expansionism by nation-states, Thomson at first went through a mild psychological crisis in which he tried to resist the irresistible conclusion that he himself by his explorations and writings had contributed to the growth of imperialism. Then he decided to join the 'big battalions'. In 1885 he ascended the Niger on behalf of the National African (later the Royal Niger) Company and signed comprehensive treaties with the Fulani ruler of Hausaland and his rival the Emir of Gwandu. He had thus beaten the Germans to the punch in northern Nigeria; in his own words he had 'at the expense of a few pounds and a demoralised monarch ... bloomed forth in all the glories of a diplomatist'.

After explorations in the Atlas mountains of southern Morocco, Thomson took service with Cecil Rhodes and the British South Africa Company. He travelled to Lake Nyasa and the Kafue river, and concluded fourteen treaties of cession from the local chiefs; he failed, however, to make contact with Msiri, the Yeke chief who controlled the copper deposits of Katanga. It was a costly omission: next year Leopold sent Captain Stairs into Katanga to annex the territory and thus obtained for the Congo the region's priceless mineral deposits. Rhodes saw the importance of Katanga and tried to persuade Thomson to return to Msiri's capital and repair his omission. But eleven years of virtually non-stop African travel had exhausted the tough Scotsman. His health was by now failing, even though he was not quite thirty-two. He spent the remaining four years of his life vainly trying to recover his strength, in South Africa and on the Mediterranean. The exhaustion and early 'burn-out' in the 1890s of Stanley and Thomson, the two explorers who most clearly straddled the eras of exploration and imperialism, perhaps points to the moral that the 'outsiders' who went where no white men had gone before were all uneasy bedfellows with the money-men of London, Brussels and Glasgow who did so much to power the machine of conscious imperialism.

15

Reputation and Impact

If we are to assess the explorers from an African, as well as European, viewpoint, we need to ask what traces they left in local legend, folklore and tradition. What kinds of reputation did they enjoy? Beyond that, what was their impact on the indigenous societies? Were the contacts between aboriginals and Europeans mutually beneficial? What were the unintended consequences of the explorers' filling in the vast empty spaces on early nineteenth-century European maps of Africa?

To answer these questions we need first of all to examine the views generally received among Africans at the time about the nature of the white man. The most basic general proposition was that white men were spirits, came from the land of the dead, and could work magic spells. On one linguistic analysis 'Mpoto' – 'the land of the white man' really means 'the land of the dead'. In 1884 the missionary George Grenfell discovered and explored the Oubangui river, a huge tributary of the Congo. Having travelled 130 miles up the Oubangui, Grenfell was greeted by cries of 'Bidimo, Bidimo' – 'Spirits'. Charles Bateman, who worked for Leopold on the Kasai, reported that the Bashilele people called him 'Chienvu' – the reincarnation of a former chief of that name. An associated idea was that white men had powers over death since they came from the land of the dead itself. Harry Johnston was once asked by a chief to send back a man from his village who had just died. White faces as the mark of a spirit also suggested that to work for such a spirit was to give oneself up to death. And in a curious inversion of European beliefs about the African, white men were widely considered to be cannibals.

The belief in white sorcery was so widespread that even some of the explorers' porters thought that their tin boxes contained spare, fold-up white men, ready to be assembled in an emergency! Since the white spirits were deemed to have magic powers, the braver Africans sometimes tried to enlist these powers on their behalf. Many whites played up to them and used mirrors, watches, umbrellas, etc, as a magic show. Baker arrayed himself in kilt, sporran, glengarry and plaid of Atholl tartan to astonish and impress Kamurasi's people. When governor of Equatoria, he took a wide range of 'miracle-working' items on his great expedition: musical boxes, magic lanterns, a magnetic battery, fireworks, and silver balls that mirrored surrounding scenes. Baker indeed claimed that Africans were so fond of music that 'I believe the safest way to travel . . . would be to play the cornet, if possible without ceasing, which would ensure a safe passage. A London organ-grinder would march through Central Africa followed by an admiring and enthusiastic crowd, who, if his tunes were lively, would form a dancing escort of the most untiring material.'

Thomson was a specialist in the art of bamboozling the locals: he bedazzled Africans with effervescent 'potions' – in reality Eno's Salts – and the firing of guns simultaneously with his flash photography. Other explorers' gimmicks included Teleki's favourite device of firing rockets at night around his camp to give it a magic aura of protection: Petherick's filling a pipe with gunpowder so that when it exploded he appeared like a wizard; and Chaillé-Long's stratagem of writing ahead to Mutesa to tell him a great prince would be visiting him, and then appearing on horseback in gold lace and red pantaloons. The traveller MacDonald coaxed an African to try to catch the second hand on his watch. In 1871 Stanley gave one tribe concentrated ammonia to sniff. This produced the comment: 'Oh, these white men know everything. The Arabs are dirt compared to them.'

But items such as cameras, sextants, theodolites, magic lanterns and magnifying glasses had to be used with care lest they bring on a charge of witchcraft. A better bet was to awe the African with amazing demonstrations of long-range shooting with the latest rifle, or to pretend to control the weather. The well-known eclipse of the sun incident in Rider Haggard's *King Solomon's Mines* was probably inspired by an exploit of Charles Bateman. Arriving at a strange village in the middle of a thunderstorm, he claimed to have started it by 'white fetish'.

There can be little doubt that the coming of the explorers initially terrified tribes who had never seen a white man before. Winwood Reade described one such encounter in West Africa:

> Here stood two men, with their hands upon each other's shoulders, staring at me in mute wonder, their eyes like saucers, their mouths open like sepulchres. There an old woman, in a stooping attitude with her hands on her knees, like a cricketer 'fielding out'; a man was dragging up his frightened wife to look at me and a child cried bitterly with averted eyes.

Du Chaillu confirmed these West African attitudes:

Then came numerous questions about the white man. How they stared when I told them that our houses were made of stone, the same material as was found on their mountains. The last question was a delicate one; it was, 'do white men die?' I wished them to remain in their present belief that we did not die, for their superstitious feeling towards me was my best safeguard, so I feigned not to hear the question and turned their attention to another subject.

Livingstone had a similar experience on the Zambezi:

There must be something in the appearance of the white man frightfully repulsive to the unsophisticated natives of Africa, for, on entering villages previously unvisited by Europeans, if we met a child coming quietly and unsuspectingly towards us, the moment he raised his eyes, and saw the men in 'bags', he would take to his heels in an agony of terror, such as we might feel if we met a live Egyptian mummy at the door of the British Museum. Alarmed by the child's wild outcries, the mother rushes out of her hut, but darts back again at the first glimpse of the same fearful apparitions. Dogs turn tail, and scour off in dismay; and hens, abandoning their chickens, fly screaming to the tops of the houses. The so lately peaceful village becomes a scene of confusion and hubbub, until calmed by the laughing assurance of our men, that white people do not eat black folks; a joke having oftentimes greater influence in Africa than solemn assertions.

Familiarity with the white devil eventually bred contempt. In the early days Africans thought that to kill a white man would bring down upon them some mysterious calamity. But by the 1880s after the killing of Leopold's men Carter and Cadenhead by Mirambo without subsequent retaliation and, even more impressively, the assassination of Bishop Hannington in Buganda, such fears were no longer entertained. A breakthrough event was the arrival of European women. On the Congo the hostility of the Bolobo tribe was assuaged when the missionary Bentley's wife and baby came upriver in 1887. Until then the white man had been looked upon as a demon, not born and bred like humans, but a semi-supernatural creature without a mate.

One 'magical' view of the white was that he might have some connection with the spirits of dead ancestors. The horrors of the slave trade could be palliated by the notion that slaves went to America, died, then as spirits worked at producing sums of wealth unknown in the land of the living. When the distinction between Europe and America began to impinge, a different variant of legend appeared. This was that when rich Africans died they went to Europe and became white; the cloth with which they were buried was their merchandise when they came back to trade. In this way the differential wealth of European and African traders could be explained in magical terms.

A large cluster of African beliefs derived from the customary mode of arrival in the riverine areas: on board steamers. It was widely believed that the pale-faced strangers lived beneath the sea, where they wove cloth in large quantities. It has been suggested that this belief arose because Africans would see an approaching ship mast first, then hull, and only finally the entire ship. The idea of the white man as water-spirit gained circumstantial weight from the Christian rite of baptism, which seemed to the tribes a form of sympathetic magic involving the European's true element. In some areas of Africa the local term for white man – usually some variant of *muzungu* – literally denoted a sea monster. It was therefore believed that a white man should always be buried in water, lest a spirit entombed on land rise up and haunt its undertakers.

The first steamers seen by the Bangala tribe on the Congo made them think their owners were water kings, and that the ships were drawn by huge fish or hippos; the engine room was envisaged as a giant cooking-pot where food was prepared. But the steamers were not the only source of wonderment to the Bangala. Since they often saw the white man go down into the hold of the ship to get pearls, *mitakos* and other merchandise, they believed that the men of the *Mpoto* (the 'far land' or Europe) descended into the bowels of the steamer to open up a door and thence fetch their treasures up from the bottom of the river.

An interesting variation on this theme on the Congo was related by the traveller J.H. Weeks. In this version white men did not weave their own cloth but had it woven for them beneath the waves by water-sprites. The legend was that the white man had found an opening to this oceanic factory and that, whenever cloth was needed, the captain of the steamer went to this aperture leading to the ocean and rang a bell. The sprites, without showing themselves, pushed up the end of a piece of cloth into the hole; the captain's men would pull it through the hole into the steamer; the process would then be continued until at the end of three days or so the white men had all they needed. As payment the captain would throw the sprites bodies of dead blacks. Those so thrown into the sprite-hole became the slaves of the sprites, making things for them and generally doing menial labour. Enamel, cutlery and other such items were, therefore, not manufactured by the white man, as he mendaciously claimed, but were the products of black men spirited away as slaves. As 'proof' of this, the Congo tribes pointed out that the cloths traded by the steamers were too finely woven to be the work of white men with two eyes. They were clearly made by sea-sprites who, having only one eye, had the sight-power of two concentrated in it and could therefore weave such fine textures. For this reason when Stanley arrived among the Bangala in 1883, they refused to trade with him, fearing that if they accepted his gifts, the *Likundu* or evil spirit would in future restrict their wealth to those exact gifts.

The wealth of the white man was legendary, not just in terms of the goods he brought with him, but because whenever he wrote a letter, in return bales of cloth, boxes of goods and cases of provisions would arrive soon after. So far the Africans had done little more than, as it were, apply Hume's sceptical view of causality: the constant conjunction of event A with event B. But they muddied this very reasonable conclusion with a misunderstanding of 'growth' and 'wealth' in European terms. Trying to fathom where such apparently boundless wealth could come from, they concocted the legend of the sea spirits and the black myrmidons; this was one of the powerful undercurrents in the early hatred of the white man for his wealth.

The steamer motif also reinforced the notion of whites as spirits since it gave them the power to go away and come back again at great speed. In 1883 the first name given Stanley by the Bangala was *Midjiji* (Ghost). On balance, Africans reacted gloomily to the coming of these spirits. One of the most powerful African myths was that of a golden age before the coming of the white man. In this era all animals lived together peacefully. But the golden age was shattered by man's sinfulness; animals turned and rent one another and the final apocalypse was denoted by the coming of the *Ibanza* or white wizards.

But in *some* localities the coming of the white man was received more sanguinely. In the Yoruba country in the 1830s the Landers were treated as demigods. At Acboro the chief sent a gift of a sucking pig together with a message: 'White men do nothing but good, and I will pray that God may bless you, and send more of your countrymen to Yoruba.' Yet even in areas hostile to the white man and depressed by his advent, the old myths offered some hope. The myth of the apocalypse was lightened by another that spoke of a new dawn, when the elements or wild animals would destroy the interlopers and usher in a new Eden in Africa. The high mortality of Europeans in Africa raised hopes that such prophecy might be more than dream-wish, while in some tribal societies it forced a revaluation of Europe as a paradise; after all, if its inhabitants preferred to come to disease-ridden Africa, conditions in Europe must be truly diabolical.

The early explorers, then, were at the very least perceived as beings with enormous knowledge and talents deriving from magic and superior fetish. In an ironical but poetically justified inversion of European cultural chauvinism, Africans actually expressed surprise that the strangers had human feelings. Significantly, they began to perceive them as human beings only when the later wave of missionaries and travellers brought women to the Dark Continent.

All the great explorers left behind them traces in the local folklore of their coming and a reputation that could vary from saintliness to aggression and brutality. As a general proposition we can say that the reputation of the explorers in Africa depended on the length of time they stayed in a given locality, and the extent to which they seemed to be men of wealth, power or justice. Also, as Schweinfurth pointed out, the African had no sense of 'news' as understood by journalists in Europe and the United States; what stayed in their memories and what they communicated was what interested *them*. In Timbuktu in 1826, for example, Laing found that Mungo Park had the name of being a ruthless murderer of defenceless men, and that this 'reputation' was apparently common coin throughout West Africa.

Speke, on the other hand, made a very favourable impression on the tribes and chiefs with whom he came in contact, with the possible exception of Mutesa himself. Some have gone so far as to assert that he was the most popular of all the explorers in Central Africa. The missionaries Wilson and Felkin found his fame widespread throughout Uganda, while Frank Pocock, Stanley's lieutenant on the 1874–7 expedition, reported that Speke was 'all the rage' in Karagwe and Buganda. Livingstone confirmed this during his last expedition: 'Speke's name is one of generosity, compared with Burton the stingy white man.' Baker provided an even more striking confirmation. While he was marching on Bunyoro in 1872 he met envoys from Mutesa. When they heard the news of Speke's death they were much cast down and continued to exclaim for several minutes: 'Wah! Wah! Speekee! Speekee! Wah! Speekee!' However, Chaillé-Long reported that Mutesa still bore a grudge towards Speke ten years later because he had sat in his presence. And other oral traditions from Mutesa's court indicate that Speke's success there was probably a close-run thing. 'Lord, let us kill this prodigy!' was one piece of advice received by Mutesa from his priests and officials while Speke was in Buganda in February 1862. Moreover, Speke benefited from his long sojourns in powerful kingdoms with dense populations. Writing forty years after Speke's exploits, the traveller J.E.S. Moore found Livingstone's fame still incandescent among the old people at Ujiji; Burton and Speke, however, were unknown.

Burton's reputation was almost bound to be either unflattering or non-existent after two key decisions he made: to spend most of his time in the interior with the Arabs of Tabora, and to refuse payment to his porters at the end of the expedition. He also despised blacks, which made it impossible for any reputation born of affection or respect to develop. Baker also despised Africans but, unlike Burton, he made his mark on them by his bellicosity. We have already seen that the Nyoro regarded him as one of the mythical Bachwezi – the early rulers of the land – returning to their former dominions. His wife's presence caused further unease, for to the African women primarily meant child-bearing, and this in turn meant the possibility of a 'Bachwezi' dynasty being raised up. In some ways Baker caught the imagination of the tribes more than any other explorers. His belief in force impressed people used to powerful warrior-chiefs. Frederick Jackson reported that Baker was remembered with admiration, affection and gratitude by the Bari, Mali and Achole because he smashed their bitter enemies the slave traders. Among the Latooka he had a reputation as a wizard. This derived from a prophecy he made that a body of deserters from his caravan would soon have their bones picked clean by the vultures. These men were later killed while taking part in a disastrous raid on the Latookas. The prophecy immensely swelled Baker's prestige: he was looked on as a magus who had 'caused' the disaster by his sibylline words.

Men of peace tended to have lesser reputations, unless they stayed for a long time in a particular area or possessed particular charisma. So Harry Johnston learned that Thomson's reputation was high among the Wataveita, and in Mandara's country, but he was scarcely known elsewhere. The Wataveita, among whom Thomson had stayed on his way through Masailand, took the view that since Thomson and Johnston were white men with virtually identical names (Jansan and Tamsan), they must be brothers – they were 'of one mother'.

The irony was that the greater the Africanist and the more capable the explorer of blending with the culture, the less he would be noticed and hence the less his reputation. But even this could depend on which tradition was later sampled. One view of Heinrich Barth was that after spending four years immersed in Africa without speaking a European language, and on many indices the most complete Africanist of all, he left little trace in local legend. But Lt Emile Hourst, who travelled in complete safety from Dakar to Timbuktu and then from the Niger to the Bight of Biafra pretended to be Barth's nephew and 'I was thus able to emerge safely from every situation.'

To be a bull in a china shop, like Baker, guaranteed a place in African memory. Nevertheless, careful, conscientious work in a sympathetic milieu could pay dividends. Du Chaillu was known to the Africans as *Mpolo* (Paul), and they later praised his skills as hunter and linguist to Burton. Lupton Bey had a considerable reputation in the Jabir kingdom of the Welle river, which made things easier for the Belgians when they penetrated the region in the early 1890s. It also helped to have striking physical features like the heavily set, bearded Baker, or the corpulent Falstaffian Teleki, whom the Africans dubbed (despite the fact that his was one European name easy for them to pronounce) 'Bwana Tumbo'. Teleki's reputation owed much to the primitive surgery he performed on the mangled arm of a man who had been mauled by a crocodile. When the patient recovered and regained the use of his arm, Bwana Tumbo had a firm reputation as thaumaturge.

Livingstone had a reputation among the Africans as a true friend, to the point where they came to him freely with important information during the Zambezi expedition. The years 1858–63 were those when his fame with Africans was at its height. Many oral traditions recall Livingstone at that time. He was remembered in the Chikwawa area as unwavering in keeping the Sabbath holy; he even forbade his men to hunt on Saturdays. In the Mwase Kasungu traditions Livingstone is said to have liked the Mwase because they redeemed slaves from passing Arab caravans. He also liked the chief's encouragement of ancestor worship. It is recorded that the chief and Livingstone exchanged gifts: an ox for needles and cloth respectively.

The two most persistent traditions involve the Makololo and Livingstone's friend chief Marenga. Oral histories are adamant that Livingstone caused the local ascendancy of the Makololo. The key was the powder and guns Livingstone gave them. Initially given so that the Makololo could defend themselves, the guns enabled them to gain hegemony over the indigenous Mang'anja. The fact that the Makololo later attacked Tengani also muddied the oral tradition of his visit there, so that he was remembered as a treacherous interloper. 'Had it not been for these men [the Kololo], Livingstone would probably have gone down in Mang'anja oral history as some mythical visitor from distant lands who came to converse with their ancestors.'

Another tradition says that Livingstone met chief Marenga in 1863. An exchange of gifts followed: Livingstone gave Marenga a china plate and an umbrella; Marenga gave him a sheep. In 1913 an eyewitness to the meeting recalled that the white men were not regarded as human beings but as spirits of the lake – visitors from another world who had arrived on earth by a wonderful boat. When Livingstone took Marenga aboard his boat, this caused alarm among Marenga's people: '*Viwanda vyambaya fumu ya weni?*' ('Are the spirits going to kill other people's chief?') But all ended well with the exchange of goods. When E.D. Young headed an expedition in 1867 to find out if Livingstone was still alive, he met Marenga, who gave him gifts and testified to the high esteem that existed towards the doctor in African communities: 'Marenga rushed towards me, and, seizing me by the hand, shook it heartily, saying, 'Where have you come from, and where is your brother that was here last year?'

Despite his great achievements, Stanley did not acquire a solid African reputation on his first two expeditions, except in Mutesa's Buganda. He did not stay long enough in one place to acquire an aura; the journalistic urgency of his assignments from Gordon Bennett meant that he tended to fight his way through hostile country and travel at great speed. Only during his five-year sojourn in the Congo while in Leopold's service during 1879–84 did his reputation acquire a stability and fixity. His fame was mixed: some oral traditions emphasised his dark side, others his positive aspects. But in the main his legend boiled down to three things: he was hard and ruthless, he was just, he was wealthy.

The hardness and ruthlessness were known among Africans as early as 1871, during the stopover with Livingstone at Ujiji. One of Stanley's *wangwana* said to Livingstone's servants: 'Your master is a good man – a very good man; he does not beat you, for he has a kind heart; but ours – oh! he is sharp-hot as fire.' Many an African who had tasted the lash from the 'little master' could tell the same story. In the 1920s there were still Africans alive who had known Stanley and could provide vivid testimony to his hardness. Despite the lack of overt hostilities, the 1883 expedition by Stanley's flotilla to Stanley Falls, and his demonstration of the power of the Krupps gun, left him with a local reputation as an aggressor, second only to Tippu Tip in ferocity. On the Emin Pasha expedition, oral tradition credited him with having cut a swathe of destruction through the Ituri rainforest. Colonel George Williamson, a US Civil War veteran in the service of Leopold's Congo in the 1880s, reported that Stanley's name 'produced a shudder among the simple folk when mentioned; they remember his broken promises, his copious profanity, his hot temper, his heavy blows, his severe and rigorous measures by which they were mulcted of their lands'. Some missionaries too testified along the same lines.

Yet this aspect of Stanley has to be seen in perspective. Congo missionaries were violently divided for and against Stanley, according to whether he helped or impeded their work. And some of the later dreadful reputation of Leopold's 'red rubber' state rubbed off on Stanley, partly through association of ideas, partly because *'Bula Matari'* ('the breaker of rocks') was an ambiguous term, used to denote both Stanley himself and the Belgian state he created. Nor could Stanley seriously have been compared to a real man of blood such as Carl Peters. Where Stanley fantasised about revenge on the 'insolent' Gogo tribe who charged him such extortionate *hongo*, Peters made Stanley's word flesh and 'solved' the Gogo problem by machine-gunning them in droves – an exploit that won him from Africans the title of *Mkonowa-Damu* ('the man with the blood-stained hands').

Moreover, it has to be appreciated that hardness and ruthlessness impressed the African more as qualities than some of those applauded in European salons. Justice and fair dealing, highly prized among whites, at least in theory, had little cachet among the Africans. On the other hand the Africans were wholly free from the morbid fear of sexuality that so exercised the Victorians, and applauded the sexual 'laxity' of the early white settlers that upset the missionaries. Selous declared that the widespread European effort to impress Africans with their moral courage, endurance and stoicism backfired. Africans worshipped power and wealth; they interpreted stoicism as weakness and asceticism as poverty. Of the Europeans, they admired most the shiftless, lazy Portuguese, who got others to do their dirty work for them. But what is bred in the bone . . . Selous ignored his own advice when he dived into a crocodile-infested river to retrieve the body of a hippo he had shot just to impress the Africans by the power of example.

'Bula Matari' (properly Matadi – the *wangwana* slurred Swahili consonants as much as the Argentines do Spanish ones), Stanley's nickname, which he himself thought referred to an incident when he blasted a road through Ngomi mountain, was in fact a soubriquet that denoted his ruthlessness – an individual whose head was so hard that he could break rocks with it. This seems to suggest that it was always the ruthlessness that predominated in the African legends about Stanley.

Against this can be set Stanley's reputation for justice. The missionary A.M. Mackay reported: 'Whenever I find myself in Stanley's track, I find his treatment of the natives had invariably been such as to win from them the highest respect for the face of a white man.' Herbert Ward found that his name 'acted as a talisman throughout the Congo country. By millions of these savages his name is uttered with respect almost akin to fear.' Harry Johnston concurred: 'No disparaging word has ever in my hearing fallen from the lips of an African. He was generous, kindly, sympathetic and just, only severe to wrongdoers; absolutely uncursed with that odious British pride and snobbishness which seals up the black men's sympathies and confidences.' In some ways the most telling testimony came seventy-five years later from the independent Congo's first prime minister, Patrice Lumumba, no friend of Leopold and all his works: 'Stanley gave us peace, human dignity, improved our standard of living, developed our intelligence, made our spirit evolve.'

The two strands of harshness and fairness represented Stanley's Janus face, and he sometimes traded on this ambiguity to achieve his goals. The Congolese suffered from a certain confusion about his identity, since he had appeared on their river in two very different guises. In 1877, travelling at great speed and dealing death from a hundred firesticks he was 'Tandelay', the Ibanza or wizard. Yet six years later a very reasonable and conciliatory man appeared, interested in trading and building stations – Bula Matari. Since in African society a man *was* his deeds, a real problem of philosophical identity arose when Tandelay claimed to be one and the same with Bula Matari – a puzzle not unlike that faced by third-century theologians when trying to establish the identity of God the Father with God the Son. Similar, yes, but identical, never. Both were white men, it was true, but Tandelay was bellicose, travelled in a canoe, traded in brass rods, fired his guns first and asked questions later; Bula Matari, on the other hand, was peaceful, did not fire his guns even under great provocation, traded in cloth, and had appeared on the Congo in 'the house that walks on water'. The only judicious conclusion was that Tandelay was a vizier or lieutenant of Bula Matari, just as the Christian heretics concluded that the Son must be inferior to the Father. Stanley cleverly turned all this to his own advantage during the 1883 Irebu civil war. Reluctantly 'conceding the truth', he warned the Irebu that although he, Bula Matari, was a man of peace, if they did not compose their differences, he would summon his war-chief Tandelay from the lower river to chastise them with his host of deadly 'lightning sticks'.

The third aspect of Stanley's reputation among Africans – that of a man of wealth – was the most important and the most firmly embedded in African oral tradition. Stanley related the mixture of awe and cupidity with which the Irebu greeted the steamer *En Avant*. They thought the paddle-wheels must be turned by some twenty men concealed at the bottom of the ship. More sophisticated observers divined that the secret must be the 'big pot' (the boiler) because the engineer was forever stoking up the fire. 'Perhaps,' concluded the Irebu, 'if we had also big pots in our canoes, and we had some of the white man's medicine, we need not toil any more with tired arms at our paddles, and suffer from aches and pains in our shoulders.'

Wealth was crucial in establishing the reputation of the white man in general and Stanley in particular. In Usukuma in 1889 Stanley, driving vast herds of cattle through East Africa on his way to the coast with the Emin Pasha column, acquired the prestige of being a harbinger of meat and plenty. The local folklore said that for this reason, if he ever returned, men would flock to him. Among the Bangala Stanley had a reputation as a man who introduced the *ntaku* or brass rod as a unit of currency, thus contriving a dual system, as before his coming they used the *manyango* (copper). Riches were considered a logical concomitant of the white man. For this reason the early missionaries, white men without wealth, and thus a freak of nature, had a thin time of it until their medical expertise regained them some prestige.

Africans could never understand the secret of European wealth, for they operated on a kind of proto-Marxist labour theory of value, in terms of which, with limited human labour to add to natural resources, the store of wealth available to a community could grow only slowly. With barter, too, they were limited to a circulation of existing goods. Western notions of credit were unknown. It was not surprising, then, that when Stanley tried to explain to the Irebu how a complex trading system worked, they were mystified and exclaimed: 'We know how to trade but our wealth does not increase.' Convinced that the total wealth of an area could not be augmented by trade, they concluded that Stanley's riches must ultimately derive from magic.

The stories and legends about Stanley in African oral tradition invariably concentrate on some aspect of this trio of attributes: hardness, justice, wealth. He was particularly famous on the Congo, where he had spent a leisurely five years founding the Congo State for Leopold. Here his fame was such that oral histories used his first coming in 1877 as a historical marker, a kind of African '1066'. Glave related that if a thief was hauled before a village council for chicken stealing, he would give an account of his personal history by invoking the universally known formula *'Arlekaki Tendele mboka bis kaza kala'* ('When Stanley passed our village a long time ago').

Reputations could also be acquired by the lesser explorers and travellers if they stayed long enough in one area and had the skill, talent or charisma to impress their hosts. This happened to the more able station chiefs on the Congo in the 1880s, where it was said that to claim to be one of Stanley's 'children' guaranteed safe passage on the river. Among the Bangala Herbert Ward was known as *Nkumbe* ('the black hawk') for his skill as a hunter. But in other parts of the Congo his reputation derived from a 40-mile trek he completed in a single day on terrible roads from Kimpete to Lukungu. This won for him the title *Mayala Mbemba* ('the wings of an eagle').

E.J. Glave, another of Stanley's favourites, was known at first as *Mwana Tendele* ('son of Stanley'). An alternative title, among those whose principal emotion was fear, was *Barimu* ('ghost') as it was suggested he was originally an African who died and returned to earth with a white skin. Sharing the common belief that all white men came from the sea, the Congolese also thought that his clothes were made from the skins of unknown sea animals. But after distinguishing himself as a hunter Glave acquired the nickname *Makula* ('arrows') and enjoyed fame as a man who kept the village at Lukolela well supplied with the meat of hippo and buffalo. He was also considered a wizard. The novels he read were taken to be books of spells, and he was once asked to look into his mirror where the future was stored and see if a certain sick child would recover. Glave

put to good use his reputation as a wizard. One day at Lukolela he was
visited by 250 warriors in canoes, who stole his family heirloom knife and
fork. Glave knew that in the normal way he could retrieve his goods only
by bloodshed. He therefore used 'sorcery'. First he solemnly announced
to the warriors that he wanted his knife and fork back. Then he threw
some magnesia into a still pool of water. It effervesced and bubbled
alarmingly. He then informed the warriors that if they left without
returning the cutlery, he would cause such a storm over the entire Congo
and overwhelm their canoes. They at once returned the knife and fork.

So much for the reputation of the explorers. Their *impact* on African
society was very different. Not only does the latter category subdivide into
direct and indirect effects, but it is logically separate from *reputation*. An
explorer's reputation could be great but his impact nil, or his impact could
be great and his reputation nil. As we have seen with Stanley and
Livingstone, reputations required concentrated activity in a restricted
locale over a period of years. Explorers 'lacked the built-in fame
perpetuating machinery' later available to the colonial bureaucracies.
This explains the paradox that European historical nonentities often
occupied a greater place in oral tradition than many of the great explorers.
Colonialism perpetuated the memories of obscure officials and district
commissioners simply by impinging so closely and continuously on the
lives of African societies, in a way the explorers could not.

Arguably, though, something of the same rule of thumb holds good for
impacts as for reputations: an explorer's impact tended to be greatest
where he stayed longest. But an inverse relationship obtained with the
more advanced societies. Whereas Speke, Baker and Stanley entered oral
tradition in a significant way by their visits to Buganda and Bunyoro, their
impact there was nugatory. Baker claimed to have wiped out the slave
trade and extended Egypt's boundaries to the tropics. In fact he had done
neither. Nor had he placed steamers on the lakes or set up a chain of
stations on the model of the Hudson's Bay Company, as in his
instructions from the Khedive. The greatest impact of Baker's mission
was in Britain itself, where the very scale of his expedition aroused
economic, strategic and philanthropic interest in the southern Sudan.
Stanley, who in some parts of Africa was able to transform weaker social
systems almost overnight, was a marginal figure in Buganda, unless we
count his influence on the later missionary effort there. The stronger,
more cohesive African societies resisted the incursions of Europe much
longer, and it was not until the 1890s that Buganda and Bunyoro came
under the imperialistic thumb.

It is the category of *impact* rather than *reputation* that establishes a true
claim to historical significance. One index of greatness in an African

explorer is when the reputational curve intersects the impactive one, as it does in the case of Stanley and Livingstone. But most explorers' impacts were inconsiderable. They were mistaken for Arabs or regarded as quaint barbarians, much as George III's envoy was at the Chinese court in 1793. Some achieved a niche, limited in space and time. The well-known frontiersman Carl Wiese achieved a high position among the Ngoni as adviser to their chiefs. Explorers were often welcomed as potential protectors. Glave was offered several tusks of ivory if he would live among the Malinga tribe and protect them from Lufembe raiders. But in general the short-term effect of the explorers was deleterious. It may be, as the missionary Mackay reported, that Stanley had an effect in mitigating the harshness of Mutesa's rule, and that Robert Moffat achieved the same with Mzilikazi, but in general the short-term result of contact with the white man was that the tribes became richer and were able to buy more slaves, and that they became more powerful through the spread of firearms. The explorers contributed to the rise of some African empires by enabling them to get hold of guns and powder.

Exploration alerted Africans to a wider world, of wealth and superior technology. It broke up their tight tribal structures and destroyed their traditional religion, if only by showing that white man's 'fetish' was stronger. Brazza's journey on the Ogowé showed all these results occurring at once. His Winchester repeater, which could fire fourteen shots in a row, became a legend. He impressed the locals with magnesium cones and pretended that when using the sextant and the theodolite he was conversing with the moon. As he went upstream each tribe tried to prevent him from continuing, as they feared breaking the fetish that prevented them from going upstream themselves or, that if Brazza broke the fetish, retribution would fall on *them*. His safe return dispelled such superstitions over the length and breadth of the river. He also broke up the traditional system of middlemen, allowing Europeans to buy directly from the producers. 'Quelle différence,' commented Brazza on his homeward trip down the Ogowe in 1878. His impact had been remarkable. Trade was flourishing where before it had been moribund or blocked by inter-tribal jealousies.

But Brazza's peaceful example was not usually followed by the French in West Africa. Some of the later explorers were fire-eaters of the Peters stamp. Paul Crampel spread fire and sword in the Cameroons. Jean Dybowski, sent to avenge Crampel's slaying by the Snoussis on the Oubangui, executed five men in cold blood as reprisal. The bloody impact of French explorers and pioneers was one of the reasons why wars in Oubangui and Chad continued into the twentieth century. France, hoping to emulate Leopold's military successes in the Congo in the

1890s, found West Africa a much tougher nut to crack; until 1898 the religious solidarity of their Muslim enemies was reinforced by the Islamic kudos of the *mahdiya* in the Sudan.

When explorers opened up an area for colonial conquest, the bloody military campaigns often led to social chaos and devastation by disease. Harry Johnston, who tried to put the blame on to Kabbarega, described thus the consequences of the British invasion of Bunyoro: 'As if the misdemeanours of their fellow negroes were not sufficient for their misery and destruction . . . Providence . . . visited this wretched country with epidemics of disease.' Among the scourges of Bunyoro at this time were plague, dropsy, dysentery, smallpox, leprosy and syphilis. The opening up of tight tribal areas invariably led to epidemics. Stanley's penetration of the Congo added a seventh, sleeping sickness, and his journey across Africa in 1887–9 spread the disease across the continent.

Exploration also led to exogamy and mingling of the races. Tribes who had rarely stirred outside their ancient territories supplied labour for the explorers and were thus transported far from their motherlands. Ganda porters followed Stanley to the mouth of the Congo, Yao headmen went with Thomson to Masailand, Makololo with Livingstone to the Zambezi. In extreme cases the miscegenation was intercontinental. In the 1850s, 1860s and 1870s numerous Beluchi (natives of Beluchistan) traders, soldiers and adventurers accompanied or followed the explorers inland from Zanzibar. There were Beluchis in Burton and Speke's caravan. They represented a tall, light-skinned, hirsute, rather handsome type of northern Dravidian. These Beluchi adventurers were greatly admired by African women for their full beards and handsome features, and begat a numerous progeny in the regions east and south-west of Lake Tanganyika, leaving a distinct trace in the population there.

Livingstone's impact was greatest on the Mang'anja people of the Zambezi with whom he was in contact for nearly five years (1859–63). Livingstone encountered a centuries-old state system that had fragmented internally. The awesome complexity of African politics can be appreciated when a modern political-science microscope is applied to the Mang'anja chiefs. It turns out that there were four distinct areas with recognisable power bases: south-west, east, south-east and north-west. In the first of these alone there was conflict between three groups: traditional chiefs, middlemen and rebels. Headmen in the villages asserted their independence from the paramount chiefs by becoming middlemen in the slave trade. Into this maelstrom came the first of the explorers. When Livingstone reached the Shire, he encountered Tengani, one of the powerful Mang'anja chiefs who had retained power over his area by turning back the Portuguese. But Livingstone, by putting on a massive show of force, forced passage into Tengani's lands. By so doing he inadvertently opened the area to the slave traders.

Worse was to come. By refusing to believe that Mankhokwe was paramount chief, Livingstone further muddied already turbid waters. Mankhokwe was offended when Livingstone did not recognise how important he was. He was also apprehensive about the possible effect of this group of white men on his tenuous food supply. Livingstone then exacerbated the situation by making friends with Chibisa, who was using him as a dupe to further his ambitions. Even when Livingstone realised what was afoot, he refused to disown Chibisa, since he was the doctor's only friend and his territory was strategic for his aims. Livingstone's final interventionist act was to dismiss his Kololo porters for insubordination, while allowing them to retain their arms. In effect he failed in his human relations with them, then transferred to them the blame for the ultimate fiasco of his expedition. The Kololo story was that Livingstone had made wild promises to them which he could not keep, so they in turn were disappointed with him. When he returned to the area in 1861, he found that with the aid of their superior firearms the Kololo had made themselves a power in the land.

Later still, Livingstone's missionaries used their guns on the side of the Mang'anja against the Yao. The missionaries also sided with the Kololo, who were regarded by the Mang'anja as the Yao equivalent in the Shire highlands. This further alienated the Mang'anja. Finally, finding themselves pawns in local politics and thus faced with the choice of either pulling up sticks or entrenching themselves as an armed theocracy, the missionaries quit the area in 1862.

In 1863 both Tengani and Chibisa died. The valley was opened to invaders from south and west. At about the same time the Universities' Mission to Central Africa was withdrawn and Livingstone's expedition recalled. In the power vacuum left the Kololo, together with Yao gunmen and Mang'anja quislings, gained control and thus finally provided a strong central direction for the Mang'anja area. 'The ruthless force that the Mang'anja needed to unite again . . . was provided by Livingstone.'

To sum up, despite his official policy of non-intervention, Livingstone used threats against Tengani, spurned the authority of Mankhokwe, lent support to the upstart Chibisa, fired on the Yao, settled the foreign Kololo in the heart of the country, and opened the area to the ravages of the slave trade.

Such was Livingstone's *direct* impact. His indirect impact, especially after his death and apotheosis by Waller and others, was immense, since the Livingstone mystique affected the way entire generations of Britons thought and felt about Africa. Enterprises triggered by his heroic death on his last expedition included Cameron's crossing of Africa in 1873-5, Stanley's epic journey from the Indian Ocean to the Atlantic in 1874-7, Gordon's anti-slavery drive in the Sudan, and a host of missionary activity, including the establishment of Scottish missions in the Lake Nyasa area and a protective Livingstone trading company to shadow the missions there, a renewed mainland thrust by the Universities' Mission to Central Africa, and the setting up of missions on Lake Tanganyika by the London Missionary Society and the Church Missionary Society. Whatever local disruption Livingstone caused in the Shire by his *direct* impact, his indirect effect on African society was incalculable because of his fame and influence in England, and the missionary and other endeavours this engendered.

As with Livingstone, so with Stanley: it was not the moments of high drama that enabled them to make the most impact on Africa. What may be termed Livingstone's 'high adventures' were a product of the missionary travels up to 1856 and his last journey from 1866 to 1873. The stirring events of Stanley's life took place on the first (1871-2), second (1874-7) and fourth expeditions (1887-90). In the case of both men it was the intermediate time in Africa – (Livingstone's Zambezi expedition (1857-63) and Stanley's Congo sojourn (1879-84) – that enabled them fully to understand the African mind.

While Stanley was still a technical explorer, his impact was as limited as that of any other occasional visitor to the great African courts. But his return as Leopold's henchman sent a shiver through the Congo, whose tribes braced themselves for the expected shock. 'The return of Stanley to the mouth of the Congo in 1879 had caused a tremendous wave of anxiety to pass up and down the coast of Equatorial West Africa. The white man was coming again to interfere with this region.' Unwittingly, Stanley was about to deliver Central Africa to the most blatant system of exploitation the world had seen since the Ancient World.

The first ten years saw the preparation for 'take off' of Leopold's 'red rubber' state. The rate of change was rapid: the traveller Albert Thys declared that in the ten years from 1877 to 1887 the Bangala were transformed out of recognition. It was the classic dislocating effect of modernism on a primitive economy and society. When the white man first came to the Congo, the principal currency on the lower Congo was the 'gun', that is, the trade price of a gun. On the upper Congo, from Stanley Pool to Stanley Falls the basic unit of exchange was the *ntaku* or brass rod (plural *mitaku*) – in shape very like a small croquet hoop or an enormous hairpin. By bringing in large amounts of brass Stanley and his European aides caused a devaluation of the brass rod currency even as they introduced it to tribes where it had been unknown before. Usually it arrived from Europe in coils of about 60 lb weight, in thickness like a brass stair-rod. It was then cut into lengths of 10 in. and bent for convenience of transport. In the 1880s the *mitaku* became shorter and prices rose. The value of the brass rod was declining in proportion to its length, causing general price inflation: at the same time prices were fluctuating in real terms because of changing supply and demand in response to the arrival of European traders. After the Berlin Conference the Powers got down in earnest to the business of strangling indigenous competitors; on the Congo the Bobangi in particular felt the lash, in the form of 'punitive' campaigns in the late 1880s and early 1890s.

Stanley himself played a part in the process. In 1883 he gave medals and payment in kind to the chiefs of Kinkanza to encourage them to be local managers and suppliers of labour, especially porters. The payment in kind was a pig and a goat to those in the existing tribal hierarchy. But when some of the chiefs protested that the medals were 'bad medicine' and refused to co-operate, Stanley simply went behind their backs and supplanted them with more pliant individuals prepared to do his bidding. This tied tribal hierarchies to a cash nexus rather than old customs and traditions and eventually had the effect of replacing matrilineal succession by succession through the deceased chief's younger brother or sister's son. Stanley was impatient with all mores, customs or folkways that interfered with his purposes. One of the traditions on the lower Congo was the maintenance of political clientelism through the import and distribution of alcohol. When a chief demanded rum in return for his services, Stanley was able to seek general European legitimation for his destruction of the ancient ways by portraying the chief as a bibulous rascal.

White men soon began making inroads on middleman monopolies on the upper Congo: the so-called 'Great Congo Commerce' that governed the flow of trade from the Atlantic to Stanley Falls whereby ivory was exchanged for goods imported by European traders at the Congo estuary. The Berlin Treaty intensified the white man's incursions. The Congo Free State declared itself the owner of all land not actually in use by the 'natives' and reserved for itself the definition of 'use'. While formal slavery was abolished, *corvée* and the requisitioning of labour were introduced. Local traders were crushed, the tribal chiefs bought off by making them managers. Local cults were suppressed in favour of Christianity. All Africans were assigned menial tasks or roles in the new system.

Such were the momentous consequences of Stanley's return to the Congo in 1879–83. Yet his indirect impact was even greater. By venturing into the unknown in 1876, against Tippu Tip's advice, and then overcoming all obstacles, Stanley opened up a highway from Lake Tanganyika to the Atlantic. Tippu Tip and his slavers then moved into the previously unknown land. The net effect of Stanley's 1876-7 journey, therefore, was to force a switch from the historic long-distance trade routes. Until Stanley opened up the Congo and the Aruwimi, the tribes lived in security from Tippu Tip and his Arabs. But by the mid-1880s Tippu was using his 'Manyema hordes' to crush the Soko and other peoples in the Stanley Falls area.

The same pattern was repeated on the Emin Pasha expedition when Stanley unwittingly opened up the Ituri forest to the slavers. Stanley, in short, repeated on a large scale Livingstone's blunder when he browbeat chief Tengani into opening up the Shire river. But Stanley's indirect impact was greater in kind as well as degree. By removing the physical and psychological barriers to the Congo, and thus letting in Tippu Tip and the Arabs, Stanley also triggered a minor version of the disastrous *mfecane* of Southern Africa in the early nineteenth century, whereby a domino effect is caused by one tribe fleeing an aggressor, so that the successive tribes are shunted out of their traditional lands until they are crushed between two forces, in this case Tippu Tip and the Luba empire of Katanga.

Stanley's impact becomes even more significant if we regard the long-distance trade that he so disastrously affected as an 'African mode of production' analogous to the Asiatic mode that Marx explicitly recognised. It has been cogently argued that long-distance trade was itself a mode of production, possibly *the* dominant mode of production in pre-colonial Africa. Here we return in effect to the debate on wealth between Stanley and the Irebu, and its implications. According to the Western view, a mode of production by definition must produce a surplus value. Long-distance trade, on the other hand, is a mere transfer of wealth from one society to another. What we confront here is a clear conflict between African and European notions of what constitutes wealth.

The long-term cultural impact of Europeans, especially missionaries, takes us too far from the consequences of the explorers' journeys. There was a poignancy about the hopeless, unequal struggle of the African against the interloper that the more sensitive explorers sometimes noticed. Certainly the cultural traffic seems to have been mostly one way. Many English and French words were incorporated into African languages in a bastardised or bowdlerised form. Very few African words entered the European languages. 'Palaver', 'piccaninny' and 'fetish' are all corruptions of the Portuguese. 'Kraal' is from the Spanish 'corral'. 'Askari' and 'safari' are Arabian, 'ju-ju' is French 'jou-jou' and 'compound' is from Malayan 'kampong'. 'Mumbo-jumbo' is one of the few authentically African words. It is therefore all the more fitting that there is no one generic word or proper name in English that has the same denotation as *wangwana* – the largely unsung heroes of all African exploration.

16

The Psychology of the Explorers

African exploration was a highly dangerous business. Mungo Park died while fighting hostile tribesmen. Livingstone died at Ilala in the heart of the continent. Burton was a hair's breadth away from death during the night fight at Berbera. Baker had a narrow escape while fleeing Kabbarega and survived an assassination attempt. Stanley ran the gauntlet of some fifty battles during his four expeditions. Speke met an untimely and violent end. Most explorers died before reaching their fiftieth year, weakened and worn out by the toll Africa took. Livingstone and Stanley, who died at, respectively, sixty and sixty-three, had constitutions which would surely have made them nonagenarians had they stayed in Europe. Tropical diseases cut a swathe through both white men and their black porters. Fatalities on African expeditions were terrific: famine, drought and the elements added to the miseries of bacteria, viruses and insect-borne sickness. Virtually every explorer of any significance fought at least one battle with hostile tribes. There was an ever-present threat from wild animals, especially crocodiles. Why, then, did these men run such awesome risks? What was there in their psychological make-up that made them prefer the Dark Continent and all its perils to life in Europe?

The psychology of the explorers is best approached at three levels. In the first place, there are the explorers' own accounts of their motivations. These constitute valuable evidence but for obvious reasons can rarely be taken at face value. The second level of motivation consists in what we might call the 'objective interests' of the explorers. From an examination of their social status, their idiosyncrasies and their neuroses, we can see clearly the ways in which African exploration might well have served their interests better than a conventional life in Europe. The third, and most problematical level, concerns the unconscious drives and impulses of the explorers. It is here that the Dark Continent becomes the perfect

objective correlative for the dark side of the men who prised it open to the
outer world.

The psychology of explorers is as yet almost virgin territory. There are
very important distinctions to be drawn between the mental worlds of the
explorer proper and the traveller. Travelling can be viewed as a romantic
refuge from boredom and the mundane world of 'fumbling in a greasy
till'. It does not require particular acumen to see that travelling in the
Amazon with a view to writing a book which will then finance another
voyage, say to the Congo, is a rational means of enjoying life and escaping
the nine-to-five grind in the Circumlocution Office, or whatever the
alternative is. Travelling appeals to those with a low boredom threshold,
determined to hold at bay *noia, angst* and *ennui*. There is an exhilaration in
knowing that one is living fully by living life on the edge; arguably there is
an element also of holding depression at bay.

But when we contrast an accomplished traveller with a genuine
explorer, a whole new psychic world opens up. This can be seen in
contemporary terms by a casual examination of the career of two famous
Etonians, Sir Fitzroy Maclean (traveller) and Wilfred Thesiger
(explorer). Freud described exploration as a metaphor for proper
preparation for life. The principal motive for exploration is the healing of
some psychic wound, a quest for identity, or a 'bracketing' of one's own
reality. Burton's *obiter dicta* make this clear: 'Man wants to journey and he
must do so or he shall die'; 'Voyaging is victory'; 'Discovery is mostly my
mania'. The end result of the exploration is comparatively unimportant.
This basic point has entered the bloodstream of our understanding. 'To
travel hopefully is better than to arrive,' said Stevenson. *'N'importe
où, pourvu que ce soit ailleurs'* was Rimbaud's contribution. Wilfred
Thesiger made the same point in different words: 'I set myself a goal on
these journeys and although the goal itself was unimportant, its
attainment had to be worth every effort and sacrifice.'

The explorer, unlike the traveller, is afflicted by what Jakob Wassermann, in his analysis of Stanley, described as action neurosis. It is a
symptom found in many restless males (rarely in females); and accounts
for the phenomenon of early death after retirement in the case of many
thrusting businessmen. In the explorer such restlessness is raised to a new
power of monomania.

The corollary of this is a feeling of profound gloom and anticlimax
when the exploit draws to a close. After three years of intense hardship
and suffering, Stanley greeted the Indian Ocean, the terminal point of the
Emin Pasha Relief Expedition in December 1889, with a feeling close to
despair. After his Harar exploit in 1855 Richard Burton's feelings were
the same:

I had time, on the top of my mule, for musing upon how melancholy a thing is success. While failure inspirits a man, attainment reads the sad prosy lesson that all our glories 'are shadows not substantial things'. Truly said the sayer, 'disappointment is the salt of life' – a salutary bitter which strengthens the mind for fresh exertion, and gives a double value to the prize.

The influence of Romanticism clearly imbues the reasons given by the explorers for their quests. Here is Richard Lander:

'There was always a charm in the very sound of Africa that always made my heart flutter on hearing it mentioned whilst its boundless deserts of sand, the awful obscurity in which many of the interior regions were enveloped, the strange and wild aspect of countries that had never been trodden by the foot of a European, and even the failure of all former undertakings to explore its hidden wonders, united to strengthen the determination I had come to.

René Caillie wrote as follows:

The history of Robinson Crusoe, in particular, inflamed my youthful imagination. I was impatient to encounter adventures like him; nay, I already felt an ambition to make myself famous by some important discovery ... Geographical books and maps were lent to me: the map of Africa, in which I saw scarcely any but countries marked as desert or unknown, excited my attention more than any other. In short, this predilection grew into a passion for which I renounced everything. I no longer joined in the sports and amusements of my comrades. I shut myself up on Sundays to read all the books of travels that I was able to procure. I talked to my uncle, who was my guardian, of my desire to travel. He disapproved of it, forcibly representing the dangers which I should incur at sea, and the regret I should feel far away from my country and my family.

Sometimes the ostensible motivation seems a bit thin, as this *apologia* from Winwood Reade:

If I have any merit it is that of having been the first young man about town to make any bona fide tour in Western Africa; to travel in that agreeable and salubrious country and with no special object and at his own expense; to *flâner* in virgin forest; to flirt with pretty savages; and to smoke his cigar among cannibals.

But it is surely significant that Winwood Reade was not really an explorer in the true sense of one who genuinely blazes trails; Reade was more a *traveller*, or one who makes an expedition to the *little-known* as opposed to the absolutely *unknown*.

The desire to be 'first', to tread virgin soil, chart *terra incognita*, 'to boldly go where no man has gone before' was clearly a powerful conscious motive with most explorers. Cornwallis Harris, an early traveller in the Transvaal, said that there was something God-like about being the first white man in an area; it was like presiding over a new creation. Livingstone declared, 'The mere animal pleasure of travelling in a wild unexplored country is very great.' On the eve of reaching Lake Albert, which he believed to be the only true source of the Nile, Samuel Baker wrote: 'I hardly slept. For years I had striven to reach the "sources of the Nile". In my nightly dreams during that arduous voyage I had always failed, but after so much hard work and perseverance the cup was at my very lips, and I was to *drink* at the mysterious fountain before another sun should set.'

In Richard Burton's case, an insatiable quest for the novel and the exotic was combined with an almost existential sense of freedom when travelling in the African forests or the Arabian sands. He felt that departure 'upon a distant journey into unknown lands' was one of 'the gladdest moments in human life' and that Man was only truly happy when he had shaken off 'the fetters of Habit, the leaden weight of routine, the Cloak of many Cares, and the slavery of Homes'. He developed the theme as follows:

> Excitement lends unexpected vigour to the muscles, and the sudden sense of freedom adds a cubit to the mental stature. Afresh dawns the morn of life; again the bright world is beautiful to the eye, and the glorious face of nature gladdens the soul. A journey, in fact, appeals to the Imagination, to Memory, to Hope – the three sister Graces of our moral being.

A similar 'existentialist' outlook was embraced by Stanley, who confessed that only in Africa was he truly himself, only there did he have independence of mind. In Africa the human spirit 'is not repressed by fear, nor depressed by ridicule and insults . . . but now preens itself, and soars free and unrestrained, which liberty, to a vivid mind, imperceptibly changes the whole man'.

Complexities naturally arise when the motivation is more mixed. Here the *locus classicus* is Livingstone. There has always been debate about whether he was primarily explorer or missionary. 'I view the end of the geographical feat as the beginning of missionary enterprise', was his own view on the matter. But it is clear that in the 1840s he gradually became impatient with the slow, tedious life of a saver of souls and developed a passion for exploration, which his enemies stigmatised as self-aggrandisement. His 'missionary travels' of the late 1840s, when he discovered Lake Ngami, were really disguised explorations. Livingstone never made a single clear convert to Christianity. He quarrelled bitterly with the London Missionary Society and proved incapable of getting on with his white peers on the 1857–63 Zambezi expedition. In truth he was very far from the saint of the Livingstone legend. In so far as he wanted to preach the Gospel, Livingstone wanted to do so in very special circumstances: that is to say, in *unknown* parts of Africa and *alone*, without white companions as on the Zambezi expedition.

Waller, Livingstone's most devoted disciple, summed up the doctor's motives as follows: dissatisfaction with the artificiality of life in Britain; the opportunity to do good and to be left to one's own devices; and the enjoyment of a simple natural existence, without bustle and hurry, in 'state of nature' conditions – 'the nearest approach to what I suppose was one of the happiest of lives, the patriarchal form'. For Livingstone there was a more subtle form of psychological well-being than that enjoyed by those, like Stanley, who derived pleasure from the exercise of authority and the morality of strenuousness. This was the asceticism that came from a rejection of European material advantages, the authenticity of the 'purely religious' (as he saw it) life, the sense of moral trusteeship over the 'inferior' African, the contentment that came from doing good, and the consciousness of superiority exercised justly. Livingstone indeed enjoyed an 'overdetermined' satisfaction in his work, since he combined the missionary's perception of engaging in strenuous and dangerous tasks in Africa for Christ's sake with the secular lure of adventure that fired the imaginations of 'ordinary' explorers and hunters. On the eve of setting out on his last journey, when conditions seemed especially propitious – no white companions, no missionary constraints, the prospect of virgin territory – Livingstone expressed his euphoria:

> Now I am on the point of starting on another trip into Africa I feel quite exhilarated: when one travels with the specific object in view of ameliorating the condition of the natives every act becomes ennobled . . . No doubt much toil is involved, and the fatigue of which travellers in more temperate climes can form but a faint conception; but the sweat of one's brow is no longer a curse when one works for God: it proves a tonic to the system and is actually a blessing.

Livingstone also had a double source for his feelings of confidence and superiority. Not only was he, as an explorer, backed by the British Empire which dominated the world and to enforce credibility was quite willing to send expeditions against unruly potentates who harmed its subjects – as happened with Emperor Theodore in 1868 – he was also convinced that he had divine support for his mission and this provided a powerful psychological bulwark against loneliness, hostility, discomfort and disease. This consciousness of being an agent of Providence and thus one of God's elect (his enemies called it self-satisfaction) gave Livingstone a peculiar strength and self-sufficiency which seemed to Stanley, when he observed it in 1871–2, to be almost solipsistic:

> He has lived in a world which revolved inwardly, out of which he seldom awoke except to attend to the immediate practical necessities ... then relapsed again into the same happy inner world, which he must have peopled with his own friends, relations, acquaintances, familiar readings, ideas and associations; so that wherever he might be, or by whatsoever he was surrounded, his own world always possessed more attractions to his cultured mind than were yielded by external circumstances.

Livingstone himself spoke of the sustenance he received from the realisation that he was doing God's work:

> I have lost a great deal of happiness, I know, by these wanderings. It is as if I had been born to exile; but it is God's doing ... I am away from the perpetual hurry of civilisation, and I think I see far and clear into what is to come; and then I seem to understand why I was led away, here and there, and crossed and baffled over and over again, to wear out my years and strength.

If these were the kinds of motives actually expressed by the explorers, how far were they compatible with their real interests? It is unquestionable that African exploration offered a unique opportunity for social advancement to the underprivileged of Europe and a rapid means of ascent of the greasy pole for the already privileged. In this respect it may be likened as a safety valve to the role of the frontier in nineteenth-century North America or to twentieth-century sport vis-à-vis the proletariat. Livingstone and Stanley both rose from spectacularly humble origins. Stanley was the illegitimate son of a promiscuous mother and was raised in a Welsh workhouse; Livingstone rose from Blantyre poverty and an apprenticeship in a Lanarkshire cotton mill. Even for those not so disadvantaged by birth, exploration provided a short cut to the glittering prizes. Stanley, Baker and Johnston became territorial governors. Lugard, following a failed love affair, thought first of suicide or death in action. He decided to solve his problems through Africa, and tried to join the Italian army on its way to the invasion of Abyssinia; as a schoolboy he had written an adulatory essay on Livingstone. Arriving in Africa penniless, Lugard found himself caught up in the struggles in the Lake Nyasa area, published a series of important books, and ended up as a famous pro-consul.

Africa was also good to many on the fringes of exploration. Missionaries who at home would have been obscure parsons wielded immense power and influence. Others used exploration as a stepping stone to wealth and fame. Alfred Sharpe progressed from exploring to governor of Nyasaland: Frederick Jackson did the same in Uganda. John Kirk, the other 'Zambezi doctor', moved from exploration to the Zanzibar consulate. Selous became an intimate of Theodore Roosevelt. Even a failure like Livingstone's son Charles secured a consulate at Fernando Po.

African exploration also provided an outlet for those whose psychology was affronted by, alien to or incompatible with mainstream European civilisation. Within the context of Great Britain this often meant Celts, 'outsiders' in terms of the dominant Anglo-Saxon culture. Livingstone, Stanley and Burton represented, respectively, the Scots, Welsh and Irish strains. Scotland was particularly to the fore in African exploration. It supplied Bruce, Park, Livingstone, Cameron, Grant, Thomson, Clapperton, Moffat, Mackay, as well as many lesser travellers and missionaries. This fact fascinated Stanley and he tried to make sense of it by postulating that the English were contemptuous of the notion of duty, while the Scots took it seriously. Writing to Alexander Bruce, who married Livingstone's daughter Agnes, he said:

> Apropos of Scotchmen, can you tell me why they succeed oftener than other people? Take Moffat, Livingstone, Mackay, real Scotchmen with the burr. They stand pre-eminent above all other missionaries no matter what nationality. It is not because they are Scotchmen that they succeed. It is not because they are better men in any one way or the other, physically, mentally or morally – of that you may rest assured – but it is because they have been more educated in one thing than all others. While I say this, I reviewed mentally all whom I know and have met – and I repeat the statement confidently. That one thing is duty.

But alienation did not need to be racial or cultural. A powerful psychological precipitant towards adventure in the wilderness in general, and African exploration in particular, was nineteenth-century disgust for industrialisation and urbanisation. The most cursory examination of Dickens' novels illustrates how the great city in the mid-nineteenth century bred aversion, alienation and feelings of inauthenticity. Some responded to the challenge of the cities by burrowing into its secrets, exposing the dreadful lives of its slum dwellers and generally laying bare the 'Dark Continent' right in the heart of civilisation; this was the method of Dickens, Zola and the Goncourt brothers.

Personalities otherwise so very different as Herbert Ward and Frederick Lugard shared a distaste for urban life. Joseph Thomson confided that he could not settle to life in Great Britain after being in

Africa. He regretted that the advent of trade, civilisation and imperialism to Africa meant that the romance was going out of African travel. He let his readers know that if people were henceforth going to look on palm trees as sources of profit rather than things of beauty, he would prefer to travel in the Polar regions, In his novel *Ulu* he described civilisation as 'the most monstrous fraud and imposture in the world' and was deeply sceptical of the long-term benefits of introducing this charlatan into Africa. Conversely he thought of many African societies as veritable Arcadias: one of his favourite peoples were the Taveita, a mixed community of settled Masai and Akamba and Chagga who lived on the lower forested slopes of Mt Kilimanjaro. He praised their stockaded town with its representative form of government as a perfect society. Harry Johnston and the newspaper correspondent Thomas Stevens, who cycled round the world and reported the latter stages of the Emin Pasha expedition, concurred in this judgement. Another similar Thomson utopia was among the Wankonde at the north end of Lake Nyasa.

For those repelled by urbanisation, Africa provided the perfect release. A.J. Swann expressed the feeling well:

> The silence of the forest is a welcome change from the noisy city and one's manhood seems to assert itself much more when entirely cut off from European associations. Perhaps the sense of individuality is the main attraction. In the constant whirl of civilisation the personal element is somewhat lost in the mass. Out in the forests of Africa you are *the* man amongst your surroundings.

Since the explorers' response to the challenge of industrialisation and urbanisation was to get out of Europe as fast as possible, it is no surprise to find that they regarded with contempt those who tried to solve such problems. Particular animus was directed at socialists and egalitarians. The psychology is clear. Collaborationist solutions in a sense threatened the explorers' very identity. Exploration was self-help raised to the power of infinity. Civilisation meant *interdependence*; what the explorers wanted was *independence* – the knowledge that success or failure depended entirely on one's own efforts.

The desire for solitude, for the wilderness undisturbed by sign or sentinel of civilisation, the preference for the savage, noble or otherwise, pessimism about the potential of one's fellow humans, a belief in original sin and the efficacy of force, these are all signs of the romantic reactionary. It is no surprise, then, to find that explorers, in the main, occupy the Far Right end of the political spectrum. The 'explorer as reactionary' syndrome is best typified in our own time by a man like Wilfred Thesiger, who ascribed the Ethiopian revolution of 1974, which overthrew Haile

Selassie, to the indoctrinating influence of English and American 'communist' schoolteachers. When the explorer is, additionally, a man of humble origins, we observe the familiar Nietzschean reaction that socialism is for the weak and the cowardly, for those unable to make it to the top by their own strength or courage.

All these currents are observable in Stanley. He believed in the smiting vengeful Yahweh of the Old Testament rather than Jesus Christ and the law of love. He had a strong antipathy to socialism, predictable in a workhouse brat made good, for we have already observed that such individuals invariably feel that 'levelling down' diminishes their own status and achievements. Stanley in any case had a peculiar perception of socialism. He regarded it as a form of degeneration or atavism, whereby Man longed to return to the classlessness of primitive societies before the division of labour. In particular he equated it with the technically classless primitive societies of Africa, before the rise of a State in which the task of government becomes the responsibility of full-time officials, like the kabaka's prime minister or *katikiro* in Buganda. Stanley's conception of socialism was influential: Herbert Ward reproduced it almost word for word in his reflections on Africa.

At various times in his life Stanley made clear his distaste for the dispensations of the Left. In correspondence with him in 1885 Dorothy Tennant, his future wife, made the mistake of sympathising with the plight of the Durham miners and saying she thought the future of England lay with the working man. Stanley hit back at once with a homily about the superiority of Nature to society – a clear hint that he thought social inequality a phenomenon as natural as gravity. During the 1893 coal strike he launched a bitter attack on the miners. 'If I had any money to spare at the present time, it would not be given to men who were determined to be sulky and who, to spite the coal owners, preferred to starve.'

Even the 'saintly' Livingstone was a political reactionary, His prejudice against the Irish was notorious. And this is what the man who as a boy had toiled fourteen hours a day in a mill had to say about revolution:

> The masses of the working people of Scotland have read history and are no revolutionary levellers. They rejoice in the memories of 'Wallace and Bruce and a' the lave' who are still much revered as the former champions of freedom. And while foreigners imagine that we want the spirit only to overturn capitalists and aristocracy, we are content to respect our laws till we can change them, and hate those stupid revolutions which might sweep away time-honoured institutions, dear alike to the rich and poor.

But perhaps the most clear-cut example of the explorer as political reactionary is Burton. He was a deep-dyed pessimist about his fellow-man, and this led him to embrace many hard-line 'right-wing' positions. He had no qualms about the supreme penalty, and thought that all punishment for civil offences should be severe: hefty fines for the rich and corporal punishment for the poor. He was no believer in civil rights: 'Perhaps if the police of civilised England were backed by the powers that be in the same way that the *Zaotiyeh* is protected in barbarous Turkey, we might have less of Fenians, Bradlaugh, Beadles, park-rioters and other treasonable demagogues.' He was a convinced social Darwinist and quoted approvingly Carlyle's 'Nature herself is umpire and can do no wrong.'

Burton detested egalitarianism and socialism and hated even more the 'do-gooding' humbug of humanitarians and missionaries. He thought England was bedevilled by a 'rage for equality' among people and classes born unequal; for him democracy was always synonymous with mediocrity. But since the entrenched power élite of England had to defend itself against the demands of mass society, it did so by paying lip service to 'equality' while fighting fiercely for the hereditary principle. The net consequence was that there was no place in the sun for men of real talent: society's most valuable members were caught in a vice between the rhetoric of 'levelling down' and the reality of aristocratic privilege.

Like almost all conservatives of a nostalgic, reactionary stripe, Burton sought inspiration in a mythical 'golden age' in the past. For Burton this was the Middle Ages, when the martial ethos was uppermost, when gentlemen settled disputes by the 'code of honour', and when skill with the sword gave victory to the most valiant. The age of firearms was for him the technological equivalent of the age of liberalism, since both gave victory to the weak, the cowardly and the mediocre, in one case through guns, in the other through the voting system. Burton's writings are full of nostalgic laments for the bygone days when his beloved sword was sovereign.

The coming of a modern industrial society caused the Victorians acute anxiety and trauma, and they sought a return to authentic human roots in a number of different ways. Typical solutions can be found in Ruskin, Carlyle, Morris, Kingsley and Matthew Arnold. Burton's solution and that of the other explorers was, to use Mark Twain's words, to 'light out for Indian territory': to escape to virgin territory, unknown lands, to experience at first hand something of the flavour of a heroic age, when technology did not give victory to the weakest and most cowardly – not that this ever prevented Burton and the others from making sure they were equipped with the latest weaponry before venturing into the Dark Continent.

Yet the explorers were not simply impelled towards their exploits by rational motives of self-interest, improvement and idealism or by conscious distaste for and dissatisfaction with nineteenth-century European society. Irrational impulses and unconscious drives also powered them on their quest. Roughly speaking we may distinguish three deep psychological motives: a desire to return to the pleasure principle of childhood, a death drive, and a displaced, transmogrified or sublimated sexuality.

Before looking at each of these in turn, it may be interesting to note an ambitious attempt to combine all three unconscious drives in a general psychoanalytical theory of exploration. The author of this general theory is Melanie Klein. Some may feel that her explanation is slightly too pat and contrived. After all, it is *a priori* unlikely that *all* African explorers would follow a common pattern. Her theory transcends space and time and seems to apply to *all* explorers in *all* epochs. By failing to account for the specificity of African explorers it presents, much like Erich Fromm's theory on the psychology of fascism, an explanation for a phenomenon detached from its specific chronology. Nevertheless, it does indicate some broad lines of enquiry and does make the important point that the psychology of explorers cannot simply be reduced to their own utterances as to motives.

> In psycho-analytic work it has been found that phantasies of exploring the mother's body, which arise out of the child's aggressive sexual desires, greed, curiosity and love, contribute to the man's interest in exploring new countries.

Klein then explains that the child's aggressive impulses give rise to strong feelings of guilt and to fear of the death of the loved person:

> In the explorer's unconscious mind, a new territory stands for a new mother, one that will replace the loss of the real mother. He is seeking the 'promised land' – the 'land flowing with milk and honey'.

Klein hypothesises that the child turns away from the earlier intense feelings he entertained for the mother through fear of her death. He is then led to recreate her in new endeavours. In exploration both the escape from her and the original attachment find full expression. The child's early aggression stimulates the drive to restore and to make good, to put back into his mother the good things he robbed her of in fantasy. These wishes to make good merge into the later drive to explore, for by finding new land the explorer gives something to the world at large and to a number of people in particular. In his pursuit the explorer gives vent to both aggression and the drive to reparation. Aggression comes in the form of struggling against disease, the elements and hostile tribes. Klein gives the following explanation for the frequent battles of the Stanleys and Bakers: 'Some of the early phantasised attacks against the imaginary babies in the mother's body, and actual hatred against new-born brothers and sisters, were expressed in reality by aggression against the natives.' The wished-for restoration, however, finds expression in repopulating the country with people of the explorer's own nationality.

Much of this is highly speculative. But what does seem clear and unexceptionable is that in exploration various impulses and emotions – aggression, feelings of guilt, love and the drive to reparation – can be transferred to another sphere, far away from the original person. Hence the importance of the trio of motifs mentioned above: childhood, death and sexuality.

The psychobiographer Fawn Brodie, after examining the motivations of Livingstone, Stanley, Burton and Baker and in particular noting the many references to the sources of the Nile as the 'cradle' of Africa, concluded that a flight from the reality principle was a principal unconscious drive of the explorers of Africa: 'For all these men the escape into Africa seems to have been a return, if not all the way back to the cradle, at least to childhood. The childish nightmares too were real, for no voyager travelled without the constant possibility of treachery and massacre.'

The classic expression of exploration as return to childhood and the pleasure principle comes in Mannoni's theory that the prime attraction of areas of 'primitive' culture to nineteenth-century Europeans was found in what he called a 'Prospero' complex, the desire to live in a world where one's individuality is enhanced by the possibility of ignoring the personalities of others. Just as Prospero had his Caliban, so Livingstone had his 'faithfuls', Stanley his *wangwana* and so on. The one thing they never had was *equals*, or when they did the result was disaster. All five white men who accompanied Stanley on his first two expeditions perished. European fatalities in the 1879–84 Congo period were well into double figures, to the point where Leopold, no 'bleeding heart', felt it necessary to send Stanley a warning. Two of Stanley's British officers on the Emin Pasha expedition met tragic deaths. Livingstone, for his part, could not collaborate with any other white man; hence the débâcle of the Zambezi expedition.

There was, then, a pervasive assumption by the explorers that Africa was a kind of colossal playground where the individual human personality could express itself in a fashion impossible in civilisation. Missionaries, with the idealism of adults, wanted to *introduce* civilisation into Africa; the explorers, with the cynicism and selfishness of children, wanted to *escape* from the same civilisation. The notion of a 'Prospero' complex also receives support from other sources. The early explorers liked to bamboozle the tribes with 'magic' and to encourage the idea that white men were wizards. Only when it was accepted that both sides were genuine human beings, with the same basic emotions and pre-occupations, could real progress in relations between the races commence. So too Prospero is redeemed as a genuine human being only when he renounces his magic staff and learns acceptance. Also of great significance is the frequent reference in explorers' memoirs to the childhood influence of *Robinson Crusoe*. The *beau idéal* of living simply and alone, or with a subservient Man Friday, far from civilisation alerts us that the Rousseauesque interpretation of Crusoe as man in a state of nature had a far more powerful resonance than Defoe's simple fable of Economic Man (Crusoe alone) and Political Man (Crusoe with Friday).

It does not take exceptional insight to see that the desire to joust with the manifold perils of the 'Dark Continent' masks an unconscious attraction towards death. Some of the missionaries came close to making such a latent drive manifest by sanctifying death in Africa as a kind of martyrdom. With other explorers darker forces still may have been in operation. One study of Mungo Park sees him as a typical product of a Lowland Scot sensibility obsessed with notions of death and evil, 'a little people on a dark little stage, an unhappy questing people haunted by the unpleasant after-effects of death'. James Hogg and Robert Louis Stevenson are the obvious literary figures here, but it is of more than passing interest that Livingstone confessed to having given up the study of astrology, to which he was deeply attracted, because he thought that to proceed further with such arcane knowledge was to make a Faustian pact with the devil.

The classic 'death drive' candidate among the explorers was Speke. Speke was a repressed homosexual with a mother fixation. His intense relationship with his mother led to a profound unconscious jealousy of his siblings. The few extant remarks of Speke about his elder brother bear this out – 'an idle country squire' is how he characterised him. This hatred of siblings extended to all who would have fraternal relations with him, whether of rivalry or dominance as with Burton, or even of deference and submission as with Grant (who, three weeks older and with a more distinguished military record, counted as 'elder brother'). Speke 'solved' the sibling problem by pathological behaviour when out hunting. To the horror of his African bearers, who correctly intuited that the white man's action was some sort of blow struck at fertility and childbearing in general, Speke evinced a taste for eating the embryos of the pregnant female animals he killed. The unconscious impulse for this strange behaviour is likely to have been 'revenge' against his siblings for being rivals for his mother's affections.

Speke's latent homosexuality, which was the undercurrent beneath his famous quarrel with Burton, also derived from mother fixation and consequent narcissism. The externalising of the replaced mother in the form of homosexual lovers never occurred with Speke. Instead he remained trapped at the level of auto-eroticism where the oedipal boy puts himself in his mother's place as love object. This explanation would account for two motifs, occurring respectively in Burton's accounts of Speke and in Speke's own books. The first is Speke's unconscionable and limitless self-esteem that Burton found buried just beneath a veneer of shyness and gaucherie. The second is the mother leitmotif found throughout Speke's published (and unpublished) work.

Maternal images haunted Speke's dreams. Sometimes he confused and conflated his own mother and Queen Victoria. Naming his greatest discovery the Victoria Nyanza, which in another man would have been a simple act of royalist devotion, could then have been a transmogrification of his intense feelings for his mother, as both Fawn Brodie and Alexander Maitland, keen students of Speke, suggest. And Speke, insensitive to the sight of blood and the many horrors of Africa, could be stirred to indignation at any example of lack of maternal feelings. He contrasted the lack of motherly sensitivity exhibited by African women unfavourably with the gallant protection of cubs by she-bears he had shot.

Rivalry with his siblings for mother love and the awful suspicion that he might not be his mother's favourite explains both the foetus fetish and a recurring childhood recollection which he described as follows: 'My old nurse used to tell me with great earnestness of a wonderful abortion shown about the fairs of England – a child born with a pig's head; and as solemnly declared that this freak of nature was attributable to the child's mother having taken fright at a pig when in the interesting stage.' The recurrence of this story in Speke's mind hints of fears that he could have been that child, and even figuratively – in point of his mother's affections – might have been. It is certainly intriguing that Speke uses porcine imagery far more than events warrant. A buffalo he had mortally wounded is described as 'standing like a stuck pig'. Even more interestingly, the Queen Mother of Buganda is described as drinking 'pig fashion'. Significantly, Burton identifies Speke's most self-destructive piece of behaviour as being the occasion when he (Burton) had to stop Speke buying and killing a pig, since roasting such an animal would have lost the expedition all credibility with the Arabs and the Muslim *wangwana*.

What makes Speke such a fascinating psychological study is that alongside the homosexuality and the mother fixation was a pronounced death drive. During his very first African expedition, in Somalia, he told Burton that he had come to Africa to be killed. Burton regarded this merely 'as a kind of whimsical affectation', but a close study of Speke shows that there was more to it than that. After all, on each of his three African expeditions, Speke came within an angel's brush of death, quite apart from the risks he continually ran when hunting dangerous animals. His narrow escape at Berbera was followed in 1857–8 by a fever so severe that Burton admitted that he regarded his companion as all but dead and buried. At the court of Mutesa in 1862 Speke was at one point a hair's breadth away from execution. And Africa did, in a sense, kill him in the end. It was on the day before he was due to debate the sources of the Nile with Burton at a meeting of the British Association in Bath in September 1864 that he had his fatal accident and shot himself. It was often queried, especially in the light of the many obscure circumstances surrounding the death, whether the 'accident' might have been suicide. A genuine conscious attempt at self-slaughter seems unlikely. What is much more likely – and certainly more plausible than that a man with twenty years' experience of heavy guns, who had always been observed to be meticulous in the way he handled firearms, should have shot himself by accident – is that in a mood of depression and anxiety about the coming encounter, where he was sure to be dialectically worsted by the quicksilver Burton, Speke's conscious mind relaxed its controls over the unconscious death drive.

The classic sign of a death drive is an excessive aggression directed towards the external world. Speke's slaughter of wildlife provides an almost textbook illustration. There is something very disturbing about the hippo hunting scene on the Pangani after the visit to Fuga, where Burton shows Speke in his element. The lust for slaughter is excessive even by Victorian 'sporting' standards and the killing is gratuitous, for Burton makes it clear that the carcasses could not be retrieved for meat. On one day Speke killed six hippo and mortally wounded a dozen others.

Whenever a head appears an inch above water, a heavy bullet 'puds' into or near it; crimson patches marble the stream; some die and disappear, others plunge in crippled state; while others, disabled from diving by holes drilled through their snouts, splash and scurry about with curious snorts, caused by the breath passing through wounds. A baby hippo, with the naïveté natural to his age, uprears his crest, doubtless despite the maternal warning; off flies the crown of the little kid's head. The bereaved mother rises for an instant, viciously regards the infanticide, who is quietly loading, snorts a parent's curse, and dives as the cap is being adjusted.

Many similar passages can be extracted from Speke's own work. One of the reasons he got on so well with James Grant on the 1860–3 expedition was that Grant shared his enthusiasm for shooting and was prepared to indulge his murderous frenzies more readily than Burton. Speke's rapport with Mutesa of Buganda was at least partly explained by their common lust for blood, though in Mutesa's case it was the human variety. And it was on the same expedition that Bombay, on questioning an order, had his front teeth smashed out by three vicious blows from Speke.

Numerous incidents attest to a feeling in Speke that all purposeful activity must be crowned by death. His biographer describes thus the moment of his discovery of Lake Victoria in 1858:

> Having attained the southern extremity of the lake, Speke celebrated the event in his customary fashion. As he trotted along, his 'trusty Blissett made a florikan pay the penalty of death for his temerity in attempting a flight across the track'. It is as if the brooding spirit with whom Speke held intensely private communion demanded a sacrifice of blood in return for its favours, if not to compensate some transgression. In this and other similar killing there is evidence of a primitive submission to ritual, for their pattern is constant and clearly defined.

In some ways even more impressive evidence for Speke's death drive comes from the record of his feverish dreams, so unlike those of Burton on the same journey. Burton had a sensation of divided identity – of being two distinct people who opposed each other. In his delirium he felt he had wings and could fly. Speke dreamt of 'tigers, leopards, and other beasts harnessed with a network of iron hooks, dragging him like the rush of a whirlwind over the ground'. It seemed that the animals he had killed so wantonly were returning for their revenge. The flight symbolism of Burton's dreams spoke of sexuality and creative endeavour hampered by an unintegrated personality. It was anxiety mixed with hope. If Burton's dreams spoke of Eros, those of Speke pointed to Thanatos.

Sexuality is an obvious candidate as prime mover among the explorers' unconscious drives, if only because libido so often breached the surface of consciousness. Exploration, after all, can almost be said to entail instinctual renunciation. The most successful explorers were those who evinced clear patterns of sexual repression, anxiety and sublimation: Speke, Burton, Livingstone, Stanley.

It is here that we see important evidence for the distinction made earlier between the psychology of the traveller and the explorer proper. Many travellers in Africa were prepared to accept sex with local women on a temporary or permanent basis. It was generally agreed that African women, if not disfigured by the lip-ring or worn out by frequent childbirth, were physically attractive. The travellers Thomas Baines and Frank Mandy particularly extolled the charms of Matabele girls, and there are similar encomia in the works of Faulkner and Chaillé-Long.

Because of Victorian prudery, the isolated areas where hunters and travellers followed the trail-blazing of the genuine explorers, and the fact that most travellers were too prudent to tell the unvarnished truth to an audience of Mrs Grundys, it is difficult to establish the extent of miscegenation, dalliance and temporary 'marriages'. But to judge from tell-tale passages in Livingstone's works, it is likely to have been widespread and commonplace. Oral tradition endorses this judgement, as does common sense. Indeed, one of the motives for living on the frontier was to escape from the trammels of civilisation, its discontents and its prudery. The greatest freedom available on the frontier was sexual freedom and indulgence.

Many hunters, traders and travellers saw sexual liaisons with African women as expedient as well as pleasurable. One could get inside a culture so much more easily and learn its indiosyncracies, unspoken codes and deep structures. The ill-fated Stokes was one trader who used this method. Francis Galton reported that the only way to know what was really going on in Africa was to have a close relationship with an African woman. Burton openly advocated female camp-followers, on the grounds that they were a safety-valve for the *wangwana*; angry and frustrated porters beat their women to let off steam but if there were no women present they fought each other, thus complicating the explorer's task.

In the midst of such easy sexuality, it is not surprising that white men with inhibitions or moral scruples about promiscuous intercourse were prone to deep anxieties. Missionaries, in particular, were constrained both by their own moral code and by the monitoring of their lives from London; a single peccadillo could lead to recall and disgrace. In the case of highly sexed heterosexual males like Livingstone, the anxiety hardened into neurosis and depression.

Exact scholarship does nothing for the hagiography of Livingstone, or for the 'Saint David' of Victorian legend. Curiously, an appreciation of Livingstone's dark interior ultimately makes him seem a greater figure than ever, a recognisable human being rather than a plaster saint. After Graham Greene we are better acquainted with the sinner who is closer to God than the pious 'unco guid'. Livingstone fits such a matrix very well, for he had more than his share of human failings. Principal among these were an inability to get along with other white men (the 'father–son' relationship with Stanley is the exception that proves the rule) and a pathological determination to be 'first' in his explorations and not to have to share the credit with co-workers. Livingstone on the Zambezi expedition provided an almost textbook example of failure in 'man management'. Here is recent judgement on his behaviour towards his European companions: 'He was unconcerned for their interests and lacked insight into their problems. He viewed their illnesses as malingering, disagreement as insubordination, and failure as culpable negligence.' Kirk, having suffered the rough edge of Livingstone's tongue, recorded this opinion in 1862: 'I can come to no other conclusion than that Dr Livingstone is out of his mind.'

The desire to be the first to discover everything and the refusal to share glory with other Europeans led Livingstone to downgrade the contributions of his companions and, if necessary, to be 'economical with the truth' in order to discredit them. On his early travels he failed to acknowledge the contribution, both financial and in terms of exploration, made by the self-effacing and altruistic William Cotton Oswell, or to salute the discoveries and travels of the Hungarian Lazlo Magyar and the Portuguese Candido Cardoso. On the Zambezi he lied about the Makololo missions and traduced the missionary Roger Price to escape censure for having grossly misrepresented the situation with Sekeletu in Barotseland.

At the limit Livingstone was even prepared to be as violent as Stanley. In 1859 he beat an insubordinate Makololo with a cook's ladle. Nine days later he thrashed a troublesome stoker and told Kirk he would 'break the heads' of any troublemakers. Even Stanley, who worshipped Livingstone, could not conceal the doctor's monomania and fantasies of violence towards the white men on the Zambezi expedition who had 'betrayed' him. In March 1872, after four months in his company, he wrote: 'I have had some intrusive suspicious thoughts that he was not of such angelic temper as I believed him to be during my first month with him.'

The most recent research establishes Livingstone as a victim of cyclothymia or hereditary manic depression. The cyclical nature of this illness led to his notable persecutions of European assistants such as Richard Thornton and Thomas Baines. It may be speculated that a trigger for the depressive downturn was sexual anxiety, for there are many explicit references to sex in Livingstone's work, unusually for a Victorian Christian. He liked to keep his wife with him during his African travels, and was heavily censured for his 'selfishness' in exposing her to the fever that killed her. He was mortified when it was known that his wife became pregnant during the voyage out from Britain to Africa, as this demonstrated to the world that he could not control his 'lusts'. His mother-in-law attacked him for insisting that his wife be at his side in Africa. 'O Livingstone . . . will you again expose her and them [his children] in those sickly regions on an *exploring* expedition? All the world will condemn the cruelty of the thing.'

Livingstone's work reveals persistent sexual anxiety. Sexual frustration loomed large in his world-view. He condemned African women for their practice of refusing their men intercourse while breastfeeding. He fulminated that male colonists were unable to find wives among 'the healthy, hardy, blooming daughters' of the 'honest poor' because workhouse 'hussies' were sent out on emigration schemes instead. And there is a sense of protesting too much in his declaration that he had never met an African woman beautiful enough to tempt him to sexual intercourse; even the prettiest, he added, were as nothing to a British servant girl.

Livingstone was simultaneously fascinated and horrified by sexuality – a typical Victorian neurosis. He castigated African women for using abstinence as a contraceptive but condemned miscegenation as a great evil: he thought that Arab men who lived with African women degenerated and took on the peculiar odour of the African. He also considered that when Portuguese officers took black 'wives', a transfer of colour as well as vitality was the result. He was morbidly obsessed with the consequences when a young person slept with someone much older. He thought of this as a kind of vampirism, whereby the young partner lost vitality while the older one gained it. He went so far as to discuss these ideas with Professor (later Sir) Richard Owen. Owen suggested that married couples too might develop similar features, as when the pregnant woman carried 'the blood of a being only half her own circulating through every part of her system.'

Sexuality was also the prime mover with Richard Burton. Burton's sexual personality was fundamentally bisexual but he had 'sex in the head' in a more overt way than Livingstone, as his learned interest in sexology and his many translations of erotica suggest. It appears that his heterosexual proclivities may have been blunted after his liaisons in India with local mistresses or *bubus*, who laughed on discovery that European males ejaculated quickly and had not learned the 'retaining art' of prolonging intercourse for an hour or more. It is significant that, though Burton subsequently took mistresses, as among the Gogo women in 1858, he was inept at the art of seduction and married a 'safe', unchallenging, virginal Catholic. There is no evidence of a white mistress at any stage in his life.

The homosexual side of his personality, probably caused by over-developed bonding with his brother Edward in the vacuum left by his feckless parents, seems to have been active only rarely. But it is clearly present both in his writings, especially in the learned notes to his famous translation of *The Arabian Nights*, and in the long line of brother-surrogates (among them, temporarily, Speke) that marked his passage through life. Nobody reading Burton can be unaware that libido in all its manifestations lurks just below the surface.

In the case of Stanley we confront the most difficult psychological conundrum of all. Stanley's life has always attracted psychobiographers. Jakob Wassermann saw him as in the grip of 'action neurosis', a mania for action where ends and means become confused. John Bierman concludes that he was a repressed homosexual. Emyr Wyn Jones has speculated that he was in the grip of a 'Phaethon complex'. Gerben Hellinga sees him as 'a choleric with a personality disorder which Adler designates the Ruling Type'.

My own view is that Stanley suffered from a schizoid personality disorder. The schizoid personality classically combines a desperate need for love with a desperate fear of intimacy. This is the syndrome observable in Stanley. There must be doubt whether he ever consummated his marriage with Dorothy Tennant, but before contracting it he had managed to contrive his own rejection by her. With the three previous 'romances' in his life he followed the same pattern. With Virginia Ambella in 1868, Katie Gough-Roberts in 1869 and Alice Pike in 1874, Stanley felt deeply attracted, but the 'civil war' within led him to self-destructive actions such that he did not have to consummate the romance. In a word, unconsciously he willed his own rejection. The origin of Stanley's fear of sex lies in his disastrous childhood – a childhood that featured his own illegitimacy, a promiscuous mother and his daily witness of every manner of vice in St Asaph's workhouse: amateur prostitution, casual dalliance, child abuse and sodomy.

If Stanley was a repressed heterosexual he was also a repressed homosexual. At every period of his life, even on his honeymoon in 1890, he liked to have the company of the current young male of his choice. There is a long line of these, beginning with Lewis Noe in the 1860s and ending with Mounteney-Jephson in the 1890s. Part of Stanley's schizoid profile, then, is a kind of repressed bisexuality. Seeking an outlet, his libido finally found expression in the yin and yang of sado-masochism. The masochism was satisfied by the suffering in Africa, especially during his triple crossing of the Ituri forest in 1887–9. 'I was not sent into the world to be happy, nor to search for happiness,' he confessed. The sadism manifested itself in vicious floggings of his men, his hounding of recalcitrants to death, and the abandonment of 'disobedient' men to the mercy of savage tribesmen. Anyone arguing that Stanley was not a sadist will need to explain the (rationally) unexplainable: his frenzied beating of Noe in 1866, or Selim in 1871, his hounding to death of his white comrades Shaw and Farquhar in 1871, his delivery of the Sudanese Fathel Mullah to a loathsome death during the Emin Pasha expedition, and much else.

The analysis of schizoid personality disorder explains many other facets of Stanley that his contemporaries found disturbing or objectionable: his inability to accept blame, the maniacal desire always to be 'first', the doling out of grudging blame for a job well done, but vituperative criticism for the slightest lapse by his subordinates, his habit of dining alone and hoarding all the best food for himself. This is the classical schizoid 'lone wolf' in action. Such a man has decided that since nobody cares for him, he in turn will care for nobody; other people are then viewed as obstacles to desires or objects of gratification.

Stanley was also a notorious liar. He lied to the world about his background and origins, he lied to Tippu Tip in 1876 about the rewards that would accrue if the Arab helped him, he lied about the circumstances in which he left behind the rear column in 1887, the reasons for the enormous death toll, and about the 'treaties' he had signed with chiefs on his way to Bagamoyo. He even lied to himself in the privacy of his own journal. But Stanley was different in his mendacity only in degree, not kind.

All the explorers lived in fantasy worlds of their own: in this limited sense Melanie Klein is right to point to a *universal* neurosis underpinning exploration. It was more than just an accident that Thomson was a close friend of J.M. Barrie, that tortured exponent of lost children and lost childhoods. Count Teleki put his finger on it. When Frederick Jackson told him he hoped he would stick to the facts in his account of the discovery of lakes Rudolph and Stephanie, the portly Teleki roared with laughter: 'My dear Mr Jackson, all African travellers are liars, my old friend Burton was a liar, Speke and Grant were liars, Stanley is a liar, we know our friends Thomson and Johnston are liars and I am going to be a liar. If I do not discover a lake, I shall say I did, and who will disprove it, until long after I have received the credit?'

In the case of those for whom exploration was a quest for identity, as with Burton, uncertainty about the true meaning of an exploit led almost inevitably to fantasy. When Burton returned from his famous voyage to Mecca, he concocted a story that he had swaggered into Shepheard's Hotel in Cairo still in Arab garb. The very identity crisis and self-doubt that led so many men to seek out unknown territories and defy death can be seen as part of the propulsion behind the curious desire to add the Ossa of make-believe to the Pelion of solid achievement. Stanley's finding of Livingstone was a great enough real achievement for any man. Yet Stanley felt the need to embroider his own feats with downright lies. A similar compulsion was at work with Burton, except that with him, appropriately for a master Sufi, the boundaries between reality and illusion were always hazier. Burton, superior in intellect and intellectual curiosity to all other African explorers, was a creative artist *manqué*. Life for him was a drama and as such it obeyed Aristotle's rules. The dramatist told not just what did happen, but what might have happened and even what *ought* to have happened.

Notes on Sources

p. 7   'Fatal Africa!' H.M. Stanley, *Autobiography* (1909) pp. 296–7

p. 8   'One of the most magnificent sights in the creation'. James Bruce, *Travels to discover the source of the Nile in the years 1768, 1769, 1770, 1771, 1772 and 1773* (1804) 7 vols., Vol. V.

p. 44   'Who shall describe' H. Capello & R. Ivens, *From Benguela to the Territory of Yacca*, 2 vols (1882), i. pp. 99–100

p. 44   'I am a *Lekoa*' Livingstone, *Missionary Travels* (1857) p. 593

p. 45   'Missionaries ought to cultivate' G. Seaver, *David Livingstone: His Life and Letters* (1957) p. 186

p. 46   'Perpetual wood-cutting' *Journal of the Royal Geographical Society* 31 (1861) p. 273

p. 49   'Sic gloria sailing' Livingstone to Waller, 8 August 1863, Waller Papers, Rhodes House

p. 60   'At length by ejecting' R.F. Burton, *The Lake Regions of Central Africa*, 2 vols (1861), i. p. 51

p. 61   'The whole scene' ibid. ii. p. 42

p. 62   'The fortunate discoverer's conviction' ibid. ii. p. 204

p. 68   'I got up a bit' J.H. Speke, *Journal of the Discovery of the Source of the Nile* (Edinburgh, 1863) p. 231

p. 69   'We were well rewarded' ibid. p. 461

p. 75   'It is the rapacity' Samuel Baker, *The Albert Nyanza*, 2 vols (1866), ii. p. 73

p. 75   'Drawing my revolver' ibid. ii. p. 77

p. 75   'The glory of our prize' ibid. ii. pp. 94–6

p. 76   'When the paddles ceased working' ibid. ii. pp. 141–3

p. 77   'Kamurasi was a remarkably fine' ibid. ii. pp. 173–9

p. 78   'I always knew the Bari' Samuel Baker, *Ismailia*, 2 vols (1874), i. pp. 300–13

p. 79   'This was Kabba Rega' Baker, ibid. ii. p. 187

p. 79 'The negro idea' ibid. ii. p. 210

p. 80 'The treachery of the negro' ibid. ii. p. 315

p. 80 'I have lately had a painful' ibid. ii. p. 404

p. 86 'Guns were fired into' Livingstone, *Last Journals* ed. Horace Waller, 2 vols (1874), 8 August 1871

p. 87 'Dr Livingstone, I presume?' *New York Herald*, 10, 15 August 1872

p. 92 'I am pale and weak' Livingstone, *Last Journals*. 10 April 1873

p. 92 'Nothing earthly' ibid. 25 April 1873

p. 92 'Oh dear, dear' ibid.

p. 92 'They saw the doctor' *Last Journals*, ii. pp. 299–308

p. 94 'What would I not have given' V.L. Cameron, *Across Africa*, 2 vols (1877), i. pp. 269–302

p. 94 'A strong and sweeping current', ibid. i. p. 374

p. 98 'Dear Livingstone' Stanley, Journal, 25 Feb. 1874

p. 110 'I travelled – always on foot' Paul du Chaillu, *Explorations and Adventures in Equatorial Africa* (1861) p. viii

p. 112 'But our task was not' Napoleon Ney, *Conferences et lettres de P. Savorgan de Brazza sur trois explorations effectués dans l'Ouest Afrique 1876–1885* (Paris 1887) pp. 28–9

p. 114 'He reminded me a little' Marie von Bunsen. *The World I Used to Know 1860–1912* (1930) p. 185

p. 116 'I took no personal share' G. Schweinfurth, *The Heart of Africa*, 2 vols (1874), ii. p. 176

p. 116 'As an explorer he stands' Winwood Reade, introduction to Schweinfurth, *Heart of Africa*, i. p. vii

p. 117 'Famine and disease are' Wilhelm Junker, *Travels in Africa during the Years 1875–1878* (1890) p. 470

p. 117 'The numbers of skeletons' ibid. p. 483

p. 119 'Neither Stanley nor Linant' C. Chaillé-Long, *Central Africa* (1876) p. 195

p. 121 'No better organised caravan' Joseph Thomson, *To the Central African Lakes and Back*, 2 vols (1881), i. p. 86

p. 123 'Hard constant work' ibid. i. p. 123

p. 124 'Africa is going to be ready' ibid. ii. p. 279

p. 125 'My fondest boast' Robert I. Rotberg,' Joseph Thomson: Energy, Humanism and Imperialism' in Rotberg, *Africa and its Explorers* (Boston 1970) p. 306

p. 125 'The only circumstance' quoted in ibid. p. 314

p. 127 'A black man might do so' H.H. Johnston, *The Kilimanjaro Expedition* (1886) p. 201

p. 127 'This man plenty devilly' ibid. p. 257

p. 127 'Acted the part of a Paris' Ludwig von Hohnel, *Discoveries of Lakes Rudolph and Stephanie* 2 vols (1894), i. p. 59

p. 128 'It was very bad' Frederick Jackson, *Early Days in East Africa* (1930) p. 127

p. 133 'It is all very well' Alfred J.Swann, *Fighting the Slave Hunters in Central Africa* (1910) pp. 45–6

p. 133 'It was with a genuine' Joseph Thomson, *To the Central African Lakes and Back*, 2 vols (1881), i. p. 122

p. 134 'The donkey ran away.' Ludwig von Hohnel, *Discovery of Lakes Rudolph and Stephanie*, 2 vols (1894), i. p. 40

p. 137 'To be shut up ill' Joseph Thomson, *To the Central African Lakes*, i. p. 38

p. 141 'Look out! Drop that box' H.M. Stanley, *How I Found Livingstone in Central Africa* (1872) p. 642

p. 141 'The distribution of loads' Thomson, ibid. i. pp. 81–2

p. 142 'It is astonishing' Alfred J. Swann, *Fighting the Slave Hunters*, p. 25

p. 144 'What other race' H.H. Johnston. *The Kilimanjaro Expedition* (1886) p. 46

p. 146 'The natives having the trouble' Pruen, *The Arab and the African* (1891) p. 184

p. 151 'This useful person' Norman R. Bennett, ed. *Stanley's Despatches to the New York Herald* (Boston, 1970) p. 10

p. 154 '*Wasungu kwenda wapi?*' Arkell-Hardwick p. 310

p. 154 'Nothing can exceed' James Augustus Grant, *A Walk Across Africa* (1864)

p. 155 'The virtue of a good whip' H.M. Stanley, *How I Found Livingstone* (1872) pp. 139–40

p. 156 'I at once proceeded' Bennett, *Stanley's Despatches* p. 71

p. 157 'Two or three days after' Bennett, *Stanley's Despatches* pp. 158–9

p. 159 'Now was the crisis' Harry H. Johnston, *The Kilimanjaro Expedition* (1886) p. 49

p. 162 'He lifted Speke' Livingstone Papers, NLS 10729 f. 83

p. 163 'Bombay, after misunderstanding' Richard Burton, *The Lake Regions of Central Africa* (1860) II p. 208

p. 163 'Bombay with all his honesty' Speke to Rigby, 12 December 1860, RGS archives

p. 163 'A man has but one life' Speke, *Journal of the Discovery of the Source of the Nile* (1863)

p. 164 'Extremely sorry to hear that' Sir John Gray, 'Speke and Grant' *Uganda Journal* 17 (1953) pp. 146–60

p. 164 'It was only the natural cowardice' Stanley, *How I Found Livingstone* p. 487

p. 165 'Stupid Bombay' Stanley, Journal, 8 May 1872, SFA

p. 165 'Neither the "Angel"' Verney Lovett Cameron, *Across Africa*, 2 vols (1877), i. p. 331

p. 166 'Chuma and Wekotani' Livingstone Papers NLS 10720 ff. 34–5; 10722 ff. 35–6

p. 166 'It is just what boys will do' Livingstone to Waller, 3 November 1866, Waller Paper, Rhodes House, Oxford

p. 166 'Blushed if a black man' Livingstone Papers NLS 10725 ff. 22–3

p. 167 'Susi for no confessed reason' Dorothy Helly, *Livingstone's Legacy* (1987) pp. 172, 190

p. 167 'I resolved to reinstate' Livingstone Papers NLS 10734

p. 168 'He was, perhaps' Joseph Thomson, *To the Central African Lakes and Back*, 2 vols (1968 edn), i. pp. 33–4

p. 168 'Among the guild' *Proceedings of the Royal Geographical Society* N.S. 2 p. 722

p. 170 'Livingstone's great march' Andrew Roberts, *A History of Zanzibar* (1976) p. 131

p. 170 'Genuine sympathy' Livingstone Papers NLS 10719

p. 170 'The Zanzibaris are thieves' *The Times*, 10 April 1890

p. 170 'I cannot express' Robert I. Rotberg, *Joseph Thomson and the Exploration of Africa* (1871) p. 107

p. 171 'As a rule' Harry H. Johnston, *The Kilimanjaro Expedition* (1886) p. 46

p. 172 '*Bunduki*' E.J. Glave, *Six Years of Adventure in Congoland* p. 231

p. 173 'Had been the first' Karl Marx, *Communist Manifesto* (1848)

p. 175 'The universal effect' Livingstone, *Missionary Travels* p. 200

p. 176 'Would be of valuable service' A. Bott, *Our Fathers 1870–1900* (1931) p. 122

p. 176 'Whatever happens' H. Merivale, *Lectures on Colonization and Colonies* (1928) p. 561

p. 177 'Knowing that the slaughter' F.C. Selous, *A Hunter's Wanderings in Africa* (1895) p. 418

p. 178 'I seized a fowling piece' John Petherick, *Egypt, the Sudan and Central Africa* (1861) pp. 458–62

p. 181 'Slavery and its attendant cruelties' Glave, *Six Years* pp. 229–30

p. 182 'Each of these tribes' Paul du Chaillu, *Explorations and Adventures in Equatorial Africa* (1861) p. 10

p. 184 'I turned from the spectacle' *Missionary Travels* p. 562

p. 184 'Ivory is not likely' V.L. Cameron, *Across Africa*, 2 vols (1877), ii. pp. 322–4

p. 184 'The traders from East Africa', Joseph Thomson, *To the Central African Lakes and Back*, 2 vols (1881), ii. pp. 286, 18

p. 185 'What unspeakable miseries' Wilhelm Junker, *Travels in Africa*, i. p. 304

p. 185 'Stop the shooting' Stanley to de Winton, 10 September 1884, SFA

p. 185 'Having planted' Mark Twain, *More Tramps Abroad* (1897)

p. 186 'No resource for escape' G. Schweinfurth, *The Heart of Africa*, 2 vols (1874) pp. 438–9

p. 186 'It seems dreadful' Frederick Courtenay Selous, *A Hunter's Wanderings in Africa* (1895) p. 182

p. 187 'The tally of slaughtered' quoted in Mark Cocker, *Richard Meinertzhagen* (1989) p. 159

p. 187 'I have an uncomfortable feeling' W. Buckley, *Big Game Hunting in Central Africa* p. 49

p. 189 'A most complicated system' Edward Coode Hore, *Tanganyika* (1892) p. 74

p. 189 'Slavery has been an' Frederick Lugard, *The Rise of Our East African Empire*, 2 vols (1893), i. p. 181

p. 190 'The Arabs are said to treat' Horace Waller, ed. *Livingstone's Last Journals*, 2 vols (1874), i. p. 7

p. 191 'One of the mission girls' H.H. Johnston, *George Grenfell and the Congo*, 2 vols (1908), i. p. 244

p. 191 'The servitude rendered' I. Schapera, ed, *Livingstone's African Journal, 1853–1856* 2 vols (1963), ii. pp. 320–1

p. 192 'An old person' Duff MacDonald, *Africana; or, the Heart of Heathen Africa*, 2 vols (1882), i. p. 147

p. 192 'My slave, Ndobo' E.J. Glave, *Six Years of Adventure in Congoland* (1893) pp. 132–3

p. 193 'One of my slaves saw' H. Brunschwig, *Brazza l'explorateur, L'Ogooué, 1875–79* (Paris, 1966) p. 161

p. 194 'The Portuguese government has not generally' Livingstone, *Missionary Travels* p. 342

p. 195 'This is now almost the only spot' Livingstone to Clarendon, 11 June 1866, SP 1868–9 No.17

p. 197 'I was living with my husband' E.J. Glave, *Six Years*, p. 191

p. 199 'It is our deliberate opinion' David and Charles Livingstone, *Narrative of an Expedition to the Zambezi and its Tributaries* (New York 1866)

p. 199 'The system of slavery is diabolical' quoted in S. Tristram Pruen, *The Arab and the African* (1891), p. 252

p. 202 'Slavery is a great evil' *Livingstone's Last Journals*, pp. 222, 225–6, 232, 302

p. 203 'This is a den of the worst kind' ibid.

p. 205 'Nowhere in the world' G. Schweinfurth, *The Heart of Africa*, 2 vols (1874), ii. p. 305

p. 205 'I will murder you' ibid. i. p. 383

p. 205 'Untruthfulness has become to them' ibid. ii. p. 322

p. 206 'Hardly had he entered the gateway' Baker, *The Albert Nyanza*, 2 vols (1866), ii. p. 268

p. 206 'It is impossible to describe' Baker, *Ismailia*, 2 vols (1874), ii. p. 136

p. 207 'That a tried traveller' *Edinburgh Review* 141 (January 1875) p. 242

p. 207 'Compare the bloody march to Gondokoro' *British Quarterly Review* 61 (1875) pp. 398–420 (at pp. 419–20)

p. 208 'Tippu Tip and many Arab traders' V.L. Cameron, *Across Africa*, 2 vols (1877), ii. p. 27

p. 208 'The chains were ponderous' Stanley, *How I Found Livingstone* (1872) p. 92

p. 209 'Curiously enough the European power' H.H. Johnston, *The Kilimanjaro Expedition* (1886) p. 99

p. 210 'They kill us all with the gun' Guy Burrows, *The Land of the Pygmies* (1898) p. 128

p. 211 'A slave here is not in worse' Charles New, *Life, Wanderings and Labours in East Africa* (1873) p. 335

p. 211 'Of the horrors of the slave trade' Thomson, *To the Central African Lakes*, ii. pp. 18, 75

p. 211 'If the latter was unable' ibid. ii. p. 75

p. 213 'The ranks became broken' Stanley, *Through the Dark Continent*, 2 vols (1890), i. p. 66

p. 214 'Mr Stanley is much pleased with us' *New York Herald*, 1 March 1875

p. 216 'Had an enemy lurked in the jungle' Richard Stanley & Alan Neame, *Stanley's Expedition Diaries* (1961) p. 31

p. 218 'Hearing cries outside' ibid. p. 39

p. 219 'Farewell to it' ibid. p. 40

p. 219 'The day brought us into' *New York Herald*, 11 Oct. 1875

p. 221 'Bull, my British bulldog' *Daily Telegraph*, 15 Nov. 1875

p. 222 'You can better imagine our perils' *New York Herald*, 11 Oct. 1875

p. 230 'There can be no doubt' Winwood Reade, *Savage Africa* (1863) pp. 495–7

p. 230 'The same proceeding' John Buchanan, *The Shire Highlands* (1885)

p. 230   'Every step I take' Livingstone's Journal, 20 February 1867, Horace Waller, ed. *The Last Journals of David Livingstone*, 2 vols 1874

p. 231   'Standing in one spot' Samuel Baker, *The Albert Nyanza*, 2 vols (1866), ii. p. 85

p. 232   'I shall never forget' Isabel Burton, *The Life of Captain Sir Richard F. Burton*, 2 vols (1893), ii. p. 425

p. 233   'One of the chief objects' M. Gelfand, *Livingstone the Doctor: His Life and Travels* (Oxford 1957) p. 60

p. 233   'I would like' I. Schapera, ed. *Livingstone's Private Journals 1851–1853* (1960) p. 132

p. 234   'The limited experience' J.P.R. Wallis, ed. *The Zambezi Expedition of David Livingstone 1858–1863*, 2 vols (1956) p. 312

p. 235   'Began with a burning sensation' Richard Burton, *The Lake Regions of Central Africa*, 2 vols (1860), ii. pp. 233–5

p. 236   'The mind drifted away' Stanley's private journal, microfilm at British Library from originals at MRAC, Tervuren

p. 237   'I think each European' *Proceedings of the Royal Colonial Institute* 1890–1, p. 23

p. 238   'They tried to cook' Paul du Chaillu, *Explorations* p. 280

p. 241   'The wounds on Petherick's legs' John Petherick, *Travels in Central Africa*, 2 vols (1869), ii. p. 17

p. 245   'Ngoma, especially' Paul du Chaillu, *A Journey to Ashangoland* (1867) pp. 130–1

p. 245   'Each village' ibid. p. 134

p. 247   'His eyes were suffused' Samuel Baker, *The Albert Nyanza*, ii. pp. 334–7

p. 248   'There were hideous sights.' Richard Burton, *Zanzibar*, 2 vols (1972), ii. p. 345

p. 258   'Advised Kamurasi not to talk' Samuel Baker, *The Albert Nyanza*, 2 vols (1866), ii. op. cit.

p. 258   'When they were seated' Ruth Fisher, *Twilight Tales of the Black Baganda* (1970 edn) p. 157

p. 259   'Can you kill a man' ibid. p. 158

p. 260   'And Kabbarega sent back' ibid. pp. 162–3

p. 261   'Thousands of armed natives' Samuel Baker, *Ismailia*, 2 vols (1874), ii. p. 295

p. 264   'I wish the black sympathisers' Samuel Baker, *The Albert Nyanza*, i. p. 153

p. 266   'This will greatly distress' *New York Herald*, 17 Sept. 1877

p. 267   'He only wished' W.R. Fox-Bourne, *The Other Side of the Emin Pasha Relief Expedition* (1891) p. 19

p. 267 'Its black possessors' *Pall Mall Gazette*, 11 Feb. 1878

p. 267 'A system of exploration' C. Tzusuki, *H.M. Hyndman and British Socialism* (1961) p. 18

p. 269 'Down the natives came' *Daily Telegraph*, 12 Nov. 1877

p. 270 'The natives had never heard' *New York Herald*, 24 Nov. 1877

p. 271 'Anyone who knows the people' W. Holman Bentley, *Pioneering on the Congo*, 2 vols (Oxford, 1900), i. p. 64

p. 271 'We should be ashamed' ibid. i. p. 65

p. 271 'As for the hostility' *Globe*, 6 April 1889

p. 271 'Depend upon it' J.P.R. Wallis, ed. *The Zambezi Expedition of David Livingstone 1858–1863*, 2 vols (1956), ii. pp. 420–5

p. 272 'In him religion' H.M. Stanley, *How I Found Livingstone* (1872), op. cit.

p. 272 'I am of the opinion' H.H. Johnston, *The Kilimanjaro Expedition* (1886) p. 288

p. 272 'It was curious to look' ibid. p. 177

p. 273 'The shells of my Reilly' C. Chaillé-Long, *Central Africa* (1876) p. 177

p. 273 'It is quite a mistaken motto' Carl Peters, *New Light on Dark Africa* (1891)

p. 277 'I take it to be evident' Livingstone, *Missionary Travels* pp. 161–2

p. 277 'I confess on occasions' A. St. H. Gibbons, *Exploration and Hunting in Central Africa 1895–96* (1898) p. 227

p. 279 'If a man is killed' Fred Puleston, *African Drums* (1903) p. 108

p. 280 'The shouts and cries' Thomson, *Through Masailand* (1968 edn) p. 188

p. 281 'Since then several Kaffirs' Frederick Courtenay Selous, *A Hunter's Wanderings in Africa* (1895) p. 36

p. 281 'I saw the lion's tail' Livingstone, *Missionary Travels* pp. 11–12

p. 285 'The buffalo's head' Thomson, *Through Masailand* pp. 305–7

p. 287 'No redeeming qualities' Puleston, *African Drums* pp. 244–5

p. 288 'Of all the larger' Emil Holub, *Seven Years in South Africa*, 2 vols (1881), i. pp. 129–30

p. 289 'There must have arrived' Stanley, Journal, 2 Nov. 1871, SFA

p. 290 'The essence of all that is' *African Drums* p. 249

p. 290 'Suddenly he disappeared' ibid. p. 324

p. 290 '*Owi na nlorli*' Glave, *Six Years of Adventures in Congoland* p. 127

p. 292 'It is remarkable' H.H. Johnston, *George Grenfell and the Congo*, 2 vols, i. p. 228

p. 294 'The huge monster writhed still' C. Chaillé-Long, *Central Africa* (1876) p. 193

p. 295 'I was suddenly awakened' ibid. p. 288

p. 296 'A huge snake' H.H. Johnston, *George Grenfell and the Congo*, i. p. 270

p. 299 'Not an instant seemed' Livingstone, *Missionary Travels* p. 430

p. 299 'He began with exceeding' J.H. Speke, 'Journal of a Cruise on the Tanganyika Lake, Central Africa', *Blackwood's Edinburgh Magazine* 86 (1859) pp. 339–57 (at p. 349)

p. 307 'The Nile sources' W.G. Blaikie, *The Personal Life of David Livingstone* (New York 1881) p. 444

p. 307 'To make Africa north' John R.Wallis, *The Zambesi Expedition of David Livingstone 1858–1863*, 2 vols (1956), i. pp.136–7

p. 308 'I am very unwilling' Tim Jeal, *Livingstone* (1973) p. 222

p. 309 'Played out to its logical' Dorothy Helly, *Livingstone's Legacy* (1987) p. 215

p. 309 'Like ours in India' J.H. Speke, *Journal of the Discovery of the Source of the Nile* (Edinburgh, 1963) pp. 8, 45

p. 309 'Almost unspeakable richness' V.L. Cameron, Journey across Africa from Bagamoyo to Benguela', *Proceedings of the Royal Geographical Society* (1875–6) p. 323

p. 309 'Why are not steamers' V.L. Cameron, *Across Africa* (1877) pp. 473, 776–80

p. 309 'Now this country' V.L. Cameron, 'Colonisation of Central Africa', *Proceedings of the Royal Colonial Institute* (1873–76) pp. 274–82

p. 310 'By their own unaided efforts' H.H. Johnston, 'The Development of Tropical Africa under British Auspices', *Fortnightly Review* Nov. 1899, p. 705

p. 311 'A chief of more than' David and Charles Livingstone, *Narrative of an Expedition to the Zambezi* (1866) p. 199

p. 311 'The very rocks' Livingstone, *Missionary Travels* pp. 213–14

p. 311 'We are thrown back' I. Schapera, ed. *Livingstone's Private Journals 1851–1853* (1960) p. 156

p. 311 'Suppose you get to' Samuel Baker, *The Albert Nyanza*, 2 vols (1866), i. p. 148

p. 311 'It is strange to see' J.H. Speke, *What Led to the Discovery of the Source of the Nile* (1864) pp. 349–50

p. 311 'O ye sentimentalists' Charles John Andersson, *The Okango River* (1861) pp. 124–5

p. 312 'Great as our Indian Empire is' H.H. Johnston, 'The Development of Tropical Africa under British Auspices', *Fortnightly Review*, Nov. 1899, p. 688

p. 312   'As his fathers' J.H. Speke, *Journal of the Discovery of the Source of the Nile* p. 18

p. 312   'Whatever Europeans have done' Joseph Thomson, 'The Results of European Intercourse with the African', *Contemporary Review*, March 1890 p. 340

p. 313   'So the caravan' R.P. Ashe, *Two Kings of Uganda* (1889) pp. 122–4

p. 314   'Living like an animal' H.H. Johnston, *British Central Africa* (1897) pp. 182–3

p. 315   'Events in Africa between' Jeal, *Livingstone*, p. 382

p. 315   'We come upon them' ibid

p. 315   'The Congolese system' Neal Ascherson, *The King Incorporated* (1963) p. 203

p. 316   'Mr Stanley has warned you' Lady Cecil, *Life of Robert Marquis of Salisbury*, 4 vols (1932), iv. pp. 284–6

p. 317   'At the expense of' James B. Thomson, *Joseph Thomson: African Explorer* (1896) p. 162

p. 320   'I believe the safest' Samuel Baker, *Ismailia*, i. p. 261

p. 320   'Oh these white men' Stanley, *How I Found Livingstone* p. 259

p. 320   'Here stood two men' Winwood Reade, *Savage Africa* pp. 145–6

p. 321   'Then came numerous questions' Du Chaillu, *A Journey to Ashangoland* (1867) p. 186

p. 321   'There must be something' David and Charles Livingstone, *Narrative of an Expedition to the Zambesi* pp. 181–2

p. 324   'Speke's name is one' Livingstone Journal, 19 November 1868, NLS 10734

p. 324   'Wah! Wah! Speekee!' Baker, *Ismailia*, ii. p. 284

p. 325   'I was thus able' Emile Hourst, *French Enterprise in Africa* (1898) p. viii

p. 326   'Had it not been for' Bridgal Pachai, *Livingstone, Man of Africa* (1973) p. 120

p. 326   'Are the spirits going to' ibid. p. 51

p. 326   'Marenga rushed towards me' H. Faulkner, *Elephant Haunts* (n.d.) p. 148; cf. also E.D. Young, *The Search After Livingstone* (1868)

p. 327   'Your master is a good' Stanley, *How I Found Livingstone* p. 435

p. 327   'Produced a shudder' *New York Press*, 15 April 1890

p. 328   'Whenever I find myself' W.R. Fox-Bourne, *The Other Side of the Emin Pasha Relief Expedition* (1891) pp. 13–14

p. 328   'Acted as a talisman' Herbert Ward, *Five Years with the Congo Cannibals* p. 239

p. 328   'No disparaging word' Johnston to Lady Stanley, 10 May 1904, SFA

p. 328 'Stanley gave us peace' Patrice Lumumba, 'Un explorateur incomparable', *La Voix du Congolais* 10 (1954) pp. 516–22

p. 329 'Perhaps if we had also big pots' Stanley, *The Congo and the Founding of its Free State*, 2 vols (1895), ii. p. 29

p. 330 *'Arlekaki Tendele'* E.J. Glave, *Six Years of Adventures in Congoland* (1893) p. 44

p. 332 'Quelle différence' H. Brunschwig, *Brazza l'explorateur, L'Ogooué 1875–79* (Paris, 1961) pp. 192–3

p. 334 'The ruthless force' Pachai, *Livingstone, Man of Africa* p. 127

p. 335 'The return of Stanley' H.H. Johnston, *The Story of My Life* (1923) p. 160

p. 340 'Man wants to journey' Burton, *Personal Narrative of a Pilgrimage to El-Medinah and Meccah*, 2 vols (1893), i. pp. 16, 49; *The Carmina of Gaius Valerius Catullus* (1894) p. ix

p. 340 'I set myself a goal' Wilfred Thesiger, *Arabian Sands* (1959) pp. 259–60

p. 341 'I had time' Burton, *First Footsteps in East Africa* (Waterfield, ed. 1966) p. 205

p. 341 'If I have any merit' Winwood Reade, preface to *Savage Africa*

p. 342 'The mere animal pleasure' W.G. Blaikie, *Personal Life of Dr Livingstone* p. 370

p. 342 'I hardly slept' Alan Moorehead, *The White Nile* pp. 91–2

p. 342 'Upon a distant journey' Burton, *Zanzibar*, i. pp. 16–17

p. 342 'Is not repressed by' Stanley, *Autobiography*, p. 533

p. 342 'I view the end' Livingstone, *Missionary Travels* p. 673

p. 343 'The nearest approach' Owen Chadwick, *Mackenzie's Grave* (1959)

p. 343 'Now I am on the point' Horace Waller, ed. *Livingstone's Last Journals*, 2 vols (1874), i. pp. 13–14

p. 344 'He has lived in' Stanley, *How I Found Livingstone*

p. 344 'I have lost a great deal' George Seaver, *David Livingstone* (1957) pp. 583, 594

p. 345 'Apropos of Scotchmen' Stanley to Bruce, 15 October 1889, NLS 10705 f. 87

p. 346 'The most monstrous fraud' Joseph Thomson & Miss E. Harris-Smith, *Ula: an African Romance*, 2 vols (1888), i. p. 148; ii. pp. 212, 216, 217

p. 346 'The silence of the forest' A.J. Swann, *Fighting the Slave Hunters* p. 45

p. 347 'If I had any money' quoted in Frank McLynn, *Stanley: Sorcerer's Apprentice* p. 373

p. 347   'The masses of the working people' Livingstone, *Missionary Travels* p. 7

p. 348   'Perhaps if the police' Burton, *Unexplored Syria*, 2 vols (1871), ii. p. 191

p. 348   'Nature herself' Thomas Carlyle, *On Heroes and Hero Worship* (1841) p. 100

p. 349   'In psycho-analytic work' Melanie Klein, *Love, Guilt and Reparation* (1975) pp. 333–4

p. 350   'For all these men' Fawn Brodie, *The Devil Drives* (1967) p. 142

p. 351   'A little people' Lewis Grassic Gibbon, *Niger: The Life of Mungo Park* (Edinburgh, 1934) p. 18

p. 352   'My old nurse' Alexander Maitland, *Speke* (1971)

p. 353   'Whenever a head appears' Burton, *Zanzibar*, ii. p. 374

p. 354   'Having attained the southern' Maitland, *Speke* pp. 82–3

p. 355   'He was unconcerned' Oliver Ransford, *Livingstone: The Dark Interior* (1978)

p. 356   'I can come to no other' ibid. pp. 142, 164, 206, 211

p. 356   'I have had some intrusive' Stanley, *Autobiography*, p. 274

p. 356   'O, Livingstone, will you' I. Schapera, ed. *Livingstone's Private Journals 1851–1853* (1960) pp. 70–1

p. 357   'Healthy, hardy, blooming' Blaikie, *Personal Life* p. 261

p. 357   'The blood of a being' Dorothy Helly, *Livingstone's Legacy* (1987) p. 140

p. 358   'I was not sent into' Stanley, *Autobiography*, p. xvii

p. 359   'My dear Mr Jackson' Frederick Jackson, *Early Days in East Africa* (1903) p. 126

Bibliography

INTRODUCTION

There are many studies of African exploration but none with the approach adopted here. Christopher Hibbert, *Africa Explored, Europeans in the Dark Continent, 1769–1889* (1982) is an excellent straightforward account. Timothy Severin, *The African Adventure* (1973) deals selectively with the moments of high drama in the European exploration of Africa, and includes adventures that have little to do with exploration proper. The most informative general study is the collection of essays edited by Robert I. Rotberg, *Africa and its Explorers* (Boston, 1970), but this is a book for people who already have a reasonable knowledge of the subject.

1 WEST AFRICA AND THE NIGER

All of the West African explorers left detailed accounts of their journeys. Of the modern overviews Christopher Lloyd, *The Search for the Niger* (1973) is highly recommendable. C. Howard and J.H. Plumb, *West African Explorers* (1951) makes a good introduction. Robin Hallett has done important work: *The Penetration of Africa: European Enterprise and Exploitation, Principally in Northern and Western Africa* (1965); *Records of the African Association, 1783–1831* (1964) and his edition of *R.L. and J. Lander's Niger Journal* (1965).

Of studies of the individual explorers, the most recent are Kenneth Lupton, *Mungo Park: The African Traveller* (1979); Mercedes Mackay, *The Indomitable Servant* (1978) (on Richard Lander); A.H.M. Kirk-Greene, *Barth's Travels in Nigeria* (1962). Barth in particular has attracted scholarly attention and there are some useful journal articles: E.A. Ayandele, 'Dr Henry Barth as a Diplomatist and Philanthropist', *Ibadan*

25 (1968) pp. 9–14; E.W. Bovill, 'Henry Barth', *Journal of the African Society* 25 (1926) pp. 311–20; R.M. Prothero, 'Heinrich Barth and the Western Sudan', *Geographical Journal* 124 (1958) pp. 326–39.

2 FROM THE CAPE TO THE ZAMBEZI

The most approachable study of the Great Trek is by Oliver Ransford, *The Great Trek* (1972). For Livingstone's early years his own *Missionary Travels and Researches in South Africa* (1857) is fundamental. This can be supplemented by the best of the Livingstone biographies: Oliver Ransford, *Livingstone: The Dark Interior* (1978) and Tim Jeal, *Livingstone* (1973). Any scholarly approach to Livingstone must take account of the four magisterial tomes edited by I. Schapera: *David Livingstone: Family Letters 1841–1856*, 2 vols (1959); *Livingstone's African Journal 1853–1856* (1963); *Livingstone's Missionary Correspondence 1841–1856* (1961) and *Livingstone's Private Journals 1851–1853* (1960). Judith Listowel, *The Other Livingstone* (1974) points up Livingstone's selfish side. There is a considerable bibliography on the Zambezi expedition. A good starting point is J.P.R. Wallis, *The Zambezi Expedition of David Livingstone 1858–1863*, 2 vols (1956). Apart from Livingstone's own account (in David and Charles Livingstone, *Narrative of an Expedition to the Zambezi* (1966)) the two volumes edited by Reginald Foskett: *The Zambesi Journals and Letters of Sir John Kirk 1858–63*, 2 vols (Edinburgh 1965) and *The Zambesi Doctors: David Livingstone's Letters to John Kirk 1858–1872* (Edinburgh 1964) are indispensable. For Mauch see E.E. Burke, ed. *The Journal of Carl Mauch: His Travels in the Transvaal and Rhodesia 1869–1872* (trans. F.O. Bernhard) (Salisbury 1969).

3 THE MOUNTAINS OF THE MOON

Richard Burton has attracted many biographers. Frank McLynn, *Burton: Snow upon the Desert* (1990) is the latest attempt to make sense of this enigmatic figure. Edward Rice, *Captain Sir Richard Burton* (New York 1990) concentrates on Burton's Indian career and contains nothing significant about his African adventures. Robin C.H. Rinsley provides an excellent précis of Burton's 1857–8 journey in 'Burton: An Appreciation', *Tanganyika Notes and Records* 49 (1957) pp. 257–93. J.N.L. Baker deals with the knotty subject of the Nile in 'Sir Richard Burton and the Nile Sources', *English Historical Review* 59 (1944) pp. 48–61.

Alexander Maitland's *Speke* (1971) is the most recent biography.

Speke has been unusually well served by journal articles, whose titles are self-explanatory. J.N.L. Baker, 'John Hanning Speke', *Geographical Journal* 128 (1962) pp. 385–8; Roy Bridges, 'Speke and the Royal Geographical Society', *Uganda Journal* 26 (1962) pp. 23–43; J.M. Gray, 'Speke and Grant', *Uganda Journal* 17 (1953) pp. 146–60; Kenneth Ingham, 'John Hanning Speke: A Victorian and His Inspiration', *Tanganyika Notes and Records* 49 (1957) pp. 301–11. Speke's complex relations with Mutesa are the subject of Ham Mukasa, 'Speke at the Court of Mutesa', *Uganda Journal* 26 (1962) pp. 97–9; J.M. Gray 'Mutesa of Buganda', *Uganda Journal* 1 (1934) pp. 22–49, and Frederick B. Welbourn, 'Speke and Stanley at the Court of Mutesa', *Uganda Journal* 25 (1961) pp. 220–3.

The most recent biographies of Baker are Dorothy Middleton, *Baker and the Nile* (1949) and Richard Hall, *Lovers on the Nile* (1980). Particular aspects are dealt with in J.R. Baker, 'Samuel Baker's Route to the Albert Nyanza', *Geographical Journal* 131 (1965) pp. 13–20 and Aidan Southall, 'The Ahur Legend of Sir Samuel Baker and the Mukama Kabarega', *Uganda Journal* 15 (1951) pp. 187–90.

4 THE LUALABA AND THE CONGO

Livingstone's last journey can be followed in his *Last Journals*, 2 vols (1874) and in the excellent work by Reginald Coupland, *Livingstone's Last Journey*. Cameron is best followed in his own *Across Africa*, 2 vols (1877) but see also W. Robert Foran, *African Odyssey: The Life of Verney Lovett Cameron* (1937) and James R. Hooker, 'Verney Lovett Cameron' in Robert I. Rotberg, ed. *Africa and its Explorers* (Boston, 1970) pp. 257–94. The various stages of Stanley's career can be traced in his own books. There is a large Stanley literature, either in the form of discrete studies of his expeditions or formal biographies. The most comprehensive study is Frank McLynn, *Stanley: The Making of an African Explorer* (1989) and *Stanley: Sorcerer's Apprentice* (1991). For the later Congo expeditions see H.H. Johnston, *George Grenfell and the Congo*, 2 vols (1908).

5 THE HEART OF AFRICA

Not surprisingly, perhaps, the German explorers have not found biographers in English, although their major travel books have all been translated. The best guide to Rohlfs is Wolfe W. Schmokel, 'Gerhard Rohlfs: The Lonely Explorer', in Robert Rotberg, ed. *Africa and its*

Explorers (Boston, 1970) pp. 175–222. For the French see Richard West, *Brazza of the Congo: European Exploration and Exploitation in French Equatorial Africa* (1972), Jean Autin, *Pierre Savorgnan de Brazza* (Paris 1985), Rosaline Nuoye, *The Public Image of Pierre Savorgnan de Brazza and the Establishment of French Imperialism in the Congo 1875–1885* (Aberdeen 1981).

There is an excellent biography of Thomson by Robert Rotberg, *Joseph Thomson and the Exploration of Africa* (1970). This should be supplemented by the reminiscences of his brother: James B. Thomson, *Joseph Thomson, African Explorer* (1896) and the short portrait by J.M. Barrie in *An Edinburgh Eleven* (1924) pp. 101–8. Harry Johnston is the subject of a good biography by Roland Oliver, *Sir Harry Johnston and the Scramble for Africa* (1957). Johnston's autobiography *The Story of My Life* (1923) is also revealing.

6 TRANSPORT AND PORTERAGE

On the hopes of using ox-waggons in tropical Africa itself see the works of Harry Johnston, especially *Livingstone and the Exploration of Central Africa* (1891) and *The Kilimanjaro Expedition* (1885). For the relationship between oxen and tsetse fly see Edwin W. Smith, *Great Lion of Bechuanaland: The Life and Times of Roger Price, Missionary* (1957). On porterage see S.C. Lamden, 'Some Aspects of Porterage in East Africa', *Tanzania Notes and Records* 61 (1963) pp. 155–64; H.B. Thomas, 'The Logistics of Caravan Travel' in M. Posnansky, ed. *The Nile Quest* (Kampala 1962); *Private Journal of Guy C. Dawnay* (n.d.); Donald Currie, 'Thoughts upon the Present and Future of South Africa and Central and Eastern Africa', *Proceedings of the Royal Colonial Institute* 8 (1877). For some outstanding contemporary scholarship on the trade goods of cloth, beads and wire see Richard Burton, 'The Lake Regions of Central Equatorial Africa', *Journal of the Royal Geographical Society* 29 (1859) pp. 1–454. See also François Coulbois, *Dix Années au Tanganika* (Limoges, 1901); J.R. Harding, 'Nineteenth-Century Trade Beads in Tanganyika', *Man* 62 (1962). For the Nyamwezi see R.G. Abrahams, *The Peoples of Greater Unyamwezi* (1967); *The Political Organization of Unyamwezi* (Cambridge 1967); Edmund Dahl, *Nyamwezi-Wurterbuch* (Hamburg 1915). For the Gogo see Peter Rigby, *Cattle and Kinship among the Gogo* (Ithaca, NY, 1969); Heinrich Claus, *Die Wagogo* (Leipzig, 1911). For the Ha see J.H. Scherer, 'The Ha of Tanganyika', *Anthropos* (1959) pp. 841–904.

7 'Dark Companions'

Donald Simpson, *Dark Companions* (1975) is fundamental. The explorers' assessments vary from journal to published accounts. Therefore Livingstone's *Last Journals* are best supplemented by his manuscript journals in the National Library of Scotland, Stanley's *How I Found Livingstone* by his newspaper reports in the *New York Herald* and his private journals, Speke's *Journal of the Discovery of the Source of the Nile* by manuscript sources in the RGS and elsewhere. For Speke's relations see also Sir John Gray, 'Speke and Grant', *Uganda Journal* 17 (1953) pp. 146–60. There is a wealth of material on 'dark companions' in A.E.M. Anderson-Morshead, *The History of the Universities' Mission to Central Africa* (1955). Further material on Livingstone's followers can be found in Norman R. Bennett, 'Livingstone's Letters to William F. Stearns', *African Historical Studies* 1 (1968); François Bontinck, 'Voyageurs Africains: David Abdallah Susi', *Zaire Afrique* 162 (Feb. 1982) pp. 99–118; 163 (March 1982) pp. 169–85. For the visit of Susi and Chuma to England in 1874 see A.Z. Fraser, *Livingstone and Newstead* (1913) which should be supplemented by François Bontinck, 'Le diaire de Jacob Wainwright', *Africa* (Rome) 32 (1977) pp. 399–434.

8 Guns and Ivory

For technology in general see Daniel Headrick, 'The Tools of Imperialism; Technology and Expansion of European Colonial Empires in the Nineteenth Century', *Journal of Modern History* 51 (1979) pp. 231–63 and his later *The Tools of Empire* (1981). A particular example of the use of technology to overawe Africans is given in A. McMartin, 'Sekeltu's Sugar Mill', *Geographical Journal* 1139 (1973) pp. 96–103. R.W. Beachey, 'The Arms Trade in East Africa in the Late Nineteenth Century', *Journal of African History* 3 (1962) pp. 451–67 is illuminating as is Gavin White, 'Firearms in Africa: An Introduction', *Journal of African History* 12 (1971) pp. 173–84. See also the other articles on guns in Africa in that issue. On the superiority afforded by the repeating rifle see David S. Landes, 'Some Thoughts on the Nature of Economic Imperialism', *Journal of Economic History* 4 (1961) pp. 496–512. For the machine-gun see John Ellis, *The Social History of the Machine Gun* (1975) and G.S. Hutchinson, *Machine Guns: Their History and Technical Employment* (1938). On ivory R.W. Beachey, 'The East African Ivory Trade in the 19th Century', *Journal of African History* 8 (1967) pp. 269–90 is fundamental. The situation in the Congo is explained in Max Buchler, *Der Kongostaat*

Leopolds II, 2 vols (1912). The best explorers' accounts for elephants and ivory are Wilhelm Junker, *Travels in Africa 1882–86*, trans A.H. Keane, 3 vols (1892) and Gaetano Casati, *Ten Years in Equatoria with Emin Pasha*, 2 vols (1891).

9 SLAVERY AND THE SLAVE TRADE

Some of the best interpretive material is tucked away in learned articles. See, for example, Frederick Cooper, 'The Problems of Slavery in African Studies', *Journal of African History* 20 (1979) pp. 103–25; Martin A. Klein, 'The Study of Slavery in Africa', *Journal of African History* 19 (1978) pp. 599–609; Lewis Gann, 'The End of the Slave Trade in British Central Africa 1889–1912', *Rhodes-Livingstone Journal* 16 (1954).

There are numerous excellent monographs and collections of scholarly articles, as for example: R.W. Beachey, *The Slave Trade of Eastern Africa* (1976); Edward Alpers, *Ivory and Slaves: Changing Patterns of International Trade in East Central Africa in the Late Nineteenth Century* (Berkeley, 1975); Suzanne Miers & Igor Kopytoff, eds. *Slavery in Africa: Historical and Anthropological Perspectives* (Madison, 1977); Paul Lovejoy, ed. *The Ideology of Slavery in Africa* (1981); Claire C. Robertson & Martin A. Klein, *Women and Slavery in Africa* (Madison, 1983).

10 AN OBJECT LESSON IN OBSTACLES

This chapter is based entirely on the three different accounts by Stanley, in his book *Through the Dark Continent*, his private journals (the majority of which were published as *The Expedition Diaries of H.M. Stanley* (1961) under the editorship of Richard Stanley and Alan Neame), and his reports to the *New York Herald* (also published in book form under the editorship of Norman Bennett as *Stanley's Despatches to the New York Herald* (Boston, 1970). Supplementary material comes from the unpublished diaries of Frank Pocock, in the possession of Rhodes House Library, Oxford.

11 THE IMPACT OF DISEASE

An outstandingly lucid introduction is Oliver Ransford's *Bid the Sickness Cease* (1983), to which I acknowledge my debt. G.W. Hartwig & K.D. Paterson, *Disease in African History: An Introductory Survey and Case Studies* (Durham, NC 1978) contains many valuable essays germane to our subject. On mosquitoes and African fevers a useful trio of books is Michael Colbourne, *Malaria in Africa* (1966); Paul F. Russell, *Man's Mastery of Malaria* (1955); Jaime Jaramillo Arango, *The Conquest of Malaria* (1950). There is much detail on quinine and 'Livingstone's rousers' in Philip Curtin, *The Image of Africa: British Ideas and Action, 1780–1850* (NY, 1964). Naturally, Livingstone's own *Missionary Travels* is a goldmine as a source for African diseases. Sleeping sickness is dealt with in John Ford's scholarly, *The Role of the Trypanosomiases in African Ecology: A Tsetse Fly Problem* (Oxford, 1971). More approachable perhaps is John J. McKelvey Jr. *Man Against Tsetse: Struggle for Africa* (Ithaca, 1973). Useful journal articles are R. Hoeppli & C. Lucasse, 'Old Ideas Regarding the Cause and Treatment of Sleeping Sickness Held in West Africa', *Journal of Tropical Medicine and Hygiene* 67 (1964) pp. 60–8; K.S.R. Morris, 'The Movement of Sleeping Sickness Across Central Africa', *Journal of Tropical Medicine and Hygiene* 66 (1963) pp. 59–76. On the virus and bacteria diseases James Christie's pioneering study *Cholera Epidemics in East Africa* (1876, reprinted 1970) is invaluable. Asa Briggs, 'Cholera and Society in the 19th Century', *Past and Present* 19 (1961) pp. 76–96 provides an overview of political and social implications. Some interesting articles on smallpox are: Frederick Quinn, 'How Traditional Dahomian Society Interpreted Smallpox', *Abbia* 20 (1968) pp. 151–66; Eugenia W. Herbert, 'Smallpox Innoculation in Africa', *Journal of African History* 16 (1975) pp. 539–59; Douglas L. Wheeler, 'A Note on Smallpox in Angola 1670–1875', *Studia* 13–14 (1964) pp. 351–62. Rinderpest is dealt with in C. Van Onselen, 'Reactions to Rinderpest in Southern Africa 1896–97', *Journal of African History* 13 (1972) pp. 473–88. The spread of infectious diseases in Africa is covered by Philip Curtin, 'Epidemiology and the Slave Trade', *Political Science Quarterly* 83 (1968) pp. 190–216; Clarke Brooke, 'The Heritage of Famine in Central Tanzania', *Tanzania Notes and Records* 67 (1967) pp. 15–22; 'Economic Consequences of Long-Distance Trade in East Africa: the Disease Factor', *African Studies Review* 18 (1975) pp. 63–73.

12 Armed Clashes

The attack on Burton at Berbera is recounted in his *First Footsteps in East Africa* (1856). Stanley's adventures at Bumbire in 1875 and on the Laulaba in 1876–7 can be followed in his *Through The Dark Continent*, 2 vols (1878), in Norman R. Bennett, *Stanley's Despatches to the New York Herald* (1970) and in Richard Stanley & Alan Neames, eds. *The Exploration Diaries of H.M. Stanley*. Oral traditions about Stanley on the

Congo are collected in Camille Coquilhat, *Sur le haut Congo* (Paris, 1888); W. Holman Bentley, *Pioneering on the Congo*, 2 vols (Oxford, 1900) and John L. Brom, *Sur les traces de Stanley* (Paris, 1958). Baker's accounts in *Ismailia* (1874) and *The Albert Nyanza* (1876) should be supplemented by the traditions in Ruth Fisher, *Twilight Tales of the Black Baganda* (1970). Other stories, legends and traditions are gathered in K.W., 'The Kings of Bunyoro Kitara', *Uganda Journal* 3 (1935) pp. 155–60; 4 (1936) pp. 75–83; 5 (1937) pp. 53–68; A.W. Southall, 'The Ahur Legend of Sir Samuel Baker and the Mukama Kabarega', *Uganda Journal* 15 (1951) pp. 187–90; R. Oliver, 'The Baganda and Bakonjo', *Uganda Journal* 18 (1954) pp. 31–3; 'The Royal Tombs of Buganda', *Uganda Journal* 23 (1959) pp. 124–33; 'The Traditional Histories of Buganda, Bunyoro and Nkole', *Journal of the Anthropological Institute* 85 (1955) pp. 111–17. There is an outstanding Swahili work utilising oral histories, J. Nyakatura, *Abrakama ba Bunyoro Kitara* (St Justin, PQ, 1947). This should be supplemented by J.H.M. Beattie, *Bunyoro: An African Kingdom* (New York, 1960). For Europeans who were prepared to believe Kabbarega against Baker see G. Schweinfurth, ed. *Emin Pasha in Central Africa* (1883); G. Schweitzer, *Emin Pasha: His Life and Work*, 2 vols (1898); J. Roscoe, *The Soul of Central Africa* (1922). For Lugard's swallowing whole of the Baker version see Frederick Lugard, *British East Africa and Uganda* (1892). For the difficulties caused Gordon by Baker's actions against Kabbarega see L.T. Wilson & R. Felkin, *Uganda and the Egyptian Sudan*, 2 vols (1882).

13 ANIMALS DANGEROUS TO MAN

This is based entirely on the accounts in the explorers' own books.

14 EXPLORERS AND IMPERIALISM

The most seminal article in the literature on imperialism in Africa is Eric Stokes, 'Late Nineteenth-Century Colonial Expansion and the Attack on the Theory of Economic Imperialism: A Case of Mistaken Identity', *Historical Journal* 12 (1969) pp. 285–301. The implications of this have been followed up with admirable lucidity by Norman Etherington, *Theories of Imperialism: War, Conquest and Capital* (1984). See also Wolfgang J. Mommsen & Jurgen Osterhammel, eds. *Imperialism and After* (1986). On the scramble for Africa Ronald Robinson & John Gallagher, *Africa and the Victorians: the Official Mind of Imperialism*, 2nd edn (1981) is fundamental. W.R. Louis, ed. *Imperialism: The Robinson and Gallagher Controversy* (1976) is a useful adjunct. Thomas Pakenham, *The Scramble for Africa* (1991) is a magisterial overview. It can be supplemented by the regional studies in D.M. Schrender, *The Scramble for Southern Africa 1877–1895* (Cambridge 1980) and an article by C.W. Newbury & A.S. Kanya-Forstner, 'French Policy and the Origins of the Scramble for Africa', *Journal of African History* 10 (1969) pp. 253–76. Particular aspects of imperialism can be followed up in Darrell Bates, *The Fashoda Incident* (Oxford 1984) and A.N. Porter, *The Origins of the South African War: Joseph Chamberlain and the Diplomacy of Imperialism, 1895–1899* (Manchester 1980).

Much of the best material on imperialism written by the explorers themselves is hidden away in articles. From Verney Cameron there is 'Colonisation of Central Africa', *Proceedings of the Royal Colonial Institute* (1873–6) and 'Journal Across Africa from Bagamoyo to Benguela', *Proceedings of the Royal Geographical Society* (1875–6). From Joseph Thomson there is 'Downing Street versus Chartered Companies in Africa', *Fortnightly Review* 46 (1889) pp. 176–85; 'East Central Africa and its Commercial Outlook', *Scottish Geographical Magazine* 2 (1886) pp. 65–78; 'Note on the African Tribes of the British Empire' *Journal of the Anthropological Institute* 16 (1886) pp. 182–6; 'Mohammedanism in Central Africa', *Contemporary Review* 50 (1886) pp. 876–83; 'East Africa as it Was and Is', *Contemporary Review*, Jan. 1889 pp. 45–6; 'East Africa and its Commercial Outlook', *Scottish Geographical Magazine*, Feb 1886. The prolific Harry Johnston produced 'The Results of European Intercourse wth the African', *Contemporary Review*, March 1890; 'The Development of Tropical Africa under British Auspices', *Fortnightly Review* Nov. 1890 p. 688; 'The Value of Africa: A Reply to Sir John Pope-Hennessy', *Nineteenth Century*, July 1890 (for the reply see John Pope-Hennessy and E.V. Dicey, 'Is Central Africa Worth Having?' *Nineteenth Century*, Sept. 1890). Lugard threw his weight into the controversy with 'The Extension of British Influence (and Trade) in Africa', *Proceedings of the Royal Colonial Institute* (1895–6); 'A Glimpse of Lake Nyasa', *Blackwood's Magazine*, Jan. 1890 p. 28. The railway advocacy of J. Conyers Morrell is in 'On the Advantage of Railway Communication in Africa as Compared With Any Other Mode of Transport', *Journal of the Society of Arts* 27 (1879); that of Donald Currie on the steamship is in 'Thoughts upon the Present and Future of South Africa and Central and Eastern Africa', *Proceedings of the Royal Commonwealth Institute* 8 (1877).

15 REPUTATION AND IMPACT

The best introduction to the problem of oral history is Jan Vansina, *Oral Tradition in History* (Wisconsin, 1985). There are some good articles on the subject by Wyatt MacGaffey, 'Oral Tradition in Central Africa', *International Journal of African Historical Studies* 7 (1974) and 'The West in Congolese Experience', in Philip Curtin, ed. *Africa and the West* (1972). See also Joseph C. Miller, ed. *The African Past Speaks: Essays on Oral Tradition and History* (1980) and MacGaffey's books *Custom and Government in the Lower Congo* (Berkeley, 1970) and *Religion and Society in Central Africa: The Bakongo of Lower Zaire* (Chicago, 1986). Baker's reputation in oral tradition is dealt with in Ruth Fisher, *Twilight Tales of the Black Baganda* (1970); Livingstone's in Bridglal Pachai, ed. *Livingstone: Man of Africa* (1973). There is a good essay on Stanley by François Bontinck, 'Les deux Bula Matari', *Etudes Congolaises* 12 (1969) pp. 83–97. Also useful is Michel Colin,'Quelques anecdotes sur Stanley', *La Voix du Congolais* 10 (1954) pp. 338–43 and the highly interesting piece by Patrice Lumumba, 'Un explorateur incomparable', *La Voix du Congolais* 10 (1954) pp. 516–22.

On Livingstone's impact see especially the essay by J.M. Schoffeleers, 'Livingstone and the Mang'anya Chiefs' in Pachai, *Livingstone: Man of Africa* op. cit. For Stanley see Jan Vansina, *The Tio Kingdom of the Middle Congo 1880–1892* (1973) and Frank McLynn's *Stanley: Sorcerer's Apprentice* (1991). For the discussion on long-distance trade routes and modes of production see Jan Vansina, 'Long Distance Trade Routes in Central Africa', *Journal of African History* 3 (1962) pp. 375–90, and Curtis A. Keim, 'Long Distance Trade and the Magbetu', *Journal of African History* 24 (1983) pp. 1–22. There are two outstanding articles by Catherine Coquery-Vidrovich, 'Research on an African Mode of Production', in Martin Klein & G. Wesley Johnson, eds. *Perspectives on the African Past* (1972) and 'The Political Economy of the African Peasantry and Modes of Production', in Peter Gutkind & Immanuel Wallerstein, eds. *The Political Economy of Contemporary Africa* (1976) pp. 90–111. See also Samir Amin, *Unequal Development* (1976).

16 THE PSYCHOLOGY OF THE EXPLORERS

The two titles dealing with this topic most generally are O. Mannoni, *Prospero and Caliban: The Psychology of Colonization* (1956) and Melanie Klein, *Love, Guilt and Reparation* (1975). Robert I. Rotberg, ed. *Africa and its Explorers* (Boston, 1970) contains some tentative thoughts, but a much more profound examination of the drives at work in a trail-blazer is his *Cecil Rhodes: The Founder* (1988).

On the explorers' own accounts of their motivations three articles by Thomson are useful: 'East Africa as it Was and Is', *Contemporary Review*, Jan. 1889; 'The Results of European Intercourse with the African', *Contemporary Review*. March 1890; 'Notes on the African Tribes of the British Empire', *Journal of the Royal Anthropological Institute*, 1886. For placing Livingstone's view on sex in their Victorian context a useful article is F. Barry Smith, 'Sexuality in Britain, 1800–1900: Some Suggested Revisions,' in Martha Vicinus, ed. *A Widening Sphere: Changing Roles of Victorian Women* (Bloomington, Indiana, 1977) pp. 182–98. On Burton there is a splendid but little-known essay by Jonathan Bishop, 'The Identities of Sir Richard Burton: The Explorer as Actor', *Victorian Studies* 1 (1957–8) pp. 119–35.

The explorers have attracted many biographies of a more or less psychoanalytical orientation. On Burton there is Fawn Brodie, *The Devil Drives* (1967) and Frank McLynn, *Burton: Snow Upon the Desert* (1990). On his ill-fated companion, Alexander Maitland's *Speke* (1971) is the best available. Tim Jeal's *Livingstone* (1973) contains many shrewd insights, but the most searching examination of Livingstone's psychology is Oliver Ransford, *Livingstone: The Dark Interior* (1978). Stanley has spawned many psychological interpretations. Among the most interesting of these are Jakob Wassermann, *Bula Matari* (1932), Emyr Wyn Jones, *Sir Henry M. Stanley, the Enigma* (Denbigh 1989), John Bierman, *Dark Safari* (New York, 1990) and Gerben Hellinga, *Henry Morton Stanley: Een Individualpsychologische Interpretatie* (Brussels, 1978). Frank McLynn's massive two-volume 'psychobiography' *Stanley: The Making of An African Explorer* (1989) and *Stanley: Sorcerer's Apprentice* (1991) aims to be definitive, but there are sure to be other investigations of this most puzzling man.

Index